Inkling, Historian, Soldier, and Brother

Photo of Warren Lewis sitting in a chair with pipe at the Kilns, circa 1970.
(Used by permission of Douglas R. Gilbert)

Inkling, Historian, Soldier, and Brother

A Life of Warren Hamilton Lewis

DON W. KING

Don W. King

The Kent State University Press   Kent, Ohio

To Isaac, Avila, Ezra, and Elliott

ISBN 978-1-60635-450-6
Manufactured in the United States of America

Cataloging information for this title is available at the Library of Congress.

27 26 25 24 23   5 4 3 2 1

Those who do not look upon themselves as a link,

connecting the past with the future,

do not perform their duty to the world.

—Daniel Webster

Contents

Acknowledgments

I have many persons to thank for assistance in writing this book. Nathan King, the Library Director at Montreat College, and his staff, especially Phoebe Maa, have been endlessly patient and helpful in securing materials. I am grateful as well to the staff at the Marion E. Wade Center, particularly David Downing and Marjorie Mead, who not only encouraged my research and made me comfortable during my many visits to the Wade Center, but also labored diligently to help me determine which excerpts from Warren's writings that I could cite in the biography. I also owe debts of gratitude to Paul Maurer, President of Montreat College, and the Faculty Scholarship Committee for their encouragement and a summer research grant, as well as the Appalachian College Association for awarding me two summer research grants. Thanks are due as well to my student research assistants Emily Erlien, Lexi Hudson, Fiona Brown, Lily Queen, and Zoe Evans. I am also deeply grateful to Joanna King-Yost, Corrie Greene, and George Musacchio, who read and commented upon early drafts of the manuscript. Joel Heck comes in for special thanks as he shared a good deal of his expertise and knowledge regarding Warren Lewis's life and writings with me at critical points along the way. I am most appreciative of the excellent editorial advice of the Kent State University Press, especially my editors Susan Wadsworth-Booth and Mary Young. Finally, I owe my wife, Jeanine, a great debt since I spent so many hours away from her while working on this book.

All copyrighted material of Warren Lewis is used by permission of the Marion E. Wade Center, Wheaton College, Wheaton, Illinois. Excerpts from *Surprised by Joy, Collected Letters of C. S. Lewis, Volume I: Family Letters 1905–1931* (London: HarperCollins, 2000), *C. S. Lewis, Collected Letters, Volume II: Books, Broadcasts, and War, 1931–1949* (London: HarperCollins, 2004), and *C. S. Lewis, Collected Letters, Volume III: Narnia, Cambridge, and Joy, 1950–1963*, edited by Walter Hooper (London: HarperCollins, 2006), are used by permission of the C. S. Lewis Company.

Appearing in this book is adapted material originally published in the following articles:

"Warren Lewis, Mrs Janie King Moore, and The Kilns," *Journal of Inklings Studies* 7:1 (Apr. 2017): 103–18.

"The Early Life of Warren Hamilton Lewis (1895–1913)," *Journal of Inklings Studies* 8:1 (Apr. 2018): 1–30.

"Warnie at War (1914–1918)," *VII, Journal of the Marion E. Wade Center* 35 (2018): 87–110.

"When Did the Inklings Meet? A Chronological Survey of Their Gatherings: 1933–1953," *Journal of Inklings Studies* 10, no. 2 (Oct. 2020): 184–204.

"Warren Lewis and the Lewis Papers," *VII, Journal of the Marion E. Wade Center* 37 (2020): 111–22.

"Warren Lewis: The Soldier Sailor," *Journal of Inklings Studies* 11, no. 1 (Apr. 2021): 58–69.

Introduction

Although Warren Hamilton Lewis (1895–1973) is best known as the beloved brother of C. S. Lewis (1898–1963), a biography of his life is necessary (not only for the importance of that role but also) because of his intimate involvement in the military, social, and cultural history of twentieth century England. Lewis fought in World War I as a young, untried officer in the Army Service Corp. His experience in history's greatest bloodbath mirrored that of thousands of others. In addition, his nightmarish days in northern France call to mind the war poetry of Edmund Blunden, Ivor Gurney, David Jones, Wilfred Owen, Siegfried Sassoon, and Edward Thomas as well as the prose of Sassoon and Robert Graves and their German counterparts Ernest Jünger and Erich Maria Remarque. Moreover, as a career army officer later serving in Sierra Leone and Shanghai, Lewis's Eurocentric sensibilities made him incapable of seeing the ways in which British colonialism shaped and hampered his understanding of the native African and Chinese people among whom he lived. Retiring from the army at the relatively young age of thirty-seven, Lewis spent the remainder of his life resolved to beginning what he called "the business of living," by which he meant finding satisfaction and meaning in a life outside the world of billets and barracks.

In addition to what has been noted, five particular matters underscore the importance of this biography. First, Warren Lewis's life sheds new light on his famous brother, including the warm and loving relationship between the two brothers that lasted throughout their lives. As young boys, they bonded quickly, in part as a response to the loss at early ages of their mother, Flora Lewis (1862–1908), and their corresponding complicity against what they believed to be the emotional, intellectual, and social intrusions upon their lives by their father, Albert Lewis (1863–1929). C. S. Lewis's autobiography, *Surprised by Joy* (1955), as well as *Collected Letters of C. S. Lewis, Volume 1: Family Letters 1905–1931* (2000), provide ample evidence of this complicity; however, scholars have yet to explore in depth Warren's responses to his mother's death and his father's role in his early life. In addition, Warren's struggle with alcoholism is well known, but its origin, influence on his life, and impact on his brother's life has not been explored in any detail. Moreover, after the death of C. S. Lewis, Warren lived another ten years—years that became increasingly dark as he grieved the passing of his beloved brother

Second, this biography explores Warren as an accomplished "amateur" historian—that is, he was not a university-trained and university-educated scholar. Nevertheless, he researched and wrote seven books on seventeenth-century French history:

The Splendid Century: Some Aspects of French Life in the Reign of Louis XIV. London: Eyre & Spottiswoode, 1953.

The Sunset of the Splendid Century: The Life and Times of Louis Auguste de Bourbon, Duc de Maine, 1670–1736. London: Eyre & Spottiswoode, 1955.

Assault on Olympus: The Rise of the House of Gramont between 1604 and 1678. London: Andre Deutsch, 1958.

Louis XIV: An Informal Portrait. London: Andre Deutsch, 1959.

The Scandalous Regent: A Life of Philippe, Duc d'Orleans, 1674–1723, and of His Family. London: Andre Deutsch, 1961.

Levantine Adventurer: The Travels and Missions of the Chevalier d'Arvieux, 1653–1697. London: Andre Deutsch, 1962.

Memoirs of the Duc de Saint-Simon. London: B. T. Batsford, 1964.

In addition, Warren collected, edited, and wrote the eleven-volume typescript manuscript, *Memoirs of the Lewis Family: 1850–1930*, and after the death of his brother in 1963, Warren published the *Letters of C. S. Lewis* (London: Geoffrey Bles, 1966). These volumes continue to be consulted today by researchers wanting to learn more about the life of C. S. Lewis. Yet no work has been done on the nature of these writings, Warren's strengths and weaknesses as a researcher and writer, and how these works contribute to our understanding of him and his famous brother.

Third, this account of Warren's life examines his role as an original member (along with his brother and J. R. R. Tolkien) of the Oxford Inklings—that now famous group of novelists, thinkers, churchmen, poets, essayists, medical men, scholars, and friends who met regularly to drink beer and to hear written compositions read aloud and to discuss books, ideas, history, and writers. In his diaries,

Warren often wrote summaries of what occurred at the various gatherings of the Inklings; in addition, he often shared insights about and commentary regarding the characters of the other Inklings. For instance, he was great friends with one Inkling in particular—Charles Williams—and after the unexpected death of Williams, Warren experienced a shattering sense of loss.

Fourth, this biography delves into Warren's participation as an active member of the household at the Kilns, the residence in Headington that he co-owned with his brother and Mrs. Janie Moore. In fact, after his retirement from the army in the early 1930s, two rooms were added to the Kilns that served as his study and bedroom for the rest of his life. In the only significant publication about Warren's life, *Brothers and Friends: The Diaries of Major Warren Hamilton Lewis*. Eds. Clyde S. Kilby and Marjorie Lamp Mead (San Francisco: Harper & Row, 1982), we learn something of the everyday life of the household, especially of Warren's increasing dislike of Mrs. Moore and how living there became something of drudgery and burden for him. However, *Brothers and Friends* is not the complete diary; in fact, it contains only about ten percent of Warren's complete 1.2-million-word daily record. This biography draws extensively from both *Brothers and Friends* and the remaining unpublished portions of Warren's diaries and yields new insights about life at the Kilns, especially the relationship between C. S. Lewis and Mrs. Moore; between Warren and his brother; between Warren and Mrs. Moore; and between the various other members of the household.

Lastly, this life of Warren Lewis reveals the important role he played in the relationship between his brother and the woman he married, Joy Davidman. As his brother's secretary, Warren read Joy's initial correspondence to his brother. A confirmed bachelor, Warren might have resisted Joy's overt efforts to develop a friendship with his brother, perhaps seeing her as a "gold-digger." Yet this was not the case, and despite his awareness that Joy wanted more than just friendship with his brother, Warren was not jealous or protective. In fact, he came to love Joy deeply, noted the "divine" irony that as Mrs. Moore was gradually removed from his brother's everyday care, Joy was slowly becoming an important part of that life, admired her courage as she fought the cancer that eventually took her life, and grieved deeply when she died.

Three final notes. In writing this biography, I tried as much as possible to re-sist writing yet another biography of C. S. Lewis. Many good ones already exist. At the same time, because the lives of the two brothers were so intertwined, it is evitable that at certain points I may have strayed perilously close to sketching too much of the life of Warren's younger brother. I hope readers will forgive these lapses. Second, the question of how to refer to the two brothers throughout was a thorny one. I knew that constant references to C. S. or CSL (or the even more

unforgiveable Clive) would become both tiresome and an irritation. The solution
I adopted was convenient, appropriate, and efficient, but not, however, without
risk. Because C. S. Lewis's family name was Jack—it was also the one most often
used by Warren—and because Warren's family name was Warnie, I decided to
risk the ire of some readers who might believe my use of Jack and Warnie as suggesting an intimacy with the two men that could not have been mine. Again, I
beg the indulgence of my readers and trust that they will soon come to be at ease
with my use of Jack and Warnie.

Third, as already noted, Warren's diary is the primary source for this biography. A crucial value of keeping a diary is that it affords the diarist the forum for
honest candor. On the one hand, the diarist can unashamedly confess doubt, fear,
joy, prejudice, delight, lust, empathy, anger, satisfaction, envy, and so on. On the
other hand, the diarist can explore the surprising truths that rise to the surface by
writing that is free, open, and unchecked. This means the diary writer can "see"
what he or she thinks, not just "think" it. Thoughts are fleeting, ephemeral, and
wispy things—and often jumbled, garbled, incoherent. One may "think" he or
she holds certain beliefs housed in a personal mental strongbox. However, it is
only when the thoughts are written down to "see" that one can begin to consider
the following: Do I really believe that? Does that actually represent me at my
deepest core? Does this cause me to live my everyday life the way I do? Or has
seeing written down on paper what I say I believe actually exposed my beliefs
as absurd, unsupportable, ill-formed, and hypocritical? Sometimes a diarist may
shock himself or herself when the answer to these questions is the opposite of
what he or she had always assumed. Thus, the chief value of keeping a diary is
that the written word trumps fuzzy, nonlinear, imprecise thinking. Words on
paper are clear, objective, and solid, so the diarist can explore with no restraint
every facet of his or her belief system. Furthermore, a diarist is self-absorbed. It
follows that we should not be overly critical of a diarist for his or her self-focus.
Every self is self-centered; at least the diarist admits as much.

In Warnie's case, he read other diaries voraciously and often reflected upon
the diarists. For instance, he read Arthur Ponsonby's *English Diaries* (1923) and
discovered what was to be the guiding principle for his own diary keeping. Ponsonby argued that what was important in a diary was not the account of one's
daily actions and events, but the psychology of the diarist. Warnie completely
rejected Ponsonby contention, implying on the contrary that he intended his
diary to be an objective one.[1] Nonetheless, inevitably what he thought, felt, and
believed comes through in the pages of his diary. As we read, we learn Warnie's
unfiltered opinions, convictions, and prejudices. Indeed, the insight we gain into
Warnie's psychology is the central reason we read him. His was a life of existential

loneliness. The early death of his mother, his emotional estrangement from his father, the lack of a long-term romantic relationship, his psychological reliance upon his brother, the absence of many deep and sustained male friends, and his dependence upon alcohol are markers of this loneliness. Accordingly, in this biography I have drawn extensively from Warnie's diaries—including both the published and unpublished portions.

I conclude with one caution: it would be a mistake to assume that Warnie's life can primarily be understood as the only sibling of Jack. Undoubtedly, the relationship between the two brothers plays a central role in both their lives, and I do not neglect the importance of their relationship. However, Warnie was also a soldier, an Inkling, and a noted French historian of the seventeenth century; these three "lives" are given careful attention in the pages that follow, as they are the central shaping influences in his life.

Montreat, NC
March 2022

Abbreviations

AMR	*All My Road Before Me: The Diary of C. S. Lewis*
BF	*Brothers and Friends: The Diaries of Major Warren Hamilton Lewis*
Bone	*Out of My Bone: The Letters of Joy Davidman*
"Diaries"	Warren Lewis's unpublished diaries
CL1	*Collected Letters of C. S. Lewis, Volume I: Family Letters 1905–1931*
CL2	*Collected Letters of C. S. Lewis, Volume II: Books, Broadcasts, and War, 1931–1949*
CL3	Collected Letters, of C. S. Lewis Volume III: Narnia, Cambridge, and Joy, 1950–1963
LP	Memoirs of the Lewis Family: 1850–1930
"Memoir"	"Memoir of C. S. Lewis," in *Letters of C. S. Lewis*
SJ	*Surprised by Joy: The Shape of My Early Life*

Chronology of the life of
Warren Hamilton Lewis (1895–1973)

June 16, 1895	Warren (Warnie) Hamilton Lewis is born in Belfast to Flora and Albert Lewis
November 29, 1898	Clive Staples Lewis (Jack) is born
April 21, 1905	The Lewis family moves to a new home, Leeborough (a.k.a. Little Lea) in Belfast
May 10, 1905	Warnie enrolled at Wynyard School, Watford, England
August 23, 1908	Flora Lewis dies
September 1908	Warnie and Jack begin attending Wynyard together
September 1909	Warnie begins attending Malvern College, Malvern, England
May 24, 1913	Warnie commits to a career in the Army Service Corp (ASC)
September 1913	Warnie begins studies with W. T. Kirkpatrick in Great Bookham, England
January–February 1914	Warnie wins a prize cadetship and enters the Royal Military Academy at Sandhurst
August 5, 1914	WWI begins

September–November 1914	Warnie is commissioned as a second lieutenant in the ASC and is sent to France with the British Expeditionary Force
September 1916	Warnie is promoted to lieutenant
October 1916	Warnie is promoted to temporary captain
November 29, 1917	Warnie is promoted to full captain
1918	The Army Service Corp is renamed the Royal Army Service Corp (RASC)
November 11, 1918	The Armistice is signed, ending WWI
April 1919	Warnie serves in Namur, Belgium
March 1920	Warnie purchases the first of several motorcycles and sidecars and begins attending training courses at Aldershot Military Garrison, England
March 1921–April 1922	Warnie serves in Sierra Leone, West Africa
August 5, 1922	Warnie meets Mrs. Janie Moore for the first time
October 4, 1922	Warnie serves as assistant to the officer of supplies for the RASC in Colchester, England
May 20, 1925	Jack becomes a Fellow of Magdalen College, Oxford
October–December 1925	Warnie serves as officer in charge of supplies for the RASC in Colchester
January–March 1926	Warnie serves as commanding officer for the No. 17 Mechanical Transport Company, RASC, in Woolwich, England
October 1926–March 1927	Warnie completes an economics course at London University
April 1927–April 1930	Warnie serves in China with the RASC, spending much of his time in Shanghai
September 25, 1929	Albert Lewis dies

April 17, 1930	Warnie returns to England
May 1930	Warnie begins editing the *Lewis Papers* and serves with the RASC at Bulford, England
October 10–11, 1930	Warnie, Jack, and Mrs. Moore move into the Kilns in Headington that they jointly purchased
January 1–4, 1931	Warnie and Jack take their first walking tour along the Wye Valley
May 1931	Warnie returns to Christian belief
October 1931	Warnie returns to Shanghai, China, and serves with the RASC
December 25, 1931	Warnie (in Shanghai) and Jack (in Oxford) take Communion for the first time in many years
December 14, 1932	Warnie returns to England
December 21, 1932	Warnie retires from the RASC, moves permanently into the Kilns, and continues editing the *Lewis Papers*
January 3–6, 1933	Warnie and Jack complete the second leg of their walking tour along the Wye Valley
January 1–6, 1934	Warnie and Jack complete the third leg of their walking tour along the Wye Valley
March 26, 1934	First documented meeting of the Inklings occurs with Jack, Warnie, and J. R. R. Tolkien present
December 19, 1934	Warnie completes editing the eleventh and final volume of the *Lewis Papers,* now titled *Memoirs of the Lewis Family: 1850–1930*
January 3–5, 1935	Warnie and Jack take their fourth walking tour, this time in the Chiltern Hills not far from Oxford
January 13–16, 1936	Warnie and Jack take their fifth walking tour, this time through Derbyshire.

July 3, 1936	Warnie has the *Bosphorus* built and begins to cruise the canals around Oxford
January 5–9, 1937	Warnie and Jack take their sixth walking tour, this time in Dulverton, Somerset
January 10–14, 1938	Warnie and Jack take their seventh walking tour, this time in Wiltshire
November 1938–June 1939	Warnie publishes eight essays about his trips onboard the *Bosphorus* in the *Motor Boat and Yachting* magazine
January 2–6, 1939	Warnie and Jack take their eighth and final walking tour, this time through the Welsh marshes
September 1, 1939	WWII begins
September 4, 1939	Warnie is recalled to active military service with the RASC and serves in France
September 1939	Regular Thursday evening and Tuesday morning gatherings of the Inklings commence; Charles Williams begins to attend
January 27, 1940	Warnie is given the temporary rank of major
August 16, 1940	Warnie is transferred to the Reserve of Officers and sent to Oxford, effectively ending his service in WWII; he serves aboard the *Bosphorus* as a part of the "floating" Home Guard
1943	Warnie begins to serve as Jack's secretary
April 13, 1944	Warnie reads his essay, "The Galleys of France," at the Thursday evening meeting of the Inklings
May 9, 1945	WWII ends; sometime this year he sells the *Bosphorus*
May 15, 1945	Charles Williams dies
1947	Warnie's essay "The Galleys of France" is published in *Essays Presented to Charles Williams* (Oxford: Oxford University Press, 1947); this

	essay later appears as a chapter in *The Splendid Century: Some Aspects of French Life in the Reign of Louis XIV*
March 29, 1947	Warnie completes his service in the Reserve of Officers
June 20, 1947	Warnie is hospitalized in Drogheda, Ireland, due to alcohol poisoning
October 30, 1949	The Thursday evening gatherings of the Inklings cease; Tuesday morning meetings continue at the Eagle and Child pub
January 10, 1950	Jack and Warnie receive Joy Davidman Gresham's first letter
January 12, 1951	Mrs. Moore dies
Summer/Fall 1952	Jack and Warnie meet Joy for the first time
1953	Warnie publishes *The Splendid Century: Some Aspects of French Life in the Reign of Louis XIV* (London: Eyre & Spottiswoode, 1953).
1955	Jack accepts the chair of Medieval and Renaissance Literature at Magdalene College, Cambridge
	Warnie publishes *The Sunset of the Splendid Century: The Life and Times of Louis Auguste de Bourbon, Duc de Maine, 1670–1736* (London: Eyre & Spottiswoode, 1955)
April 23, 1956	Jack and Joy are married in a civil ceremony
October 1956	Joy diagnosed with bone cancer
March 21, 1957	Jack and Joy are married in an ecclesiastical ceremony in her room at the Churchill Hospital, Oxford; Joy's health begins to improve
1958	Warnie publishes *Assault on Olympus: The Rise of the House of Gramont between 1604 and 1678* (London: Andre Deutsch, 1958)

1959	Warnie publishes *Louis XIV: An Informal Portrait* (London: Andre Deutsch, 1959)
October 1959	Joy's cancer returns
July 13, 1960	Joy dies
1961	Warnie publishes *The Scandalous Regent: A Life of Philippe, Duc d'Orleans, 1674–1723, and of His Family* (London: Andre Deutsch, 1961)
1962	Warnie publishes *Levantine Adventurer: The Travels and Missions of the Chevalier d'Arvieux, 1653–1697* (London: Andre Deutsch, 1962)
October 1962–February 1963	Warnie writes a biography of the "teenage Louis XIV" for the *Horizon* magazine in New York; it is never published
November 22, 1963	Jack dies
1964	Warnie publishes *Memoirs of the Duc de Saint-Simon* (London: B. T. Batsford, 1964)
May 19, 1964	Warnie moves from the Kilns to 51 Ringwood Road, only a few blocks away
1965	Warnie has a minor stroke
1966	Warnie publishes *Letters of C. S. Lewis* (London: Geoffrey Bles, 1966)
April 18, 1967	Warnie moves back to the Kilns
August 1970	Warnie's health worsens and he can no longer take long walks
January 1972	Warnie has a pacemaker installed
August 1972	Warnie enters Our Lady of Lourdes Hospital, Drogheda, Ireland, for a month of rest; while there, gangrene in both feet occurs, leading to minor surgery
April 1973	Warnie returns to the Kilns from Ireland
April 9, 1973	Warnie dies peacefully at the Kilns

CHAPTER ONE

Early Life
(1895–1914)

In the opening pages of C. S. Lewis's autobiography, *Surprised by Joy: The Shape of My Early Life*, he relates a story that explains the genesis of what he calls *Sehnsucht* or joy: "Once in those very early days my brother brought into the nursery the lid of a biscuit tin which he had covered with moss and garnished with twigs and flowers so as to make it a toy garden or a toy forest. That was the first beauty I ever knew. . . . As long as I live my imagination of Paradise will retain something of my brother's toy garden."[1] While the impact of this story has long been recognized as marking the central theme in the life and works of C. S. Lewis, what has not been noticed until now is how significant this incident is to the life and works of Lewis's brother, Warren Hamilton Lewis (1895–1973). That is, in the making of that toy garden we see the defining characteristic of Warren's life: an approach that was tactile, practical, and utilitarian. While for Warren's younger brother the toy garden awakened a powerful, nurturing aesthetic sense, for Warren the episode illustrates that he was given to working with things, with objects in the world before him, and with the matters of everyday life. He fabricated the toy garden for his brother with no idea of how it would impact his imagination; rather, Warren put together the toy garden because he delighted in making, constructing, and assembling.

Indeed, throughout his life Warren took a pragmatic and hands-on view of life; he was concerned with "how things work." The continuous flow of life, the day to day, and the present and pressing matters of the moment captured his attention. This vision of life explains his penchant for history (he wrote seven books on seventeenth-century French history), his interest in current events, his keen awareness of what was happening in contemporary English society, and his primary focus on the matters of everyday experience. He was a careful observer, a sharp-eyed reporter, and an active doer. His mind was prosaic rather than poetic, pragmatic rather than imaginative, and engaged rather than detached. If his brother was romantic, reflective, and intuitive, Warren was realistic, practical, and commonsensical. In short, if C. S. Lewis was right-brained, Warren Lewis was left-brained.

The best example highlighting the difference between the two brothers is the fact that Warren chronicled his life for over sixty years by keeping a diary; it runs to 1.2 million words (almost 1,400 single-spaced typed pages). In an early diary entry, he explained that he decided to keep a diary because it gave him immense pleasure to be able to look back over the notes he had taken in the previous year. While an outsider might find his notes "like eating sawdust," they helped him to remember precisely what had happened on each day. He could scan a few lines and be able to remember the place, how the sun shone through the trees, the whine of an artillery shell, the sound of his friends' voices, and the card games he played after supper. Things that would be insignificant to other people would bring him great delight. Accordingly, he wrote that he would make an effort to stick doggedly to the drudgery of keeping his diary. He admitted that his daily entries would not be witty or sparkling, but he knew it would be fatal if he decided to put off a day's writing.[2] Most telling was his conviction "that all I write is going to be a cinematograph which can be seen at will in the years to come."[3] Now contrast this with what C. S. Lewis said about keeping a diary in SJ: "If Theism had done nothing else for me, I should still be thankful that it cured me of the time-wasting and foolish practice of keeping a diary. (Even for autobiographical purposes a diary is nothing like so useful as I had hoped. You put down each day what you think important; but of course you cannot each day see what will prove to have been important in the long run)."[4] The two brothers could not have had more opposing notions about diary keeping. For Warren, the "every day" served as a stimulus to his memories; for his brother, the "every day" was uninteresting and time-wasting. Much of the remainder of Warren's efforts as a diarist was devoted to creating a verbal cinematograph by which he could replay and stimulate memories that recalled his past daily life.

Interesting parallels can be drawn between Warren's utilitarian approach to life and to the city where he was born on June 16, 1895: Belfast, Ireland. Belfast was a thriving center of industry, well known for its linen manufacturing and its exploding population. In the period from 1810 to 1900, Belfast's population swelled from 20,000 to 350,000, a more than seventeen-fold increase.[5] Moreover, and most crucial for Warren, was the fact that from the middle of the nineteenth century through World War I, Belfast was the most important shipbuilding center in the United Kingdom. Hundreds of vessels were conceived, designed, and constructed in the new shipyards that sprang up in the harbor of this port city. Leading up to WWI, the Belfast shipyards "were producing up to 10% of British merchant shipping output."[6] Most notable were the firms of Harland & Wolff, Workman Clark, Bibby and Sons, and MacIlwaine and Lewis; collectively, they manufactured vessels that were purchased locally and internationally.[7] Of special note is the fact that Richard Lewis (1832–1908), Warren's paternal grandfather, had once been intimately involved in the Belfast shipbuilding industry. While working for the ship repair firm of Walpole, Webb, and Bewley in Dublin, Lewis met John MacIlwaine. Together they decided to move to Belfast in 1868 and created their company, MacIlwaine and Lewis: Boilermakers, Engineers, and Iron Shipbuilders.[8] For reasons that are not entirely clear, Lewis left the firm in 1886 to work for the Belfast Harbour Board.[9]

Albert Lewis (1863–1929), who was the sixth child of Richard and Martha Lewis, and Flora (1862–1908), who was the second child of Thomas and Mary Hamilton, provided a warm, loving, and comfortable home for their two sons, the family growing with the arrival of Clive Staples Lewis on November 22, 1898.[10] Warren's younger brother threw overboard his given name by the time he was three or four, insisting on being called Jacksie, then Jacks, and finally Jack. Warnie—as he was known to family and friends—and Jack would have been able to look down into the Belfast Lough and witness the busy harbor and the ship manufacturing. Warnie's attention was drawn to and entranced by all this energy, and he was particularly fascinated with the shipyards, often drawing pictures of the many ships he saw being built.[11] As Jack later put it in *SJ*, the Belfast Lough, filled with shipping, was delightful to both him and his brother, but especially to Warnie.[12] Related to Warnie's interest in the vessels he saw in the harbor were the trains that traveled in and around Belfast. The expansion of rail service in Belfast had not been without controversy. According to J. L. McCracken: "When the Ulster Railway was opened [in 1839] the Belfast presbytery declared that Sunday trains would result in an increase of vice and wickedness. One clergy man told his congregation that he would rather join a company for theft and murder than the Ulster Railway Company, because its business was sending souls to the devil at the rate of sixpence a-piece: 'Every sound of the railway whistle,' he said, 'is answered by a shout in hell.'"[13] Regardless, the movement of things mechanical—particularly huge ships and rushing trains—imprinted itself powerfully upon Warnie's developing mind and psyche, so much so that for the remainder of his life he retained a fascination with the way machines worked. Belfast's "hands-on," busy, functional ethos was a perfect match with Warnie's down-to-earth, pragmatic approach to life.

During one of his business trips to London, Albert, knowing of Warnie's interest in how things worked, purchased a globe of the world and mailed it home. Flora wrote to Albert on May 8, 1900, that the globe arrived safely, and "Badgie" was delighted with it.[14] This gift foreshadowed the fact that Warnie would later travel the world during his military career.[15] Later that same summer, while Flora and her two sons were vacationing down by the sea in Castlerock, she wrote to Albert about another instance of Warnie's tactile approach to life, telling him that their oldest son was drawn to the brickmaking that took place below the railway near where they were staying; she added that Warnie was always wanting to go there because there was a waterwheel that worked a circular saw.[16] The following summer, again writing from Castlerock, Flora told Albert of Warnie's fascination with the movement of the waves. Most telling, however, was her letter of June 27, 1901: "When we were up to see the train yesterday, one of the engine drivers invited Badgie up to see his engine; I did not half like letting him go, but he was so anxious that I let him; they showed him all the things, and he was greatly delighted."[17]

It was during these early years together that Warnie and Jack bonded. Warnie says that by the time they moved to their new home, Leeborough, on April 21, 1905, he and his brother had "laid the foundations of an intimate friendship that was the greatest happiness of my life and lasted unbroken until his death fifty-eight years later."[18] One marker of their intimacy from these early days was their lifelong nicknames for each other: Warnie was A. P. B. and Jack was S. P. B.—shortened versions of the threat their nurse used to make about spanking their "piggiebottoms," with Warnie as "Archpiggiebotham" and Jack as "Small-piggiebotham." Driven indoors frequently by the damp Irish weather as well as the unhealthy living conditions of Belfast, the two boys—feeling at times like housebound prisoners—developed elaborate fictional worlds where they freely exercised their creative imaginations.[19] Both boys learned how to draw, and Jack made his first attempts at writing; together they fashioned imaginary worlds. Worth noting is that while Jack created stories and populated them with his drawings of anthropomorphic animals, Warnie's contributions tended to be functional, including maps, ships, and railways. Another way to put this is that Jack's early imagination was creative and interactive while Warnie's was practical and constructivist. In *SJ*, Jack notes that the Animal-Land he and his brother created had to be modern, containing trains and steamships if he hoped to share it with Warnie.[20] Warnie was fascinated by India, so the boys created a geographical relationship between India and Animal-Land: "We made [Warnie's India] an island, with its north coast running along the back of the Himalayas; between it and Animal-Land my brother rapidly invented the principal steamship routes. Soon there was a whole world and a map of that world."[21] Eventually

Animal-Land became Boxen, and at one point Warnie began a Boxonian newspaper. From their earliest days together, Warnie was purposeful—focused on the matters of everyday life, especially transportation routes, geography, and news reports—while Jack was intuitive—focused on the matters of the imagination, especially narrative stories, fascinating characters, and adventurous episodes.[22] This bifurcation of sensibilities marked the two throughout their lives.

It is important here that I clarify a distinction I am drawing between Warnie and Jack. Both were voracious readers; however, the ends for which they read were different. In general, when Warnie read, he was essentially exercising what might be call an applied imagination—meaning that he enjoyed reading and writing toward serviceable ends. His later work on the *LP,* his diary, his essays about boating in the canals in and around Oxford, and his books on French history are expressions of his applied imagination.[23] Moreover, although he was a devoted reader throughout his life, for him reading was primarily for pleasure and information. Witness his later dogged reading of Shakespeare's plays, even when he was not particularly enjoying the play at hand.[24] Reading was a great enjoyment for him, but primarily it was a way to expend time and to move life along—not as a particular source of inspiration, imaginative interaction, or literary development. In the words of Samuel Taylor Coleridge, for Warnie reading was an expression of his primary imagination: that is, "the living power and prime agent of all human perception." When Jack read, however, he was exercising a creative imagination—he enjoyed reading and writing toward intuitive, reflective, and aesthetic ends. Certainly, his deep reading of the towering figures of Western literature—Homer, Virgil, Dante—and of English literature, especially Chaucer, Spenser, Shakespeare, Milton, George Herbert, Samuel Johnson, Jane Austen, William Wordsworth, George MacDonald, William Morris, and G. K. Chesterton served as the wellhead of his creative imagination. He read and wrote in order to explore, express, and nourish his already rich imagination. Again, in the words of Coleridge, for Jack, reading was an expression of his secondary imagination: "an echo of the former, coexisting with the conscious will, yet still as identical with the primary in the *kind* of its agency, and differing only in *degree,* and in the *mode* of its operation. It dissolves, diffuses, dissipates, in order to recreate; or where this process is rendered impossible, yet still, at all events, it struggles to idealize and unify."[25]

But to return to Warnie's early life, his childhood relationship with his parents was warm. Flora was loving, attentive, and caring. While not strict with Warnie and Jack, she did watch over her sons protectively. More even-tempered and available than Albert, Flora saw to their daily needs, as well as their educational and spiritual development. Albert, conversely, was consumed with work—something not unusual for a solicitor, especially one assigned to cases involving the police. His work required that he travel extensively, a necessity that troubled both Flora and the boys. In her letters to Albert while he was away, she often wrote of her longing to be with him, how much she missed him, and the queries from the boys regarding when their father would be home. To his credit, Albert loved his wife and sons, and was a wonderful provider. However, he was a workaholic, unable to relax and enjoy the company of his family, particularly when on holiday. Warnie recounts what may be the quintessential portrait of Albert. Recalling their annual holidays at the seaside, Warnie notes that two pictures remain in his memory. The first was of his father's gloomy detachment. Albert might visit his family on the weekend, but he would never stay for the fortnight. His excuse would be the urgent business he had as a police solicitor. Warnie believed, however, that the real reason his father did not stay for the entire holiday was that he needed a break from family duties. In the second picture, Warnie suggests that his father's reluctance to enjoy a holiday may have gone deeper than that: "I never met a man more wedded to a dull routine, or less capable of extracting enjoyment from life. A night spent out of his own home was a penance to him: a holiday he loathed, having not the faintest conception of how to amuse himself. I can still see him on his occasional visits to the seaside, walking moodily up and down the beach, hands in trouser pockets, eyes on the ground, every now and then giving a heartrending yawn and pulling out his watch."[26] Thus, while Albert worked hard to give his family all the material comforts he could, it was left to Flora to nurture, educate, and refine her sons. Given the brothers' affinity for assigning nicknames, it is not surprising that they soon came to refer to their father as the O. A. B.—short for the "Old Air Balloon."

WYNYARD SCHOOL

On May 11, 1905, Flora, after she and Albert had vetted a number of English preparatory schools, enrolled Warnie at Wynyard School, Watford, in Hertford-shire, roughly 30 miles west of London.[27] This move to Wynyard for Warnie was momentous; it was less than one month after the family had moved into their new home, Leeborough, and he was still a month shy of his tenth birthday. Although Albert and Flora were following the typical pattern of middle-class Irish parents in sending Warnie away to an English public school, why they chose Wynyard—which initially was not even on their short list—is a mystery. To be fair, Albert and Flora used the services of Messrs. Gabbitas and Thring, a popular and frequently consulted London vetting agent for prep schools. George Sayer assumes in his biography of Jack, *Jack: C. S. Lewis and His Times*, the deciding factor in favor of Wynyard was financial—it was affordable.[28] However, nothing in the *LP* confirms Sayer's argument nor do any of Albert's or Flora's letters. In the *LP*, Warnie expresses his own uncertainty over the choice, writing that he finds it difficult to understand how his parents chose such a poor school since they made careful and exhaustive enquiries; they had narrowed the choice to three or four schools and Wynyard was not one of that group.[29]

Whatever the reason, Wynyard was a decidedly poor choice. Warnie wrote that Wynyard was a grotesque throwback, even for unknowing parents like his own. In all honesty, Warnie added, parents who sent their children to Wynyard certainly did not have their comfort in mind.[30] The school proved to be disastrous, first for Warnie, and then later for Jack. Readers will know of Jack's opinion of Wynyard through *SJ*. Suffice it to say here that his view of Wynyard is expressed succinctly through the name he gives it: Belsen, among the most notorious and cruel concentration camps of World War II.[31] However, few readers will know the devastating impact Wynyard had on Warnie. Indeed, his years there forever scarred him psychologically and hobbled him academically. Many forces were at work at Wynyard that harmed Warnie. The food was poor, the housing spartan, and the sanitation abysmal. Warnie wrote later that even in 1905 a Sanitation Inspector would have condemned the toilets since one of his most abiding memories was their noxious odor in summertime.[32] Jack gave some idea of how poor the food was, writing in his diary of November 1909: "I had a shop egg [not fresh] for my breakfast today, being Sunday; for breakfast most week days we had bad ham." And several days later: "By the way I might mention dinner. We had enormous helpings of boiled beef, with thick, sickening, yellow fat, and little grey puddings, sometimes known as slime balls, not to mention an adjoining complement of black, adamantine parsnips."[33] Also telling is the fact that there were no playing fields, gymnasium, laboratories, workshops, or library. Organized games, except cricket, ceased to exist shortly after Warnie arrived, their places taken by pick-up games of rounders and conkers.[34] Warnie also affirmed that the bullying of weaker boys by the stronger ones frequently occupied free time.

The monotony of life at Wynyard was deadening, leading Warnie to reflect that for a boy who would eventually make his way through public school, it would be hard to imagine a worse place.[35] The headmaster, the Rev. Robert Capron (whom the boys nicknamed Oldie) made no effort to engage the boys in genuine learning; he did not try to draw out or even to understand the kinds of things the individual boys were interested in learning. Instead, Capron was essentially a warder, ruling his boys—and his family—as a tyrant and making use of intimidation, terror, and physical beatings. Warnie later wondered whether Capron was a sadist or merely a willful, brutal bully, citing as one example Capron's casual comment to one of his charges at the end of morning classes: "And after lunch ... if I'm not too tired, I shall give you a good drubbing."[36]

Moreover, what little instruction Capron employed relied upon rote learning over a small range of repeated subject matter. For instance, the boys spent hour after hour doing repetitive arithmetic sums. Warnie noted that in his case he spent the better part of the school year doing the same four sums over and over again every day in rotation, observing that it was little wonder that he ended up having an extremely difficult time passing the elementary mathematics entrance test when he later applied to attend Malvern College.[37] History and geography were similarly handled, so that Warnie insisted subsequently he could not re- member one single instance of learning that he achieved while at Wynyard. As far as Warnie was concerned, Capron maintained the school primarily as means of assuring himself of a livelihood. However, Warnie's early letters home to his mother and father did not reveal the misery of his days at Wynyard. Often, he would write his parents and say that he thought the school was nice, or that he was getting on pretty well in his lessons, or that he was having a good time; the only hint of dissatisfaction was the frequency with which he would communicate how many days were left before the term would be over, and he would be back again at Leeborough. In letters home to Jack, he underscored how he longed to be home for the holidays, and his continuing fascination with ships; in one instance, he wrote Jack that he had just bought two delightful postcards of the *Lusitania* and the *Mauritania*.[38] Later, Warnie offered more details on his inter- est in the *Lusitania* when he attended a Franco-British Exhibition at a nearby museum. He noted that he most enjoyed the shipping and the railway hall; he was particularly attracted to its models of the *Lusitania* and a river ferry, as well as a real, full-size railway engine. He also disagreed with Jack, who thought all the models of the steam ships looked the same.[39]

In the *LP*, Warnie noted that letters to parents from schoolboys were not to be trusted because to be honest and complain risked being revealed to the school authorities. In looking back twenty years later over the letters he wrote at Wynyard, Warnie said he was surprised by the inaccuracy of his letters while there, including claims that he was content, that he liked this or that person, and that he was learning a great deal.[40] In the novel *The Harrovians* (1913), which both Jack and Warnie read, art imitated their lives since in the novel we find this same kind of schoolboy denial. The main character, Peter O'Neil, "was not happy. He hated [games] and he lived in fear of being whooped [caned]. Of all this he wrote nothing in his letters home. . . . A boy takes the worst of surroundings for granted, and though he will grumble among his friends, he will rarely or ever complain to his people."[41] Eventually, however, toward the end of his time at Wynyard, Warnie did begin to complain about Capron. On February 12, 1908, he wrote his mother that one day, as he was doing algebra with Capron and could not answer one of the questions, the headmaster exploded in anger and ridiculed him before the other boys. Another thing Warnie disliked was how Capron linked his poor academic performance to his nationality. In one instance when Warnie failed to answer a question correctly, Capron belittled him and told him that he did not want any of his "Irish wit."[42] Eight months later and not long after Flora's death, Capron wrote a blistering letter to Albert about Warnie. While complimenting Jack, who only recently had begun to attend Wynyard, Capron denounced Warnie, complaining that he was reluctant to engage in either mental or physical effort. His indolence, he wrote, was so marked that Capron believed it to be more a disease than a conscious choice. Capron also described Warnie as a liar and prevaricator. The letter cited a recent incident where, he claimed, Warnie tried to cheat on his algebra assignment. Capron's censure of Warnie concluded with his assessment that the only reason the boy returned to school was to follow his own whims, break rules, and flout Capron's will.[43] Capron did not connect the recent death of Flora on August 23, 1908—it had been less than two months since she had succumbed to stomach cancer—to Warnie's alleged behavior. It may be that a hundred years ago in England adults such as Capron made little allowance for a child's grief.[44]

Albert, too, failed to see how the death of Flora may have adversely affected Warnie. In a letter to Jack of October 26, 1908 (Jack had written to his father and defended Warnie against the charge of laziness), Albert wondered why Warnie was always in trouble and doing so poorly at Wynyard. He could not fathom why Capron was no longer friendly toward Warnie, as he once had been. Warnie's unhappiness was a terrible trouble to him, in a life, Albert added, that was already so full of trouble that he found it very hard to bear.[45] In other letters, Warnie complained to his father about Capron accusing him of being greedy and gluttonous—in one case blaming Warnie for stealing a piece of another boy's cake and then lying about it; Capron had flown into a rage, cursed Warnie for being insubordinate, and called him a huge swine.[46] Warnie also told his father that Capron publicly derided and disparaged him—once calling him a cheater and a bully, and on another occasion singling him out before the class and claiming that he was guilty of spending his holidays idling around shipyards and smoking cigarettes.[47] Albert, sensing that at least some of Warnie's unhappiness at Wynyard was merited, sent Annie Hamilton, his sister-in-law, to investigate the school in October 1908. After hearing the reports from his sister-in-law, Albert came to believe that the fault lay more with Capron than Warnie. Inexplicably, however, Albert did not immediately pull his two sons from Wynyard.[48] Warnie remained there until July 28, 1909, and Jack until July 12, 1910.

Warnie later wrote in his "Memoir" that he and his brother could never adequately convey the dismal story of Wynyard and Capron.[49] Ernest Benson, who, along with his brother Joe, "went to that hateful place [Wynyard] in the winter term of 1896," confirmed in his own autobiography the horrors of the place and the cruelty of Capron. Because both Jack and Warnie were forever damaged by Capron, Benson's Wynyard experience is worth referring to at length. During his first meeting with Capron when he was being interviewed to become a student at Wynyard, Benson was struck by Capron's "wide forehead and a very thin nose, the rest of his features concealed by a heavy moustache, side whiskers, and a long beard of almost ginger color coming right down to his navel." About Mrs. Capron, Benson said he "never heard her laugh and seldom saw her smile, there was a grayness about her whole appearance. She was probably a sick woman, an unhappy woman, and an embittered woman all the years I knew her." In the tea that accompanied the interview, Capron called Benson his "little manikin," while Mrs. Capron kissed him and said, "So this is the little man, how we shall love to look after him and make him happy." Benson then described a schoolroom and the "very subdued" chatter of the boys there; moreover, there was a "complete absence of the smiles and geniality I had experienced a few minutes previously in the drawing room." Unfortunately, on his first night at the school, Benson and another boy wet their beds. Benson painfully recalled Capron's response: "He carefully selected one of the canes which had been cunningly concealed behind the bookcase, out of sight of any possible visitor. Then seizing the [other] boy roughly by the collar, exclaimed, 'Come out you filthy pig' . . . and administered four almighty strokes, after which he shouted, 'Pigs don't eat with gentlemen.'" Benson continued: "It was quite usual for the boys to be abused as cads, skunks, or pigs, and even parents came in for wild abuse on occasion, especially if some parent should have the impertinence to . . . insist that their son's breakfast should be supplemented by an egg."

About geometry class, Benson had unforgettable memories: "A wrong answer was sufficient for a flogging, but the treatment meted out during the afternoon Euclid classes exceeded everything in brutality. . . . A boy became completely mesmerized by fear. Standing in front of the blackboard with chalk in one hand and cane in the other, [Capron] would demand the problem to be solved. . . . The result was invariably the same." Capron would scream "'Good Lord deliver us' . . . [and] would shout as he brutally flogged them just for being petrified. I saw boys' hands deeply incised by vicious strokes, and I saw my brother [Joe] so treated." Even sixty years later, Benson remembered "that (one victim) suffered from curvature of the spine and frequent bouts of severe nose bleedings made no difference. . . . I once saw [Capron] severely flog a day boy who was a cripple, and who died a few years later of his infirmities. . . . I never knew any boy utter a sob or a sound during these floggings." Benson was incensed to recall that on Sundays Capron would "have every appearance of a jovial *pater familias*[50] escorting [his] family to Church." Capron eventually cut out all Sunday visits by the boys to their own homes; they became "less and less frequent, finally ceasing. . . . Excuses were given to our parents, but probably the main reason was that we carried the telltale marks of [Capron's] canings on our bodies; significantly, I never knew a caning to take place during the last fortnight of the term." During Lent, Benson was "thankful that [Capron] made no attempt to deny himself beer or tobacco. What might have happened if he had, I shudder to think."

In addition, Benson had flashbacks about the pervading sense of evil at Wynyard: "[Capron] was a light sleeper. . . . Once I [Benson] was forced to visit the toilet in the night . . . situated alongside his bedroom. I succeeded in getting there in my bare feet, but I had not bargained for a temperamental plug [toilet backup]. . . . [Capron] rushed out [exclaiming that] 'it was a case of sheer laziness on my part' and I was for it. But I got so accustomed to being caned that I became almost immune to pain although my skin would often be lacerated and my pants would stick to my flesh." However, Capron's verbal abuses scarred Benson more than the physical punishments. Once he wrote his mother: "Mr. C. said I was a cad and that nobody likes to speak to Joey [his brother] at Wynyard because he is a cad, and that our ancestors were lumps of yeast and beer bands. All this because I was last [to finish] my dinner." The greatest crisis experienced by Benson at Wynyard came during the Lent term in 1901 when Capron heard that he and another boy, Punch, had been shooting birds:

[Capron] stormed into the schoolroom in the worst rage I had ever seen. He literally rushed for his cane and almost dragged Punch and myself into his study. . . . He started immediately to knock Punch about the head with fists and down on to the floor. He thrashed and thrashed him unmercifully. His fury knew no bounds when Punch sobbed out, "I will tell my father." Whether out of exhaustion or realization that he had gone too far or for fear of the consequences, he suddenly stopped. Punch was by then in a pitiable and disheveled condition, his face showing the signs of the blows, his collar almost torn off and his calves covered with welts. He was allowed to have his breakfast in the schoolroom. . . . When breakfast was over . . . there was no Punch."

Punch, of course, had run away; once found, he was expelled, but "fear descended on [Capron]. The treatment of boys ... had been seen outside [the school], and it was certain that nothing could prevent it being talked about." A sequel soon followed:

> Not many days after, [Capron] came into the schoolroom before breakfast and in the most subdued manner that I had ever known, said (to me) "Ernie, come along and see me." It was something unusual to be addressed in this appealing way.... He sat down with pen and paper ... and started to suggest to me what had happened in this same room a few days earlier. Of course I readily agreed that he had given Punch only a few light strokes, and had done nothing more than box his ears two or three times quite softly.... Punch's family however held entirely different views of what had happened.... So legal proceedings were instituted against [Capron] in the High Court. Being the only independent person present, I became the principal witness ... I was interviewed by the solicitor for the defense.... Of course I stuck to [Capron']s account, I was far too frightened to do otherwise. The old lawyer obviously saw through all this.... On the day of the hearing of the case [Capron] and three or four of us boys ... left for London. Swaggering up and down the platform ... was a boy who had been removed by his father from the school some years earlier because of the rough treatment he had received; he was a hostile witness and [Capron]'s feelings were obvious.... My father was there (in the Law Courts), the old solicitor was there ... and a conversation was taking place in a quiet corner between my father and [Capron]. Then the old solicitor disappeared with [Capron]. When he reappeared he told us it was all over. It was not until some years afterwards that I knew that the case had been settled out of Court. [Capron] had to pay £50 to a charity, meet all the legal expenses, and give Punch a character.... The case was too strong against [Capron], and the old solicitor knew it.... There is no doubt that the case started a decline in the school, for it was impossible to prevent people or boys from talking, and this specially affected the intake of new boys."

After this incident, Benson no longer feared Capron because "I now knew that he was a coward."

Benson ended his recollection by commenting on Mrs. Capron's death: "The boys irritated her and, as if to soothe [her husband's] erotic craving, I often heard her urge him on by saying, 'cane him hubby.' She was the only woman I ever met who was devoid of every vestige of feminine tenderness or affection." He then added a story about Capron that neither Jack nor Warnie had ever heard: "With a rapidly declining income from the school," Capron tried hard to marry the widowed mother of a former student. However, he was unsuccessful, so he accepted a position as a minister in a country church where "he seems to have lost all control of his sadistic cravings, for, deprived of the means of satisfying his erotic passions through the floggings of boys, he turned his attentions to the choir and Churchwardens. As a result, he was quickly put under restraint, certified insane, and within a few months died, incapable of recognizing his former associates."[51]

After spending several thousand words in the *LP* describing his own unhappy years at Wynyard, Warnie concluded: "I have failed [in my description] . . . if I have not shown you a powerful, violent, brutal man, without intellectual tastes or attainments, regarding his school as at once a mere livelihood, and a safety valve for his ill temper, who by secluding himself from all who were not under his domination, had reached such a degree of tyranny that the kindest verdict I can pass on him is . . . that he was not quite sane."[52] Essentially cruel and unstable, Capron comes across as a compilation of several characters out of the novels of Charles Dickens: Mr. M'Choakumchild, the ruthless teacher in *Hard Times*; Bill Sykes, the brutal criminal in *Oliver Twist*; Mr. Murdstone, David Copperfield's cruel stepfather in *David Copperfield*; and Wackford Squeers, the sadistic, manipulative schoolmaster in *Nicholas Nickleby*. One other literary character may have influenced Warnie's portrait of Capron: Dr. Grimstone, the autocratic headmaster of Crichton House, who appears in another novel Jack and Warnie read, *Vice Versa: A Lesson to Fathers* (1882) by Thomas Anstey Guthrie. At one point, when Grimstone is about to cane a boy in front of the school for having passed a note to a girl in church, he pontificates:

> See him as he cowers there before your gaze, in all the hideousness of his moral depravity. . . . You do well to shun him as a moral leper . . . [as] the impious wretch has availed himself of the shelter of a church to cloak his insidious advances. . . . If I can succeed in bringing this coward, this unmanly dallier in a sentiment which the healthy mind of boyhood rejects as premature, to a sense of his detestable conduct; if I can score the lesson upon his flesh so that some faint notion of its force and purport may be conveyed to what has been supplied to him as a heart, then I shall not have lifted this hand in vain! He shall see whether he will be allowed to trail the fair name of the school for propriety and correctness of deportment in the dust of a pew-floor, and spurn my reputation as a preceptor like a church hassock beneath his feet![53]

Grimstone's tirade and public humiliation of the offending note passer captures well the atmosphere Capron created at Wynyard.[54]

Under Capron, Warnie came to view learning as an absurd joke at best and as a mindless, tortured penance at worst. Equally telling was Warnie's summary of Albert's part in this educational debacle: "With his uncanny flair for making the wrong decision, my father had given us helpless children into the hands of a madman."[55] Both Warnie and Jack were intellectually and psychologically traumatized by their experience with Capron. Warnie emerged from three years at Wynyard devoid of the requisite academic skills he needed when transitioning to Malvern College in September 1909; Jack was psychically wounded by Capron's cruelty, and it was not until near the end of his life that he was he able to forgive Capron, in spite of many concerted efforts to do so.[56] Compounding their terrible experience at Wynyard was the untimely death of their mother—after a painful and prolonged struggle with stomach cancer. On how his mother's death affected him, Jack wrote with stark clarity in *SJ*: "With my mother's death all settled happiness, all that was tranquil and reliable, disappeared from my life. There was to be much fun, many pleasures, many stabs of Joy; but no more of the old security. It was sea and islands now; the great continent had sunk like Atlantis."[57] In addition, he ascribed to her death not only his own sense of crushing loss, but also the beginning of a lifelong estrangement from his father. While their mother's death drove Warnie and Jack closer together, it also drove a wedge between the two and their father.[58]

In Warnie's "Memoir," he was much less forthcoming about the impact of his mother's death. He did note that 1908 was an unhappy year marked by death, since his father first lost his father, then his wife, and finally his brother, Joseph.[59] If he tried to give an account of his mother's extended illness and death, Warnie said it would be an inadequate paraphrase of what his brother had already written in *Surprised by Joy*. Adding to the hurt, his mother died on his father's forty-fifth birthday, August 23, 1908. Warnie remembered that there was a Shakespearean calendar hanging on the wall of the room where she died with the quotation "Men must endure their going hence."[60] His father preserved the page of that calendar for the remainder of his life, and the quote later surfaced several other times in Warnie's life.[61] Although neither brother lingered over the impact of their mother's death, Jack was deeply impaired by the loss. Warnie, by comparison, had much less to say and treated the event almost matter-of-factly. If Jack gave us an "inside view" of his response to losing his mother, Warnie gave us an "outside view." Jack felt the event internally while Warnie held the event at arm's length. In drawing this distinction, I am not arguing that Warnie was less feeling, less tender, and less devastated than Jack; however, I am suggesting that he was reticent to go over the old wound, to dwell on what may have been the most painful experience in his life. At this point in their lives, Jack internalized and Warnie externalized. It is significant to note that even in later life the two brothers almost never wrote about their mother's death. Other than in *SJ*, Jack rarely referred to his mother, and Warnie, in spite of his lengthy diary, seldom mentioned her. In brief, Flora's death seems to have been so traumatic that both brothers repressed the pain and avoided consciously reflecting on their loss.[62]

MALVERN COLLEGE

It is reasonable to believe that Warnie entered Wynyard as a capable student—albeit not as bright as his younger brother—but he left the school with poor study habits, a tendency toward indolence, and a distaste for academic rigor. Sensing this was the case, as early as October 1908 Albert had begun searching for a new school for Warnie. This time he was more careful than he had been with Wynyard, seeking the advice of William Thompson Kirkpatrick (1848–1921), his former headmaster at Lurgan College, in county Armagh, where Albert had been a student from 1877 to 1879. Among the many schools considered were Winchester, Cheltenham, Rugby, and Shrewsbury. Ironically, however, Albert ended up taking the advice of Capron, who recommended that Warnie be sent to Malvern College, located in Malvern, Worcestershire, England, close to the border of Wales and 70 miles northwest of Oxford. Writing Albert on June 1, 1909, Capron claimed that he could not do any better than to secure Warnie a place in Reverend Sydney Rhodes James's house at the college. Capron then added, blindly unaware of the damning testimony to his and Wynyard's failure to educate Warnie, that he knew a little Greek, Latin, English, and French, but was hopeless at mathematics and knew no German. He told Albert to expect that his son would enter Malvern at a very low level; this probability would be quite embarrassing for Warnie.[63] Albert wrote the Headmaster at Malvern College, Mr. James—a Trinity College, Cambridge scholar—on June 2 and inquired if there might be a place for Warnie; he was delighted to hear back from James on June 4 that Warnie would be welcomed to Malvern College.[64] The news was a huge relief to Warnie; he wrote his father on June 16, his fourteenth birthday, and requested books about steam ships or railway engines.[65] Almost certainly the best birthday news he got was that he would be going to Malvern College. Blessed relief came when he left Wynyard for the last time on July 28, 1909.

Warnie began life at Malvern College on September 16, 1909. Among the most immediate contrasts to Wynyard was the character of Headmaster James. Affectionately known to the boys as Scrubby, James was very popular, in part because of the origin of his nickname. Whenever he was angered, he had the facile ability to substitute for bad language an innocuous euphemism. Soon the boys were themselves using James's substitute expletives. Among his favorites were "scrubby toad" and "measley squirm." Moreover, James was conscious of his peculiar practice and readily laughed at himself;[66] he could not have been more different than the maniacal Capron. A second notable contrast to Wynyard was the food. In a later essay, Warnie recounted the excellence of the food at Malvern. During breakfast, students found tables piled high with bacon, sausages, and fish, as well as bread, butter, sugar, and pots of teas. One could eat all one wanted. During tea, bread and butter, with cake or jam, seemed to be supplied endlessly. For supper, there was bread, butter, and cheese, and milk and beer flowed freely.[67] Regarding the easy access to alcohol, he added that dinner went down better when they snuck to town and had a glass of sherry afterward at the local hotel. He also observed that many people began to drink at a younger age in those days; moreover, they drank more.[68] In addition, excursions to the countryside meant they could have a pint of inexpensive but excellent hard cider along with the first smoke of the day.[69]

A third contrast to Wynyard was the physical facilities. Not only was there a chapel, a well-stocked refectory, hiking paths, playing fields, study rooms, clean toilets, and comfortable sleeping rooms, but also there was the delightful Grundy Library. Warnie recalled that he loved to slip unobserved into the Grundy and spend the afternoon there. His delightful memories of relaxing summer afternoons included his first encounters with Swinburne, Tennyson, Ruskin, Arnold, de Quincy, and many other great writers.[70] He also remembered that when he was at Malvern there was a golf course that kept the more sharp-eyed teachers occupied, when they might have otherwise been on the lookout for the mischievous activities of the boys.[71] Also of note and a significant facilities contrast to Wynyard was the science laboratory, although Warnie indicated he made little academic use of it. As long as they did not burn down the building or create enough noise to rouse suspicions, the boys could do whatever they wanted in the laboratory. His own discovery was that on a hot, summer afternoon when he put a lump of ice in a container of water and added just the right amount of sulfuric acid, he could concoct a passable substitute for lemonade.[72]

A fourth contrast to Wynyard was social life. Spartan, limited, and uninspired as it was under Capron, Warnie's school life among his fellows at Malvern was comparatively friendly, diverse, and exciting. For instance, he claimed there was little bullying, and the supposed all-absorbing interest in sports exaggerated.[73] The key, according to Warnie—who was no athlete, disliking both cricket and football—was feigning interest and offering enthusiastic support of those who were athletes. Furthermore, if one could secure a written excuse from the house-

master, the captains of the sports teams did not even care if one did not show up
to the games to offer support. Warnie's duplicity soon overcame the difficulty
of securing a leave off since he learned how to forge the housemaster's name.[74]
Related to an enjoyable social life was a relatively easy academic life, particularly
because of a clandestine system of specialization, in which a student who was
strong in one subject would do the work for the others. Thus, a student strong in
Latin would do the Latin homework for all. Similarly, a student strong in math
would do math for all. Since Warnie was best suited to write English essays, that
was what he did for his fellows; it became, he said, almost a fulltime job.[75] This
kind of specialization was common in English public schools. In *The Harrovians*,
one of the athletes, Cadby, "who believed firmly in the nationalization of brains,"
enforced a weekly "raffle" that assigned his housemates to do his schoolwork.[76]
Each drew "slips of paper headed 'Greek Prose,' 'Mathematics,' 'English essay.'"

> Cadby explained the essential justice of the system to Peter: "You don't do a thing for
> the House, and, by the way you show up at footer, don't look as if you ever would.
> Now, I've played for the House for years, and not only at footer, but at cricket and
> rackets. See? That's what I do. And you? Not a dam' thing. The one thing you've
> got is a head for [academics]. . . . Well, then, make yourself some bally use. If you
> can't play for the House, at least you can help me to keep fresh."[77]

Warnie went on to say that while he did learn from his teachers, he began to feel
that scholarship should come to an end, and so he retreated from it quickly.[78]
Ever the pragmatist, Warnie arranged his academic life at Malvern not around
scholastic rigor and intellectual inquiry, but around practical efficiency and
creature comfort. The desultory habits he learned at Wynyard did not fade away
after he left; if anything, they worsened. Indeed, for much of the rest of his life,
he often followed the path of least resistance.

With the considerable improvements of Malvern over Wynyard, it might be
expected that Warnie would have flourished in his studies; such was not the
case. Letters from Albert to Warnie expressed displeasure at the school reports
he began receiving during Warnie's second term. On March 6, 1910, Albert
voiced his disappointment upon learning that Warnie had actually regressed
in his academic progress, having fallen from twelfth to twentieth in his form.
According to the reports, Warnie's poor work was the result of inattention.
Albert concluded that Warnie was either doing his best or not doing his best. If
the former, then Albert was wasting his money, and so he should send his son
to a less expensive school; if the latter, Warnie was acting dishonestly.[79] Warnie
deflected his father's criticism, claiming he had been placed into a higher form

than the one for which he was prepared. In addition, he said that he had been working hard and that some of his poor work was due to poor teaching. Warnie's explanations were guileful at best and fabrications at worst; as has been noted above, Warnie was not a self-motivated scholar, and he took every opportunity to engage in academic short cuts. The pragmatic side of his personality controlled whatever sense of personal integrity he had as a schoolboy.

However, although Albert was deeply troubled by Warnie's academic regression, he was much more worried that homosexuality was common among the boys, his fears primarily related to withdrawal of one of his friend's sons from Malvern under suspicious circumstances—at least suspicious from Albert's point of view. On May 18, 1910, he wrote Warnie and asserted that his friend would not have removed his son from Malvern without good cause. In trying to gain Warnie's confidence, Albert said he wrote because he wanted to be both his son's father and best friend. He reminded Warnie that he had warned him that in nearly every school there were perverse, wicked boys who tried to lead others into sinful, unhealthy, disgusting, criminal activities. Accordingly, he implored Warnie to be open and honest with him, so that if he ever became aware of things going on that he knew his father would condemn—and that he as a Christian gentleman should reject—he would tell his father at once.[80] In his May 21, 1910, reply, Warnie told his father he really did not know much about the case of the withdrawn boy since he did not live in Warnie's house. Furthermore, he tried to calm Albert's fears, writing that his own house was known for the virtuous conduct of its occupants; he also promised to tell his father about everything, no matter what the subject.[81] Even though Warnie prevaricated about his academic performance, I think we can take him at his word regarding this matter. Nowhere in his letters, diaries, and other papers does he show any interest in or fascination with homosexuality, and it is likely that he did not, in fact, know much about this case.[82]

At the same time, it is worth noting that in *SJ*, Jack wrote extensively about the pederasty he found rampant at Malvern.[83] Warnie took umbrage with Jack's claims on this matter, writing that while he did not deny there was immorality at Malvern, when he later went to Sandhurst, the Royal Military College he attended after Malvern, and talked with other boys who came from other public schools, he found that Malvern was no different from the others in that regard.[84] He went on to say that a first year boy rarely knew what was really going on, relying on scandal and rumor and imagining immorality any time there was a close relationship between an older and younger boy. Warnie pointed out that such associations were not surprising, given that eighteen-year-old boys were isolated from female relationships for two-thirds of the year. In addition, such relationships, although unwise and fatuous, were usually not sexual, something that his brother was unwilling to see or admit.[85]

A final contrast between Wynyard and Malvern was the relatively quick and deep friendships Warnie forged at the latter. There is no indication that Warnie made friendships with any of his fellow sufferers at Wynyard; arguably, all of them were simply holding on, trying to endure their misery as best they could. Thus, he never wrote of any confidences he had at Wynyard. However, Warnie made deep friendships with two of his classmates at Malvern. Edward Goodwyn Hilton (1895–1938?) arrived at Malvern at the same time as Warnie, and they both left at the end of the summer of 1913. Hilton, nicknamed "Blodo," was in some ways an unlikely friend for Warnie since he was a star athlete and had little interest in intellectual matters. Despite these seeming incompatible temperaments, a warm friendship developed that lasted well beyond their Malvern days. Robert Bull Olphert (1894–1915) was a year senior to Warnie; after Malvern, Olphert and Warnie were fellow cadets at Sandhurst.[86] The three young men spent many hours together—often doing schoolwork together, but more frequently engaging in unapproved social activities including smoking, drinking, and leaving the school grounds.

Hilton and Olphert were welcomed friends to Warnie; however, Jack was his best friend. Although the two brothers were often apart physically, when with each other they banded together—in part because of their deep love and affection for one another and in part as a defensive front against their father whom they viewed as intrusive, opinionated, and dogmatic.[87] One comical example of their joint front against the world dates from their 1911 Easter holidays. Warnie was home from Malvern and Jack was home from Cherbourg Schools (where he had arrived in January 1911). After they found their midday meal prepared by one of the servants inedible, Jack proposed that they bury it in the garden. In full view of the servant, the brothers carried the food outside, dug a grave for it, and covered it over. Throughout this mock burial, Jack had carried the family gramophone playing Chopin's "Funeral March."[88] An equally comical episode occurred during their August 1911 vacation to the Scottish coast with their father. Albert had looked forward with great anticipation to the holiday, but their hotel was terrible—the food was bad, the rooms uncomfortable, the scenery uninteresting, and the swimming unpleasant. Jack wrote that he and his brother had to share a double bed; however, the bed was so uncomfortable that every night they flipped a coin to see who should sleep in the bed and who should sleep on the floor. The loser had to sleep in the bed.[89]

An important milestone in Warnie's life as a writer occurred in January 1912: for the first time he began keeping a diary. Most of his initial entries were prosaic, brief ticking-offs of the day's highlights. A closer look at his diary of 1912 reveals his matter-of-fact assessment of daily life: where he was, who he was with, what he did, and so on.[90] However, several details are noteworthy. Among the jetsam and flotsam of a day's events, he would often note shipping details, including the names of various ships under construction, their tonnage, how close they were to being completed, the likelihood of the purchaser, their initial sailing date, how long they had been out of port, and so on. In addition, he paid careful attention to money matters, particularly the investments he was making, their chances of success, and possible future investments; his interest in finance and investing was one he shared with his father. He also admitted to his academic cutting of corners, including times he was discovered being dishonest. For example, on January 29, 1912, one of his favorite teachers, Henry Wakelyn Smith (aka Smewgy or Smugy), caught him cheating but treated him fairly over the incident; somewhat cynically, Warnie resolved to be more careful in his deception in the future.[91] In all these respects, Warnie differed from his brother; Jack would have no more kept logs of shipping matters, financial investments, and academic compromises than Albert would have enjoyed weeks of casual, relaxing holidays. Furthermore, Jack, because of his intellectual curiosity and deep commitment to learning, would never have engaged in academic dishonesty.

Four months short of his seventeenth birthday, Warnie wrote his father about possible career choices; not surprisingly, his intentions were practical, not academic, telling his father that he thought the best thing he could do was to begin working for one of the railways as the utilitarian aspects of a railway career were particularly attractive.[92] He went on to ask if Albert would fund his staying at Malvern for an extra two terms, having him leave in summer 1913 rather than Christmas 1912. Warnie pointed out that then he could shift his plan of studies from the Classical track to a more down-to-earth one, emphasizing mathematics, shorthand, book-keeping, business writing, and German. He suggested that after a few years working at one of the Irish railways, he might transfer to a Canadian one. But Warnie also revealed that a secondary reason for wanting to stay at Malvern until summer 1913 was social: most of his friends would be staying on until then. The bonds of friendship with Hilton and Olphert were particularly strong, hence his appeal to Albert. After some discussion back and forth, Albert agreed with Warnie's request, and at the start of the May 1912 term Warnie commenced studies in the science curriculum.[93] As a part of Headmaster Smith's midterm evaluation of Warnie's academic progress, he confirmed this course of action: "[Warnie] is the most helpless boy at Greek and Latin that I have come across in longish experience ... [and in this regard] is attempting the impossible. Outside Classics he is easily interested, and can write English. I suggest [he take a] science curriculum."[94]

Warnie's last year at Malvern was marked by three important milestones. First, after several years of deception, since he and Jack had been smoking for some time, Warnie asked his father for permission to smoke when not at school; he assured his father he would not smoke at school since it was against the rules.[95] He further assured his father that he smoked not because of peer pressure, but because he enjoyed it. In his lengthy reply of December 14, 1912, Albert noted that an estrangement had already occurred between the two of them during the recent holiday because Warnie had "pinched" some of Albert's tobacco; accordingly, it was not news to Albert that Warnie was smoking. Although he pointed out that smoking was habit-forming (Albert was an occasional smoker himself), he acquiesced to Warnie's request, reiterating only his condemnation of smoking at school. On other occasions, such as at dinners when it would make Warnie feel like the odd man out, Albert told him to smoke with a clear conscience.[96] As in the matter of writing essays for others, Warnie was not able to keep his father's confidence; on December 20, 1912, less than a week after receiving the admonition that he not smoke at school, Headmaster James wrote Albert to inform him that Warnie had been found smoking on school grounds.[97]

Warnie's second milestone in his last year at Malvern was his appointment as a prefect on March 9, 1913. A prefect was a school leader expected to set a positive example for the younger boys through his good character and leadership; among other things, a prefect was to model responsibility by ensuring fair play, faithfully carrying out assigned duties, following school rules, and setting a virtuous example. In regard to the younger boys, a prefect was expected to display benevolent paternalism. Prefects were also expected to model good manners, respect for authority and school traditions, an even temperament, and good taste. In short, they were to represent the qualities of a perfect gentleman. Given Warnie's breaking of the smoking regulation, it is somewhat surprising that he was appointed a prefect; it may have been that there were few other choices or perhaps Headmaster James hoped by giving Warnie more responsibility, he would rise to the occasion. Unfortunately, Warnie did not merit James's appointment. Two weeks after becoming prefect, Warnie wrote Jack about a motorcycling incident that—had he been caught—would have resulted in his being expelled; he also mocked how his father would have railed against him if he had been caught.[98] Warnie soon discovered that he did not like being a prefect, writing to his father that he was disappointed with his new position. As the lowest-ranking prefect, he had to handle all the hard work and enjoy little of the fun.[99] He went on to use his prefecture as a reason to ask a second time to stay longer at Malvern, this time until Christmas 1913, when most of his friends would be leaving. Ancillary to this motive were two others. First, Warnie argued, perhaps somewhat guilefully, that by staying an extra term he could help Jack during his first term at Malvern. Second, and surely the most important one from Warnie's perspective, he would have seniority in the fall term and thus enjoy the increased perks of being a prefect; Warnie admitted that it was unrewarding to be a prefect if one could not enjoy its perks.[100]

The final milestone in Warnie's last year at Malvern carried with it lifetime implications: he decided to forego a career in the railways, opting instead to seek an appointment to the Army Service Corp (ASC). This shift in career focus occurred because he knew that that military service was probably inevitable anyway, and a future in the railways would be difficult to secure. As early as his May 12, 1913, letter to Albert, Warnie began talking about joining the ASC, writing to his father that staying at Malvern until Christmas would give time to decide between the ASC and the Railway.[101] The immediate challenge Warnie faced was how to enter the ASC. After writing letters to various friends and family acquaintances, he learned there were three options: the first was by attending the Royal Military College at Sandhurst; the second was by joining the Special Reserves; and the third was by entrance to a university where he would almost certainly be sent to officer training school. The weight of the advice he received urged him to opt for Sandhurst. One family friend, Captain George Harding, wrote that Sandhurst was the best method of entry, and it would be up to Malvern to prepare Warnie for the entrance exam. Harding assured Warnie that the entrance exam was relatively easy when a person was well prepared. Moreover, once admitted to Sandhurst, Warnie would almost certainly pass into the army if he paid close attention to the lectures. After that, it would be up to Warnie to earn his way into the ASC.[102]

Albert consented to Warnie staying another term at Malvern, in part because he believed the additional time would help his son prepare for the Sandhurst entrance exam. More importantly, however, although he had some reservations about the ASC, Albert believed Warnie was actually committed to the idea of an army career—a serious undertaking that struck Albert as a new and welcomed change in Warnie's character. In his letter to his father of May 24, 1913, Warnie told him that he had finally decided upon the ASC, and that for the first time in his life he sincerely felt a definite excitement for a career. He confessed that up until that time he had been passive about the future, but now he would make amends, believing that the ASC life would entirely suit him.[103] Warnie's decision to work toward an army career was entirely consistent with his both feet on the ground approach to life. Misplaced into an academic curriculum that stressed Latin and Greek, he thrilled at the idea of a life given over to the day-to-day exercise of accomplishing important, real-world tasks. Indeed, his academic focus at Malvern was shifted toward helping him to pass the Sandhurst entrance exam, including more focus upon mathematics, history, and French. All might have gone well for Warnie, but, despite repeated warnings by Albert, Warnie continued to smoke at school, and only weeks into June 1913, he was caught smoking and lost his status as a prefect. Although Headmaster James eventually restored Warnie to his prefectship, he would not allow Warnie to return to Malvern once the term ended, thus throwing a wrench into Warnie's plans. On July 30, 1913, Warnie ended his education at Malvern. Years later, he succinctly summarized his years at Wynyard and Malvern: "Wynyard was simply a swindle, a cruel prison, and though on the whole I enjoyed my time at Malvern, what did I bring away from it? An Old School Tie and a ready-made stock of prejudices."[104] One especially painful memory was his "bitter" poverty at Malvern: "I will never forget, nor has anything ever made up to me for the penniless days at [Malvern], surrounded by, and trying to live with boys whose parents treated them with some understanding of the feelings of adolescence in a conformist society."[105]

Before we turn to how Albert solved the problem of getting Warnie prepared for the Sandhurst entrance exam—it was set to be given in the first week of December 1913—it is important to note that Jack moved the few hundred yards from Cherbourg School to Malvern College on September 18, 1913. One unexpected result of Warnie and Jack's experiences at Malvern was that it served to create a wedge between the two brothers. Initially, of course, the distance between them was merely spatial: Warnie was at Malvern and Jack was first at Wynyard, and then at Cherbourg. But the divide between the brothers had more to do with their personalities than their proximities. Warnie, ever the pragmatist, soon embraced the society of his fellow students. In addition, he freely joined in the overall life of Malvern students. He was not a loner; indeed, he was gregarious, a joiner, and something of a "hail fellow well met."[106] Another way to put it was that he was "clubbable," eager to blend in and ready to make friends.[107] This desire to be a part of a greater whole may have gone deeper. With the death of his mother still something of a fresh wound, Warnie's coping mechanism was to focus outward rather than inward. Instead of musing internally on how devastating the loss of his mother was, Warnie chose to focus upon the day-to-day, in one sense using the continuous flow of daily life to deaden the pain. By keeping busy, blending in, and making new friends, Warnie did not have to face the sobering truth that he would never see his mother again.

Jack, however, scorned the social life he found at Malvern. While his brother had eagerly joined in the school ethos, Jack stubbornly resisted. Unlike Warnie, Jack was a loner, a thinker, an outsider. By temperament, he stood to be a marked person. In *The Harrovians*, we find something of Jack's situation at Malvern: "Harrow is a network of traditions designed to curb the arrogance of the new-comer.

You may not walk down the middle of the road, wear your hat on one side, nor carry your umbrella furled unless you are an established 'blood.'"[108] Jack cared little for the social life of his fellow students, and he hated the way the Bloods and all they stood for dominated school life. Then, too, he may have found it more difficult to push aside the terrible loss of his mother. Unlike Warnie, Jack internalized almost everything that happened to him. By nature reflective, intuitive, and reserved, Jack found almost nothing at Malvern to nurture him. Other than the Grundy Library and his favorite teacher, Henry Wakelyn Smith, Jack despised Malvern.[109] While Warnie was clubbable, Jack hated the collective; instead, he was detached, independent, and self-contained. In *SJ*, he notes how their differing attitudes toward Malvern created a division between them: "And now a terrible thing happened. My reaction to [Malvern] was perhaps the first great disappointment my brother had ever experienced. Loving the place as he did, he had looked forward to the days when this too could be shared between us. . . . Instead he heard, from me, blasphemies against all his gods; from [Malvern], that his young brother looked like becoming a Coll Punt [a pariah, an unpopular person]. The immemorial league between us was strained, all but broken."[110] Warnie's irritation with Jack at this time surfaced in letters to his father where he began referring regularly to his brother with the affectionately derisive nickname, "It."[111] Later, in his "Memoir," Warnie noted that Jack never should have been sent to public school because even as a young student he would have connected more easily with undergraduates than with public school boys. In addition, "he was something of a square peg in a round hole . . . and by his temperament he was bound to be a misfit, a heretic, and object of suspicion within the collective-minded and standardizing Public School system."[112]

One other matter is worthy of note at this point. When we come to evaluate Warnie's spiritual life during his years at Wynyard and Malvern, we have little to go on. Jack's *SJ*, which is essentially the story of his conversion to Christianity, is filled with reflections marking the various stages of his spiritual journey. Of course, *SJ* was written by Jack the older man, not Jack the young boy; accordingly, it is not entirely surprising that it offers an inside view of his spiritual life. He was by nature given to internal exploration. In *SJ*, we find the older man looking back and exploring in great detail his early spiritual life. Filters of all sorts slant Jack's retrospective; however, the key point is how comfortable he is when looking back and recalling his spiritual maturation. This looking back by the older man upon his younger self regarding his spiritual life is something Warnie does not do, at least not with any intensity or depth. Accordingly, Warnie's early spiritual life is veiled. Nevertheless, we should not view Warnie's disinterest in his early spiritual life as a weakness or as a deliberate aversion. An outer-oriented, external approach to life was intrinsic to his nature and temperament; accordingly, matters of faith played little role in his daily life at Wynyard or Malvern.

While Jack in *SJ* provided a lengthy, detailed examination of his childhood loss of faith, Warnie never did, most probably because he never had a faith to lose. On the occasions when he wrote about attending church services, he commented disinterestedly about the sermons, almost like a movie reviewer discussing a recent film. For the most part, his was an external, ritually oriented faith; following the example of his father and his older relatives, Warnie submitted to the necessity of church attendance.[113] His faith, at that time, was largely a matter of social enculturation, not that of a fully realized personal experience. In none of his early letters or diary entries did he suggest that religion was anything other than a necessary social contrivance, one that must be observed in order to avoid censures, denunciations, and recriminations. On occasion, he wrote about specific dates associated with the church calendar. For instance, on March 23, 1913, he wrote Jack and wondered how he made it through Good Friday, complaining that in his case he had to listen to a detailed description of the sufferings that a crucified man endured; it was so vivid that Warnie almost threw up.[114] Here we find nothing about Warnie being moved spiritually by Christ's sacrifice; instead, his focus was upon physical details of the crucifixion and how they made him feel. Jack was given to internal reflections regarding the things important to him—musing, cogitating, and mulling things over; he was comfortable accessing and writing about his interior life. Warnie, however, maintained a focus upon his exterior life. Issues of faith, therefore, played little role in his early daily life. Warnie's view of matters involving Christian faith may conceivably have been similar to those given by the boys in *The Harrovians*: "Most boys say their prayers as a matter of course. Nor are their communications punctuated by the traditional sponge. The boy performs certain rites carelessly and without any emotion, vaguely conscious that there may be more in them than meets the eye. . . . [Faith is] believing in what you know isn't true."[115]

Although Warnie had entered Malvern happy to be away from Wynyard, he was both relieved to be rid of Malvern and anxious about the coming Sandhurst entrance exam. Ever the pragmatist, he worried about how he would prepare himself for a test that would likely determine his future. Fortunately, he was rescued by the same tutor who would later play such an important role in Jack's intellectual development, William Thompson Kirkpatrick.[116] By all accounts, Kirkpatrick, known affectionately by the Lewises as the Great Knock, was a gifted teacher. Robert M. Jones, a Lurgan College student at the same time as Albert, wrote:

No boy and no man could be in his company for even a very short time without being impressed by the fact that he was in the presence of a man of unusual power and grasp, of an overmastering influence on the mind, and of an intellectual honesty and vigour before which pretence and make-believe were dissipated like smoke before a strong wind. None who knew him could be surprised that it was he who subsequently made Lurgan College for many years one of the most remarkable and successful schools in Ireland. He became an almost incomparable teacher, and under him the boys swept on to victory over their work and to mastery of their subjects and of themselves. His pistol never missed fire; but he gave you the impression that, if it did, as [Oliver] Goldsmith said of [Dr. Samuel] Johnson, you would be knocked down by the butt-end.[117]

Albert, anguished by what to do about Warnie and recalling the excellent teaching he had received at Lurgan College, wrote to Kirkpatrick—he had been serving as his former teacher's solicitor for some years—in August 1913 and proposed that he tutor Warnie in preparation for the Sandhurst exam. Kirkpatrick had been retired from Lurgan since 1899, but he had been tutoring one or two students a year for university entrance exams from his home, Gastons, in Great Bookham in Surrey.

Kirkpatrick replied on September 4, 1913, and agreed, noting he could help Warnie with Classics, mathematics, modern language, and English; the only sticking point was that Kirkpatrick had neither the physical facilities nor the requisite knowledge to tutor Warnie in science.[118] Notwithstanding this potential difficulty, Albert was so relieved that he sent Kirkpatrick a telegram on September 6, 1913, thanking him, and followed that up with a longer letter the same day. The letter was noteworthy because Albert unburdened his worries about Warnie. He explained to Kirkpatrick that because he had no female to help bring up his sons, he was despondent, fearing that he had made a mess of it. Yet, he added, that he did his best with a task that he was not equipped to handle. He enjoined Kirkpatrick to write to him forthrightly about Warnie and to criticize him from every standpoint as the occasions arose. In a particularly telling passage, Albert noted that one painful effect of sending his boys to English Public Schools was that they had drifted away from him. The intimacy and comradeship that the three of them might have enjoyed through daily intercourse had atrophied. What his sons once were to him, they were no more.[119]

Warnie's initial reaction to meeting Kirkpatrick foretold what Jack wrote in SJ about in his own first meeting with Kirkpatrick.[120] He expected the old man would be sentimental, shedding tears over meeting with the son of his former student. Not so, as Kirkpatrick was dry-eyed, and all about teaching Warnie. His physical description of Kirkpatrick also anticipated Jack's later account, noting that he was a tall, lean old man with side whiskers, unkempt clothes, and bright, penetrating eyes; at the same time, he radiated physical strength and mental energy. When Warnie first saw Kirkpatrick, he seemed familiar, and Warnie soon recognized in him a slender and more alert version of the Emperor Franz Joseph of the House of Habsburg.[121] As was later the case with his brother, Warnie assumed his studies would be put off until some introductions and settling in took place. Instead, he wrote that within an hour of entering his house, Warnie was having to confront mathematical problems with an urgency he had not experienced before.[122]

Immediately, then, Warnie found himself engaged in serious, sustained, and targeted academic study, the very thing he had not experienced at either Wynyard or Malvern. Given his previous desultory approach to learning, he might have shrunk under Kirkpatrick's onslaught. Instead, Warnie blossomed, not only because of Kirkpatrick's expectation that Warnie take up the academic challenge before him, but also because the old man knew how to encourage Warnie's spirit. Warnie later recalled Kirkpatrick's deft touch, particularly because he helped him realize that a good deal of his poor academic work was the result several factors, including an inferiority complex, due to his time at Wynyard, his own indolence, and the lax curriculum of Malvern. Within only a few weeks, Kirkpatrick's encouragement restored Warnie's belief in himself. Warnie realized that while he was not necessarily brilliant, his poor school record had resulted from his indolence and not stupidity.[123] From Kirkpatrick, Warnie learned how to think rigorously, logically, and clearly. No casual remark was allowed to go unchallenged, and Kirkpatrick was a formidable adversary. Warnie wrote that Kirkpatrick was as unassailable as a band of Genghis Khan's cavalry, often adopting the same tactics. For instance, Warnie might go to bed thinking he had argued Kirkpatrick to a stalemate, but the next morning at breakfast Kirkpatrick would immediately reopen the debate. Noisily drinking his cup of tea, Kirkpatrick would suddenly pounce, make his trenchant arguments, and completely rout whatever feeble argument Warnie might still have left.[124] Warnie's most generous remark about Kirkpatrick—and one betraying deep affection—was simple: "I owe more to him than to any other person I have ever met."[125] Under Kirkpatrick's firm hand, Warnie buckled down and studied hard.[126] He and Albert were both rewarded when Warnie passed the Sandhurst entrance exam in early December 1913, placing twenty-second out of 201 students; his high score earned him a "Prize Cadetship," resulting in admission to Sandhurst at half the normal fees and a grant of £50 upon obtaining his commission.[127]

On February 4, 1914, Warnie entered the Royal Military College at Sandhurst. Tracing its beginnings to 1799, Sandhurst—located in Surrey near the village of

Camberley, 34 miles southwest of London—was created to train "Gentleman Cadets" for the British Army. The need for better trained officers had been highlighted by British losses in the Boer War, also known as the South African War (1899–1902); some contemporary critics claimed that the British officers were so inept during the war that the soldiers had been betrayed by their leaders, leading to the criticism it was "an army of lions led by donkeys."[128] The eighteen-month course of study at Sandhurst for subalterns—junior officers below the rank of captain—had been truncated to six months in anticipation of the certainty of an impending European war.[129] During the four years of WWI, 5,131 "Gentlemen Cadets" passed through Sandhurst; 3,200 (over 60 percent) of them were killed during the war.[130] Appallingly, according to Anthony Morton, the life expectancy of subalterns on the Western front was only six weeks.[131]

Warnie found his experience at Sandhurst challenging and invigorating. Although he likened it in some ways to being in a public school such as Malvern—especially with regard to the character of other young men there—the biggest difference was that it was a place meant for hard work. Indeed, while slackers at public schools were usually popular, at Sandhurst they were ostracized; instead, everyone toiled to make his company the finest in the battalion. Days began at 6:30 in the morning and went on until 10:30 at night. Field drills, rifle inspection, cleaning, and shooting, field tactics, revolver shooting, war lectures, and night marches comprised a typical day. A concerted effort was made to create in the new cadets an *esprit de corps*, and the training officers impressed upon the young men the sense that they were the smartest body of soldiers in the British army, congratulating them on having had the good sense to have chosen the finest calling in the world. In letters to his father, Warnie confided throughout his months of training that he had selected the best possible career. Only two matters concerned him. First, and ironically, Warnie was surprised and offended by the general lack of spiritual interest among his fellows. Most were religiously apathetic, and a few were openly irreverent, even during mandatory church services. In one instance, a cadet lit a cigarette during the middle of a church service, intending it as a joke. Warnie did not find it funny, noting that "even looking at it from an heathen point of view, I should call it rather bounderish to come into Some one else's house while He was holding a reception and start smoking while not being invited to do so."[132] Second, he worried about his chances of getting a commission to the ASC because only two were going to be offered during his time at Sandhurst; he figured that at least ten other cadets would be applying for one. However, he labored tenaciously, passed all the necessary exams with high marks, and on September 30, 1914, he was rewarded by receiving as commission as a second lieutenant in the ASC.

When Warnie attended Wynyard and Malvern, he was in his boyhood and young teenage years. Living a sheltered, middle-class Irish life, he knew little of the greater world. His few months with Kirkpatrick marked an initial change in his view of the world; he quickly learned that if he wanted to get on, he had to buckle down, study hard, and perform well. This knowledge served him well during his military training where he was molded into an officer. Leaving Sandhurst, he soon faced the trenches of northern France and was compelled to grow quickly into manhood, while engaged in a war of unimaginable horrors, mind-numbing blood baths, and battlefield disasters. His systematic, orderly, commonsense ethos would serve him well as he plunged into the nightmare known as the Great War.

CHAPTER TWO

The Great War
(1914–1918)

At the onset of World War I, Warnie and his fellow soldiers—friend and foe alike—had no idea of the coming apocalypse. Indeed, the mind-numbing butchery of WWI is without equal in the history of warfare, so grotesque it borders on being an outrage to the imagination; estimates place the number killed on the battlefield at 8,750,000 (including 750,000 British), with another 21,000,000 wounded. George Mosse points out in *Fallen Soldiers* that more than twice as many men died because of battlefield action or wounds during the 1914–1918 conflict than were killed in all major wars between 1790 and 1914.[1] Barbara Tuchman in *The Guns of August* notes that when the war was over "the known dead per capita of the population were 1 to 28 for France, 1 to 32 for Germany, 1 to 57 for England, and 1 to 107 for Russia."[2] Even those brought up during World War II, Korea, Vietnam, and the Gulf Wars, wars with their own particular evil dreams of death, recoil at this incredible loss of life and the seemingly absurd battlefield tactics. As Paul Fussell puts it in *The Great War and Modern Memory*, "Every war is ironic because every war is worse than expected." If that is true, then World War I is history's greatest irony.[3] In this chapter, I explore Warnie Lewis's involvement in history's greatest irony by reviewing his years of military service from 1914 to 1918, including what branch of the British Army he served in, the dates of his various postings, the record of the divisions he served with, his ambitions for promotions, his everyday duties as an officer, how his attitude toward the war changed over time, how the war may have influenced his later alcoholism, and when he was under active fire and how he responded.[4] In addition, I examine how he reacted to his brother's decision to join in the fight, what his fears were once Jack was directly involved in battlefield action, and, most significantly, the critical things Warnie took away from his service during the Great War.[5]

On October 2, 1914, Warnie recorded his first letter after his commission as a second lieutenant from his barracks at Aldershot—the military headquarters in England, about 32 miles southwest of London—expressing his delight at sitting in the anteroom after mess and writing to his father. He said it almost seemed too good to be true, and he was happy that he had relieved his father's worries about his future since he was embarking on his career in the Army Service Corps.[6] Although Warnie went on to express some misgivings about not having sought to serve in a fighting unit, his delight with his situation overcame any second thoughts. He added that the work was harder than at Sandhurst, but it was more interesting. Like thousands of other subalterns, Warnie was excited finally to be nearing action. As was the case with many soldiers, Warnie approached the conflict with fervor and optimism, captured in the poem "Vitai Lampada"[7] by Henry Newbolt (1862–1938), which likened the determination necessary to win the war to that of a hard-fought cricket match:

There's a breathless hush in the Close to-night—
Ten to make and the match to win—
A bumping pitch and a blinding light,
An hour to play and the last man in.
And it's not for the sake of a ribboned coat,
Or the selfish hope of a season's fame,
But his Captain's hand on his shoulder smote
"Play up! play up! and play the game!"

The sand of the desert is sodden red,—
Red with the wreck of a square that broke;—
The Gatling's jammed and the colonel dead,
And the regiment blind with dust and smoke.
The river of death has brimmed his banks,
And England's far, and Honour a name,
But the voice of schoolboy rallies the ranks,
"Play up! play up! and play the game!"

This is the word that year by year
While in her place the School is set
Every one of her sons must hear,

And none that hears it dare forget.
This they all with a joyful mind
Bear through life like a torch in flame,
And falling fling to the host behind—
"Play up! play up! and play the game!" (1897)

In response to Warnie's October 2, 1914, letter, Albert was of two minds. On the one hand, he was pleased that Warnie had finally begun his career, writing him on October 8, 1914, and congratulating him that he had won a commission in His Majesty's army. He praised Warnie for having done so well at only nineteen years old, looked forward to his future, and promised to pray daily that he would be a courageous and dedicated soldier.[8] On the other hand, Albert warned his son against excessive drinking, arguing that there were two truths about drink that Warnie should never forget: alcohol was stronger than the strongest man, and once a person began drinking heavily, it was almost impossible to stop.[9] A month later, Albert repeated this warning after receiving a letter from Warnie in which he boasted about having sat at a local boulevard café in France drinking cheap red wine. Albert told his son that such drinking episodes were just showing off, and he cautioned him against frequent escapades. He pointed out that repeated bouts of this kind of drinking were not only frivolous but also injurious because they could lead to habitual drinking. Once that happened, the next stage was often damnation in both this and the next world.

Albert then contrasted the dangers of drink with two other common pitfalls for soldiers. Gambling might impoverish a man, said Albert, yet he might be able to recover. Associating with prostitutes might ruin a man's health, and he might develop sexually transmitted diseases; but at least he might die repenting of his actions. However, Albert claimed that alcohol was the worst and most addictive of the three.[10] While Warnie may have found this kind of advice an unwanted encroachment—both he and Jack had long resented their father for his intrusive-ness—Albert had seen in his work as a solicitor many examples of men whose lives had been blighted by alcoholism. This was not the last time Albert wrote Warnie about the risks of excessive drinking; however, notwithstanding Albert's many warnings, Warnie eventually became an alcoholic. Were these early warnings un-intended catalysts of Warnie's problem or did Albert see early on that his son was constitutionally prone to an excessive use of alcohol? As subsequent events suggest, Warnie's life as a soldier—surrounded by many hard-drinking companions—was certainly a contributing cause of his alcoholism.

With his father's cautions in mind, Warnie began service in the ASC, the military unit responsible for keeping the British Army supplied with all its provisions. The role of the ASC in the war effort cannot be overstated, as the military faced an enormous logistic challenge with regard to feeding, housing, and transporting both its men and livestock.[11] "Hundreds of tons of equipment, ammunition and food had to be loaded, moved, unloaded and distributed every day to keep the men at the front fed and armed. The ASC was responsible for keeping the horses and lorries [trucks] on the road as they carried supplies from bases along the French coast to the front line."[12] According to the *King's Regulations and Orders for the Army 1912*, "the officers of the ASC [were] entrusted with furnishing transport, provisions, fuel, light and supplies, for the use of all branches of the army, and with the allotment of barracks and quarters and their equipment, as laid down in the Regulations for Supply Transport and Barrack Services."[13] Among other things, the ASC was responsible for land, coastal, and lake transport, air dispatch, barracks administration, the Army Fire Service, staffing headquarters's units, and supplying food, water, fuel, and domestic materials such as clothing, furniture, and stationery, and the supply of technical and military equipment.[14] Like other newly arrived soldiers, Warnie spent his initial training at the Le Havre base depot and then transferred to the advanced depot at Rouen for posting. During this training, Warnie received instruction "in [horse] riding, driving, drills and general duties in addition to passing through the prescribed courses . . . [and he underwent] practical courses of instruction in the farriers', wheelers', and saddlers' shops."[15]

It may surprise some that part of Warnie's training included horse riding and related skills. However, the ASC was organized into four sections: Horse Transport, Mechanical Transport, Supply, and Remount. Warnie's ASC initial posting on November 4, 1914, was to a Horse Transport division, the Fourth Company, Seventh Divisional Train.[16] This meant he had to have some level of knowledge and expertise regarding horses since over fifty-three thousand riding and draught horses were with the British Expeditionary Force (BEF) when Warnie reached France.[17] Such a large number of animals meant that a good deal of time, money, and effort went into caring for them. Warnie gave some idea of this when he recounted his daily routine in a letter to his father of December 12, 1914. He noted that the weather was frigid and wet, very dangerous things for horses since they had to stand out in the open. However, working with his commander, Captain T. A. Prendergast, the two of them arranged to get the horses stabled in a nearby bombed out cottage, losing only one to pneumonia.[18] Together they fixed a hole in the roof and found sufficient straw to bed down the horses comfortably. Warnie told his father that a typical day for him involved rising at 5 A.M.; riding and caring for horses from 6 to 7:30; breakfast at 8; convoy work from 9:30 to 2:30 P.M.; lunch, smoking, and relaxing until 3:30; work in the stables until tea at 4:30; office work until 7; and then in bed by 9. He indicated that although he was not under fire like those serving in the trenches, he was not living an easy life.[19] Warnie's comments about the difficulties he faced were echoed by thousands of others. Indeed, most subalterns, only recently removed from English public schools and universities, found the conditions hellish.[20] They "suffered from the isolation of the trenches, the deafening noise of persistent artillery fire, the fatigue brought on by nights without continuous sleep, the filth of the living conditions, the undivided attention of lice, the stench of decaying corpses, the scurrying of rats grown fat on human flesh, and the boredom of trench routine."[21]

While Warnie's description of his daily duties gives some idea of his tasks, the prescribed obligations of a second lieutenant in the ASC were extensive. According to the *Regimental Standing Orders of the Army Service Corps*, an officer in Warnie's position would "command half a company. They [would] make themselves thoroughly acquainted with the qualifications of the men . . . under their command. They [were] responsible to the commanding officer for the efficiency of their half companies, and [would] instruct all non-commissioned officers serving under their orders in their respective duties."[22] Since a company normally consisted of two hundred men, this meant Warnie would have had roughly one hundred men under his training and command.[23] Some additional obligations of a second lieutenant included opening all official letters addressed to the soldiers in the company or arranging for another officer to open official letters in cases of unavoidable absence. Moreover, second lieutenants published "all casualties affecting the pay, service, and documents of all warrant officers, non-commissioned officers, and men under their command" as well as making recommendations for good-conduct badges.[24] Another task was assisting in the stipulated course of training for recruits in a Horse Transport company. This instruction took place over fourteen weeks and included physical workouts, foot drills, marksmanship, barracks duties, proper dress, semaphore signaling, care of equipment, practical horsemanship (saddling, fastening up, pack saddlery, and harnessing), pitching and striking tents, horse welfare and disease, stables daily routine, and improvising repairs."[25] The challenges of these daily obligations were ones that Warnie—with his practical, pragmatic approach to life—found invigorating.

Once he settled into the life of his company, Warnie wrote and told his father that he had become the officer in charge of the company's baggage. In addition, Warnie, who had been learning French since his days at Wynyard and Malvern, told his father how much more he was learning French; in fact, he said that it was critical that he had become more fluent in French so that he could readily secure supplies from local farmers.[26] Other letters included requests for cigarettes, pipe tobacco, chocolate, and books as well as explanations about how an army division was organized. On other topics, Warnie criticized the clergy back home who had no idea of what was going on in France. He hoped, that because of the war, the church would come alive and be led by real clergymen who learned firsthand about the realities faced by soldiers in the field.[27] One early crisis in the war was concern about the sobriety of soldiers. Fearing that the war effort was being hampered by drunkenness, Lord David George, the Chancellor of the Exchequer, began a public campaign against the consumption of alcohol and recruited the leaders of the British government to take a pledge against the use of alcohol. In April 1915, King George V supported the campaign, promising that no alcohol would be consumed in the Royal household until the war was over. On April 23, 1915, Warnie wrote his father and complained about the King's pledge, claiming the King let himself be influenced by a small group of prohibitionist fanatics. Warnie asserted that he was not a big drinker and did not see any harm in drinking in moderation. He also explained that he was thankful to have received his daily ration of rum during the winter.[28] Warnie's reference to himself as not being a big drinker was both ironic and dishonest, yet it did reflect his desire to prevent his father from worrying about him. He also complained about not hearing from Jack: "Why has 'It' not written to me since I have been out here? I tried a little heavy sarcasm the other day on a field service post card, but so far it has not had any result."[29] Later letters repeat common themes of bad weather, boredom, and the daily monotony of maddening duties.[30]

On September 15, 1915, Warnie was transferred to the Third Company, Seventh Divisional Train, under the command of an Irishman, Horace Stratford Collins. The transfer was fortuitous since Collins became Warnie's closest wartime friend:

> [He] was the most intimate of my war time friends, and our long association prevented both of us from sinking into the merely animal existence led by so many officers at the back of the front. . . . He was one of the most "alive" persons I ever met, and endowed with a liberal curiosity. He could be reckless in dissipation, but was a most competent company commander; he could gamble all afternoon and insist in breaking off to admire a sunset. He loved the beauty of nature, the open air, a horse to ride; he also loved bar parlours, and less reputable establishments. Few war memories carry with them any happiness—but I still remember with keen pleasure nights in quiet French villages, far from the front, when Collins and I, whisky on the table, kettle on the hob, and our pipes drawing evenly, would range over the little field of English literature we knew, the conversation gradually widening into a reconstruction of the post war heaven which was going to be built when we had won the war.[31]

Unfortunately, soon after his transfer to Collins's unit, Warnie contracted influenza and was admitted to the Rawalpindi General Hospital, Wimereux, on September 24, 1915.[32] While there, he healed quickly and enjoyed the time away from active duty. However, he did see things in the hospital that exposed him to some of the terrors of war that heretofore he had no way of understanding. He wrote his father on October 4, 1915, that "some of the wounded are ghastly sights. . . . The most pitiful sight I have come across was a gunner . . . ; he was absolutely uninjured, but he is playing about on the floor of his room like a little child and his intelligence is about that of a 5 year old. God knows what he saw to drive him into that state of mind."[33] In this same letter, he wondered how Jack was doing. Moreover, Warnie's worries about Jack grew increasingly acute as he neared eligibility for war service. Five weeks later, Warnie wrote his father that he did not want to postpone his coming leave because he wanted to see Jack and was afraid this might be his last leave.[34] Although Warnie was mistaken about it being his final leave, the ominous tone of the letter shows that he was eager to see his brother in case he might not survive the war.

As the war dragged on, Warnie's feelings toward Germany, not surprisingly, turned bitter. Writing his father on February 27, 1916, he said that Germany had relinquished any right to be treated with mercy and argued that after the war it should be divided between Russia, France, and England and settled with non-Germans, forcing the native Germans to either leave or subsist in squalor. Any German discovered to have weapons would be subject to execution. He surmised that after two hundred years of such treatment, the German threat would be no more.[35] He also had little sympathy for able-bodied men back home looking for ways to avoid serving in the army. In the same letter, he expressed scorn at the flimsy appeals being made for military exemption, including one from a Scoutmaster who claimed his troop would fall apart if he were to leave it. Calling such requests shameless, Warnie insisted that men should be trying to do their duty, not scheming to avoid it.[36] He also hoped that Jack could win a scholarship to Oxford as result of his studies with Kirkpatrick.[37] Weather was a constant topic, and Warnie underscored how difficult battlefield conditions were, writing that the weather was brutal—snowing during the day and freezing at night. As a result, it was almost impossible to get the wagons to move on the roads. Since the country was hilly, the horses could not maintain their footing, and so they slipped and slid all over the place. At the same time, he told his father that compared with those fighting in the trenches he and his men were most fortunate.[38]

In his March 12, 1916, letter to his father Warnie shared about a recent camp move where he found a good billet for all the horses and men. As he compared his present quarters with his last one, he complained about the many rats in his previous bedroom, noting that they would often drop onto him just as he was falling asleep. Not surprisingly, he had not been getting much sleep, complaining that of everything they had to put up with, the rats were the worst.[39] He also mused about how close he might be to a promotion to full lieutenant. He worried that his promotion might be delayed or hampered because he was serving with the ASC. However, an important step to his promotion occurred when three weeks later he was put in charge of the supply section, the senior job in the company.[40] In addition, his letters to his father increasingly highlighted the almost apocalyptic conditions of the battlefields.

I went up today and saw the ground over which desperate fighting has been taking place for the last week:[41] do you remember the Biblical phrase "the abomination of desolation?"[42] I never realized before what it meant—in a strip of ground perhaps not three miles broad, there is no living thing—not a blade of grass, not a tree, not a building which stands more than three feet high: one cannot walk over it without difficulty, for there are no two square yards which do not contain a shell hole. And all round are men who look as if they were asleep, and things which were once men. There was one particularly vivid picture which I shall never be able to forget—a boy asleep on a bank and the mess by his head was his brains. But although these things have moved me deeply, they are in reality the ordinary incidents in a successful advance.[43]

In a letter to his wife, Paul Nash, another WWI soldier, although not stationed with Warnie, described a similar battlefield:

No pen or drawing can convey this country. . . . Sunset and sunrise are blasphemous, they are mockeries to man; only the black rain of the bruised and swollen clouds all through the bitter black of night is fit atmosphere in such a land. The rain drives on, the stinking mud becomes more evilly yellow, the shell holes fill up with green-white water, the roads and tracks are covered in inches of slime, the black dying trees ooze and sweat and the shells never cease. . . . It is unspeakable, godless, hopeless.[44]

On September 24, 1916, Warnie was promoted to full lieutenant, and on October 1, 1916, he was made temporary Captain.[45] However, Warnie's promotion was not without hardships; he thought he would take over command of his former company (Fourth Company, Seventh Divisional Train), but instead he was assigned to the Thirty-Second Divisional Train and found himself serving under a terrible commanding officer, Major Ronald Maclear.[46] He groused to his father that Maclear would not let him do his work as the transport Captain, insisting instead that Warnie follow behind all day long ready to laugh at his jokes. Warnie claimed Maclear was the biggest bore he ever met.[47] His later character sketch of Maclear was withering:

> He was short, and sturdily built, with a square head covered with grey hair, very closely cropped except in front, where one lock usually hung down over his fore-head. His ruddy, weather beaten face contained a blunt nose, a close clipped little moustache, and a pair of very small grey eyes, partially concealed by lids which were always half closed. He spoke in a low querulous monotone, surprisingly at variance with an appearance which seemed to call for a loud voiced, peremptory self-assertiveness. . . . He was never seen to open a book, or even look at a newspaper. . . . He never left camp unless compelled to do so in the course of duty. . . . One speedily realized that the man was a mass of hate; hatred of almost everyone was to him the normal condition of existence—a banked up, smouldering hatred, always active, never flaring into temper, reasonless, and as intractable as the forces of nature. . . . If for any reason, or no reason, he took a dislike to a man, he was extraordinarily ingenious and painstaking at making his life a hell to him by a thousand carefully thought out vexations and inflictions. He was in fact that worst of all types, the nagging bully. . . . He was an interminable talker of the disjointed stop and start again variety, and conversation—or rather his monologue—was generally of how men of his acquaintance had come to ruin and disgrace, told with a relish which was sickening. In short, [he was] a sort of [terror] from Hell. He gloated on stories of British atrocities committed on Germans. . . . He frequently lectured his men on Germany and the Germans in the style of an Old Testament prophet, finishing off with "The only good Hun is a dead 'Un.'" . . . In the course of a somewhat picaresque life I have met a good many men of all classes and types; it raises my faith in human nature when I reflect that of all I have met, I can only recollect four . . . whom I would describe as bad men. Ronald Maclear is one of the four.[48]

Warnie was so disillusioned by his promotion that he longed to be a second lieutenant back in his old company.

This letter also revealed Warnie's growing and discomforting realization that his brother was going to have to serve in the war. He told his father that he had been thinking about "It" almost continuously, and while he could not advise that his father try to keep Jack out of the war, he did strongly urge Albert to keep Jack out of the fighting until he was at least nineteen. Warnie added that the idea of Jack taking an officer's commission with his lack of experience was both ludicrous and prosecutable.[49] Yet within two weeks, Warnie was more upbeat, in part because learned his brother won a scholarship to Oxford, but even more so because he had been made a temporary supply officer, a job with a good deal of logistics responsibilities. He disclosed to his father that he had 3,000 men and 2,500 horses to feed and keep warm.[50] The work of a transport unit such as Warnie's finds expression in Robert Graves's *Goodbye to All That* (1929). Having been declared medically unfit for trench service, Graves took command of a headquarter company and lived with a transport unit: "My company consisted of regimental clerks, cooks, tailors, shoemakers, pioneers, transport men, and so on, who in a break-through could turn riflemen and be used as a combatant force.... I used to go up to the trenches every night with the rations . . . about a twelve mile walk there and back."[51] As in the case of Graves, Warnie's work as a supply officer brought him under frequent enemy fire.

Warnie's assumption of additional responsibilities coincided with Allied advances on the battlefield. From February 23 to April 5, 1917, the German armies, employing a scorched earth policy, withdrew to the Hindenburg Line in order to take up a defensive position intended to hold back the forward momentum of the Allied armies.[52] Warnie offered his assessment of the German withdrawal in a letter to his father of April 5, 1917, where he mocked the idea of German chivalry during this retreat. He cataloged how devastating the German destructive retreat was, noting that they burned every house, cut down every fruit tree, and mined all the roads. In each village, the German soldiers gathered all the plates and dishes and then smashed them to pieces; in a particularly petty action, the Germans even broke up all the children's toys. Worst of all, they poisoned every single well.[53] German soldier Ernest Jünger, who participated in the retreat, confirmed the German army's actions in his diary, *Storm of Steel:*

The villages we passed through on our way had the look of vast lunatic asylums. Whole companies were set to knocking or pulling down walls, or sitting on rooftops, uprooting the tiles. Trees were cut down, windows smashed, wherever you looked, clouds of smoke and dust rose from vast piles of debris.... With destructive cunning [soldiers] found the roof-trees of the houses, fixed ropes to them, and with concerted effort, pulled till they all came tumbling down. Others were swinging pile-driving hammers, and went around smashing everything that got in their way, from flowerpots on the window-sills to whole ornate conservatories. . . . Every village was reduced to rubble, every tree chopped down, every road undermined, every well poisoned, every basement blown up or booby-trapped, every rail unscrewed, every telephone wire rolled up, everything burnable burned; in a word, we were turning the country that our advancing opponents would occupy into a wasteland. As I say, the scenes were reminiscent of a madhouse, and the effect of them was . . . bad for the men's morale and honour. . . . Among the surprises we'd prepared for our successors were some truly malicious inventions. Very fine wires, almost invisible, were stretched across the entrances of buildings and shelters, which set off explosions at the faintest touch. . . . Or there were spiteful time bombs that were buried in the basements of undamaged buildings. . . . One such device blew up the town hall of Bapaume just as the authorities had assembled to celebrate victory.[54]

Later, in his April 5, 1917, letter, Warnie's increasing hatred for the enemy came into focus, as he declared that he had not despised the Germans until he saw the things they did during their retreat. Three weeks after this letter Warnie worries about Jack were eased to some degree when his brother matriculated at University College, Oxford, and joined the Officers' Training Corps billeted at Keble College.

As the Allies advanced, Warnie found himself increasingly exposed to artillery fire. On June 8, 1917, he admitted to his father that one night he had just gotten into bed when a shell whizzed right over him. Startled, he jerked up as a second shell fell, covering his tent with mud and debris, so he and those with him jumped out of bed, led the horses away, and then spent the rest of the night huddled in a low spot in the field a few miles away.[55] They had only returned to camp several hours later when the shelling began again, and they had to make another hasty evacuation. He and his commander, Major John Hunter Shaw, dashed down a cart track, but almost immediately the bombing was so intense that they had to drop into a ditch. Warnie pointed out this was very fortunate, since a shell then exploded only twelve yards away. The two of them stayed in the ditch for another forty minutes while the Germans bombed them relentlessly. Albert must have been alarmed reading this, especially when Warnie added with grim humor that he was bringing home a piece of the shell as a souvenir. He had dug it out of a nearby tree and was keeping it as a reminder that if it had been three inches more left and one lower, his fledgling career in the ASC would have been over. He concluded the letter uneasy about his brother, so two weeks later he urged Albert to use his political connections to get Jack into the artillery if possible, but added—probably wishfully—that even if Jack went into the infantry, his chances of surviving were very much better now than in the early days of the war.[56] Over the next six months, Warnie continued his duties with the Thirty-Second Divisional Train and persisted in his apprehensions about his brother. At his father's urging, during part of a leave that he spent in Oxford with Jack, he tried to talk Jack into joining the artillery rather than the infantry, but he had no success.[57]

Later, in his "Memoir," Warnie recalled a critical incident that caused the relationship between Jack and his father—already a difficult one—to be further strained. After pointing out how foreign the war seemed to those living in Ireland, Warnie recorded that on November 15, 1917, Jack sent his father a telegram informing him that he was about to leave to serve in the trenches in France and asking Albert to meet him in Bristol before he disembarked. Warnie noted: "My father simply wired back that he could not understand the telegram, and asked for leisured explanations: he made no attempt to keep the rendezvous in Bristol—proposed clearly enough by Jack—for what might well have been a last meeting, and Jack had to sail for France and the war without seeing him again. This must have been felt as a rebuff, though it was probably due to a genuine misunderstanding, a failure in 'communication.'"[58] The tenuous bond between Jack and his father, already fraught with distrust, suspicion, and doubt, was further fractured by Albert's bungled handling of Jack's departure to the front.

However, good news came to Warnie when he was finally promoted to full Captain on November 29, 1917. His promotion—and his liberation from serving under Maclear—set the stage for a major change in his military career: a move from the Horse Transport section to the Mechanical Transport section of the ASC, something that he had applied for in March 1917. Only three days after his promotion, Warnie confessed to his father that since he had not been raised around horses, he did not think a future career would involve working with them. However, now that he was in the Mechanical Transport section, he could imagine a twenty-year or so career in the ASC and then retiring with a comfortable pension. He would be in his mid-forties, a relatively young man, and knowledgeable about automobiles. Accordingly, he believed he would be able to secure employment with a car company and an income to supplement his retirement subsidy. Warnie also responded to Albert's news that Jack decided to stay in the infantry, comforting his father by arguing that Jack would almost certainly never make it to the front lines. At the same time, he was fatalistic, telling his father that most soldiers believed that if one's name was written on a German shell or bullet, it would find him out, regardless. He ended by telling Albert that he was sure Jack would survive the war.[59] On December 21, Warnie also wrote his father noting that if his brother decided to stay with the infantry, then it was feasible that he would not be thrust into front line duty because of his health.[60]

Contiguous with these persistent misgivings about his brother, Warnie reported to the Mechanical Transport School of Instruction at St. Omer where he underwent training from December 23, 1917, to March 4, 1918. The need for a concentrated period of training was acute since his duties as a Captain of a Mechanical Transport Company included taking charge of the company workshop. The additional responsibilities of a captain meant Warnie "is responsible that all repairs are carried out properly and that no material is wasted. He will see that the company is always supplied with the necessary stores and equipment to meet all requirements. He will prepare the annual estimates for all stores, and will constantly satisfy himself that the company equipment is in a thoroughly serviceable condition. He will take steps to ensure that artificers are not permitted to undertake private repairs for officers and others in company or station workshops, or during working hours."[61] Up until now, Warnie had served solely with Horse Transport units, so this change required that his ASC skills be completely retooled. For the next ten weeks, Warnie was schooled about steam vehicles (although this sounds arcane, steam vehicles played a major role in WWI), all aspects of steam engines and boilers, changing gears, internal combustion engines (names and functions of all parts of cylinders, carburetors, water pumps, radiators, different systems of ignition, distributors, spark plugs), clutches, gears, and gear boxes. He also had to know about differentials, axles, different systems of lubrication, brakes, and removing and repairing tires. Other things he had to master were steering backward and forward, driving up and down hills, cleaning up and readying vehicles for the next day, extricating vehicles when stuck in soft ground, estimating fuel requirements, and driving the most common vehicles, including heavy trucks, cars, and motorcycles.

While his time at the Mechanical Transport School of Instruction was not without some difficulties, for the most part Warnie welcomed the new challenge. He wrote in his diary on January 1, 1918, that he attended lectures on differentials and was driving various kinds of vehicles; he complained in particular about a Saurer lorry, lamenting that it was the worst vehicle he had ever driven because the clutch jammed and the gears would not shift properly.[62] He also admitted to excessive drinking—something he had hidden from his father—noting that when he had awakened that morning he was incredibly tired with a terrible headache, the result of "one whiskey too many."[63] Unfortunately, he failed the weekly theory test, missing a passing grade by three points. However, he resigned himself, noting that he did not fail for lack of trying.[64] As the weeks pass, he studied hard, took and passed written tests, and drove many other vehicles, including Lelands, Daimlers, Straker Squires, Dennises, Douglases, and motorcycles; he was particularly elated when he passed his first lorry driving test.[65]

Soon Warnie was given permission to go out driving on a Triumph motorcycle, in part in order to prepare him to take the motorcycle driving test. He also began taking apart various parts of trucks and motorcycles, learning on each occasion detailed information about them. However, it was not all work, as several diary entries referred to a local restaurant, Kitty's, where he noticed several beautiful women. When he wrote his father about his new posting, Warnie was generally upbeat, and his diary also reflected his relative happiness during this training.

Of special note was his new friendship with Herbert Denis Parkin (1886–1958), who had joined the army in 1908, the Army Service Corps in 1911, and was taking the same course as Warnie at the Mechanical Transport School of Instruction. In his diary, Warnie noted his almost daily contact with Parkin, including time spent together studying, listening to the gramophone, riding motorcycles, gambling, eating, drinking, and dating girls. Over the next forty plus years, the friendship between Warnie and Parkin flourished, and they encountered each other frequently in various posting throughout their military careers. On January 28, 1918, Warnie wrote that it was a beautiful sunny day—one in which it was delightful to be alive.[66] In his summary of his first month of training, he admitted that as he looked back over the diary entries, he was surprised to see how often he had referred to being bored. In fact, he conceded that he had a really interesting time, noting that all his activities had shaken him out of his lethargy. At the same time, the sooner he was finished with the course, the better because he was spending too much money and drinking too much.[67]

Albert wrote to Warnie on February 3, 1918, noting he was not surprised at Warnie's success with motor vehicles, pointing out that he naturally had strong mechanical and engineering gifts, explaining that from his great grandfather down, nearly every member of the Lewis family was connected in some way with mechanical work. In the same letter, Albert expressed deep discouragement about the progress of the war, certain that it would never end, and continued to fret obsessively about Jack.[68] In order to allay his father's discouragement, Warnie advised him that his depression was a result of his isolated life; for Warnie's part, he admitted that Jack was always on his mind, but he was confident Jack would be fine. In addition, Warnie offered a somewhat brighter view of the war. Using a poker metaphor, Warnie declared that most soldiers in the field believed the Germans were about to gamble and put all their money in the pot via a major offensive. Even though the Germans held some powerful cards, Warnie assured Albert that their hand was not as good as the Allies'. He asserted that everyone with him believed the Germans would bet their success on a huge offensive before America entered the war. Then when that failed, even the most devoted German soldier would recognize that *unser Kaiser*[69] was not what he claimed to be.[70] The Germans had been so badly depleted by the war, that even though they might be able to amount a new offensive, their losses had been so great that they would not be able to sustain it for long. In effect, then, the Germans were bluffing, hoping to frighten off the Allies. Warnie ended the letter by optimistically hoping for a reunion at Leeborough very soon.[71] Subsequently, Warnie's training intensified, and he passed a crucial practical test: he was given a 40-horsepower engine that had nine or ten things wrong with it, and he managed to get it running within the twenty-minute time limit.[72] Warnie finished his training at the Mechanical Transport School of Instruction three weeks later.

After receiving his orders to report to "D" Siege Park, an ammunition column of the Royal Garrison Artillery, on March 7, 1918, Warnie shipped out by train, noting the ruined landscape in and around the Somme.[73] When he was there in 1916, he could hardly move because of all the troops, but now there was almost no one. The one overriding sight was No Man's Land, large swathes of ground that he described as bleak and depressing.[74] His duties as captain of the company included distributing pay to the men, authorizing leave, and censoring the mail. One disconcerting side of serving with the ammunition column was that he was under frequent enemy fire; after one attack, he divulged that he was caught under an enemy barrage with large hunks of earth raining down on him. This was terrifying because he had forgotten to wear his steel helmet.[75] Warnie's experience under fire was typical of ASC soldiers. One fellow officer wrote: "Our Brigade has suffered heavily in the severe fighting, and some of the very best fellows, with whom we were dining on the previous night, have fallen on Hill 60. Never in my life do I wish to hear such a terrible shaking of the earth as we are experiencing now, and still less do I want to see such awful, unmentionable sights as I saw at Ypres three days ago. Thank God, I got my supply company out without casualty. I recommended two of our fellows for conspicuous coolness and courage."[76]

Warnie was increasingly conscious that the major German offensive was imminent. When it came, he conceded in his diary on March 21, 1918, that the initial success of the German attack was frightening. He had been awakened by heavy fire around 5 A.M. with four 5.9 bombs falling close by; it was a misty morning with heavy showers of shrapnel and high explosive bombs falling nearby. Also unsettling, news had come that the Germans had broken through the Allied lines to a distance of 3 miles and captured the town of Vaulx, less than 5 miles away. For the next eight days, Warnie and his company were under almost constant shelling, as well as machine gun fire, and fell back a number of times in order to avoid being overrun. During this period, Warnie undoubtedly saw scenes such as the one described by Ernest Hemingway in his short story, "A Way You'll Never Be":

The attack had gone across the field, been held up by machine-gun fire from the sunken road and from the group of farmhouses, encountered no resistance in the town, and reached the bank of the river. . . . [The dead] lay alone or in clumps in the high grass of the field and along the road, their pockets out, and over them were flies. . . . In the grass and the grain, beside the road, and in some places scattered over the road, there was much material: a field kitchen . . . stick bombs, helmets, rifles,

sometimes one butt up, the bayonet stuck in the dirt . . . intrenching tools, ammunition boxes, star-shell pistols . . . medical kits, gas masks, empty gas-mask cans, a
squat, tripoded machine gun in a nest of empty shells . . . mass prayer books, group
postcards showing the machine-gun unit standing in ranked and ruddy cheerfulness
as in a football picture annual; now they were humped and swollen in the grass.[77]

Despite the sobering reality of such scenes, Warnie reported better news in his
diary on March 29, 1918, noting that while the Germans had inflicted a terrible
hole in the middle of the Fifth Army, they were not able to break through.[78]

In his diary summary of March 1918, Warnie affirmed candidly how near to
breaking and being overrun his company and the Allies had been in the face of
the German offensive: "This has been a most eventful month. On [March] the
4th I . . . found myself a fully-fledged M[echanical] T[ransport] officer. Then I
was only beginning to feel settled up the line when the retreat started. For about
24 hours I went through agonies; I really thought the unspeakable thing had
happened, and the Army was broken. I never realized before how much it all
meant to me. Now however I think that thanks to God we are safe again, but it
has been a bad fright."[79] A more constant theme in his diary at this time was the
amount of time he spent censoring the mail of the men in his company who were
writing home. For some in Warnie's position this became a tiresome obligation,
especially handling the inordinate number of love letters being sent back home.
One ASC officer, Lieutenant C. Smallpiece—not in Warnie's company—came
up with a novel solution: "It became part of my duties to censor all the letters
the men wrote home . . . and the censoring became a very serious business for
me, as I frequently had at night to wade carefully through 150 love-letters. So I
. . . bought a football, which I took back for my men to play with. The result was
quite marvelous. . . . The men took to it so keenly that they played football all
day, and had very little time left in which to write love-letters. . . . [Soon] I never
had more than five love-letters to censor at night."[80]

Warnie's letters and diary entries for April 1918 were somewhat contradictory.
At times he sounded optimistic about the Allies repelling the German offensive
when he wrote his father. On April 14, 1918, he related to his father that he would
be glad to know that his company was well, although they did have some close
calls.[81] However, his diary entry for the same day was sober and dark. He pro-
fessed that the morning news was bad because the German army was continuing
its northern attack. Indeed, it was a profoundly distressing day. He hoped that
unified Allied efforts would be able to halt the German offensive.[82] In the April
14 letter, Warnie also praised the bravery of the infantry, and he wondered what

everyone back home thought of the progress of the war. Where he was, everyone was optimistic, although they admitted that the Germans managed a first-rate attack and came close to breaking through. He predicted the war would be over in three or four months, with his only real worry continuing to focus upon Jack.[83] Yet in his diary entry for April 15, he revealed that there were frightening rumors about the war. Over the next week, the news about the war was better, and Warnie was less anxious in his diary. However, on April 24, he received a telegram from Albert saying that Jack had been severely wounded and was in the hospital at Étaples.[84] Warnie immediately borrowed a motorcycle and rode the 50 miles to Étaples in just over three hours; when he arrived, he discovered that Jack had only suffered minor wounds and was able to make light of his injuries. Warnie was greatly relieved, happy that Jack would now be out of the most dangerous action.[85] Returning to his base around 9 P.M., Warnie related to his father with some pique that his brother had been falsely described as severely wounded; he was not sure who had given such a dire report, but it had given Warnie the horrors.[86] He went on to say Jack was actually in good spirits—the two of them had cracked jokes and looked forward to Jack getting out of the thick of fighting. Warnie then related his understanding of the wounds, noting that a shell had exploded near Jack, killing a Sergeant; however, luckily for "IT," Jack had non-life-threatening shrapnel wounds in one of his cheeks and two his hands.[87]

Warnie's diary summary for April 1918 was marked by sober optimism: "A month which might have been better but could certainly have been worse. From a selfish point of view the great news was undoubtedly [Jack's] wound. It will be a very long time before I forget that ride to Étaples and waiting in the hospital hall to see him. But the mental and physical pain was more than counterbalanced by the joy and thankfulness of seeing him sitting up in bed." Then he added: "It's funny how relief from fear turns to irritation. I really was angry at having to go through four such hours for nothing." When he turned to writing about the war, he was very sober. Warnie admitted that while it had been a tenuous month, it did not compare to the terrible days following March 21. He genuinely regretted the loss of several northern French towns since he had come to know many of the people well, but he also recognized that if such losses shortened the war, then such sacrifice was worth it.[88]

Warnie's letters and diary of May 1918 were cheerier, recognizing that the fortunes of the war were turning against the Germans and toward the Allies. Entries in his diary delight in the beauty of the weather, his learning how to play badminton, rides on his motorcycle, pleasant visits with Collins, noticing pretty women, lively dinner parties—often with neighboring French forces—and his being transferred from the Royal Garrison Artillery ammunition column, Siege Park, to the Thirty-First Divisional Mechanical Transport Company.[89] On May 13, 1918, he revealed to his father that that his own unit was the center of several ASC sections in charge of guns and ordinance; as a result, they were usually only 7 or 8 miles from the fighting. Furthermore, all his comrades agreed that whatever might happen next, the Germans could never mount an attack like that of March 21. Warnie's pride in being a part of the ASC was also mentioned when he recounted that an ASC lorry driver had been awarded the Victoria Cross.[90] Warnie and his fellow ASC comrades were pleased that one of them, and the entire corps by extension, had been given such a recognition.[91] Warnie informed Albert he could bring this award to the attention of anyone back home who believed all the ASC did was hide behind the lines using up coal rations and stealing strawberry jam.[92] With his transfer to the Thirty-First Divisional Mechanical Transport Company in late May 1918, Warnie was upbeat, writing in his diary that Jack was safe in London.[93] The next day, he wrote his father and shared that he was no longer under heavy shell fire. In fact, he thought his job cushy, as he was overseeing two subalterns, thirty-two lorries, a mobile workshop, and two motorcycles. Together they were responsible for looking after the food supply for the men and the shells for the artillery.[94] Since the outbreak of the war, Warnie had matured in many ways, not the least of which involved his expertise and responsibilities as an ASC officer.

From May 27 to June 6, 1918, the Third Battle of the Aisne, the third phase of the German spring offensive, was fought. Although the Germans made some initial gains, their advance soon was paralyzed. In anticipating this battle, Warnie wrote on May 20, 1918: "Tomorrow is the supposed date of the German offensive—600,000 infantry and marksmen in rear with 150,000 cavalry. Think they'll get it in the neck if they do come."[95] The beginning of June 1918 marked the beginning of the end for the German army. Although four separate German battles in the spring offensive led to some minor territorial advances against the Allies, the German successes were marked by heavy losses and a weakened supply line. For example, the Battle of Matz, occurred June 9 to 12, 1918, and, despite substantial territorial gains, the Germans did not achieve their strategic goals. The tipping point came from July 15 to August 6, 1918, with the Second Battle of the Marne and last German offensive on the Western Front. The Germans were vigorously counterattacked by the French, and from August 8 to November 11, 1918, the Allies engaged in the Hundred Days offensive. Beginning with the Battle of Amiens, from August 8 to 12, 1918, the Allies launched a series of offensives that pushed the Germans out of France, highlighted by the Battle of the Hindenburg Line from September 18 to October 17, 1918. After this victory, the

Allies broke the German lines and forced them into the retreat that eventually led to the end of the war.

For Warnie, the last five months of the war were relatively quiet. His evenings were marked by games of drinking and bridge (in which he regularly lost small amounts of money), while his letters and diary recounted days of routine work, his increasing fluency in French, and brief comments on the books he was reading. Most importantly, he read James Boswell's *The Life of Samuel Johnson* (1791) for the first time, a biography that became a lifelong favorite for both him and Jack. Warnie's tastes in reading were always broad and varied, but more and more he found himself drawn to biographies, memoirs, journals, and collections of letters. For instance, during this period Warnie read the *Memoirs* (1915) of Algernon Bertram Freeman-Mitford, First Baron Redesdale (1837–1916), British diplomat to Japan, collector, and writer. Warnie's scrutiny of Freeman-Mitford's life foreshadowed his later fascination with the life and court of Louis XIV of France. And in an act that presaged his life as an historian, he purchased a Royal typewriter—the same instrument he would later use to type out the complete eleven volume history of the Lewis family as well as his seven books on seventeenth-century French history.

In other matters, he served on the board of court-martials and discussed with his father the state of his finances, business dealings, and financial plans, all with an eye to preparing for the end of the war. Moreover, on one occasion, he wrote a speech in French for his commanding officer while another time he served as temporary commanding officer.[96] When he referred to battlefield action, he reflected the growing feeling that the end of the war was near. For example, on August 2, 1918, he avowed to his father that everything was moving along nicely, and he praised the leadership of French general, Ferdinand Foch, who was leading a new offensive against the Germans.[97] Five weeks later, he was even more optimistic, telling his father that the Allied forces had made major advances and that everything seemed to be going extremely well.[98] Letters from Albert gave him the news that Jack continued to recover and, more importantly, had a book of poems—*Spirits in Bondage* (1919)—accepted for publication. All these positive developments resulted in Warnie's diary write up for September 1918 being most ebullient. He opined that while he did not think he was being overly confident, he believed September was a month that historians would mark as the beginning of the end for the Germans. Regarding Jack, Warnie was pleased that he was recovering in England, well out of the fierce fighting. About *Spirits in Bondage,* Warnie thought that even if it did not sell well, it was evidence that Jack had achieved an important literary goal.[99]

Over the next month, Warnie shared with his father that his company advanced almost daily with little or no resistance from the German army, and both father and son celebrated that Jack was almost certainly out of anymore active combat. On the evening before the armistice was signed, Warnie described the wild celebrations marking the end of the war:

> A day which I shall not forget in a hurry. I was in the office about 9 P.M. and suddenly there was an outburst of syrens, rockets, Verey lights,[100] hooters, searchlights and all sorts of things. Hurried back to the mess and found everyone dancing round the room! . . . Everyone off their heads. Cars with people sitting all over them. Australians firing Verey pistols in the square. There were about six bonfires going with Belgians dancing and shouting round them with our lads. Cathedral and Church bells pealed most of the night. Got home and to bed about 2:30 A.M. A very great day indeed. So ends the war![101]

On November 11, 1918, the armistice was signed, effectively ending the Great War.[102] That day Warnie declared: "It seems wonderful to think that the war is really over at last. Thank God Jacks has come through it safely, and that nightmare is now lifted from my mind."[103] On November 29, 1918, he wrote his father and expanded on his diary entry from Armistice Day, again thanking God that Jack was spared. He admitted that Jack's safety was paramount, and he admitted that the biggest torment for him throughout the war was his worry about his brother. Jack had constantly been on his mind, causing him to wake up in the middle of the night wondering if he was still alive. He gushed with happiness, telling his father he simply could not believe the war was actually over.[104] After more than four years of service in their shared horror of the Great War, Warnie recounted the memorable day on December 27, 1918, when he and his brother were reunited: "A red letter day today. We [he and his father, Albert] were sitting in the study about 11 o'clock this morning when we saw a cab coming up the avenue. It was Jacks! He has been demobilized thank God. Needless to say there were great doings. He is looking pretty fit. We had lunch and then all three went for a walk. It was as if the evil dream of four years had passed away and we were still in the year 1915."[105]

The most pointed irony of WWI was expressed by Paul Fussell: "In the Great War eight million people were destroyed because two persons, the Archduke Francis Ferdinand and his Consort, had been shot."[106] Warnie's letters and diaries of 1914–1918 often touched on the many ironies he saw during his service; furthermore, they chronicled his daily life as an ASC officer, and they offered an inside view of one who experienced the war with a sensitive awareness and perceptive eye. WWI battlefield poets like Wilfred Owen or Siegfried Sassoon saw the war from a more visceral point of view. John Johnston in *English Poetry of the First World War* effectively summarized the kind of war poetry Owen, Sassoon, and others like them wrote:

> During the second winter of the war, when the true nature of the struggle was becoming apparent, poets began to react to the horrors around them with a directness almost unprecedented in verse. This literature of angry protest employed the weapons of satire, irony, and a savage realism. . . . Most frequent of all, and most significantly from a literary point of view, we have accounts of the experiences of the common soldier amidst a new kind of warfare—a warfare that utilized to the maximum every species of concentrated scientific violence. As a partial and natural consequence, we have a tentative, episodic, disconnected, emotional kind of writing, a desperate insistence on the shocking facts of life and death, a compulsive focus on the obscene details of crude animal needs and reactions, on wounds, death, and decomposition. Never before in literature had war been described with this painful compression of action and incident, with this narrowing of focus, this fragmentation of reality, this obsessive emphasis on isolated and irrelevant sensory details.[107]

Because Warnie was not directly fighting in the trenches, his war writings were less visceral, less intense, less emotional, and less angry. At the same time his writings do give us "accounts of the experiences of the common soldier amidst," as Johnston described it, "a new kind of warfare—a warfare that utilized to the maximum every species of concentrated scientific violence." Among other topics that Warnie reflected upon in his account as a common soldier, were many that I have not had time to explore; these include his periods of leave, almost always home to Ireland; his keeping up with family news back home; his deep and abiding love of classical music; his careful attention to business and investment concerns; and his discussions of the service and movements of dozens of ships during the war, many of which he had watched being built in Belfast and had known about since early childhood. He also reflected upon the friends he made among fellow servicemen; his regular attendance at army church services and detailed analyses of the sermons he heard; the many novels he read and mused upon; his growing fluency in French and knowledge of French history; and his sense that democracy was not a preferred form of government.

However, there are three important observations we can make about Warnie's involvement in the war and how he was shaped by it. First, Warnie became a man

through his service in WWI. As the child of a well-to-do middle class Irish family, next as an insulated schoolboy at Malvern College, and then as a sequestered
cadet at Sandhurst, Warnie had lived a sheltered, protected, and privileged life.
He had no firsthand knowledge of the way of the world, and despite the early
death of his mother, he had never faced the reality of existence outside the very
comfortable life his father provided him and Jack. Of course, the brutality of
WWI was something he could not close his eyes to, but as important was the fact
that for the first time in his life he rubbed shoulders with men not of his class.
Appointed a second lieutenant not long after his nineteenth birthday, he knew
nothing about leading men, and learned how to do so primarily by the positive
and negative examples he saw among the senior officers with whom he served.
By the end of the war, he was a captain, responsible for overseeing equipment,
camps, and two hundred men and officers. He began the war as a naïve teenage
boy but emerged from it as a seasoned, disciplined officer.

Second, the many allusions to drinking—sometimes seemingly benign—do
not mask the fact that he engaged in heavy episodes of alcoholic dissipation. This
fact in itself is not surprising, given the alternating periods he experienced of
long, monotonous boredom and intense, frightening peril. Most soldiers had to
find a way to cope with their service and their fears, so Warnie's drinking would
not have been an anomaly, but rather an everyday fact of life. Notwithstanding
his father's repeated warnings against excessive drinking, Warnie's lack of self-
control regarding the use of alcohol becomes an unfortunate theme in his life.
He almost certainly became an alcoholic because of the patterns of drink he
acquired during WWI and then later repeated throughout his army career.

Third, and most importantly, Warnie's life as a writer was stimulated by his
wartime service. While his many letters to his father might have been expected—
after all, what could be more comforting than to connect regularly to life back at
Leeborough where lay familiarity, warm memories of hearth and home, beloved
places and people, tender scenes of friendship, and above all normality—his other
wartime writings were coping mechanisms. They were musings where he could
process not only the simple, everyday chronicle of his life, but also where he could
explore deeper, existential questions and matters common to all human beings.
Who am I? Why am I here? Where am I going? For instance, Warnie's wartime
writings often captured the irony of the whole affair. In one letter he wrote: "Last
night there was a glorious sunset—all crimson and gold, and not a gun to be heard
anywhere. Somehow it suddenly struck me how silly the whole thing is—I don't
know if you can understand what I mean—but on a lovely spring evening, why
should some five million men be concentrating all their energy on the destruction
of another five million men?"[108] In another example, Warnie recounted: "[One

evening] we halted for the night in the same village where we were last August. I think I was happier there than I have ever been since I joined the Army. . . . The place was deserted and I went for a long solitary ramble. . . . There was the [river] bank where we used to sit and talk in the evenings. . . . Such thoughts and pilgrimages are worse than useless and yet I think very few of us can resist the temptation to make them when the chance arises."[109] In a final instance, Warnie conceded how desolate the country around the Somme had become: "The most saddening thing about the present advance is the country we are passing over. . . . The places which now are desolate stinking ruins were cheerful little towns which we all have lived in at different times during the last three years. . . . It is a dreadful thing to go to a place where you have had civilian friends and a cheery time . . . and find that there are not sufficient remnants of the roadway to . . . where your old billet was."[110]

In addition, his wartime writings also include adroit character sketches of some of his commanders, comrades, and friends. In these character sketches, Warnie shows a wonderful eye for physical description, but even more telling are the astute evaluations of the moral, spiritual, and social qualities of the individual under scrutiny. For example, about one of his instructors at Sandhurst, he notes that "though a rigid disciplinarian, he was very easy of access off the parade, and was always scrupulous in avoiding the least hint of patronage in his dealings with Cadets, whom he treated as brother officers, of course to their great delight. . . . He had a long, mobile face, with sparkling black eyes . . . [and] he had an inexhaustible supply of service anecdotes which he told extremely well."[111] He describes one of his commanders in France as "a tall, very thin, grey-haired, clean-shaven man . . . with a finely molded, sardonic face, who walked with the deliberate, rheumaticky [sic] motion peculiar to the larger birds, particularly storks."[112] In another extended character sketch, Warnie proved he could be generous with his praise of a superior officer—in this case Major Andrew Grant:

> He was under middle height, very well built, with a pale oval face, steady light blue eyes, a sharp nose, and a tiny straw coloured moustache, sharply turned up into points. He was very dapper in his turn out, and at a time when the soft service cap was fashionable he adhered to the stiffest of stiff caps which he wore very much on the side of his head. He was an excellent war time unit commander, loved by his officers and men and trusted and respected by [his] staff. . . . He was in fact the ideal leader. . . . He had a most uncanny flair for dividing orders into those which were essential and those which were not; and the latter class he disobeyed so matter of factly that he rarely got into trouble for so doing. . . . He succeeded in getting the best out of his subordinates solely by making friends with them; he

not only knew all his men by name, but knew a good deal about each of them; he regarded himself as merely *primus inter equales* [first among equals] and the result was that everyone in the Company felt that to fail to do one's best would be rather a breach of manners than a breach of discipline; no one ever dreamt of taking a liberty with him. He appeared to do very little work, yet he was always at hand to suggest an alteration in my orders which when put into effect, proved to make all the difference between passable and good work.[113]

Warnie's wartime service 1914–1918 was the central shaping influence on his life. However, his life was not defined solely by the Great War; he emerged from it scarred, but not defeated nor crippled. Indeed, he continued as an active-duty soldier until 1932, and it is to that portion of his life we turn next.

CHAPTER THREE

Army Career
(1919–1932)

Postwar Europe was in crisis. In England, France, and Germany, entire genera-
tions of young men had been decimated. Women who wanted to marry were
so numerous and without prospects that some referred to themselves as surplus women.[1] Prewar centers of authority were scrutinized with suspicion and
cynicism. The British government, once respected and trusted, was perceived
as having betrayed its young men. Both the press and the church were seen as
complicit with the government, having readily turned a blind eye to the evils
of the war, acquiescing to political machinations. For instance, C. E. Montague
damned the press coverage of the Battle of the Somme: "The most bloody defeat
in the history of Britain . . . [occurred] . . . on July 1, 1916 [60,000 soldiers were
killed or wounded], and our Press come out bland and copious and graphic,
with nothing to show that we had not had quite a good day—a victory really.
Men who had lived through the massacre read the stuff-open-mouthed. . . . So
it comes that each of several million ex-soldiers now reads . . . with that maxim
on guard in his mind—'You can't believe a word you read.'"[2] Siegfried Sassoon's
poem "They" (1917) neatly expresses how many soldiers, including Warnie, saw
the church as both clueless and ineffectual:

> The Bishop tells us: "When the boys come back
> They will not be the same; for they'll have fought
> In a just cause: they lead the last attack
> On Anti-Christ; their comrades' blood has bought
> New right to breed an honourable race,
> They have challenged Death and dared him face to face."

"We're none of us the same!" the boys reply.
"For George lost both his legs; and Bill's stone blind;
Poor Jim's shot through the lungs and like to die;
And Bert's gone syphilitic: you'll not find
A chap who's served that hasn't found some change."
And the Bishop said: 'The ways of God are strange!'"[3]

It is no exaggeration to claim that the generation of WWI survivors looked upon their elders and the age-old, honored institutions of state, press, and church with cynicism, distrust, and suspicion.

Moreover, the cumbersome and poorly managed process of British demobilization exacerbated the resentment of many soldiers. Undoubtedly, demobilization was a huge, complex, and unprecedented challenge.[4] When the war began in 1914, the British army consisted of roughly 250,000 volunteers; by the end of the war, 6.2 million men had been mobilized.[5] How to reintroduce so many soldiers into civilian life was a critical problem for the British government, compounded by fears that social unrest and labor riots would result as hundreds of thousands of former soldiers returned home looking for work. As early as 1916, demobilization plans were being discussed; however, the initial scheme was seriously flawed because it tended to favor releasing men from the military not based upon their length of service, but instead upon their perceived immediate usefulness to key segments of industry. Riots and small-scale mutinies resulted. In January 1919, Winston Churchill was appointed as the war secretary, and he quickly introduced a new and equitable plan of demobilization. According to Stephen Graubard, "the principles of the Churchill plan, stated concisely and lucidly, could be easily understood by all. When the Armistice was signed, there were about 3,500,000 men in the British Army. All but 900,000 of these were to be released. The new army was to comprise only those who had enlisted after December 31, 1915, were under thirty-seven years of age, and possessed fewer than three wound stripes. All others were to be released."[6] As Churchill put it, "if anyone has to stay, it must be those who are not the oldest, nor those who came the earliest, nor those who suffered the most."[7] To pacify further the remaining soldiers, their pay was essentially doubled.

Warnie, as a career Royal Army Service Corps officer, avoided the demobilization pitfalls common to many.[8] He went on leave on December 22, 1918, and, as was noted in the previous chapter, he was already in Belfast when he was reunited with his brother at Leeborough on December 27, 1918.[9] During his monthlong leave, Warnie relaxed, visited relatives, listened to classical music on the family gramophone, considered his financial investments, and read a number of books. He also enjoyed taking a walk almost every day. On Christmas Day 1918, for instance, he went out of his way to pass near the spot where the Harland & Wolff Company was building an extension to its shipbuilding facility. Ever the pragmatist, Warnie was keenly interested in shipbuilding and the shipping industry. He also had several long conversations with Jack; while there is no record of what they said to each other, it is safe to assume they shared stories about their wartime service, what each hoped regarding the future, and how it seemed to them that Albert was getting along. Whether or not they spoke of Jack's relationship to Mrs. Janie King Moore (1872–1951), the mother of his friend, Paddy, who died during the war, is unknown, but probably unlikely.[10] Jack and Paddy, facing the likelihood of dying on the battlefield, had made a pact, promising that if one died and the other survived, the survivor would take care of the parent of the deceased. Jack's biographers have long assumed that a romantic relationship between Jack and Janie Moore had already begun; whatever the case, Jack kept the nature of his relationship with Moore as much a secret from Warnie as he had from their father.[11]

When Warnie returned to active duty with the Thirty-First Divisional Mechanical Transport Company on January 22, 1919, he was stationed in northern France in the town of Arques, Pas-de-Calais. With hostilities over, Warnie and his fellow soldiers no longer lived on the razor edge of uncertainty as to whether they would be alive one day and dead the next. Accordingly, he concerned himself with his daily routine, noting that things were now more relaxed than they had been during combat and that his company was gradually demobilizing. In letters to his father, he expressed a great interest in financial matters, including the investments Albert was overseeing on his behalf as well the British government's promise to increase the pay of army officers. Without a significant pay increase, Warnie told his father, many younger officers would be forced to resign their commissions, although as a senior officer he would be able to get by. John Fortescue writes about the issue of RASC wages: "In July 1919, it was decided that . . . special pay, which had attracted such excellent officers before the war should be withdrawn from all except a small proportion who had been specially trained to mechanical transport. This was virtually a breach of faith, and was the more galling because the Royal Army Service Corps alone was subject to this deprivation."[12] For Warnie and many of his fellows RASC officers, this was a bitter pill.

Much of Warnie's interest focused upon Jack, his return to Oxford, and his poetry. In his letter to Albert of January 28, 1919, Warnie offered his opinion of Jack's *Spirits in Bondage*. While he agreed with Albert's praise of the book's strengths, he offered a stinging rebuke: "While I am in complete agreement with you as to the excellence of parts of 'IT'S' book, I am of the opinion that it would have been better if it had never been published. Jack's Atheism is I am sure purely academic, but even so, no useful purpose is served by endeavoring to advertise oneself as an Atheist. Setting aside the higher problems involved, it is obvious that a profession of a Christian belief is as necessary a part of a man's mental make-up as a belief in the King, the Regular Army, and the Public Schools."[13] While Warnie's opinion of *Spirits in Bondage* was condescending, it was also honest and forthright. How, Warnie implied, could one expect to get along in the everyday world without a dutiful submission to recognized governmental, military, and social forces? Of course, Warnie was not being entirely honest with his father since his own experiences in the army and public schools were hardly ones that endeared him to religious faith. In this letter, he also noted with great sorrow the death of Henry Wakelyn Smith, his beloved teacher at Malvern. He expressed deep regret that he was gone, writing that he was noble-minded and an excellent thinker and trusted confidant.[14] In other letters to Albert, Warnie alluded to the burgeoning conflict between the Irish Republican Army and the British security forces.[15] The dark shadow at home was only part of a larger darkness settling over Europe; although the war was over, its aftermath was depressing and debilitating. Warnie, as did many others, longed for his prewar life, a period frequently romanticized, yet still treasured with deep affection.[16] As he looked about him, Warnie saw a world so racked and broken that even a mentally stable person might be tempted to despair; as far as he was concerned, everything noble or valuable had been or was in the process of being destroyed.[17] Reflections such as these hinted at Warnie's gradual shift toward a profoundly depressed condition.

Warnie's letter to his father of March 3, 1919, highlighted a book that played a critical role in his life as a diarist and later as a biographer and historian of seventeenth-century French history: the *Memoirs* of Louis de Rouvroy, duc de Saint-Simon (1675–1755).[18] He had stumbled on the book while browsing a local bookstore, and he told his father he was going to read it in French, hoping that it would not be too hard to comprehend. Warnie was immediately taken by Saint-Simon's memoirs, and years later he wrote: "[I] bought it [originally] as a change from French novels, and became a life-addict to the period."[19] About Saint-Simon, Warnie said he was something of an idler, one who chronicled everything worth noting during his life and that of Louis XIV. While the events of that period interested Warnie, he was much more interested in its people. As had earlier been the case when Warnie read Freeman-Mitford, reading Saint-Simon's memoirs enthralled him. To his father he confessed the period was his favorite in history, and so he expected great pleasure from reading the memoirs.[20]

In his next letter of March 23, 1919, to his father, he shared three important developments. First, he had been offered but turned down a job involving transport at the General Headquarters; his reason for turning it down was that it primarily involved applied mathematics—never a strong academic subject for Warnie. It was also the case that he saw the job as tedious and overly insular. Second, he had applied for a transfer to the Russian Expeditionary forces, believing it would be both an adventure and financially advantageous.[21] Third, he had taken over command of his company since his commander had left for special duty in England. He also commented favorably on Jack's poem "Death in Battle."[22] Warnie added that in a bar he ran into a man named McElroy that Albert had for some reason found objectionable during his own previous encounter with McElroy. However, Warnie told his father he found McElroy civil and decent enough, and, while not the sort of person one would be intimate with, McElroy was a lot better than dozens of people Warnie had mixed with since 1914.[23] Albert's snobbish opinion of McElroy contrasted sharply with Warnie's practical and experienced worldly response.

In early April, Warnie transferred to Namur, Belgium where he became the Commanding Officer of the Sixth Company Pontoon Park. When he wrote his father on April 14, 1919, he was very pleased with his new assignment, although he admitted his unit was odd, nothing like a park and lacking any pontoons. He surmised they must have done a good job during the war, but now they did not appear to have anything to do. The country nearby was beautiful, and he was especially taken by the area around the famous battlefield of Waterloo.[24] Warnie said he had been engaged in reading multiple biographies, noting in particular a life of the Irish Lord Lawrence;[25] Warnie had been so impressed with Lawrence's bravery and leadership during a mutiny in India that for one of the few times in his life he said he was proud to be Irish. This letter ended with Warnie yet again directing his father to purchase investments on his behalf.[26] His May 4, 1919, letter to his father recounted a lovely walk he had taken in the nearby countryside and his opinion that the League of Nations—ostensibly formed to prevent future global conflicts—was doomed to failure. He also proved himself no prophet of the future when he asserted that there would not be another world war in his lifetime.[27]

Later correspondence that month reveals that both Warnie and his father were concerned about the nature of Jack's relationship with Janie Moore.[28] On some level, Moore had won Jack's affection since she regularly visited him in London at the Endsleigh Palace Hospital in May 1918 when he was recovering from battlefield wounds, motivated by an attempt to assuage her own pain since Paddy had been killed in action.[29] Albert, despite repeated pleas from Jack, had never visited him in the hospital. At best, Albert's failure suggests an appalling lack of empathy and compassion; at worst, it demonstrates a hardness of heart that is unforgivable. Whatever the case, it is hard to fathom Albert's callous disregard of his son's heartfelt requests that he come to him. What is certain is that Albert's failure to visit Jack drove the already existing wedge between them even deeper.[30] In his letter of May 10, 1919, Warnie wondered about the relationship between Jack and Moore, claiming the whole thing was a conundrum. Still, he thought his father was unduly worried. Warnie found it hard to believe that there was a serious relationship between Jack and Moore while admitting there was something bizarre about it.[31] Ten days later, on May 20, 1919, Albert replied: "It worries and depresses me greatly. All I know is that she is old enough to be his mother—that she is separated from her husband and that she is in poor circumstance. I also know that Jacks has frequently drawn cheques in her favour running up to £10. If Jacks were not an impetuous kindhearted creature who could be cajoled by any woman who has been through the mill, I should not be so uneasy. Then there is the husband whom I have always been told is a scoundrel . . . who some of these days might try a little amiable blackmailing."[32] On June 3, 1919, Warnie wrote and told his father he was relieved to find out that Moore had a husband, having believed she was a widow. That she had a husband meant she could not marry Jack and it also meant that her husband could not blackmail Jack because he had no money. Moreover, Albert could not be blackmailed because he would not stand for it.[33] As later events demonstrate, Warnie's early suspicions about Moore festered long, resulting in an intense and bitter dislike.

Other matters covered in the letters of this period included Warnie's assertion that people like Jack who were entirely sedentary and working with their brains ought to be required by the government to engage in vigorous physical exercise for an hour every day; his delight that Germany was being humiliated though the peace negotiations after WWI that eventually resulted in the Treaty of Versailles;[34] his worries about Albert's health;[35] his application for an overseas tour;[36] arrangements about taking leave so that he would be in Belfast when Jack was back from Oxford; his toying with the idea of becoming a golfer; and his having taken up photography—this latter interest being one Warnie practiced for much of the remainder of his life. Most importantly, this period marked Warnie's return to keeping a diary. The main reasons he decided to renew his commitment as a diarist were his delight in reading the diaries of others as well as the great deal of personal pleasure diary keeping gave him. Although he admitted that others reading his diary might find it tiresome, for him it was a pleasurable way to solidify past experiences. Later he could reread and enjoy them: "I remember how the sunlight looked on the trees, the whine of a shell, the voices of friends, the rubber of bridge after mess—a thousand little things which are of no interest to anyone but myself. . . . I know that all I write is going to be a cinematograph which can be seen at will in the years to come."[37] When we consider in retrospect that Warnie was keeping a diary with more or less regularity until his death in 1973, this entry is witness to his tenacious, dogged commitment to maintaining his diary.[38]

Warnie's official duties kept him busy, but much of his work was routine and provided plenty of free time, especially for reading the diary of Samuel Pepys (1633–1703), one that he had long anticipated exploring. He also made repeated visits into Brussels, noting the restaurants and shows he enjoyed. On June 24 and 25, 1919, his diary recorded a sexual liaison he had with a young woman:

> Had a delightful evening. After the show was over, went down to the Palace with the 4th Area troops people and had a nightcap and listened to the band. Just as I was going out, I ran into Allday. . . . While I was talking of old times with him, a girl who he knew came up, wanting to be taken home. So I offered to run her out to Wépion, and she accepted. Got back about 3:30 A.M., and spent the night, or rather the earlier part the morning, very pleasantly together. *Enfieu c'etait un jour qu'on n'auriat pes trouvez mol* [Finally that's a day that no one could find me]. . . . Up at 7:30 A.M., instructing my scandalized batman[39] to bring up two teas and hot waters and to arrange for two breakfasts. After breakfast saw the girl off and went down to the office where I polished off a certain amount of business.[40]

Warnie also reported a second sexual encounter, this time in Ostende, "a noisy, cheery, vulgar, casino, brothel haunted town." He secured the services of a young French woman, but she jumped out of bed after the first kiss, claiming that her mother would not let her stay out all night. Wiser but cheated of fifty francs, Warnie handled the incident stoically.[41] It is not surprising that Warnie wrote about these sexual encounters around the time he was reading Pepys's diary since Pepys himself was an opportunistic womanizer—he had sexual trysts with his wife's maid, the wives of friends and acquaintances, servant girls, shop girls, and prostitutes—and his diary is filled with accounts of his sexual machinations.[42] Warnie's use of French to describe his rendezvous was akin to the verbal code that Pepys used to disguise his own sexual liaisons.[43] For instance, on June 20, 1665, Pepys wrote: "Thence after dinner I to White-hall with Sir W Berkely in his coach. And so I walked to Herberts and there spent a little time *avec la mosa, sin hazer algo con ella que kiss and tocar ses mamelles, que me haza hazer la cosa a mi mismo con gran plaisir [spent a little time with the beautiful one, without doing anything with her other than kiss and touch her breasts which made me do the thing to myself with great pleasure]."* Warnie unquestionably enjoyed seeing pretty women, and regularly commented in his diary about the attractive wives of fellow officers. For instance, on one occasion, he was entertained by a couple named the Simpsons, and he wrote that Mrs. Simpson sang beautifully, was very good looking, and had a winsome personality. Warnie believed her husband was very lucky to have her, and he wrote that if he could find a girl like her, he would have been willing to take a shot at married life.[44]

After a good deal of wrangling with his military commanders, Warnie was granted leave from July 23 to August 23, 1919. He met Jack in Oxford and together they traveled to Great Bookham where they visited W. T. Kirkpatrick; it was the last time they saw their great tutor alive as he would be dead within the year. They arrived at Leeborough on July 26. For Warnie, the time back in Belfast was relaxing and enjoyable. On August 4, 1919, he recorded in his diary that he found it difficult to keep a daily record of their doings because one day was so like the one before. While in Belfast, they seemed to forget that time existed, so mostly they read, smoked, argued, walked, teased each other, and played the gramophone. He also visited old friends from Malvern and the Western Front. For example, at one point they went to Dublin where Jack met Collins for the first time; Warnie was delighted, especially since Jack and Collins liked each other immediately.[45] However, the visit to Leeborough also marked a severe breach between Jack and Albert when he caught Jack in a lie about money matters.[46] Jack, whose lie almost certainly was the result of trying to keep secret from his father the fact that he was financially supporting Moore, verbally lashed out his father. As Warnie put it, his brother told his father in no uncertain terms what he thought about Albert, accusing him of being meddlesome, demanding, and critical.[47] Warnie shared some of Jack's resentments regarding his father, but there was never a rupture like this in Warnie's relationship with Albert. Temperamentally, Warnie was more like his father than Jack; he understood and empathized with him to a degree that Jack could not. Then, too, he never engaged in a deception as grand and audacious as Jack's with Moore. Certainly, Warnie at times lied and deceived his father, but as he grew older, he made more allowances for Albert than Jack did.

When Warnie returned to Belgium and active duty at Namur his company was soon abolished, and on September 11, 1919, he was appointed the commanding officer of the Sixth Auxiliary Petrol Company based in Boulogne. Unlike his time in Namur, he was now constantly at work; unfortunately, he was also suffering from severe gum disease. In late January 1920, Warnie was attached to the 487th Horse Transport Company, and in early February 1920 Warnie wrote Albert and told him he had been posted to Aldershot. Soon he was rooming with Herbert Parkin at the Victoria Hotel for three months while they both took the required Second Regular Officer's Course. Warnie complained that the course, which continued until the end of November, was an awful experience because it was expensive, and he had to work so hard; as a result, in the evenings he drank heavily and spent freely, leaving him deeply in debt.[48] A major highlight of this period was Warnie's purchase of a Triumph motorcycle and sidecar that he nicknamed the Daudel; over the next seven years he almost always owned a Daudel.[49] On one occasion, he picked up Jack in Oxford and they visited their old haunts in Malvern and journeyed on into Wales. Warnie wrote: "'The joy of the open road' is a very hackneyed phrase, but it is none the less true for all that: let a man provide himself with a reliable bike and sidecar, a congenial companion, and a pocket full of money, and if he doesn't enjoy himself, it would be doing him a kindness to poleaxe him."[50] Warnie successfully completed the Second Regular Officer's Course on November 30, 1920, and was on leave from December 15 until March 9, 1921. During this leave, Warnie began reading more and more sources related to Louis XIV and seventeenth-century France, including the *Memoir of Georges Mareschal, Surgeon to Louis XIX* and the *Secret Correspondence of Louis XV*. In addition, after reading Charles Auguste, Marquis de La Fare's memoirs of Louis XIV, he noted: "His is, I think, the best, condensed history of the reign of Louis XIV which I have read: and as he disliked the king strongly and always presents him in the worst possible light he is worth reading as a corrective to the more adulatory writers of his time."[51] He also began reading the diaries of his maternal grandfather, the Reverend Thomas Robert Hamilton, a process he found distressing since the things that stood out about Hamilton were his religious bigotry, small-mindedness, evangelical zeal, self-importance, and ill-temper. Warnie admitted that he would have despised him had he been obliged to know him.[52]

His leave over, Warnie embarked for an overseas posting in Sierra Leone that he had requested. Explorers from Portugal had originally named Sierra Leone, "Serra de Leão" or Lion Mountains. In yet another ignoble chapter of European colonialism, the history of Sierra Leone from the fifteenth century onward was intimately connected with slave trading. Colluding with powerful African chiefs who became rich, Europeans traded manufactured goods for ivory and slaves. In 1787, a group of freed slaves from England tried to establish a settlement along the coast, but disease, mismanagement, poor funding, and hostility from the local population doomed their efforts. Eventually freed slaves from Nova Scotia founded the coastal enclave of Freetown under the supervision of the British government. By 1864, tens of thousands of liberated slaves made their way to Freetown. However, because this disparate group lacked a common language, culture, or religion, the British government made the calculated decision to try to mold them into a unified community. Key to this effort was the work of the Church Missionary Society (Anglican). In time, an educated and Christianized elite of Sierra Leonese developed. By the end of the century, the British government—in cooperation with the French—drew borders for the country, and in 1895 declared it a British protectorate, eager to reap the benefit of its natural resources, including cocoa, coffee, palm oil, and peanuts as well as gold, timber, bauxite, and iron ore. Despite a number of revolts by the ruling chiefs who had not been consulted about the protectorate, the native populace was quickly suppressed, and the British took over running day-to-day matters.[53]

The British Army in Sierra Leone was charged with ensuring civil and social stability and for seeing that colonial business and trade interests were not hampered. Accordingly, when Warnie arrived in Freetown on March 19, 1921, he became the RASC Officer in Charge of Supplies and Transport and was responsible for assuring that provisions needed by the British Army and government officials were in ready supply and in good condition.[54] Figuring out how to keep the sugar from turning into liquid and how to insure that the ice factory was kept running were his major challenges. He handled all his duties with great efficiency, his practical, pragmatic nature assuring that he fulfilled his responsibilities effectively. The biggest obstacle he faced, however, was not related to his official duties. Instead, he confronted a climate he came to deplore. The tropical climate of Freetown meant high humidity and an average annual temperature of 81 degrees (Fahrenheit); in the summer, the temperature was much higher, often reaching 100. Average yearly rainfall was 144 inches—twelve feet—with much of it falling during the May to November rainy season. Heavy rainstorms and tornadoes were a constant threat. Most northern Europeans struggled with these climatic conditions, and tropical diseases and maladies were common, recalling the opinion of the station manager in Joseph Conrad's *Heart of Darkness* about the similar climate of the Congo: "Men who come out here should have no entrails."[55]

Warnie's days soon fell into a predictable and tedious pattern.[56] He would generally arise between 7 and 8 and have breakfast. After that he would spend an hour or two handling perfunctory work duties, often connected with local shipping; the remainder of the day would be taken up in desultory activities, leading to long periods of boredom punctuated by drinking, gossiping, playing bridge, reading, and keeping track of the many vessels that either passed by or put in at Freeport. The persistent boredom worked little good in his character, in part explaining his frequent bouts of drinking. In diary entries, he admitted his drinking was often excessive, noting that he and his fellow soldiers drank so heavily that they often passed out.[57] At one point, he resolved to limit himself to three drinks a day.[58] When the new year came, he promised himself to cut back even more on his consumption of alcohol.[59] Despite his good intentions and resolutions, Warnie continued to drink heavily.

Most of the men stationed with Warnie were, like him, fulfilling a required, one-year foreign tour of duty; since they had few tasks to perform, petty squabbles and rumors were frequent, often about the inadequacies of this or that fellow. In addition, the few wives that were there often became the subject of tittle-tattle and table talk. Warnie had a keen eye and would give clear-eyed accounts of his companions. For example, about one married couple, he wrote that after his fellow officer introduced him to his wife, Warnie discovered her to be a stereotypical suburban woman, looking ridiculously out of place in Sierra Leone. The couple called each other "ducky" and "darling" and petted the other with playful slaps and hand-holding. Warnie found their two-year marriage both incomprehensible and nauseating.[60] Rubbers of bridge were frequent evening events (usually three or four times a week), and Warnie kept a careful accounting of the small amounts of money he won and (mostly) lost. He also kept a close inventory of the ships that came in and out of the harbor; many were ships he was familiar with either because they were built in Belfast or because he knew them from World War I. His affection for some of the vessels suggests they were like old friends to him. For instance, about the Union Castle liner *Saxon*, he noted that when it came into the harbor its coal bunkers were on fire. Despite this calamity, for Warnie it was a great treat to see the ship again.[61]

His most serious physical discomfort—beyond that of suffering with heat and humidity—was a recurring case of anal boils; when the infection was at its worst, he could not sit down.[62] Fortunately, a round of antibiotics eventually cleared up the infection and gave him considerable relief. In addition, he was very aware of the danger of snakes. One day as he passed the mission school he saw and almost stepped on a large snake that was nearly two feet long and a beautiful light blue color. When the snake saw Warnie, it wriggled away into the canal. He came to find out later that he was very lucky not to have stepped on the viper, since it was either a mamba or a spitting cobra—the two most-deadly snakes in Sierra Leone: the bite of either could have killed him in just over ten minutes.[63] Cockroaches were also a big problem, Warnie calling them disgusting creatures that ate food, books, clothes, and even human flesh.[64] The constant dearth of fresh water was also very vexing, as was difficulty sleeping because of the heat. However, despite the dangers and discomforts, Warnie found great beauty in the land and seascape. About the former, he wrote:

Even its worst enemy admits the beauty of Freetown. As seen from the sea: from a European standpoint the first and most striking characteristic is the exaggeration of every color value. The shore consists either of rich red rock or a ripe wheat color stretch of sand: over this rises a series of hills of every shade of green, of every variety of tropical tree or shrub: this is broken up by the houses scattered all over the slope, which are mainly of white or red stone with bright red roofs. The roads such as they are look like narrow slips of flame-colored ribbon, thrusting through the main pattern.[65]

He then described a picturesque palm-fringed creek spanned by a bridge. The road rose rapidly and gave a wonderful view of the sea, and when one reached the top of the hill, the entire panorama of Freetown, the harbor, and the surrounding hills was breath taking.[66]

Warnie's great solace in Sierra Leone was reading. The long-enforced periods of inactivity afforded him copious amounts of time for books. Like his brother, Warnie was a voracious reader, although his tastes were more eclectic and less academic than Jack's. A safe estimate is that Warnie read over 100 books during his twelve months in Sierra Leone. Novels, short stories, plays, and nonfiction were his main fare, but he also read Dante's *Divine Comedy* and John Milton's *Comus,* "Lycidas," "L'Allegro," "Il Penseroso," *Samson Agonistes, Paradise Lost,* and *Paradise Regained.* "L'Allegro" and "Il Penseroso" were delightfully surprising to Warnie as he had not thought Milton capable of such delicate, graceful poems.[67] He committed to read through the Bible, but he ran out of steam in the Pentateuch, calling Leviticus an amazingly dull book.[68] The novelists he most enjoyed included Fyodor Dostoyevsky, H. G. Wells, Joseph Conrad, and Rudyard Kipling. Because of his involvement in serving blindly the interests of European colonialism, Warnie never discussed or criticized the imperialism portrayed in Conrad and Kipling. Nor did he ever see his own work as integral to the avaricious expansionism of white European governments. There was no moral regret, no informed judgment, no analytical assessment. This lack of self-analysis characterized Warnie's diary keeping at this time; indeed, it would not be until the 1930s and beyond that he began to explore his inner world.

In addition, he kept reading seventeenth-century French history, particularly anything having to do with Louis XIV. Receiving mail from his father and brother was a special treat, although given the lack of regular mail service, Warnie often went weeks without hearing from either, especially Jack. Warnie's letters to them described his life at Sierra Leone, often times drawing from incidents he had written about in his diary. The bit of news from Albert that most surprised him was that Kirkpatrick had died on March 22, 1921. Warnie told his father that he was irreplaceable and one of the finest persons he had ever met; he added that there were no words that could express how much he owed Kirkpatrick.[69]

Warnie's attitude toward the Sierra Leone natives was regrettably typical of white Europeans, ranging from paternalistic amusement to scathing condescension. For instance, upon first meeting his servant, Copra, Warnie said he was clean and "almost" intelligent; but by the next day he was calling him a fool for having lost the keys to his room. Two days later, he wondered how anyone could stand the natives, claiming they were exasperating and stupid, representing the lowest level of human intelligence. In another example, in a letter to his father of April 4, 1921, Warnie described with some degree of bewilderment and horror the native practice of female genital mutilation.[70] Despite his prejudice, Warnie relied upon Copra and soon enjoyed his company. One diversion he grew to care about a great deal was a green mango monkey he bought and delighted in. Warnie would feed and play with it, and it gradually came to be comfortable sleeping on his lap.[71] Although he spent a good deal of time with the other Europeans, Warnie never developed any deep friendship; all of them seemed to be marking time until their tour of duty was over. He did find the company of a young couple, the McLellans, refreshing, and he described the wife as one of the nicest women he had ever met. It was with great relief that Warnie finished his tour at Sierra Leone on March 23, 1922, arriving home to Belfast on April 12, 1922.

One great benefit of his tour in Sierra Leone was that Warnie received six months' leave. While he spent the majority of his leave at Leeborough, one of the most important episodes of his life occurred during an extended visit to Jack in Oxford, August 3–25, 1922: Warnie met Moore and her daughter, Maureen, for the first time on August 5, 1922.[72] Such a meeting had not been planned by Warnie; indeed, when Jack initially floated the idea that he come to visit them at their home on Hillsboro Road, Warnie's reaction was decidedly negative.[73] Warnie was even more strongly opposed to the idea the following day: "During the meal I [Jack] thought I had arranged for him to come and meet the family at tea; but quite suddenly while sitting in the garden . . . he changed his mind and refused pertinaciously either to come to tea or to consider staying with us. I therefore came back to tea alone." Yet when Jack returned to Warnie after tea, Warnie had changed his mind and promised he would visit them the next day.[74] Warnie's initial negative reaction was probably the result of the continuing suspicions both he and Albert had regarding Moore. Father and son saw her a threat to Jack, believing she was taking advantage of Jack's sympathy over the death of Paddy.

Although Warnie eventually did agree to stay with Jack and the Moores, Jack's diary gives us clear grounds to believe that another reason Warnie initially balked at the idea of spending time with Moore was his jealousy. Warnie was jealous of anyone who took up Jack's time, and taking up Jack's time was exactly what he saw Moore doing. Accordingly, a week into the visit, Warnie began to press Jack to agree to return to Leeborough during some portion of his leave; when Jack refused, Warnie cut him off and threatened to return immediately to Belfast, arguing that he could bore himself for nothing in Belfast. Jack wrote: "I am now convinced that this was mere temper and not seriously to be resented from one who habitually lives (with me) in a thoroughly schoolboy atmosphere. . . . [The next morning] he continued to sulk and I was so disgusted at this childish sort of compulsion that I was tempted to reject all thought of going home."[75] Warnie further pressured Jack to come home because it would be easier for the two of them to be with their father than either one separately—something that Jack admitted to be true. Jack talked over the situation with Moore—who apparently did not stand in the way—and told Warnie he would do as he wished. At the same time, Jack told Warnie emphatically that he had not agreed to come to Leeborough because of Warnie's jealous fit of temper; he told Warnie that if he tried a similar tactic in the future, it would not work. Warnie appeared not to understand Jack's point, but it was a transparently dishonest response.[76]

Warnie had hoped his visit to Oxford would rekindle the warm friendship and comradery he and Jack enjoyed when they were growing up at Leeborough. He felt that Moore's presence thwarted his efforts to recapture those golden days when it was him and Jack against the world. While he wanted to live with Jack in "a thoroughly schoolboy atmosphere," Jack had moved on. He was living in a domestic arrangement that, on the whole, he very much enjoyed, while Warnie was living the life of a career soldier; in many ways, Warnie came across as independent, unattached, almost autonomous. Jack found great pleasure in domesticity with the Moores, as it recalled something of his life before his mother died. Warnie, conversely, found little to recommend about domestic living. Instead, he had a yearning for schoolboy larks such as he had at Malvern; for instance, during a talk he and Jack had on August 8, 1922, Warnie admitted as much when he said that one day he supposed he would grow up.[77] Therefore, it is somewhat surprising that when he reflected on his visit a month later, Warnie noted how much he had enjoyed the activities they engaged in, including bridge, ping pong, croquet, hide-and-seek, and tennis. Surprisingly, the only critical thing he had to say about the Moores was limited to a brief comment regarding Maureen on August 14, 1922, complaining that she was a noisy, irritating fifteen year old.[78] Warnie had come to recognize that his desire to recapture the old days with Jack had been wrong. In his diary, he confessed that his time in Oxford was delightful, and he was happy to have met and spent time with the Moores, primarily because he could now take part in Jack's home life. Most notably, he accepted that his old days with Jack were over, and that was the way it should be.[79] Moore's reaction to Warnie was captured by Jack on August 21, 1922: "We fell to talking of W. D. said he was nice and 'just missed being very nice indeed' but one couldn't tell how.[80] I said probably because you felt that he had no need for you. She admired his slow, whimsical way of talking, which was attractive and which one found oneself unconsciously imitating."[81] After Warnie left to return to Leeborough, Jack said his visit had been a great pleasure to him and "a great advance too toward connecting up my real life with all that is pleasantest in my Irish life. Fortunately, everyone liked him and I think he liked them."[82]

Related to the matter of Warnie's jealousy, it is important to point out his psychological dependency upon Jack. Notwithstanding the fact that Warnie was three years older than Jack, in many ways he was the "younger" brother. Jack said as much, writing in *SJ*: "Though three years my senior, [Warnie] never seemed to be an elder brother; we were allies, not to say confederates, from the first."[83] Of the two, Jack, despite his own tendency to depression, was more self-possessed; Warnie was less self-assured, less confident, less certain of himself—what today might be stated as having an underdeveloped emotional intelligence. His inner life was largely veiled to himself, causing him to rely in many important ways upon Jack. Accordingly, Warnie had a deep need to be near him; any threat to that connection was disconcerting. For example, after Jack visited his father and Warnie in Belfast from September 11 to 21, 1922, Warnie reflected on their own parting at Paddington Station in London: "I gave him a whiskey and soda and sandwiches in the refreshment room as he would be rather late at Oxford. Although the train was crowded he managed to get a corner seat, and so we parted at 6:45 P.M. For some time I wandered round the Paddington area, a prey to the depression which I have never outgrown at parting from J."[84] Certainly, Jack was in a measure dependent upon Warnie, but not in the same way nor to the same degree; Moore was Jack's psychological anchor, and Warnie's sense that this was the case undercut the old security he had in his relationship with his brother.

Two other matters are significant regarding Warnie's six months leave. The first concerns Warnie's moribund spiritual life. Nothing during his time in Sierra Leone suggested he felt anything but impatience with and disinterest in the Christian heritage his mother had assiduously tried to encourage in him; his few references to church services in Sierra Leone are critical and dismissive. While he dutifully continued to attend church services with his father back home in Belfast, he only did so in order to keep the peace and to avoid explosive scenes. Regarding one particular Sunday, Warnie wondered why the congregants showed up for the service each week, given that everything about it was lifeless, repetitive, and boring. He surmised they must not have been there actually to worship but instead were trying to enhance their public reputation for commercial reasons.[85]

The second matter concerns how the brothers found it increasingly difficult to be with their father. During Warnie's visit to Jack in August 1922, he told Jack that despite the past—the old disputes, arguments, interferences, forced conversations, and absurdities—he could have become friends with Albert if his father had a serious will to do so. Instead, his father further alienated Warnie by sneering at his profession as a soldier. Jack agreed and said that just by the slightest effort his father could have brought about a reconciliation, but no effort had been made. As a result, the distance between father and sons—moral, intellectual, and psychological—was permanent.[86] Both brothers continued to resent their father's tendency to offer outlandish opinions or to misrepresent and recast their stories into his own odd interpretations. In one instance, as they were walking to church on Christmas Day, the two brothers discussed the time of sunrise. Albert opined—absurdly as far as Jack was concerned—that the sun must have already risen because without it there would not have been any light. Once in the church, Warnie wanted to keep his coat on because it was so cold. Albert pressed Warnie to take it off at least during communion, insisting that otherwise it would be very disrespectful.[87] While the brothers often simply bit their tongues rather than cause a scene, on occasion matters boiled over. For instance, Warnie once complained that his eating expenses in in the army were made acute because there were usually few officers to share the costs. Albert then made fun of the army and its challenges. Jack confided in his diary that because Warnie was so sensitive about his lack of money, he lashed out at their father, retorting sarcastically that it was easy for Albert to be so insulting since he holed up in his study at Leeborough and spent £1,400 a year on himself.[88]

Their frustrations with their father led them to begin "Pudaita Pie," a written record of their father's most amusing—and at times maddening—remarks which eventually reached one hundred.[89] As an example, on one occasion Warnie was getting ready to take a photograph of Leeborough when Albert observed that it would not be much of a picture; in order to set things right, he inserted himself in front of the house and said, "Now take your photograph."[90] In his "Memoir," Warnie confided that as his father aged, his intrusive way of probing into the personal lives of his and Jack's lives become more autocratic and trying. In effect, Albert drove his sons away.[91] Toward the end of his life, Warnie reread the novel, *The Ulsterman: A Story for Today* by Frank Moore, and found it just as powerful as he had remembered it. The novel gave a sharp, bitter but authentic portrayal of family life in 1914 Ulster—one that Warnie connected with his own family life with his father. Warnie wrote: "The most interesting thing is to find that the dominance, the ceaseless cross-examination, the unawareness that J and I were *individuals* which we thought was Lewisianism was in fact Ulsterism. True, we were never treated so badly as the Alexander family but in what follows there is enough of our own adolescent grievances to give more than a hint of Leeborough conditions."[92]

He then cited the words of the younger son in the novel that portrayed the same feelings Warnie had toward his father:

> You know the relative position of father and son in Ulster. . . . The son is in a worse position than the errand boy. You know the way we have to give an account of ourselves wherever we may go. If I go as far as Belfast for a day, I'm cross-examined as to how I spent every hour. If I get asked out anywhere here I have to ask leave to go. I'm not supposed to make an acquaintance without father's leave. . . . I daren't smoke even now except behind his back. Well, is it any wonder when we're treated like this, we sons turn out liars and hypocrites? Is it any wonder that we try to get the better of our fathers and show them that we have souls of our own?[93]

Warnie continued with another passage from the novel and linked it to his own early experience: "The true humor of the Ulsterman . . . consists in the probing of an unhealed wound—the touching of a raw place with the broad top of a finger fresh from the pot of red pepper. In the writhings of the victims are to be found the elements of the finest humor, if the tormentor knows anything of what humor really is."[94] Warnie then recalled that his father often made fun of him for his wanting to be well dressed and would needle him for it. When Albert saw how much his badgering bothered Warnie, he would press it relentlessly: "[My father] continued to jab at the sore place for the rest of our joint lives. But worst of all was the fact that from the end of the war until the last time I visited him I doubt if he ever let 48 consecutive hours pass without some offensive sneer at my profession. . . . The recollection of these 'humorous' sallies of his still has at times the power of irritating me."[95] For Warnie, *The Ulsterman* articulated perfectly his own experienced reality with his father.

When Warnie came off leave in October 1922, he became the RASC officer in charge of supplies in Colchester, a town 50 miles northeast of London. He was stationed there until December 25, 1925, and his duties were largely routine, mainly consisting of handling correspondence and official communications, managing the budget, and overseeing all details related to supplies. In his diary, he wrote about his life at Colchester, including rumors related to promotions, frustrations with senior officers, the running of the mess, and matters related to issuing pay. Since he knew he would be required to serve another term in foreign service, he volunteered to do a tour in either Bermuda or Hong Kong.[96] As had been the case in Sierra Leone, he had a great deal of free time that permitted him to read many books; at Jack's suggestion, he read Edmund Spenser's *Fairie Queen* and, much like his surprise when reading Milton for the first time, he found it enchanting.

In addition, he reread the diary of Samuel Pepys and steeped himself deeply in seventeenth-century French history. Specifically, he read the *Memoirs of the Comte de Gramont, A Duchess of France, Histoire de Mme. De Maintenon, Correspondance Génévale de Mme. De Maintenon, Landmarks in French Literature, History of the French Monarchy, Journal de la Regence,* and *The Ascendancy of France 1598–1715.* Although he did not know it at the time, the focus of his reading in French history, memoirs, correspondence, and literature provided a fertile ground for his later books on Louis XIV and seventeenth-century French history.[97] He also indulged in his enduring interest in classical music and frequently visited bookstore and picture shops. Regrettably, he also continued to drink heavily. For instance, on September 25, 1925, he said that he woke up with "'my head aching mightily' as Pepys used to say, which I fear is proof that I drank more whiskey than was good for me last night."[98] Similarly, on September 30, 1925, he wrote that he had drunk too much and was feeling confused.[99] When the weather was warm, he would go to the coast and enjoy swimming in the salt surf. Although Warnie was not involved in a romantic relationship, he had an eye for beautiful women, preferring young, attractive ones. Regarding a new barmaid, Warnie described her as interesting, smart, musically informed, especially on Handel, and a devout, winsome Christian.[100] However, his thoughts about the new wife of one of his fellow officers—she had been a longtime barmaid—were scathing. He noted that she was a coarse, tasteless wench who valued bawdy talk. In addition, it was common knowledge that she had sexual liaisons with several fellow officers. Moreover, Warnie admitted that he flirted with her and often ran his hands along her legs.[101]

On the whole, Warnie was content with the solitary life he was leading, but at the same time he was making regular weekend trips to Hillsboro House, the home Jack and Moore shared in Headington, a village just outside Oxford. Undoubtedly, his greatest joy at Colchester was his latest Daudel; this motorcycle had a sidecar allowing Jack to accompany him on a number of road trips.[102] While Jack was usually happy to spend time with Warnie, sometimes he envied his brother's seemingly unencumbered life. After one of Warnie's visits to Hillsboro, Jack wrote: "For no assignable reason, certainly through no fault of his, I found W.'s society, which I had looked forward to with some pleasure, quite unbearable this time."[103] He attributed his feelings to Warnie's contented cynicism, dismissal of all things warm and ideal, and ironic skepticism. The next day, he worried about this change of feelings since he remembered so many of their past good times. A few months later, after Warnie had visited Jack during Whitsun, his old affection for his brother returned, although he still found himself occasionally jealous of what he saw to be Warnie's pleasant, comfortable, and worry-free life.[104] Because of his close proximity to Jack, his relatively light duties, his amiable fellow soldiers, and his ready mobility on his Daudel, Warnie's three years at Colchester were the best of his army career. He later wrote that he spent the happiest years of his military career at Colchester.[105]

This pleasant interlude came to an abrupt end when, on January 1, 1926, he was appointed the Commanding Officer of the seventeenth Military Transport Company, RASC, at Woolwich, just east of London, south of the Thames River, and 11 miles east of the Charing Cross Tube Station and the Imperial War Museum. On the one hand, the London museums and bookstores were readily accessible, so he was able to purchase many books at affordable prices. He continued to read seventeenth-century French history, as well Shakespeare's narrative poems and Tennyson's poetry. In addition, he found that visiting many cultural sites in London was fascinating, including Piccadilly, Westminster Abbey, and the National Gallery. Trips to Hillsboro and several leaves, including a ten-day visit to his father in April 1926, were great pleasures. On the other hand, the physical surroundings at Woolwich were drab, and smog was ever present as was the continual hum of noises from trams, river craft, and human voices. The overriding atmosphere was one of dreariness and squalor. Moreover, Warnie did not find kindred spirits among his colleagues as conversations were primarily focused upon sports, including hunting, football, and fishing; in many ways he felt as if he was reliving some of his worst days at Malvern College.[106] Professionally, he achieved a great coup when he applied for and was accepted to attend an Economics Course at London University. The six-month course ran from October 5, 1926, to March 24, 1927, and he moved from Woolwich to Millbank, near the Thames River, south of Westminster, just a few blocks from St. Paul's Cathedral. He found the course challenging, and even though he tired of London, he thought the whole experience was rewarding and successful. Although he could not have known it at the time, after he finished his economics course, Warnie saw his father alive for the last time during a brief leave in April 1927.

At the conclusion of the course, he learned almost immediately that his foreign tour of service would not take him to Bermuda but instead to Hong Kong, where he was to serve as second in command in the Fifteenth Military Brigade; the brigade was sent out hurriedly for fear it would be needed to be protect British interests from warring Chinese and Japanese factions.[107] On April 11, 1927, he set sail on the SS *Derbyshire*, unaware that he would be away from England for almost three years. The trip was long, boring, and very hot. At the same time, the sea voyage itself was in many ways delightful as it reminded Warnie of the geography he and Jack created for their Animal-Land some twenty years earlier. He kept himself busy reading the novels of Joseph Conrad, keeping his diary, and watching with keen interest the changing views of the sea, the skies, and the landscapes. They sailed south along the coast of Portugal and then into the Mediterranean Sea after making port in Gibraltar. Next, they traveled along the southern coast of Spain, passing Algiers in Northern Africa. A few days later, they sailed by Malta and then went on to Port Said and eventually into the Suez Canal. After traveling the canal, they made port at Aden in what is now Yemen. Then they passed along the Indian coast and made a port of call to Colombo (now Sri Lanka). The last leg of the trip took them to Singapore and then eventually to Hong Kong, where they docked on May 15, 1927.

During the voyage Warnie found little companionship to his liking, and worried in particular about his commanding officer, Colonel Gerald Badcock, whose reputation was as the "best hated man" in the RASC.[108] Warnie came to see Badcock as professionally capable but personally terrible; he was arrogant, conceited, condescending, and self-serving. Warnie said that while he treated the officers badly, he was a terror to the enlisted men. He cited the case of a clerk with a stutter; at the end of each daily conference held by Badcock, he would turn and require each man present to ask one intelligent question. Then he would inevitably turn to the stutterer and say, "And now, poor stuttering fool, what imbecility have you got for us today?"[109] On another occasion, a sergeant collapsed and had to be carried to the hospital. When Warnie told Badcock, he replied that it was a "pity he's not dead. I've made up my mind about that man: he's no use to me."[110] It is no hyperbole to claim that for the five months Warnie served under Badcock, he was on tenterhooks, and his life was miserable.

For his first several weeks in China, Warnie was the second in command of the Base Supply Depot of Shanghai Defense Force at Kowloon, on the mainland of China, just opposite the island of Hong Kong. Essentially a cross between a ship's officer and a wharf manager, Warnie worked hard supervising the unloading and organizing of cargo from ships back home or Australia and seeing that the supplies were accounted for and stored in the *godown*, or warehouse. His initial reaction to the Chinese was contemptuous. While his attitude toward the natives of Sierra Leone had been paternalistic and condescending, his attitude toward the Chinese was distasteful and repugnant. He even wondered if they were human beings, feeling that they must dropped in from another planet.[111] To his father, he wrote that he found no point of contact with the Chinese and that their customs and habits were incomprehensible; the natives of Sierra Leone, on the other hand, were, by comparison, genuine men and like brothers.[112]

Unhappily, by July 11, 1927, Warnie was seriously ill with a high fever and boils covering his entire body. Although the boils were treated and cleared up within weeks, the lingering fever was harder to cure, so Warnie remained in hospital through August. In early September, he was moved to Wei-Hai-Wei, a convalescent depot 500 miles north of Shanghai. He healed slowly and was in no hurry to return to Shanghai and service under Badcock, enjoying the tranquil atmosphere as well as the food and comfortable living conditions. Warnie also found the northern Chinese more appealing than those he had met in Kowloon, writing Jack that they were taller and more honest—in fact, fellow human beings. Warnie believed the northern Chinese were virile, manly, and dignified, and he found their pigtails and mustaches appealing.[113] As luck would have it, by the time he returned to active duty in Shanghai on September 25, the Fifteenth Military Brigade was being dissolved and Badcock was only weeks away from being recalled to England. The key result of Warnie's encounter with Badcock was his determination to work toward retiring from the army as soon as possible so that he would never again have to serve under such a lout.

By far the most important matters for Warnie during his term in China had to do with his professional, personal, and spiritual life. Regarding the former, since the Fifteenth Military Brigade had been dissolved, he might have had to return home, and as a result lost the time he had spent in China toward his required three years of foreign service (such a length of service abroad meant he would not have to do another one for six years). This difficulty was removed when Warnie learned of a nearby vacancy. He applied, and on November 1, 1927, he was reassigned as the officer in command of the Supply Depot, Shanghai. Warnie's daily duties were not onerous, and he continued to have large periods of time to read, socialize, explore, and drink. Indeed, after he recovered from his illness and got away from Badcock, Warnie on the whole enjoyed his time in China. One of his favorite after-hours pastimes was bar hopping. This might include after tea a game of billiards at the French Club or a game of badminton. Around six P.M., he and his friends would move to the bar to drink, chat, and admire the pretty women. Dinner would follow at the club grill, and afterward there would be more billiards until eleven or so. The evening would end with visits to one of Shanghai's numerous night clubs—Mumm's, Del Monte's, or Ladow's—where there would be drinking with the Russian dancing girls until two or three in the morning. Predictably, Warnie was prey to excessive drinking, especially on holidays. He recalled one disastrous Christmas Day when the colonel of the Russian Labor Corps visited him, and they entertained each other by filling alternate wine glasses, first with whiskey and then with vodka. He also referred to Armistice Day, New Year's Eve, and the Chinese New Year as other occasions that stood out in his memory as monumental pieces of dissipation.[114] One unexpected pleasure was that he was reunited with Herbert Parkin, his friend since their days together in northern France where they were stationed in 1918. In October 1928, Parkin became the commanding officer of the RASC in Shanghai, leading Warnie to write that "prospects for the rest of my tour are brighter than I had hoped."[115]

In his personal life, the matters most on his mind concerned his father's health and his plans to retire from the army. For some time, Albert had been feeling run-down and "rheumatic." His letters were less frequent, often depressing, and filled with health complaints and religious musings.[116] Both Warnie and Jack worried about him, and Jack tried repeatedly to convince him to come and stay as his guest at Magdalen College, Oxford, where he was now a lecturer.[117] However, Albert would not come. Jack and Warnie had been able to visit their father together during the Christmas holidays in December 1926; at the time, they did not know it would be their last Christmas together. Albert was so pleased with their visit that he wrote in his diary on January 18, 1927: "Warnie and Jack returned tonight … [but] as the boat did not sail until 11 o'c. they stayed with me to 9:30. So ended a very pleasant holiday. Roses all the way."[118] Sensing their father's flickering spirit, they began to urge him to sell Leeborough and move into a smaller place that would be easier to manage. Albert refused. They also suggested that he see a specialist and visit a spa. Again, Albert resisted. Jack continued to make holiday visits to Leeborough, but by July 1929, he was so concerned for his father that he went with him to Scotland, hoping that a change of air, scene, and diet might perk him up.[119]

The end came relatively quickly. Jack wrote Warnie from Leeborough on August 25, 1929, and told him that their father was seriously ill; stomach cancer, while not confirmed, was a distinct possibility. A few days later, he worsened, and for the next few weeks Jack stayed in Belfast to watch over him. In mid-September, Albert was admitted to a nursing home, and an exploratory operation discovered carcinoma of the bowel. Assured by the doctors that Albert was not in danger of dying, Jack went back to Oxford on September 22; two days later, they urged Jack to come back, but before he arrived, Albert died of a heart attack. Because mail to China took several weeks to arrive, Warnie had no way of knowing that his father was seriously ill, so he was shocked to receive a cable from Jack on the morning of September 27 telling him that their father had died two days earlier. Warnie's diary entry for that day is marked by pain, regret, tenderness, and nostalgia. In many ways, he could hardly believe that his father was gone, and he confessed that being in China had caused him to care even more for him. He seemed to recall only the good times with his father, and his heart ached also as he realized that he no longer really had a home at Leeborough: "The thought that there will never be any 'going home' for me, is hard to bear. I'd give a lot at this minute for a talk with J."[120] Telling is Warnie's admission that his tour in China had caused him to grow fonder of his father—away from him, he missed him and longed for the rose-colored past. Much that had irked him melted away and was replaced by fond memories. Albert's death also moved Warnie to do something he normally resisted: engaging in self-reflection by remembering the pain of his mother's death twenty years earlier. Moreover, he grieved for the coming loss of Leeborough as so many homely thoughts and recollections assailed him. His desire to be with Jack at this time was entirely consistent with his psychological dependence upon him. With the passing of Albert, Warnie knew that his emotional life was on the verge of radical change—without parent, without home, without old certainties.

Jack, too, was powerfully moved by his father's death, in spite of their relatively cool relationship. On October 17, 1929, he wrote Warnie: "As time goes on the thing that emerges is that, whatever else he was, he was a terrific *personality*. . . . How he filled a room! How hard it was to realise that physically he was not a very big man. Our whole world . . . is either direct or indirect testimony to the same effect. Take away from our conversation all that is imitation or parody . . . of his, and how little is left. The way we enjoyed going to Leeborough and the way we hated it, and the way we enjoyed hating it: as you say, one can't grasp that *that* is over."[121] Jack's response to Albert's death is certainly heartfelt, but it is different from Warnie's. Both brothers were surprised at how Albert's death revealed to them their genuine love for him, despite his maddening, irritating ways. But Jack's response is more about the loss of their father as a phenomenon. It is not the loss of his father as a person that strikes him; instead, it is the loss of his father as a force of nature. So much of his life had been shaped by his reactions to his father's character; with that personality gone, how would he find something to shape his conversations, his jokes, his satires, and his wit? In the death of Albert, Warnie lost much that was important to his home life; Jack lost the central foil to his way of responding to life.

The other personal matter occupying Warnie was retirement from the army. When he reached China, he had completed thirteen years of service in the RASC; in order to retire in a financially comfortable position with a pension of £200, he figured he would need to serve until the end of 1932. In a letter to Jack on December 5, 1929, he said he had enough of his life in the military and was finding it more and more tiresome.[122] He was weary of military service, at one time referring to it as a prison sentence.[123] With each day, week, and month, retirement became the end game, and much of his thinking centered around those plans. After the death of his father, it was several months before he was able to leave China, but on February 24, 1930, Warnie sailed from Shanghai on the commercial freighter *Tai-Yin;* he took this venue so that he could return to England via the Pacific and visit the United States. Highlights of the voyage—more adventurous than his journey to China—included stops at San Francisco and (via the Panama Canal) New York and Boston. He liked Boston, finding it to be similar to a pleasant English city that had been unluckily dumped on the East Coast of America. He warmed to it immediately, just the opposite of what he felt about New York.[124]

His fifty-day voyage ended on April 16, 1930, when he landed in Liverpool, having been gone from England just over three years. Since he would be on leave until June, he moved in with Jack and the Moores at Hillsboro and enjoyed a very comfortable time. Moore even invited Warnie to make his home with them whenever he was on leave. Jack welcomed this arrangement, telling Arthur Greeves "they like one another and I hope, as W gets broken in to domestic life, they may come to do so still more—but in the interval there is a ticklish time ahead."[125] After so many years as a bachelor, free of any dependents, and used to the army essentially taking care of him, where to settle after the army was often on Warnie's mind and became his overriding practical concern. Since he had visited and stayed at Hillsboro so many times, the idea of moving in with Jack and the Moores—at their invitation—began to be attractive.

As he weighed the pros and cons, he worried that his loss of liberty meant his reading would be seriously compromised; however, then he reasoned he could do the majority of his reading in Jack's rooms at Magdalen College during the day and the remainder in his bedroom at night. He also realized that even in the army his reading was often curtailed by others, interruptions, and responsibilities. A more serious issue was the personal freedom he would lose by living at Hillsboro. He envisioned having to let Jack or Moore know where he was going, what he would be doing, and how long he might be gone; moreover, he would have to take up household chores, sometimes do the shopping, or walk the dog. Warnie resolved this problem by deciding that just as his independent life had both its discomforts and luxuries, so he must see that domesticity had its good and bad. In addition, he believed Hillsboro would provide him a richer intellectual life and a healthier physical life since he would be able to eliminate many hours of army drinking.

While Warnie was still in China, Jack, although eager to have Warnie join the household, tried to make sure his brother understood what he would be getting into by writing him a lengthy letter:

I suppose you do realize that to exchange an institutional for a domestic life is a pretty big change.... Both kinds of life have their discomforts: and all discomforts are in a sense intolerable. The great thing is to choose with one's eyes open. Can you stand as a permanency our cuisine—Maureen's practicing [piano]—Maureen's sulks—Minto's burnetto-desmondism—Minto's mare's nests—the perpetual interruptions of family life—the partial loss of liberty?[126] This sounds as if I were either sick of it myself or else trying to make you sick of it: but neither is the case. I have definitely chosen and don't regret the choice. What I hope—very much hope—is that you, after consideration, may make the same choice, and not regret it: what I can't risk is your just floating in on the swell of a mood and then feeling trapped and fed up. Of course to weigh it fairly one must compare the best of this sort of life with the best of the other, and the worst of this with the worst of the other. What one is tempted to do is just the opposite—when one is exasperated in a home, to compare it with one of those splendid evenings one had in a mess or common room. Of course what one ought to do is to weigh it against the evening with the mess bore. On the whole my judgement would be that domestic life denies me a great many pleasures and saves me a great many pains. There is also this further point. I spoke above of Pigiebotianism[127] and Hillsborovianism.[128] I presume that if you join us you are prepared for a certain amount of compromise in this matter. I shall never be prepared to abandon Pigiebotianism to Hillsborovianism. On the other hand there are the others to whom I have given the right to expect that I shall not abandon Hillsborovianism to Pigiebotianism. Whether I was right or wrong, wise or foolish, to have done so originally, is now only an historical question: once having created expectations, one naturally fulfills them. All this I am sure you see: I am sure you did not entertain the idea that you and I could set up a purely Pigiebotian household with the others simple as "staff" or "chorus." One hopes of course that we should live in a "blend:" but pure, unadulterated, orthodox, high flying Pigiebotianism would naturally appear only from time to time when we were off on our own. But then again, it wouldn't be fair on the others if I allowed the 'blend' to become merely the background and our neat Pigiebotian moments to become definitely my life.... All this is very disagreeable stuff: also, once it gets on paper, it sounds terrible poetical and forbidding. I don't think really that the problems are specially difficult—quite stupid people solve them every day–but I think they had to be set out.[129]

Significantly, Jack was honest about the challenges of living with Moore and Maureen. He did not mitigate the faults and liabilities of the Hillsboro menagerie, but he explained why he had come to accept and even enjoy the life he had chosen. However, despite Jack's cautions, what tipped the balance in favor of

Hillsboro for Warnie was the certainty of a closer intimacy with his brother, so Warnie decided that as soon as it was economically feasible, he would move in with the Hillsboro household.[130]

One immediate reality was that Hillsboro would not be large enough for them; accordingly, the two brothers and Moore began to search for a permanent home of their own. By July 1930, they found a property they fell in love with: the Kilns, a small home with almost nine acres of land in the blue collar village of Headington Quarry about 5 miles from Magdalen College. The two brothers were taken with the Kilns immediately—Warnie thought it Edenic—and began planning how they might purchase it and the improvements they would make to the grounds. Pooling their money, Moore, Jack, and Warnie were able to purchase the Kilns for £3,300, and in October 1930, they moved in.[131] Initially, Warnie was very happy, although he did miss the peace and quiet of Hillsboro.[132] Within the first year, Warnie's concerns grew stronger because of Maureen's unhappiness; she resented moving out into the country and away from her friends. Additionally, the constant conflict between Maureen and her mother was wearing.[133] Warnie also found himself in awkward or maddening situations. For example, on one occasion, Mrs. Armitage, a friend of Moore's, managed to corral Warnie in the common room of the Kilns where she talked at him with such energy that he could not get away. Jack wrote Greeves about this incident:

> You wd. have been so amused if you'd been here last week end. Mrs. Armitage . . . often comes to call. I had had a pupil to tea and took him out for a walk after. Coming back at 7 I found Mrs. A. still there, seated on the same sofa with Warnie, and conducting a feverish conversation with him about married life, women, and kindred subjects, and under the impression (she is a widow) that she was making great headway. I wish she cd. have seen W., a few minutes later when she had left (for of course my return broke up the party), coming out of the front door into the twilit garden, drawing his hand across his brow, and remarking with great solemnity "I'm going down to 'the Checkers' [the local pub] to have a LARGE whisky and soda."[134]

Given that Warnie later came to regret his decision to move to the Kilns, it must be noted that he went into the arrangement with his eyes wide open.

Warnie's spiritual life also went through a transformation, related almost certainly in part to the death of his father. Serendipitously, it paralleled what was going on with Jack spiritually. The story of Jack's movement from theism to agnosticism to theism to Christianity is well known and reflected in his autobiography *Surprised by Joy,* diary entries in *All My Road before Me,* and numerous letters. What is important to note here is that he said he moved to theism in

the spring of 1929, roughly six months before the death of his father.[135] He then
suggested it was another two years before he admitted that Jesus Christ was the
Son of God, an event he connected with riding to Whipsnade Zoo in the sidecar
of Warnie's Daudel.[136] Warnie's conversion—or it would be more accurate to say
his recommitment to Christian faith—had its genesis during his return trip from
China in 1930. He had been reading about Buddhism and decided to make a
pilgrimage to the Dibutsu Buddha temple at Kyoto, the old capital of Japan. On
February 28, 1930, he visited the temple and was struck by the overwhelming
beauty of the place. When he saw the Dibutsu, it was seated on a lotus leaf at
the base of a huge wooden head of a Buddha. As he gazed at it, he found it very
difficult to leave its exquisite serenity and peace.[137]

On March 4, 1930, he journeyed to Kamakura to see the real Dibutsu Buddha—
he had learned that the one at Kyoto was only a small copy—and his search for
the real one seemed to be as elusive as finding the Holy Grail. As he entered the
shrine, he read the following notice: "Stranger whosoever thou art and whatsoever
thy creed, when thou enterest this sanctuary, remember that thou treadest upon
ground hallowed by the worship of the ages. This is the temple of Buddha and
the gate of the Eternal and should be entered with reverence." Approaching the
Buddha, he was stunned by its enormous size—fifty to sixty feet high—and even
more so by its fascinating countenance. When Warnie peered up at its huge face
looking down under half-closed eyelids, he experienced a theophany. He read in
the Buddha's face the following: "I have always known everything and have always
been here, and anything you may do or say in your little life is mere futility." He
stood there looking into its face for a full ten minutes. So taken with the Buddha
was he that he longed to stay for several days in order to come back and view the
statue at varying times during the day.[138]

This experience of the numinous became the moment in time when Warnie's
slumbering spiritual imagination reawakened, and for the rest of his life he kept
a small replica of the Dibutsu Buddha in a prominent place in his living quarters. When he returned to England, he began to attend church services more
regularly—and at about the same time Jack was moving toward faith in Christ.
Jack noted something of this in a letter to Greeves on January 10, 1931: "[Warnie]
and I even went together to Church twice: and—will you believe it—he said to
me in conversation that he was beginning to think the religious view of things
was after all true. Mind you (like me, at first) he didn't *want* it to be, nor like it:
but his intellect is beginning to revolt from the semi-scientific assumptions we
all grew up in, and the other explanation of the world seems to him daily more
probable.[139] Warnie's return to practicing Christianity was the result of a long,
slow, steady conviction that human life could not simply be the result of a cosmic

accident several millions years in the past. He noted that "with me, the wheel has now made the full revolution—indifference, skepticism, atheism, agnosticism, and back again to Christianity."[140] Coming at it from two different perspectives but at almost the same time—Jack intellectually and Warnie experientially, especially through his encounter with the Dibutsu Buddha—the brothers returned to the faith of their mother, the person most responsible for inculcating in them biblical truths, ideas, and narratives. Jack eventually became the most famous and effective Christian apologist of the twentieth century. Warnie, while certainly less known for his Christian witness, became a faithful churchman, eventually serving in the 1950s as the churchwarden for his and Jack's local parish church, Holy Trinity, Headington Quarry. Early religious instruction dies hard; in the case of Jack and Warnie, they never permanently left the protestant Christianity of their Northern Ireland heritage.[141]

Warnie's last two and a half years in the army were uneventful. After his return from China, from mid-May 1930 to October 1931, he was the assistant to the Officer Commanding Supply Company at Bulford, an army base near Stonehenge and a 70-mile drive southwest of Oxford. He renewed his warm WWI friendship with Parkin, and they often met for drinks and dinner at various hotels and pubs.[142] On one occasion, Warnie invited Jack and Parkin to dine with him at the Eastgate Hotel in Oxford. As had been the case with Collins, Jack liked Parkin, and a few days later Jack invited Parkin to dinner at Magdalen College.[143] Warnie also continued his extensive reading of seventeenth-century French history and drove his Daudel to the Kilns almost every weekend.[144] Both brothers enjoyed their efforts at improving the landscaping around the Kilns, with Jack writing Greeves: "This afternoon W and I have been at work in the wood clipping the undergrowth, he with shears and I with a sickle. I hope you can see the whole scene—the light slanting through the fir trees, the long elder branches swaying and then swooping down with a rustle of leaves, the click-click of the shears, and the heavy odour of crushed vegetation. *What* pleasures there are in the world."[145] By early May 1930, Warnie was planning to compile what later became the *Lewis Papers*.[146] He enjoyed several weekend road trips with Jack as well as visits back to Belfast and Northern Ireland. In addition, in January 1931, Warnie and Jack took a 54-mile walking tour of the Wye Valley, the first of a series of walking tours they would take during the 1930s.[147]

As early as March 1931, Warnie began arranging a return posting to Shanghai, since a second foreign tour was necessary as a precondition to a comfortable retirement.[148] Once he was certain of the posting, he felt he was in sight of the "stony road to retirement," as he would have served his prison sentence and the cell doors would be near to opening.[149] The dream of retirement was so strong that he feared some financial crisis would thwart his plan, yet he knew he would plod on if he had to do so. He set sail on the *Neuralia* for Shanghai on October 9, 1931, following essentially the same route he had taken on his first trip to China, and he arrived on November 17, 1931, when he became the officer commanding the RASC in Shanghai. He felt comfortable in Shanghai and enjoyed the old familiar sights, sounds, and smells. Most days, his work was confined to the time between ten and noon, so he had plenty of time to read and plan for the future. The men he supervised were among the best he had served with, so there were few personnel or work-related matters to handle, with the exception of the fallout from the fighting between Chinese and Japanese forces. Jack kept him informed of the happenings at the Kilns, including the fact that they were adding two rooms to the house specifically for Warnie upon his return. Warnie continued his newly adopted practice of regularly attending church, and on Christmas Day 1931 he took Communion for the first time in many years, pleased and thankful that he was again a fully communing member of the Church.[150] Providentially, on the same day, Jack also took his first Communion in many years.[151] When Warnie learned of this, he was delighted, noting that had Jack not also begun to take Communion, there would have been a lack of common interest, which Warnie would have regretted.[152] On several occasions over the next few months, Warnie's duties keep him from being able to attend the Sunday service, something he greatly missed; at the same time, he was glad he was disappointed because it affirmed the genuineness of his return to faith.[153]

Because of the increasingly volatile conflict between the Chinese and the Japanese, Warnie decided to move forward his plan for retirement. On March 24, 1932, he relinquished command of the RASC in Shanghai, and he began serving as the commander of the supply depot in Shanghai on April 4, 1932. On August 8, 1932, Warnie officially applied for retirement and requested the 108 days of leave due him.[154] Once his retirement was approved, he sailed from Shanghai on October 22, 1932, on the cargo liner *Automadon* by way of Mikki, Hong Kong, Manila, Singapore, Port Swettenham (the main gateway into Malaysia, renamed Port Klang in 1972), Penang, Colombo, Djibouti, Kamaran, Jeddah, Port Sudan, Port Said, and Tripoli, reaching Liverpool on December 14, 1932. The most memorable part of the voyage occurred one evening when there was a fierce windstorm. Warnie was awakened when he was thrown against the head of his bunk; the ship was pitching steeply, and the wind was howling. He got up and opened his curtain to a breathtaking view—the moon was bright, the sea was fiercely roiling, and the ship was bobbing up and down from front to back with unimaginable stress.[155] Given Warnie's great affection for the many ships he encountered throughout his life—sometimes almost idealizing them—the powerful experience of this night on the sea was indelibly printed on his memory.

When he finally reached the Kilns after the voyage, he was struck by its beauty and delighted to find the new wing that contained his study and bedroom. On the morning of December 21, 1932, he got up early and found a copy of the *Times* containing the announcement that he had been dreaming of for years: his retirement was effective that day. In his diary he wrote: "After eighteen years, two months, and twenty days, my sentence comes to an end, and I am able to say, like Wordsworth, that I have 'shaken off,' 'The heavy weight of many a weary day / Not mine, and such as were not made for me.'[156] But so far from grousing, I am deeply, and I hope devoutly thankful. It has been a good bargain: how many men are there, who, before they are forty, can struggle free, and begin the business of living."[157]

When Warnie entered the army in 1914, he was a young, inexperienced subaltern facing extremely poor odds for survival on the Western Front. His faithful service in the Great War illustrated his sense of duty, his devotion to his country, and his commitment to his military career. After the war, he handled well his assignments in France and Belgium, and then he competently fulfilled his first foreign tour of duty in the challenging setting of Sierra Leone. In the mid-1920s, his assignments in Colchester and Woolwich brought him additional experience and expertise. Bearing new levels of responsibilities, he served with distinction in Shanghai, finishing his career still as a young man of thirty-seven with the bulk of his life before him. Throughout, he was efficient, skilled, and honest. Above all he was a man of personal integrity as demonstrated by his fidelity to his country. The many hours of boredom with little to do sometimes led to desultory habits, including excessive use of alcohol; indeed, the major negative outcome of his military career was the grip that alcohol had on him.[158] Retirement provided him the opportunity to "begin the business of living" unfettered from the demands of military life; in addition, his newfound freedom gave birth to the next important phase of his life—his work as an historian focusing on both his family life and seventeenth-century French history. In addition, he now looked forward to many years of close living with Jack.

CHAPTER FOUR

Beginning the Business of Living
(1933–1939)

After Warnie's retirement from the army, he began "the business of living," meeting often with Herbert Parkin for drinks and meals, living with Jack and the Moores at the Kilns, reading more and more about seventeenth-century French history, and in general thrilled to be released from military life.[1] In particular, his life was marked by five significant involvements. First was his transition from the life of a soldier to that of a civilian—in his case as a member of the somewhat fluid and oddly comprised denizens of the Kilns. Although he began living at the Kilns with hope tempered by the knowledge that it would be decidedly different from regimental life, he gradually came to regret his decision, primarily because of Mrs. Moore. Indeed, by the mid-1940s he despised her; nevertheless, he willingly endured her narrow-mindedness, irascible character, and unpleasant prejudices because living at the Kilns meant he could be with Jack. Being able to see his brother daily made up for what otherwise would have been an unendurable penance. The second involvement was one of delight and deep personal satisfaction: the compiling, editing, and printing of the *Lewis Papers*—the eleven-volume collection of letters, essays, diaries, journals, sermons, and writings of his extended family covering the years 1850 to 1930. In many ways, the *LP* was the major written work of Warnie's life, notwithstanding his diary and the seven books of seventeenth-century French history he would publish later; indeed, the *LP* may have been the catalyst for his other writings since the experience of intense research and detailed cataloguing set the stage for his subsequent publications.

Shortly after finishing the *LP,* Warnie turned to a third and all-consuming activity: sailing the waterways in and around Oxford and Cambridge on the *Bosphorus,* his motorboat. From 1936 until the outbreak of WWII, Warnie spent many days aboard the *Bosphorus,* and relished hour after hour of freedom and personal satisfaction. The fourth matter that occupied him was the annual walking tour that he took with Jack. In early January of every year between 1931 and 1939—with the exception of 1932 when he was in Shanghai—the two brothers set out on a loosely planned tour of specially selected areas of the British countryside, usually with a pub or inn as the days' final destination. The walks were the highlight of every year for Warnie, rekindling the spirit of the walks he and Jack took in and around Belfast when they were boys. His fifth involvement was his role in the early development of the Inklings—that group of novelists, thinkers, churchmen, poets, essayists, medical men, scholars, and friends who met regularly to drink beer and to hear written compositions read aloud and to discuss books, ideas, history, and writers. In this chapter, I explore each of these involvements and discuss how they marked for Warnie the "beginning the business of living."

LIFE AT THE KILNS WITH MRS. MOORE

Warnie's antipathy for Mrs. Moore—nicknamed Minto by the brothers—has been well documented.[2] Yet it was not always that way. Despite Warnie's initial frustrations with numerous Minto-induced kerfuffles—episodes of agitation, alarm, commotion, conflict, disorder, dispute, or uproar—he was otherwise happy and pleased with his release from military life. Accordingly, during his first few months at the Kilns, he endured Moore's disruptions with a degree of tolerance. For instance, in his diary entry of February 8, 1933, he wrote: "My new way of life—or perhaps I should say the beginning of my real life, is still a constant source of joy to me, to be savored minute by minute. God send that it lasts: at any rate I am conscious of it & grateful for it all the time."[3] During much of 1933, he bore Moore's brouhahas and her exasperating personality with tolerance and grace. However, the frequent conflicts between Moore and her daughter, Maureen, had the cumulative effect of souring Warnie's attitude toward both, but especially Moore. For instance, the two women often quarreled over the use of Maureen's car, as well as her driving ability.[4] Warnie also found Maureen's naïveté painfully funny. On one occasion, he noted: "Over tea, when we got home, we had a characteristic Maureenism. Somehow the conversation got round to the fact of officers in the Guards wearing stays[5]—or the story that they do so, I should say. When told this, Maureen said incredulously: 'What! Just like these?' (at the same moment pulling her frock up to her chin and disclosing an ensemble of chemise, corset, blue knickers and black silk stockings). Even Minto was a trifle startled, and so was I—not that I disliked the spectacle."[6]

Two particular incidents—one in August and one in September 1933—were harbingers of the downward spiral in his relationship with Mrs. Moore. The first episode had the unfortunate collateral result of making Warnie also resent Fred Paxford, the Kilns handyman and gardener. After an evening with Moore, Warnie found himself increasingly bored by her conversation because she was developing the irksome habit of repeating Paxford's views, beginning almost every conversation with "Paxford says." Warnie was further nettled by Moore calling him Pax-Warnie, and he was finding her reliance on Paxford's adages maddening. He was also angry with himself because he was beginning to dislike Paxford, even though Warnie knew that was unfair. Nonetheless, almost everything Paxford said irritated and piqued him.[7] Later in the year, another incident occurred which furthered Warren's dislike of Paxford when Moore took Paxford's advice about which radio set they should buy. No matter what point Warnie made about the relative value of one set over the other, in the end Moore chose the one favored by Paxford. Warnie seethed silently and said to himself that if ever someone wanted to get a person disliked, be sure to include his name in every sentence spoken.[8] Regrettably, Warnie retained a strong dislike for Paxford for the rest of his life, based in part on episodes such as this.

The second incident involved a September kerfuffle when Moore believed something terrible had happened to Jack during a trip to Milford. Her panic so frightened Warnie that he believed the worst had occurred, and he joined her in a frantic search of the streets, with Moore wildly pushing people out of the way. "She has the most diabolical power of generating and communicating panic of any person I have ever met, and . . . I was feeling quite sick with fright. Fright faded into relief and relief into anger when at long last I saw J standing on the edge of the pavement gazing vacantly across the street."[9] These two episodes proved to be the turning point in Warnie's attitude toward Moore, so that from this time forward, his mindset toward her steadily deteriorated. One indication of this deterioration was Warnie's decision to avoid going on long car trips with Moore. Instead, whenever possible, Warnie would travel separately by train to their destination.[10]

Nevertheless, his diary entry of December 21, 1933—exactly one year after his army retirement—was sanguine as he evaluated his first year of living with Moore at the Kilns. Regarding Moore, much about her reminded him of his father, particularly their tendency to treat family members with an appalling lack of grace. In addition, like his father, Moore was supremely confident that her opinion regarding almost everything was the correct and final one. He was also irritated by her prejudices and selfishness, and he lamented how she dominated his brother's life: "It fills me with both admiration and irritation to see how completely the whole of J's life is subordinated to hers—financially, socially, recreationally: the pity of it is that on his selflessness her selfishness fattens."[11] In an unpublished portion of Warnie's diary for this same date, December 21, 1933, he expressed his frustrations with how Moore was stealing time from Jack and offered additional insights into the constant conflicts between Moore and Maureen. He mused on what Moore's married days must have been like that caused her to clash with Maureen so frequently. Whatever the causes, Warnie claimed that Moore never lost the opportunity of picking a fight with her daughter, and then Maureen's petulant responses made life at the Kilns tense and unpleasant.[12] To be fair, in the published portion of the diary for that day, Warnie listed several things about Moore that he actually admired, including her hospitable nature, her kindness to animals, her love of nature, her deep affection for his brother, and her welcoming him into the Kilns household. He even ended the published entry by noting that while he and Moore were not close, they were on good terms.[13] As the years went on, however, Warnie grew increasingly tired of Moore's failings and saw less and less about her to like.[14]

Regarding Maureen, Warnie admitted that his earlier dislike of her started fading, particularly because they began attending together many classical music concerts in Oxford, and she began to teach him how to play the piano.[15] When he reviewed his year with Jack, he confessed that he had not gotten as much time with Jack as he would have liked, but he had gotten as much as was possible, so he was satisfied. Regarding the actual reality of living at the Kilns, he almost gushed with good feelings, writing that he was elated to have a home where he could enjoy the changing seasons, a deep satisfaction in the pleasures of every passing moment, and thankfulness for still being relatively young.[16] One particular gratification for him at the Kilns during this period was a series of gramophone concerts covering Beethoven's symphonies that Warnie arranged on Sunday evenings. Jack said it was one of the best hours of the week: "The rush and crowd of visitors and continual flurry of the week end subsides and after a quiet supper Minto, Warnie, Mr. Papworth [their dog], and myself sit down in the study and have our music."[17] In his diary summary of December 21, 1933, Warnie commented that, all things considered, he thanked God because his first year living in the Kilns had been the happiest of his life.[18]

Unfortunately, Warnie's happiness and contentment did not last. The more time he spent around Moore—and he had many daily interactions with her—the more he came to dislike her, and this colored everything else about his life at the Kilns. In his "Memoir," he claimed she was an autocrat who ruled with stifling tyranny, and he faulted her for being the cause of so many fiascos.[19] "Mrs. Moore was one of those who thrive on crisis and chaos; every day had to have some kind of domestic scene or upheaval, commonly involving the maids: the emotional burden so created had then to be placed squarely on the uncomplaining shoulders of Jack. In this atmosphere the physical inconveniences of the household seemed relatively unimportant: notable among them was the total unpredictability of any meal-time."[20] In addition, he more and more found his brother's affection for her bizarre. Once, Warnie ventured to express his frustrations with her to Jack, but Warnie said his criticism of Moore sent Jack away stumping in a temper.[21] This was particularly problematic because Warnie saw—as noted above—striking and unflattering similarities between her personality and that of his father, leading him to observe in his diary that "the more I see of Minto, the odder I find the psychological problem of J's feelings towards her and those which he entertained for P."[22]

The final tipping point in Warnie's feelings toward Moore occurred during an August 1934 trip to Kilkeel in County Down, Ireland. As early as April 1934, Moore and Maureen were arguing over details of the trip, and once they arrived in Kilkeel their disagreements were constant. Warnie found Moore's behavior maddening, as she would take unfounded positions on almost any topic, and flatly deny anyone else's views. She was fractious, censorious, and querulous, and her comments to the others increased "in acidity to a point where it was becoming increasingly difficult to ignore them."[23] Warnie was completely exasperated by her foolishness and bickerings. Despite all the advantages she had, she spent most of her time causing quarrels and discord.[24] Several days later, Moore tried, unsuccessfully, to get Warnie to conspire with her in a plan to thwart a side trip planned by Maureen. On August 16, 1934, Moore embittered Warnie during a separate side trip to Newry by convincing him—falsely—that she knew the town very well. Afterward he kicked himself for listening to her since it turned out she knew nothing about the town and they ended up completely lost. In addition, he bristled as she went on and on about how sure she knew the way.[25] The result of the trip was that Warnie would never enjoy Kilkeel again.[26] Sixteen years later, he wrote: "I associate [Newcastle] with nothing except that truly dreadful month at Kilkeel. That holiday was—apart of course from her stealing [Jacks'] life—the worst trick that Minto ever played me. By her tantrums there she robbed me of a good half of my own precious Co[untry]. Down. . . . For never as long as I live do I want to set eyes on Newcastle [or] Kilkeel . . . ever again. Yes, yes, beautiful, beautiful, but they'll never be beautiful to *me* again."[27] Warnie coped with Moore as best he could through the 1930s; however, as we shall see in the next chapter, by the end of the 1940s he loathed her and could no longer endure being near her.[28]

THE *LEWIS PAPERS*

The second issue that kept Warnie occupied after his retirement was the matter of the Lewis family papers. As early as May 7, 1930, nine months after the death of Albert, Warnie and Jack began talking about organizing, editing, and publishing the family papers they brought with them from Leeborough. Since Warnie was nearing retirement, Jack agreed that Warnie should be the one who took on this project, although the brothers consulted frequently with each other, and they drew up a mutually agreeable plan. Metaphorically, the two brothers locked arms on this project with Warnie taking the lead by common consent. On May 10, 1930 he wrote: "On getting back to Magdalen [College from my morning's errands] I spent the rest of the morning in drawing up a scheme for the editing and arrangement of our family papers: this I discussed with J at lunch time and he approves of it: there will be a lot of work in it, and I expect it will occupy the first year of my leisure, if and when it comes."[29] Then on August 10, 1930, he added: "J dipped at random into the chest of family papers."[30] In this "chest of family papers," Warnie and Jack had an extensive, although unorganized, family archive consisting of letters, diaries, journals, essays, sermons, poems, newspaper clippings, illustrations, maps, photographs, drawings, short stories, anecdotes, legal papers, and miscellaneous documents. While the majority of the papers dealt with the lives of the four main family members—Albert, Flora, Warnie, and Jack—other documents concerned the extended Lewis and Hamilton families. Not everyone would have found family documents such as these worth the time to archive, but for Jack and Warnie these papers were a repository of critically interesting and culturally infused information about where they came from, who they descended from, and how their lives were shaped.

Warnie began this project with a vast collection of materials, including more than thirty volumes of diaries and a large cache of unsorted papers. Specifically, he drew from seven volumes of diaries and a volume with a theological essay by his maternal grandfather, the Reverend Thomas Robert Hamilton covering 1850–1868; thirteen volumes of diaries by Warnie himself covering 1912–1930; eight volumes of diaries by Jack covering 1922–1926; short, fragmentary diaries by Albert and Jack of various dates; dozens of letters by Warnie and Jack (many of the latter maddeningly undated); and a collection of unsorted papers by Albert's father, Richard Lewis, which probably came to the family in 1903 when Richard came to live with Albert and Flora.[31] However, the largest cache of material was a mass of letters written to and by Albert from the late 1870s up until the time of his death on September 25, 1929, as well as other miscellaneous papers important to Albert; this portion of the family papers was the most complete because Albert had the habit of keeping drafts of his private letters.

When Warnie set himself to start working through these materials on January 9, 1931, he faced two large trunks filled with unorganized papers. He quickly decided upon a procedure that would guide him, consistent with his penchant to organize, systematize, and synthesize; this ensured that his ordering, sequencing, and particularizing of the material would be efficient and practical. About Warnie's plan, Jack wrote him on February 21, 1932: "I thoroughly agree with your . . . [organizing idea] for the Lewis Papers."[32] Warnie's overriding organizational strategy was to arrange the documents in chronological order, thus ensuring that something of a loose narrative would result. This is nowhere more apparent than in the love letters between Albert and Edie Macown—an early love interest—and later between Albert and Flora.[33] Another principle he followed was to correct spelling and punctuation errors, something he was not always successful in accomplishing since he, like Jack, was a poor speller.

Regarding material he decided not to include, Warnie claimed that he only excised passages dealing with medical matters or others detailing intimate, private issues that he determined not fit for printing. Finally, Warnie checked with Jack and other family members whenever he was not certain of the circumstances, situations, or occasions under consideration.[34] In the epitaph on the title page of the *LP*, Warnie quoted Daniel Webster—"Those who do not look upon themselves as a link, connecting the past with the future, do not perform their duty to the world"—in the process revealing his historian-driven agenda. He then explained in the "Foreword" to the *LP* what motivated him as an editor: "The history of a given period is not exclusively, or even mainly, the history of its famous men and women. The real history of the past lies in the answer to the question, 'How did the ordinary, undistinguished man live? . . . It is with a view to providing posterity with an addition to such all too scanty material, that the papers which follow have been embodied in a permanent form."[35] Of course, when Warnie compiled the *LP*, he could not have known that his brother would be much more than an ordinary, undistinguished man; however, Warnie's lack of knowledge about Jack's future fame lends to the *LP* a certain innocent, disarming charm and facile appeal.

Warnie's work on the papers was briefly interrupted by his final tour of duty to Shanghai from October 9, 1931, to December 14, 1932. But after his retirement, he returned to his work with enthusiasm. On February 4, 1933, Jack wrote Arthur Greeves: "Warnie . . . is now *retired.* . . . He has become a permanent member of our household and I hope we shall pass the rest of our lives together. . . . We both have a feeling that 'the wheel has come full circuit,' that the period of wanderings is over, and that everything which has happened between 1914 and 1932 was an interruption. . . . We make a very contented family together."[36] On a typical day, Warnie would walk or bus in from the Kilns to Jack's rooms at Magdalen College, purchasing a pork pie or something similar along the way for lunch, usually arriving around 10:30. He would break for lunch at 1:00 and then work steadily from 1:30 until 5:30, at which time he would have a glass of beer or whiskey, ending the day by taking a bus back to the Kilns. The work was engrossing and almost hypnotic; there was nothing tedious about working with the papers, and Warnie was fascinated to find out details about his extended family that heretofore had been unknown to him and sharing them with Jack. For instance, early on he discovered evidence that Joseph Lewis, his great grandfather, may have kept a mistress after the death of his wife, Jane Ellis.[37] Jack noticed how happy Warnie was with his work, writing Greeves on March 25, 1933: "Warnie sinks deeper and deeper into the family life; it is hard to believe he was not always here."[38]

Once the papers were organized, he began the slow task of typing them on the little Royal typewriter he had purchased years before. Since he had never taken typing lessons, he used the "hunt-and-peck," or one-finger-at-a-time system, a decidedly slow and inefficient way to go about the project. Yet Warnie never tired of his work. For letters, sermons, and essays he assigned each a number, essentially helping him to arrange things chronologically; however, he did not number diary extracts, recollections, or footnotes, relying instead upon dates or internal dating clues. Another organizational technique he employed was an extremely detailed table of contents, noting a brief description of what each chapter contained, as well as a separate listing of all photos, illustrations, or maps included in each volume. He probably finished typing out Volume 1 of the papers by the spring of 1933, since he wrote in his diary on June 2, 1933, that the first volume had returned from the binders the previous day and that both he and Jack were delighted with it. In addition, he noted that he was already fifty pages into his work on the second volume.[39] Although Warnie did not list the date when he finished each of the individual volumes, I offer the following as an informed estimate:

VOLUME	DATE COMPLETED
Volume 1, covering October 17, 1850, to September 23, 1881	May 1933[40]
Volume 2, covering September 24, 1881, to July 19, 1901	July or August 1933[41]
Volume 3, covering July 20, 1901, to December 30, 1912	October 1933[42]
Volume 4, covering January 1, 1913, to July 8, 1915	December 1933
Volume 5, covering July 9, 1915, to June 20, 1918	February 1934
Volume 6, covering June 21, 1918, to June 2, 1921	April 1934

Volume 7, covering June 3, 1921, to January 10, 1923	June 1934[43]
Volume 8, covering January 11, 1923, to September 8, 1925	August 1934
Volume 9, covering September 9, 1925, to February 25, 1928	September 1934
Volume 10, covering February 26, 1928, to April 17, 1930	November 1934
Volume 11 and index, covering April 18, 1930, to Dec. 6, 1930	December 1934[44]

Over a four-year period, Warnie completed a herculean work—running to nearly 3,300 pages of single-spaced typescript—that highlighted his organizational skills, his determined commitment to a project, and his pragmatic, practical sensibilities. Without Warnie's doggedness and Jack's encouragement, the *LP* may never have happened.

By almost any measure, the *LP* are an exceptional accomplishment. They provide an unparalleled repository of primary documents about Warnie, Jack, and many other members of their extended family. As evidence of this, consider a sampling of Lewis-related books that have drawn extensively from this archive: Walter Hooper's three volumes of Jack's letters; Hooper's edition of Jack's diary, *All My Road Before Me: The Diary of C. S. Lewis, 1922–1927;* and major biographies on Jack by Roger Lancelyn Green and Hooper, George Sayer, Alister McGrath, Hal Poe, and several others.[45] In addition, the authors of scores of books and essays on a multitude of C. S. Lewis–related topics have mined the *LP* as has a recent edition of his collected poems.[46] However, the *LP* are not dominated by Jack's letters and diaries; in fact the majority of the volumes—6 through 11—are taken up by Warnie's diary entries.[47]

It remains to consider the strengths and weaknesses of Warnie's work on these family papers. The major weakness of the *LP* was inevitable: because of the massive amount of material included, there are frequent points at which one item follows another with no apparent reason, and there is no attempt to create a bridge or connection. This lack of transitions means the *LP* sometimes move abruptly and with little sense of cohesion from one incident to the next. While the chronological order does create a loose narrative, the lurch from one entry to another produces a stumbling, jumbled read. It is like a road dotted with potholes. Accordingly, it is difficult to feel one is "getting somewhere" in terms of the overall story of the Lewis family. A related weakness is the lack of explanations regarding some of the people mentioned. While Warnie does a good job of explaining who the members of the Lewis family are when mentioned, other people are not always adequately described, nor is their significance in the larger narrative noted. A final weakness—or at least oddity—is Warnie's tendency to write as a third-person narrator but then on occasion to shift to his own voice as a first-person narrator. On the one hand, writing from the third-person perspective creates a tone of objectivity and distance important in historical composition; however, since readers know that Warnie is really the author, in passages where he shifts back and forth between first and third person there is often a cognitive break, leaving readers feeling off balance. On the other hand, when he writes in first person, there is an authenticity and immediacy to the text that is effective. Deciding to write the *LP* either from either first person or third person might have been best since the mixing of the two narrative approaches is problematic and distracting.

However, the strengths of Warnie's work far outweigh these weaknesses. Chief among these is when Warnie supplements the letters and diaries with memoirs. Some of the most important episodes of his life become wonderfully imagined and detailed anecdotes. For instance, Warnie's recollections of his experiences at Wynyard offer critical insights into his and Jack's lives while there. These memories appear in *LP,* 3, 33–41, and center primarily around the headmaster, Robert Capron.[48] The most lasting impressions he has of Capron are found in his physical description and his so-called teaching methods. Capron's face, writes Warnie, "was marred by the nose, which was small, had the appearance of being varnished, and from which the lobe of the right nostril had at some time been removed." Tall, stocky, and robust, Capron moved his victims to fear, and often handed out corporal punishment with sadistic delight.[49] Also memorable was his neglect of personal hygiene, with Warnie remembering his filthy beard, dirty hands, and tobacco-stained mustache. His arresting voice struck fear in all the students and suffered no opposition. Without Warnie's carefully realized accounts of Capron, readers today would little understand the nightmarish experiences of Warnie and Jack at Wynyard. The two talked at length about Capron and their terrible memories while Warnie compiled the *LP.*

Warnie's memoir regarding W. T. Kirkpatrick—from the *LP,* 4, 61–65—is notably more sanguine.[50] As with Capron, Warnie recalls physical details about Kirkpatrick, writing that he was "a tall, stringy old man with white side whiskers, untidy clothes, and an expressive and piercing grey eye, not over cleanly as to his person and radiating physical and mental energy."[51] His overall appearance leads Warnie to identify him as a leaner and more spirited version of the Emperor Franz Joseph of the House of Habsburg. Warnie suggests that Kirkpatrick was in the main a grim man, in part because he was a hard-edged realist, opposed to cant or romanticism. At table, his manners were brusque, and though not a big eater, he ate as if half-starved, talking and eating almost at the same time. When

Warnie thinks back to his time with Kirkpatrick, he recalls not only the person of his tutor, but also his bucolic days and the arresting landscapes of Bookham.[52]

Much like Warnie's memoirs, his many character sketches—whether brief or extended—are key components strengthening the overall quality of the work. In these character sketches, he shows a sharp eye for physical description, but even more telling are his astute evaluations of the essential moral, spiritual, and social qualities of the individual under review. Regarding Henry Wakelyn Smith, his favorite teacher at Malvern, Warnie says he was "a born teacher, and few boys left his form without learning from him some love of letters. . . . He read English verse, particularly that of Tennyson, in a very beautiful way, which did not fail to make an impression even on the most materialistic members of his form." Warnie also notes that Smith initiated a system of competition among the boys culminating in a weekly prize, and that he was—unlike most of the schoolmasters—respectful of the boys: "[He] realized that boys are as sensitive to courtesy as their elders; he always addressed his form as 'Gentlemen,' and his boys loved and respected him. To attempt to rag [act disrespectfully] in [Smith's form] would have been regarded by the school at large as a deplorable breach of manners."[53] These sketches of Capron, Kirkpatrick, and Smith were certainly discussed with Jack, and in his later autobiography, *SJ*, it is clear Jack bases some of his own descriptions of these men on Warnie's profiles of them in the *LP*. Undoubtedly, Warnie was Jack's "unnamed co-conspirator" on portions of *SJ*. Warnie's predilection for writing character sketches serves him well throughout the *LP* and equips him to write effectively and convincingly about many of the persons he later covers in his books on seventeenth-century French history.

Before leaving this discussion of the *LP*, it is worth noting how Warnie's work affected the relationship between the brothers. I think that their deep affection for one another was enhanced in at least four ways because of Warnie's production of the *LP*. First, Warnie's work on the *LP* cemented their loving friendship as siblings. That is, what they had only known in part about themselves and their family was made more concrete to each other because of Warnie's work. In a very real sense, they "saw" something of who they were via the lens of the family papers. Second, the *LP* "objectified" the personalities of their closest relatives, particularly their father, Albert, with whom both (but especially Jack) had a conflicted relationship. By looking objectively and from a distance at their father's life as revealed in his letters, essays, orations, court cases, and legal papers, the brothers came to understand more about Albert—and themselves—than they ever did during his life. Third, the *LP* were compiled on the heels of each brother's return to Christian faith—a faith very much in the tradition of their Irish Protestant heritage. While both rejected in large part the rigid self-righteousness and inflexible anti-Catholicism of many Belfast relatives, they nevertheless were made keenly aware of the dangers of insular faith and social religion. Put another way, the family papers confirmed the importance of genuine, nonsectarian Christian faith while at the same time bolstering the religious bond between the brothers.

Finally, the *LP* clarified the lifelong love of writing they shared. The *LP* were completed and bound after Jack's *The Pilgrim's Regress* (1933) but before his *The Allegory of Love* (1936); both books heralded the writing skills and intellectual "muscle" that Jack would go on to evidence over the next thirty years. Although the *LP* were not (nor are likely to be) published, and despite the limitations I have identified, they nonetheless mark Warnie as a writer of some note. As children, Jack and Warnie shared a love for writing that carried over into their adult years. Warnie's work on the *LP* demonstrates that they continued as writing collaborators as adults.[54] Warnie's gifts—including a highly retentive mind, first-order organizational skills, single-minded commitment and determination, and his fine eye for characterization (as well as his years of military service in the RASC wherein he developed a deep understanding of what it takes to handle huge logistic challenges) equipped him superbly during the years he labored to produce the *LP.* Born with a pragmatic, get-it-done sensibility, Warnie's monumental accomplishment with the *LP* is impressive. Working without benefit of a computer, he produced a finely edited family archive from which readers have and will continue to benefit richly.[55]

BOSPHORUS

After completing the *LP* Warnie turned his attention to a project that fulfilled both a long-held dream and an immediate need. The latter was the creation of a place away from the Kilns where he would be free from Mrs. Moore; the former was the building of a boat where he could indulge his lifelong love of ships and being on the water. Both the dream and the need were met when in 1936 he contracted with Salters Brothers, Ltd., Oxford, to build a motorboat so that he could revel in sailing on the many canals and rivers near Oxford.[56] Drawing from the days when he and Jack created their imaginary worlds in the attic room at Leeborough, Warnie named his vessel after one of the Boxen ships, the *Bosphorus.*[57] Designed only for inland cruising, the river cruiser was built to Warnie's specifications: twenty feet long with a beam of six feet eight inches and a draft (the depth of water needed to keep the boat afloat) of one foot ten inches.[58] The interior of the *Bosphorus* was simple, with a toilet in the bow, a two-berth cabin six feet six inches long, a galley and pantry, and an open cockpit with a locker in the stern.

The *Bosphorus* was powered by an eight-horse-power marine engine.[59] While Warnie could have gotten by with a smaller engine, he believed it was the best to invest heavily in the hull and engine at the outset and then gradually upgrade the spartan interior as time went by. Commissioned on July 3, 1936, the *Bosphorus* went into immediate service and cost £200.[60]

Not only did Warnie love touring about in the *Bosphorus,* but he also found pleasure in writing about his experiences. For instance, in the first of eight essays he published about his boating days, "'But What's It Going to Cost?'" published in the *Motor Boat and Yachting* magazine in November 1938, Warnie offered a good deal of practical advice for anyone contemplating the purchase of an inland cruiser—also called a ditch crawler. He advised potential buyers to consider all the risks, especially the costs of keeping a river motorboat going after the initial investment.[61] One source he said no one should trust was the owner who gave only vague and unsubstantiated reports about the actual financial costs of maintaining a motor boat: "I regret to say . . . [that] owners of their beloved boats . . . [are no] more to be trusted than mothers talking of their children; speed is usually a little lower and fuel consumption a little higher than the proud owner is ready to admit."[62] Warnie then provided a detailed list of all his expenses for the 1936 season (a total of forty-six days in use and a total distance traveled of 528 miles), including insurance, tolls and lock dues, fuel costs, repairs, river registrations and season pass costs, routine maintenance costs, tips, food, and annual docking fees. He admitted that because he did not like to do maintenance himself, he happily paid someone else to tune up the engine, take care of painting and varnishing, and fix other problems. His total costs for the 1936 season were just under £33.[63] Warnie also included the same information for his 1937 (93 days in use, 916 miles traveled) and 1938 (92 days in use, 662 miles traveled) seasons with the costs being £76 and £80 respectively.[64]

In assessing his first three seasons of cruising, Warnie was forthright and candid. His expenses were trending higher in 1937 and 1938 because he was on the river for a longer period than in his first year. In addition, he noted several costly accidents, especially in 1938, as well as unexpected expenses; although he reckoned 1938 an abnormal season, he confessed that it was probably the case that every yachting season was financially challenging.[65] Another reason costs were increasing was because of the food he bought for guests; in 1938 he had guests on board for 43 of the 92 days he sailed. Jack would have been a frequent guest on day trips. Others, most notably Herbert Parkin, would have probably taken longer, overnight trips on the *Bosphorus.* Improvements that meant additional comfort, efficiency, and appearance added to his costs. Warnie anticipated some who might quibble with his failure to account for depreciation, but he nonchalantly dismissed their concerns: "It seems to me that unless you can afford to set aside in hard cash the amount thus written off every year, a mere paper entry of £X for depreciation is of very little value. I cannot afford to build up a depreciation fund, and therefore ignore the question. My banker is a very kind gentleman, and will doubtless build me a new boat when the time comes."[66] He ended his essay by tallying the credit side of his boating. Cruising saved him about £5 a year compared to what his household expenses would have been ashore. Moreover, taking all his normal holidays and bank weekends onboard *Bosphorus* saved him about £40 annually.[67] These practical savings aside, the main benefit of spending so much time on his boat was the immediate satisfaction he received: "But most important of all are the imponderable assets—the ever-changing panorama of river or canal, the wind and the sun, even the rain, the village inn at journey's end, still starlit nights, the birds at dawn, silent waters far from traffic routes and road-houses, one's own little floating home—who can calculate the value of all these in pounds, shillings, and pence?"[68]

The first extended canal cruise he took—a round trip of sixteen days from May 10 to 26, 1937—covered the entire length of the Oxford Canal, a distance of just under 78 miles one way and almost due north. In "Through the Oxford Canal: A Whitsun Cruise on a Secluded and Attractive Waterway, Parts 1 and 2," Warnie carefully explained how the Oxford Canal linked to other waterways, how one moved from lock to lock, the tools required to open and close the locks, the important stopping points along the way, how to negotiate cruising under bridges, the kind of landscape one sees at various spots, dangerous currents to avoid, maximum safe speeds to travel, preferred stopping places for supplies and dining, and the comradery of canal boatmen.[69] Although the two essays are long on the practical realities of such a trip, Warnie also described lovely vistas, in one instance writing: "Now I was in the heart of the real country. Cows gazed at my passing with stolid disinterest, whilst horses, on the contrary, cantered the width of the field to snort their disapproval. Heavy-coated sheep . . . drowsed by the waterside, and among them ran panic-stricken lambs who had lost their mothers. . . . A troop of ducks marching in single file along the towpath quacked a greeting, and here and there a heron flapped up out of a low green meadow."[70]

On another trip—this time a three-day sojourn from September 6 to 8, 1937—Warnie and an unidentified companion sailed the Wey, a tributary of the Thames, from Thames Lock, Weybridge, to Catteshall Lock, a distance of 19 miles one way. In "Exploring the Wey: A Three Days Cruise on a Tributary of the Thames," Warnie explained the shorter length of this voyage was due to its being so late in the season and was marked by several challenges, including the narrowness and shallowness of the navigable waterways.[71] Warnie often emphasized the need to stay in the middle of the channel, admitting that on one occasion the *Bosphorus* ran aground. In order to get moving again, he had to go overboard and push it back into the center of the river. Although the trip was a challenge, his eye for the natural beauty along the way was always open, and at one point he described "lush meadows [that] were the grazing ground of numbers of magnificent draught horses, and as the ground rose on each hand meadow gave place to gentle slopes clad in rich groves of ancient oaks from which, here and there, rose a grey tower or spire, hinting at unspoilt villages."[72]

Warnie's next extended trip was his most ambitious and led him to pen "The Great Ouse: A Week with 'Bosphorus' on Fenland Waterways." After spending his first two seasons exploring the Thames and the other waterways around Oxford, in 1938 Warnie decided to sail the groups of rivers known as the Fens and used Cambridge as his headquarters; he was especially attracted to over 190 miles of good, navigable waterways. As there was no direct way for him to sail the *Bosphorus* to Cambridge, he shipped his one and one quarter ton vessel by rail at a cost of slightly over £8—about the same amount he would have paid for fees and lock passes had he remained in the Oxford area.[73] He found in H. C. Banham's boatyard at Cambridge an excellent mooring station and sailed from Cambridge on June 12, returning on June 18, 1938. During this trip, Warnie chronicled his movements in exacting detail, intent on providing the necessary information anyone else would require who wished to make the same journey.[74] However, in the midst of sharing his knowledge of the practical realities (such as where to obtain drinking water), Warnie, as in his earlier essays, waxed eloquently on the natural beauty he witnessed. For example, he described the charm of the Old West River, noting that he loved its isolation and the young animals along its shore. He found the dearth of buildings satisfying, delighting instead with the omnipresent songs of birds and masses of flowers.[75] In another place, he noted "perfect summer mornings when a white heat haze floats on the water and everything seems all right in the best of all possible worlds" and a "countryside [that] is luscious, rich, parklike, musical with birds, slumbering, still . . . and [reflecting] nothing but · the heart of England beating drowsily under a June sun."[76] At the end of his trip, he believed he had covered some of the most interesting and beautiful country open to fellow inland cruisers.

Before his fourth season out with *Bosphorus*, Warnie penned two reflective essays. The first, "The Winter of Our Discontent: It Is Not So Bad, After All, Thinks This Ditchcrawler," is largely a reverie dealing with what the ditch crawling man can do during the winter when being on the water is impossible.[77] Warnie found any number of consolations for the boating man in the frigid off-season, including being able to while away a wet, dismal day by going to look at his boat in dry dock. Doing so gave great pleasure to the marooned boater since he could decide what new improvements he wanted to make, "talk boat" with the shipyard proprietor, pull out maps and start planning the next season's voyages, relive past trips—"on this bend of the river I hit a submerged tree trunk and nearly lost my propeller; moored along that meadow I spent the night of the great thunderstorm"—take walks along the canal, and talk with the canal keeper while keeping an eye out for ideal mooring spots.[78] Best of all, however, was armchair cruising in front of a warm fire while the cold wind moaned in the chimney and icy rain beat on the window. Any problems that might come up during such a reverie were overcome, much as Tennyson's Lotus Eaters did, living in "'a land / In which it seems always afternoon'—a fine summer afternoon, the engine running sweetly, locks which work perfectly and are never set against you, a land of warm, lovely countryside."[79] Additional wintertime cruising consolations were that no breakdowns occurred, a perfect inn appeared around the next bend with an ideal mooring, and an attractive barmaid took your order. Another delight was wondering about the exotic names one encountered along the waterways; how did Coven Heath, Stewponey, Bumble Hole, Muckfleet Dyke, and Acaster Malbis get their names? A final wintertime amusement was to imagine receiving a financial windfall and then dreaming about the kind of boat one might build if money was no object. Warnie concluded his essay by arguing that "the winter is not so black as it is often painted. And, anyway, we are more than half-way through the darned thing now."[80]

The second reflective essay, "A Ditchcrawling Discourse: Some Thoughts on Inland Waterways Cruising," mused on matters related to whether was it better to rent or to buy a ditch crawler.[81] After pointing out that renting a boat might be a good way to test the waters, he discouraged buying a used boat, especially one advertised as suitable for both sea and inland waterways: "There may be some to which the description truly applies, but there are other which would have been better described as 'equally unsuitable for either.'"[82] For Warnie, the real ditch crawler had to carry one "into the heart of England, far from towns and busy waterways, to sleepy canals and moss-grown deserted wharves; to the stillness which is so far to seek in these troubled days, to a life which he can in some sort share with the birds and cattle, the only sharers of his solitude."[83] In the rest of the essay, he gave advice with his usual pragmatic sensibilities. For example, he cautioned that the boat must not be more than twenty feet long and must offer a very low profile because of dearth of headroom under so many low hanging bridges. In addition, he pointed out that the hull would quickly lose its showroom finish since it would frequently hit the sides of stone walls and other obstructions that line the canal locks; the latter problem could be lessened, he wrote, if one installed a wooden, metal-shod fender all around the waterline of the vessel. Other items the ditch crawler ought to have were a hurricane lamp, a large winch handle for working the locks, a bathing ladder, and a long-bladed knife for cutting away weeds and debris. As for when it was best to take to the water, he said it was springtime before plants begin to grow and clog the channels. Nighttime moorings should be chosen carefully in order to avoid running aground. The larger the galley the better, and although stores and supplies could be obtained along the way, he advised carrying a large stock of drinking water, tinned milk, and gasoline.

Warnie's last essay was "'Sailing P. M. 13.th'"[84] It is a brief comic narrative about the bad luck that befell him when, after returning to Oxford late one afternoon, he made the hasty decision to take a late day cruise on *Bosphorus*. The trouble began after spending a long lunch with a friend some distance away. Too much food and too much drink were compounded by a leisurely train ride back to town. The pleasant journey along the Thames beguiled him, leading to the question: "Why go home?" He was not expected back and the fare at the Kilns would be "designed for female consumption only." The *Bosphorus* was ready to go, and, not deterred by it being the thirteenth day of the month and the possibility of bad luck, he wrote: "I pride myself on having no superstitions, and go to considerable inconvenience to walk under ladders and such-like things."[85] Thus supplying himself with the necessary provisions, he boarded his cruiser. Immediately things went badly: on his previous trip he had decided to leave the boat keys in the now locked yard office, so he had to squeeze into the boat's cabin via a small fore hatch; all his sailing tools were locked in the stern; and in the interest of safety, he had turned off the petrol valve which also was inside the stern.

After scrambling about and fortuitously finding someone who could retrieve his keys from the office, he set out on *Bosphorus* in the twilight for the overnight mooring he had set his heart on. But only a half mile from his goal, he unexpectedly ran aground: "*Bosphorus* rose like a rocketing pheasant and came solidly to rest with her stem pointing upwards at a cynical-looking star. . . . She was immovably held for about two-thirds of her length on a flat, slimy expanse of unknown dimensions."[86] All seemed to be getting better in the morning when a friendly sailor offered to help pull the *Bosphorus* off the sandbar. However, once Warnie started up the engine, his stern rope wrapped around his propeller; the other boat could not pull the *Bosphorus* on its own power, so his would-be helper promised to send help. In the meantime, Warnie decided to take matters into his own hands, and despite it being a cold, gray day, he stripped down, slipped into the icy water via his bathing ladder, and cut away the offending rope. But when he tried to get back on board, the bathing ladder broke, and he could not reboard. Eventually he was rescued and managed to get the *Bosphorus* back to the boatyard. He ended his tale of woe by citing three morals. First, do not cut corners on the river on the assumption you know which parts to avoid. Second, replace infrequently used gear like a bathing ladder. Three, do not make even short trips on the water impulsively. Warnie's ability to laugh at himself is winsome and illustrates he could find humor at his own expense. Jack surely roared with laughter at his brother's nautical mishaps.

At the risk of hyperbole, the *Bosphorus* was Warnie's Promised Land, Shangri-la, Arcadia, or Elysium.[87] Throughout his army days he sometimes grimly soldiered on, looking forward eagerly to the day when he would be free to do what he wanted to do. The move to the Kilns was the first step, and his completion of the *LP*, the next step. Having the *Bosphorus* was a further move in the direction of enjoying the business of life. Self-fulfillment and self-satisfaction were increasingly significant for Warnie. Having a boat that he could retreat to alone or with an invited guest was a dream come true.[88] In a letter years later to a friend, Warnie offered additional insights into his pleasure with the *Bosphorus,* noting especially that when boating, he would be where no one could find him; in addition, he did not have to worry about getting mail. The greatest delight, however, was the freedom to pull into shore wherever he wanted and take a stroll and enjoy the beautiful landscape.[89]

Left unspoken here is the blessed relief he also experienced away from Moore, her disruptions, and the other irritations of living at the Kilns. However, in an entry from his diary, Warnie, after having sold the *Bosphorus,* did articulate this benefit: "It is only by slow degrees that it has dawned upon me how large a part the 'Bosphorus' played in making the Kilns tolerable."[90] Later he added that he avoided going down to the river where the *Bosphorus* had once been moored: "I should keep away from the river: I never go there without a heartache for the 'Bosphorus' and the days that will never return."[91] And during a lunch along the river near Reading with Parkin on June 21, 1950, when Warnie saw several ditch crawlers , he admitted that it pained him and caused him no small amount of envy as he reflected back to his *Bosphorus* days.[92] It is important to note here that Warnie's diary keeping fell off precipitously after February 27, 1936; indeed, except for the days when he and Jack were on their walking tours in January of 1937, 1938, and 1939, Warnie's diary is silent until February 22, 1943. Accordingly, the matter of Warnie keeping a log of his trips on the *Bosphorus* is important. Clyde Kilby and Marjorie Mead write that Warnie "faithfully kept a log (unfortunately, no longer in existence), which no doubt served an equivalent to his previous diary record."[93] Without the logs, there is a gaping hole in our detailed knowledge of Warnie's life during his ditch crawling days. Warnie's eight essays on inland cruising may reflect an expansion or refinement of some of his log entries. Regardless, these *Bosphorus* inspired essays provide critical information about Warnie's seemingly idyllic life during this period. On the *Bosphorus*, Warnie the old soldier became Warnie the young sailor.

WALKING TOURS

Warnie's fourth preoccupation during the 1930s was one that fulfilled profound needs in his emotional and psychological life: extended time alone with Jack during leisurely jaunts through the British countryside. Each tour gleaned out precious minutes with Jack—moments that Warnie desperately needed. The brothers first developed their love for the natural world while growing up in Belfast and exploring the landscapes of County Down. Whether riding their bicycles or walking nearby paths, they reveled in what they saw. As noted in the previous chapter, this continued later when the two traveled in Warnie's Daudel motorcycle—Jack in the sidecar—back and forth between Warnie's posting at Colchester, on day trips out from Oxford, or longer trips in southern England. For instance, about a return trip from Bristol on April 26, 1924, Jack wrote about zipping along at a rapid speed through places such as Bickland, Kingston, Bagpuize, Fyfield, Bessels, Leigh, Cumnor, and Botley on the way into Oxford. Then he added: "It is a tame, well combed, cheerful country of tidy well growing woods, white gates, dark tarred roads, comfortable cottages, sometimes exceedingly beautiful, green hedges and flat blue distances. The speed, the sunlight, and the sense of coming home put me into an unusually prolonged fit of 'joy.'"[94] Thus, as Warnie approached retirement, they decided to take annual walking tours.[95] Later, in his "Memoir," Warnie reflected on the importance of these tramps:

> These . . . [walking] tours were a great feature of his life and mine: they were inspired by a joy in landscape that developed out of the Boxonian visions of our childhood and was—together with books—the most enduring element in cementing our friendship. Until 1939 our annual walking tour was a regular fixture: on these long days, and during the pleasant evening hours when we took our ease in an inn, Jack was always at his most exuberant, his most whimsical, his most perceptive—the overworked cabhorse released from the shafts and kicking his heels.[96]

According to Warnie, only one general principle guided the progress of the walks: Jack insisted on having tea daily around four in the afternoon.[97] Since Jack was usually free from college duties immediately after the new year, January was selected as the most convenient—though not necessarily the most comfortable—time for their marches.

The first excursion—a 54-mile trek along Wye River that straddles the border of England and Wales in order to trace its source—took place January 1–4, 1931, when Warnie was on leave from Shanghai.[98] After traveling by train from Oxford to Chepstow in Wales on January 1, they walked north for the next three days through fourteen villages and adjacent country sides and thence to their ending point, Hereford, back in England.[99] Both brothers were struck by the beauty of Chepstow Castle, a Norman stone fortification dating to 1067.[100] The highlight of their trek on January 2 was visiting the ruins of Tintern Abbey, the inspiration for many writers, especially William Wordsworth and his poem, *"Lines Composed a Few Miles above Tintern Abbey, on Revisiting the Banks of the Wye during a Tour. July 13, 1798."* Warnie was especially moved by the quiet beauty of the ruined abbey.[101] Other highlights of the day included seeing the Bristol Channel in the distance, sampling local ciders, and enjoying a charming tea in St. Briavels. Regarding the latter, they stopped at the village pub, were shown to an inner room where they took off their shoes, put on slippers, and dined on bread, cheese, and beer, followed by a pot of tea—the latter of course, a requirement of Jack's. This was Jack's standard lunch on a walking tour, so Warnie followed his brother's lead and found it to be an excellent touring diet.

On January 3, they awoke to a cold drizzle that gave way to sunshine by noon. They basked happily in beautiful scenery and explored graveyards and local churches. At Symonds Yat, they paused for a morning beer in the local pub, and Warnie was charmed by a huge Great Dane pup "so large that when I was sitting down, he could lick my nose without stretching himself: he had recently cut one of his forepaws in breaking in a window to get at another dog whom he wanted to speak to, and he went first to J and then to me and held up the injured paw for our inspection—a very jolly animal."[102] Later that day, they passed through farmland, navigated through a herd of unfriendly cows, and steered around a mound of bracken that was as large as a haystack. They finished the day by overnighting at a pub in Ross-on-Wye, with Jack reading a book by Robert Louis Stevenson and Warnie one by G. K. Chesterton. The brothers completed their walk on January 4, arriving in Hereford at midafternoon. There Warnie delighted in several encounters with local "humorists" and was impressed with a copse of holly trees.[103] During the four-day trip, Warnie made detailed notes of the places, people, and vistas they appreciated, claiming that during "this leave I found a new pleasure in life by going on my first walking tour, an expedition with which J has been threatening me for two years or more . . . [it] is one of the best holidays I have ever had in my life."[104] In addition, Warnie noted how this walking tour had brought back memories of their early school days at Malvern College.[105]

Jack reflected on this walking tour in a letter to Greeves, confiding that he was worried that Warnie's "selfish habits wd. [not] really accommodate themselves to the inevitable occasional difficulties. My fears however were quite unfounded. He has been with us all the month here and everyone says how greatly he is improved." Jack then deftly summarized a central difference between him and Warnie: "Of course I have not had and probably never shall have any *real* talks on the heart of the subject [religion] with him. But it is delightful to feel the whole lot of us gradually beginning to move in that direction. It has done me good to be with him: because while his idea of the good is much lower than mine, he is in so many ways better than I am. I keep on crawling up to the heights & slipping back to the depths: he seems to do neither. There always have been these two types."[106]

Since Warnie was in Shanghai in 1932, their next walking tour—the continuation of their effort to trace the source of the Wye River and roughly 34 miles long—did not take place until two years later, January 3–6, 1933. Warnie was in high spirits as they took the train from Oxford to Hereford where their walking tour in 1931 concluded. When the brothers neared in Malvern, they recalled memories of their school days: "When we arrived at Great Malvern, we found to our great joy, that we were having the unanticipated pleasure of traveling in the identical train by which we used to return from the Coll. in the old days, which naturally led us into much reminiscent talk."[107] Leaving Hereford, they took a train to Moorhampton. Getting off the train, Warnie felt it was a great moment, because for several, uninterrupted days it would just be him and Jack. They settled their backpacks on their shoulders—the train trundling off into the chill twilight—leaving them to ramble out into an absolute silence. As it had been a long time since he had been in the open countryside, the silence moved Warnie deeply. From Moorhampton, they set off on a westward jaunt.

On January 3 and 4 their largely west-northwest progress took them through Bredwardine, down the Golden Valley to Dorstone, and eventually to Hay-on-Wye. The tramps up the hills and elevation changes were tiring, but the views, especially down the Golden Valley which Warnie described as extraordinary, were well worth the effort. He wrote that he never saw such a country like it for brooks and streams, most of them pretty, and many strikingly beautiful. Passing rich farmland and lovely little waterfalls, they carried on in spite of a heavy rain that began to fall. Warnie found Hay-on-Wye to be ugly and depressing. On January 5 and 6, they crossed the river at Glasbury and then made their way along the Wye, arriving at Builth-Wells where they began their train trip back to Oxford.[108] The days were marked by breathtaking vistas, meetings with locals, stops in several pubs, views of castles and snug little farms, crossings and recrossings of the Wye, and securing comfortable quarters at the Greyhound Inn. Warnie called it "a capital little holiday."[109]

Their third walking tour, January 1–6, 1934—a 35-mile northwest excursion from Builth-Wells to the coastal town of Aberystwyth—was the final leg of their effort to trace the source of the Wye River.[110] The brothers had spent some time planning this portion of their tour of the Wye valley. Warnie gathered maps of their proposed route and showed them to Jack. Together they made preparations for the walk, and Warnie could hardly contain his excitement.[111] On January 1, they began their tour by returning via train to the Welsh village of Builth-Wells and stayed overnight, again at The Greyhound Inn. On the morning of January 2, they started out, with Warnie later writing that the first half day of their walking tours was particularly thrilling for him.[112] Part of Warnie's deep affection for the Welsh countryside he believed was hereditary—his great-great grandfather, Richard Lewis (1775–1845) came from the small Welsh village of Caergwrle—so it was more than just the natural beauty that moved him. Instead, it was the deeply embedded familial connection to Wales that charmed him. After lunching at a pub in Newbridge-on-Wye, they struck out across the breathtaking countryside and made their way to Rhayader where they spent the night in a comfortable pub.

The next morning, January 3, was highlighted by an encounter with several red squirrels that Warnie thought almost tame. They also came across a herd of sheep who were being tended by lads who only spoke Welsh. For tea, they stopped at Llangurig longer than they should have, so that when the afternoon turned cold and rainy and the sun began to set, they had a hard trudge to Pant Mawr, arriving at their inn just after six. After a comfortable night, they headed out on January 4 into a driving rain. Initially, Warnie did not find it troublesome: "In spite of the wind and the rain, I enjoyed the next stage of the walk: we had a good firm track under foot, with the Wye sprawling below us, now quite definitely a stream, and on either side bare hills, down the face of which little torrents showed white."[113] However, as the day went on and a heavy fog fell on them, he regretted their decision, comparing the walk to some of his worst WWI marches. Unable to convince Jack to turn back, Warnie resolved to let this be his last walking tour; fortunately, a friendly driver picked them and took them to Ponterwyd, where they spent the rest of the day in a warm, comfortable inn.

When they awoke on January 5, the weather was even worse than the day before, so they agreed to do the last leg to Aberystwyth by bus. It was a wise move because the rain came down even harder until they reached Aberystwyth when the sun came out and the sky cleared. After finding an inn, they relished exploring the town. Warnie took to it at once, glad to see and smell the sea once again. An unexpected treat was the large number of bookstores.[114] Other aspects of the town they liked were the large War Memorial, the University of Wales (for which they agreed Jack should become the principal), and the rugged cliffs overlooking Cardigan Bay. They lounged about comfortably that afternoon, engaging in a discussion on immortality: "After tea J and I fell into talk on the subject of personal immortality, J maintaining that he would understand as such, the addition of new faculties of perception etc. to the 'me,' whereas I hold that 'me' can only exist in the next life if it is quite recognizably the survival of me, stripped of course of all sensual tastes, but with a core of [myself]. It was an interesting talk."[115] On January 6, they headed back to Oxford by train, arriving in the evening around eight. Warnie's assessment of the holiday was upbeat: "In spite of the Ponterwyd day, I look back on as one of the very best I have ever had. Its only real fault is that it has given me aesthetic indigestion: I am not constituted to absorb beauty in such very large helpings."[116]

Their fourth walking tour was January 3–5, 1935. Because both Jack and Warnie were financially strapped, they decided on a shorter walking tour closer to home. Accordingly, on the early morning of January 3, they arranged to have Paxford drive them southwest 10 miles or so from Oxford to the village of Watlington, near the border of Oxfordshire and Buckinghamshire. From there, they began a 38-mile, semicircular route of the Chiltern Hills that took them southeast to through several villages, eventually finishing in Thame.[117] As usual, Warnie was filled with anticipation:

Next to the arrival at the inn in the evening, I know no better moment than the start on the first morning of a walk—the sense of adventure, the feeling of having finished with the business of life for three days, the knowledge of the personal effort that will be needed to bring one to one's journey's end, the freedom from the little unavoidable rubs and galls of domestic harness—all these combine to produce an exhilaration somewhat after the old beginning of the holiday feeling but saner and better savored: then too it is the time of the year when I see most of J. So altogether it is a good moment.[118]

The march that day was filled with the things that charmed Warnie—open vistas, encounters with locals, friendly pubs, and a comfortable bed in the evening—in this case concluding in High Wycombe.

On January 4, they headed north through poultry country and were over-joyed by an encounter with two frisky colts who ran alongside them in a field that bordered their path. The walk was a glorious one that Warnie thoroughly enjoyed.[119] Although along the way in one of the pubs they consumed "bad beer," they finished the day in Tring in a homey, comfortable inn. January 5 found them passing through beautiful beech forests and lovely valleys. In one pub where they stopped for refreshment, they met a tiresome landlord who bragged about his large map of England hanging on the wall. The day ended with Moore and Maureen picking them up in Thame as prearranged. Despite the fact that Warnie savored the three days, it was tempered by his sense that they were too close to home: "The knowledge that almost anywhere during the past three days one could have, had necessity arisen, been home for the next meal, introduced an element of make believe which was a bar to getting the fullest enjoyment out of it. There must be the adventure of a formal railway journey away from home—one must be far enough from one's base for the loss of one's money to be a serious matter. But nonetheless I enjoyed myself amazingly."[120]

For their fifth walking tour—January 13–16, 1936—Warnie and Jack decided to go north and explore Derbyshire. On January 13, they left Oxford by train and traveled to Derby via Birmingham (a city Warnie had never before visited and one that reminded him of Belfast), arriving at their point of departure at the village of Darley Dale in midafternoon. By evening they reached their overnight destination, the village of Bakewell 5 miles away to the northwest, and agreed it was the best half-day walk they had ever had, with much of the landscape in the Derwent valley reminding them of both County Down and the Wye valley in Wales. On the morning of January 14, they took a train northwest that passed through a breathtaking viaduct and disengaged near Buxton. Although the day was cold and icy, the views were magnificent. For a time, they followed Derbyshire's own River Wye to the southeast.[121] In one spot where the river was dammed and made a huge curve, Warnie marveled at the wide expanse of becalmed water since he had expected a torrent of gushing water; he was momentarily struck quite still at the sight.[122] They also passed through Miller's Dale—a nice place with an ugly, squat church—and then, veering away from the Wye, they shifted south to Taddington and Monyash where they had lunch. From Monyash, they turned back to the southwest and the village of Longnor before going south again along the River Dove via Pilsbury and ending the day at Charles Cotton, a rustic but comfortable inn in Hartington.

On January 15, Warnie awoke from one of the worst nights he ever had on a walking tour, primarily because his bed had been unusually short. Despite the persistent cold, icy weather, they continued their trek southward down the Dove valley along the Dove River. Warnie found the river "exceptionally beautiful, for wherever there were rushes or a tree trunk in the stream, there was a wonderful ice tracery to be seen. The water in these parts is most beautifully clear."[123] They had lunch near Ilam and tea in Mapleton. Both brothers grew increasingly tired because of the difficulty of the terrain, so they were thankful to overnight at the Royal Oak Inn in Ashbourne. After their 33½-mile walking tour, they returned by train to Oxford on January 16 via Uttoxter, Tutbury, Burton-on-Trent, and Birmingham. For Warnie it was the end of "the best walking tour I have ever had."[124]

For the site of their sixth walking tour—a journey of almost 60 miles on January 5 to 9, 1937—the brothers chose Devonshire and the southern coast of the Bristol Channel.[125] As usual, Warnie was upbeat about their expedition, writing on January 5 that he was delighted that they were beginning his favorite annual vacation.[126] After six hours on trains, they arrived at Dulverton. The next morning, they awoke to a rainy, misty, windy morning and began a northerly footslog toward the Bristol Channel. It turned out to be one of the most unpleasant days of all their walks, primarily because of various combes—deep, narrow, steep, barren clefts between the hills, which meant the walking was very much up and down. Moreover, the wind blew hard, rain stung their faces, and the scenery was disappointing.[127] However, the day was somewhat redeemed when they reached Dunster, a jewel of a town near the coast that compensated for the day's 17½ miles of a harsh forced march.

After a comfortable overnight, they left on January 7 on a westerly path along the River Avill, passing through the villages of Wootton Courtenay, Luccombe (according to Warnie one of most beautiful villages he had ever seen), Horner (accompanied by a friendly collie), and thence to Porlock where they lunched and imbibed with gusto a dry, draft cider that was the best either brother had ever tasted. They made the difficult climb up Porlock Hill and were rewarded with magnificent views of the Bristol Channel and vast, panoramic views of the country they had just tramped. The rest of the day took them through Oare, Malmsmead, and Brendon, where after their 21-mile odyssey they overnighted at the Stag Hunter's Inn. On January 8, they did another 21-mile hike, this time stopping at the coastal city of Lynmouth for lunch before continuing on to Martinhoe and a beautiful view of Woody Bay. They were pleased when they saw the cheery lights of the day's final destination, the Lion Inn in another coastal city, Combe Martin. The next morning, they returned to Oxford by train, with Warnie declaring their tour most pleasing.[128]

Their seventh walking tour—covering 52 miles from January 10 to 14, 1938, in Berkshire—was a southerly one. After arriving by train in Challow on January 10, Warnie and Jack relished a leisurely walk to Wantage 5½ miles away; in the church there they saw an Anglican nun.[129] Refreshed after a restful night, on January 11 they headed south; they passed through the villages of Letcombe Regis and Letcombe Bassett, and Warnie noted that the rain gradually let up. He was thrilled by this development, writing: "Far below us on our right was a ring of firs, with a clump of the same tree in the center—like an enormous faerie ring as I said: J reproved me for calling the Little People by a name that they so much dislike and threatened all sorts of catastrophe—'Why can't you keep a civil tongue in your head?' he asked. However, they apparently decided to overlook my rudeness, for the improvement in the day held."[130] They lunched at East Garston, where Warnie wistfully recalled last being there with his close Malvern friend, Blodo, in 1911. Continuing south, they trekked through pig country and finished their 14-mile walk at the very comfortable Bear Inn in Hungerford.

They rose to a drizzly morning on January 12 and headed west toward Durley. Along the way, Warnie was taken by the beauty of Littlecote House.[131] The walk from there to Durley and the Forest Hotel where they were to overnight was a challenging one; Warnie developed a blister on his heel during their 14-mile journey, leading him to say that he could not ever remember a more grueling day. January 13 began as a cold, gray morning and the brothers trudged for most of the day along a poorly kept canal towpath heading west. At one point, Warnie was excited to see a spot where he imagined berthing the *Bosphorus*. He also appreciated the character of the Salisbury Plain.[132] After lunching near Wilcot, a steady rain began to fall, and the march became a slog. At the village of Horton, they turned away from the canal path and made their way to Devizes for an overnight at the uncomfortable Bear Inn after their 18-mile odyssey. About the inn, Warnie wrote: "The lounge was bad, the bar was worse, and the lavatory, which stank, was plastered with notices regarding the cure of venereal disease; the dinner was tolerable, but the service was wretched."[133] After catching the train in the morning, they arrived back in Oxford at 1:30 P.M., agreeing that other than the night at the Bear Inn, it was perhaps the finest of all their walking tours.[134]

The eighth and what turned out to be the final walking tour—January 2–6, 1939, in the area of Shrewsbury—was 42 miles in length; it ended up being the coldest and most physically unpleasant of all. In fact, because the weather had been so cold, they almost decided to cancel their plans; despite the cold, gray skies that greeted them on January 2, they took the train from Oxford via the familiar venues of Malvern, Worcester, and Hereford. Along the way, Warnie's spirits lifted. First, because as they traveled, he and Jack "were engaged in the first intimate conversation we had had for three long months." Second, because he "had the usual never failing delight in turning mine eyes unto the hills as we drew near Malvern and then seeing the Coll. cold and silent in its winter holiday sleep."[135] They finally reached their walking starting point, Marshbrook, around 3:30 P.M. and set off north on a 4½-mile hike to Little Stretton. After an excellent overnight, they awoke to a snowy morning on January 3; however, by the time they began their hike, the sun was shining. Warnie was disappointed by the white monotony of the snow against the landscape as he preferred the grays and greens of the landscape and blue, cloud-dappled skies. They shifted east and passed through Hope Bowdler, Ticklerton, Hatton, Middlehope (where they turned south), and Corfton, where they paused for lunch. In the afternoon, they continued south through fine cattle country and passed through the charming villages of Seifton and Culmington. Before they reached their overnight destination in Ludlow, they surveyed the imposing view of Ludlow Castle. After a cold 18 miles on the road, both brothers found the beds in the Feathers Hotel gratifying. In fact, Jack said: "Whatever this may be as a walking holiday, it is undoubtedly the best *sleeping* holiday we have ever had."[136]

A heavy snow was falling on the morning of January 4, and it was bitterly cold. Because they had not planned this walking tour very well, they realized there was only one pub they could possibly reach in time for lunch. Nonetheless, bolstered by a huge breakfast and sandwiches stuffed in their packs, they took off down the hill at Ludlow, fearing every moment they would fall face first on the icy road. They kept due south and passed through Ashford Bowdler where they turned east; finding themselves pacing through almost uninhabited areas, they christened the countryside Shropshire Sahara. The weather was so bad and the walking so difficult that they abandoned plans to go farther south in favor of heading east for Tenbury where they would catch a train to Bredenbury. As they left the train station near Bredenbury, Warnie wrote that "there are few more desolate situations in a civilized land than to find oneself in the last of the daylight of a bitter day in the heart of the country, bound on foot for an unknown destination."[137] When they finally reached their inn for overnight, they realized their truncated walk for the day had been a very hard 12 miles. On January 5, they awoke refreshed and, after strolling about a bit, headed back to Oxford by train, stopping to overnight in Malvern where Warnie's affection for the place was once again renewed. The next day, they caught the train to Oxford, arriving shortly before 2 P.M. Of all the walking tours the brothers took, this is the only one that received no praise from Warnie.[138]

In total, the brothers walked over 350 miles. Warnie's diary entries about these walks illustrate once more his gifts as a writer: a sharp eye for detail; deft descriptions of landscapes and weather; astute observations about churches, hotels, and inns; and a keen ear for overheard conversations. Most noteworthy is how Warnie's walking tour entries illustrate a deep and abiding love of nature. His pure joy in its visuals and the evocative emotions nature produced in him intimate an unconscious connection to the divine—akin to Jack's concept of Joy. Warnie was never so happy as when he was with Jack. He was never so happy with Jack as when they went on their walking tours. And he was never so happy with Jack on their walking tours as when—at the end of a long day of tramping through forests, meadows, hills, often in the rain or snow—they found their way to a snug little inn and took their baths, consumed a hearty meal, a pint of beer, and then settled in for a quiet evening of reading. If Warnie could have had his way, this would have been the life he would have chosen permanently. Alone with Jack—with no distractions from Moore—would have been as close to a return to their idyllic days in the attic room at Leeborough as possible.[139]

WARNIE AND THE INKLINGS: THE BEGINNINGS

As there exist several superb scholarly studies of the genesis of the Inklings, it is not my purpose here to trace the origin of this group of like-minded writers and thinkers.[140] Suffice it to say that some believe the group may have had its inception as early as the late 1920s, but it is generally agreed that by the early 1930s the Inklings had coalesced around Jack and J. R. R. Tolkien, and they would meet regularly—usually on Tuesday mornings at the Eagle and Child pub in Oxford and on Thursday evenings in Jack's rooms at Magdalen College.[141] Joining Jack and Tolkien as the third most frequent attendee of the gatherings was Warnie; because he retired from the army in late 1932, he could not have begun attending the meetings until around that time.[142] For instance, within a month of his retirement, Warnie was spending a good deal of time with Tolkien, savoring meals and meetings. In addition, only two months after his retirement, Warnie became charmed by another Inkling, Hugo Dyson, "a man who gives the impression of being made of quicksilver: he pours himself into a room on a cataract of words and gestures, and you are caught up in the stream—but after the first plunge, it is exhilarating."[143] During a dinner several months later at Exeter College hosted by Tolkien and Dyson ("in most exuberant form, especially the former"), Warnie met Nevill Coghill for the first time, a "big, pleasant, good-looking [man] in a sort of musical comedy way, except for a vicious mouth. What I could overhear of his talk sounded good."[144]

It is possible that the first Inklings meeting Warnie attended occurred on March 26, 1934, when he, Jack, and Tolkien gathered at 4 P.M. in Magdalen to read Richard Wagner's *Walküre* (Valkyrie). Warnie reported that although his brother and Tolkien read in German, he was able to follow along and read his part in English. They broke for dinner at 6 P.M. at the Eastgate Hotel (where many meals were taken before Inklings gatherings), and then returned to Magdalen to finish the reading: "Arising out of the perplexities of Wotan we had a long and interesting discussion on religion which lasted until about half-past eleven when the car called for us. A very enjoyable day."[145] Until his WWII call up in late August 1939, Warnie would have attended these early meetings of the Inklings. Ironically, although we know the Inklings were meeting regularly between 1933 and 1939, there are only two documented meetings: the one on March 26, 1934, mentioned above and the one of October 20 or 27, 1937. We know about the October 1937 meeting from Jack's first letter to Charles Williams where he wrote: "We have a sort of informal club called the Inklings: the qualifications (as they have informally evolved) are a tendency to write, and Christianity."[146] In a follow-up letter, he urged Williams to attend a meeting: "I want you to be at the next Inklings probably on 20 or 27 October [1937]. Can you keep yourself fairly free about the time?"[147] In the next chapter, I explore in more detail the meetings of the Inklings after Warnie's WWII service since he recorded in his diary summaries of various Inklings meetings. At this point it is enough to say that whatever camaraderie Warnie experienced in the army was to pale in comparison to the friendships he developed as a member of the Inklings.

The years 1933–1939 were arguably the happiest of Warnie's life. Freed from army life, he was released to pursue the things he wanted to do—or perhaps to do the things he was meant to do: live with Jack; research and write about his family; build, sail, and live on his own water craft; traverse the English country-side on long walking tours with Jack; and come along side like-minded friends amongst the Inklings. Halcyon days indeed. While it is true that life with Moore was unpleasant, still it was better than army life. Unfortunately, much of Warnie's pleasure would evaporate late in 1939 as the gathering clouds of war assembled and then burst. Warnie had planned a canal trip on the *Bosphorus* with Jack and Dyson from August 26 to September 1, 1939. However, as the outbreak of WWII was imminent and Warnie expected he might be recalled to service in the Royal Army Service Corps at any moment, he decided he could not go. Accordingly, Jack asked, his doctor, Robert Havard, to replace Warnie as navigator.[148] As expected, Warnie received a letter from the War Office recalling him to active service.[149] Now there was nothing he and his fellow countrymen—with bitter memories of WWI still fresh—could do to stop the forces of Germany and Fascism, and their relentless pursuit of revenge for the humiliation they endured after WWI.

Despite the overall happiness Warnie experienced from 1933 to 1939, two sobering caveats must be noted. First, early in their lives—as evidenced by their experiences at Malvern—Warnie was the sociable brother while Jack was the loner. As young men, Warnie was friendly, outgoing, clubbable, and daring, while Jack was introspective, prickly, isolated, and snobbish. As the years passed, the

Captain Warren Lewis and fellow officer, Lieutenant Shiel, standing on board a ship in Sierra Leone Harbour. As officer in charge of Supply and Transport, Lewis's duties included ship inspections. Standing, *left to right*: Warren H. Lewis (white suit) and Lieutenant Shiel (dark pants and tie). Circa 1921. (Used by permission of the Marion E. Wade Center, Wheaton College, Wheaton, IL)

Warren Lewis, studio photograph, circa 1940–1955. (Used by permission of the Marion E. Wade Center, Wheaton College, Wheaton, IL)

Left to right: C. S. Lewis (standing), Mrs. Janie King Moore, and Warren Lewis, as well as two family dogs (Pat and Papworth). Outside the Kilns, 1930. (Used by permission of the Marion E. Wade Center, Wheaton College, Wheaton, IL)

C. S. Lewis, approximately 12, and Warren Lewis, approximately 15, standing outdoors in front doorway of Leeborough (Little Lea) in Belfast. Circa January 1910. (Used by permission of the Marion E. Wade Center, Wheaton College, Wheaton, IL)

Warren, Albert, and C. S. Lewis, posed indoor portrait, circa 1908. (Used by permission of the Marion E. Wade Center, Wheaton College, Wheaton, IL)

Photo of the *Bosphorus:* First published in the *Motor Boat and Yachting,* November 4, 1938, p. 482. (Collection of the author)

C. S. and Warren Lewis, standing side by side outdoors at Salterstown pier, two miles from Annagassan, Ireland. Taken while on vacation at Vera Henry's bungalow, Golden Arrow, Salterstown, circa 1949. (Used by permission of the Marion E. Wade Center, Wheaton College, Wheaton, IL)

Photo of Warren Lewis and Frank Henry, circa 1965. (Collection of the author)

Photo the Eagle and Child pub in Oxford, 2019. (Collection of the author)

Photo of Warren Lewis's typewriter, which is now at the Kilns. (Collection of the author)

CHAPTER FIVE

Turning and Drifting

(1939–1951)

Our understanding of Warnie's involvement in WWII is hampered by the fact that he did not keep a diary from January 6, 1939, to February 21, 1943. In addition, none of his letters survive from this period. His silence during this gap is more than regrettable, because it leaves us with only a scant bit of factual information, forcing us to surmise, speculate, infer, and presume. For instance, we have no way of knowing how he felt as he witnessed the march of history toward a second world war. While it is probable that he agonized at the thought of returning to the battlefield, we do not have his writings to reveal his particular thoughts and fears about the coming conflagration. Given his relief upon his retirement from active service in 1932, it is fair to assume he was depressed and unhappy about the prospects of returning to army life. He had grown accustomed to life as a civilian at the Kilns, surrounded by a small, if sometimes unpleasant, society. Having begun the business of life after his retirement from the RASC with enthusiasm and joy, the prospect of returning to barracks life and army routine at forty-four years old—overweight, out of condition, racked by anxiety—was disheartening and dismal.[1] In many ways, Warnie's life from 1939 to 1951 was a turning away from happiness toward a drifting, sobering, uncertain future.

On September 4, 1939, Warnie returned to active service with the RASC. He left the Kilns for Catterick in Yorkshire, bound for the military base that served as a staging area for new and recalled soldiers. He remembered this trip later in his diary entry of February 23, 1943, when he and Jack were on their way to Durham University, where Jack was to deliver the Riddell Memorial Lectures: "At Darlington I had the exquisite pleasure of hearing the sad harsh voice of the girl at the loudspeaker directing the unfortunate troops to the 'next train for Catterick,' and thanked God for His mercies to me since that September evening in 1939 when I got out of the London express at Darlington with my world in ruins round me."[2] However, at the time, he was immediately thrown into the war effort, assuming command of H. Company, probably attached to the Fifth Infantry Division. Jack wrote a weekly letter to his brother almost without fail, and it is primarily from these letters that we can infer the things Warnie was experiencing. Jack's letters note that while Warnie was miserable about his return to army life, he was at least safe and physically comfortable at Catterick. Still, the whole thing was awful. In one of Jack's letters to Arthur Greeves, he shared that Warnie said what made everything so terrible was "the ghostly feeling that it has all happened before— that one fell asleep during the last war and had a delightful dream and has now waked up again."[3] In another letter, Warnie proposed that his brother meet him at a pub in Darlington on Jack's way to give a lecture in Newcastle. However, the lecture was canceled, so Jack wrote that if he could manage it, he would spend a weekend with Warnie at the pub in January 1940—a kind of poor substitute for their tradition of taking a walking tour in January. On a more positive note, Warnie told Jack that the living quarters for subalterns and the handwriting of privates had considerably improved since WWI. Both brothers agreed that at least with the outbreak of war there was the great relief of not having to linger by the radio and listen to the maddening newscasts.[4]

Warnie was at Catterick less than a month, for on October 15 he was posted to Bulford for duty at No. 3 Base Supply Depot, probably attached to the Third Infantry Division.[5] After only ten days, he embarked for France with the British Expeditionary Force on October 25, and two days later he joined the No. 3 Base Supply Depot at Le Havre.[6] He wrote Jack about his recent movements, and in Jack's November 5 reply, we learn that Warnie's letter gave evidence of having been censored. More importantly, Warnie told Jack that his journey turned out to be more pleasant than either expected. Jack wrote that Warnie's story of his moonlit ride in a blacked-out train was vivid, making Jack feel as if he had taken the journey himself.[7] In Warnie's October 30 letter to Jack, we learn that the rules at Le Havre included no smoking while on duty, going to bed early, and getting up early as well. In Jack's reply he joked that it sounded as if Warnie was being incarcerated, but he was sure his brother would soon get use to the nonsmoking rule. On the plus side, Warnie was savoring French breakfasts and dinners.[8]

Initially, Warnie found his posting at Le Havre pleasant enough, but by the middle of November he was having trouble sleeping.[9] He complained to Jack that he no longer liked being involved in the transportation matters his duties required of him, leading Jack to suggest there was irony in Warnie's current job because thirty years earlier, moving about between ships and trains would have been his brother's ideal occupation. Warnie was also frustrated by the inefficiency of the railroads, likening it to malfeasance. Jack sympathized, agreeing that delaying train movement was almost criminal.[10] While Warnie certainly missed being away from his brother, it worked both ways. For example, on November 8, Jack wrote a friend, expressing his worry about Warnie: "My brother, who is a regular, has been sent to France: a sad business for us both, since he was retired and we had both hoped these partings were over."[11] Another example is found in Jack's letter to Warnie of December 3 wherein he recounted a recent incident when, as he was searching through a book, he came across Warnie's notes in the margin: "[I] have derived much 'social pleasure' from your pencillings: as I have experienced before, to read a book marked by you in your absence is almost the nearest thing to a conversation. When I read that hares turn white in winter because they eat nothing but snow . . . and see your mark, it is almost as if one of us was pointing the passage out to the other here in the study."[12]

In another letter, Jack responded to Warnie's musings about the many good benefits of being a Christian. Jack agreed and then wondered how they had formerly found themselves prizing the books they loved so much, when they had no conception that Christianity was at the center of them. Jack finished his thought by imitating Dr. Samuel Johnson, the eighteenth-century critic, essayist, poet, and novelist: "Sir, he who embraces the Christian revelation rejoins the main tide of human existence!"[13] Jack agreed with Warnie's opinion of Johnson, and affirmed that Johnson's personality had made him almost a member of the Lewis's family.[14] After reading that some of Warnie's work pressure had eased, Jack encouraged him, and concurred with his brother's ire over the German propaganda being broadcast over the wireless; still, Jack pointed out that since they were living in a time in which lies were told everywhere, it might be best not to take notice of anything.[15]

In Jack's Christmas Eve letter of December 24, 1939, he sympathized with Warnie's unhappiness at being recalled to active service since there were so many things his brother really wanted to do at home; however, Jack said many of the men of Warnie's age who had been recalled were probably glad to be relieved of their boredom. He likened Warnie's situation to being in prison, and ended the letter on a tender note, admitting that it was a sad reality that Warnie would not be with him on the morrow, and that they would not be taking their annual walking tour.[16] Jack's December 31, 1939, letter shared a picture of the domestic scene at the Kilns that would have comforted Warnie:

You will remember that while I was writing to you last Sunday I was being nearly smoked out of the study. Until the chimney could be cleaned Minto had the fire lit in the bungalow and that became my study for about half of last week. It is not really, as at present furnished, quite as comfortable as the study, and the constant putting on and off of gum-boots becomes a bore: but it's very snug and quiet and has a kind of little-end-room remoteness which you would appreciate. Its aesthetic advantages are great. Stepping out of it . . . at about 6 one evening I thought I had never seen this place more beautiful. Just behind me a moon, the colour of a harvest moon, was rising: the sky was blazing "with few, but with how splendid stars," Jupiter among them: the grass was frosty: into the dimness ahead stretched the white concrete slabs of the path leading the eye on to the dark gable-end of the Kilns proper. An absolute enchantment.[17]

Jack went on to tell Warnie that without him home they did not have much Christmas cheer. Moreover, his walk to Holy Trinity Church for the early morning Christmas service was a sad business as was his journey to an evening party the following night, since Jack always associated such times with Warnie. In a tip to Warnie's motorboating days, Jack told him that he had recently drank a bottle of the red wine on board the *Bosphorus* and found it rather good.[18] He finished the letter by recounting an incident on Boxing Day when Jack had to have a ring hacksawed off his finger after he foolishly jammed it on. Probably to Warnie's delight, Jack compared what he did to something their father would have done: "To you, I expect, the most interesting feature of this event will be the extreme P'dayta-ishness of my act in forcing the damned thing into such a position originally: it being a marked trait in the character of a P'dayta that tho' being physically rather feeble for any useful purpose such as cranking a car or lifting a log, he is subject to fits of demoniac strength when it is a question of jamming, twisting, bursting or crushing anything into ruin."[19] By sharing events like this, Jack did much to make Warnie feel missed and deeply loved.

The new year brought Warnie a new set of health crises. On January 8, 1940, he was admitted to the No. 11 General Hospital, located in Boulogne, France, at 98 Boulevard St. Beuve. Although we cannot be certain as to why Warnie was admitted, most probably it was because of a high fever. Jack's letters of this time recounted a brief walking tour with Cecil Harwood—something Warnie would both have relished and regretted not being a part of—as well his concerns about his brother's health.[20] Warnie's stay in the hospital was brief as he was discharged on January 15. Jack, of course, was relieved to hear this and that Warnie found the hospital stay a good thing on the whole, especially the bed rest and enforced leisure.[21] Less than two weeks later on January 27, Warnie was promoted to the rank of Temporary Major, suggesting that in spite of whatever doubts he had about his fitness for a return to active duty, his superiors found his work deserving of reward.[22] Unfortunately, Warnie had to be admitted to hospital again on January 30 for a high fever, and was transferred to No. 1 General Hospital in Le Havre on February 2. In his February 3 letter to Warnie, Jack—probably unaware of his brother's return to hospital—told him that he had been reading Warnie's diary about their walking tour of January 1938. Jack's recounting of their tour indicated how much he—like Warnie—loved their annual walks. In a sense, Jack's lengthy summary of the tour served as a substitute for the tour they could not take in 1940. While he took great pleasure in reading over Warnie's diary, he noted that he would have enjoyed it more if Warnie had just been away on a short holiday; however, since Warnie was back in service and unable to come home, Jack found himself lonely and depressed. He mused that it did not take long to go from a comfortable privacy to the emptiness of loneliness. The room might look the same, but without Warnie, everything about it changed.[23] As Warnie recovered in the hospital, almost certainly his spirits were revived by Jack's lengthy recounting of their 1938 walk.

In Jack's February 11 letter to Warnie, we get the first hint that his poor health might lead to his being sent home and relieved from active duty. Jack noted that Warnie's most recent letter recounting his lingering fevers gave Jack some hope that his brother's days of active service were numbered. Jack wrote that if his brother had to keep returning to hospital, surely the army would send him home.[24] Warnie was discharged from the hospital on February 12 and returned to active duty at the No. 1 General Base Depot. However, less than a week later on February 18 Warnie was admitted to No. 4 General Hospital, probably in the city of Camiers. Jack's letters of this period expressed his concerns for Warnie's persistent fevers as well as his hope that his brother would soon get leave.[25] In a letter that Warnie posted to Jack on February 28, he indicated that his treatment in the previous hospital, No. 1 General Hospital, had been ineffective, leading Jack on March 3 to express his dismay and opinion that certainly the army would send Warnie home. He also shared that Warnie's recent letter was the only bright spot that day.[26] Jack finished his letter warmly, wishing his brother a gentle recovery and telling him not to hurry the cure. Warnie remained in the No. 4 General Hospital where he did get better until sometime in mid-March when he returned to active duty on March 23 at No. 3 Base Supply Depot.[27]

Over the next two months Jack's letters to Warnie focused upon when he might get leave.[28] Leave finally came around May 7 (when Warnie's unit was evacuated from Dunkirk, weeks before the "Miracle at Dunkirk," which occurred from May 27 to June 4), and Warnie spent a happy week with Jack in Oxford. Writing to Greeves on May 9, Jack said: "Warnie is on leave at the moment: his first since he went out. He is so wholly confident about the war and so different from the people here in that respect that his presence is like a breath of fresh air."[29] Although the brothers spent hours together during the leave, it came to an end when Warnie joined the Supply Technical Training and Mobilization Center, at Wenvoe Camp, Cardiff, Wales. Jack's spirits were lowered by Warnie's departure, but the fact he was not returning to France was a positive. In fact, Warnie never returned to France. We know next to nothing about Warnie's three months in Cardiff. As he passed his forty-fifth birthday on June 16, it is reasonable to surmise that he was depressed by his experience in France during WWII, much of it spent in and out of hospitals. He was on leave in Oxford in late July and dearly longing to be out of the war for good. Jack had some sense that Warnie's days of active service were about to be over, writing to him on August 11 that he was happy to hear the "good news"; at the same time, Jack was trying not to get too excited since he knew it might turn out to be a false hope.[30] Incalculable relief came on August 16 when Warnie received a letter removing him from active service and relegating him to the army reserve. The dismissal letter, by Sergeant H. L. Wilson stated: "It is regretted that the services of Captain W. H. Lewis, currently at the Supply Technical Training and Mobilization Centre, Wenvoe Camp, Cardiff, for duty with No. 3 Base Supply Depot, cannot be retained for the Royal Army Service Corps. Captain Lewis is to be returned to the Regular Army Reserve of Officers, effective on the date of this letter. Pay will cease 28 days from the date of this letter. His name is noted in the event that a suitable vacancy occurs, and he is to be thanked for his service."[31] Upon his return to Oxford, Warnie served as a private soldier with the Sixth Oxford City Home Guard Battalion.[32] And much to his delight, he returned to life aboard the *Bosphorus* during the summer months and served as part of the "floating" Home Guard.

Several of Jack's biographers have given an ominous reading to Warnie's WWII army service, especially regarding his removal from active service. Alister McGrath, for instance, writes: "It is not clear precisely what happened to Warnie's military career, which appears to have imploded at a time when the British army was trying to recover from the near catastrophe of Dunkirk, and needed experienced officers to help with its reconstruction. Warnie's military record offers no explicit reason for his discharge, while leaving its readers wondering what is to be read into its terse statements. Inevitably, given his subsequent history, many will suspect that alcohol addiction played a part in it."[33] George Sayer is even more explicit, writing that when Warnie was recalled to active service, Jack was worried about Warnie's inclination to drink heavily when under pressure. Sayer—who knew Warnie well—argues that Warnie had already been a binge drinker for years, and it was likely he might have disgraced himself through drunkenness while on active service. Sayer concludes: "Even if the worst—a court-martial—did not happen, [Warnie] might behave in a way that he would regret for the rest of his life. Not much is known about what happened to Warnie during his eleven months of active duty. . . . He never spoke about his experiences in the Second World War, and his silence suggests deep shame. Certainly he was drinking heavily then."[34] Lacking any hard evidence from Warnie's official military record, McGrath and Sayer can offer only speculations about the role the abuse of alcohol may have played in Warnie's retirement from active service in August, 1940. Their judgments about Warnie and his removal from active service because of drunkenness are possible. But they are not verifiable. Indeed, since his dismissal letter included that "his name is noted in the event that a suitable vacancy occurs, and he is to be thanked for his service" argues against his being ousted from the RASC because of drunkenness. What we know for sure is that Warnie was not in good health throughout his eleven months of active service; accordingly, it is more likely that poor health, rather than drunkenness, led to his early exit from WWII. Nonetheless, it is important to state that much of Warnie's drinking during his WWII stint was probably self-medication. Unfortunately, rather than help him cope, it worsened things for him. Even if his discharge had nothing to do heavy drinking, his abuse of alcohol exacerbated his recurring health problems.

There are several points to make about Warnie's brief WWII service. Most importantly, his inward turn accelerated. Because there was nothing about his return to the army that he found pleasing, edifying, or profitable, the *curvatus* that began after his retirement to the Kilns in 1932 rapidly advanced. As a result, he spent more and more time in his inner world; other than his relationships with Jack and the Inklings, Warnie's turn within worked insidiously to isolate him. A second point is the way in which Jack—acutely aware of Warnie's misery and depression—went out of his way to encourage his brother by writing lengthy weekly letters, trying as much as possible to project a kind of normality and warmth. Jack's WWII letters to Warnie were purposely newsy. He included details about the arrival of child evacuees; critiques of the Vicar at Holy Trinity; meetings of the Inklings; the books he had been reading; his "public works" projects (his landscaping work around the Kilns); college politics and policies; amusing incidents, conversations, and anecdotes; air raid drills; memories of their father; tiresome domestic "scares"; the drudgery of nightly blackouts; recent local walks and descriptions of the countryside; walking tours with Tolkien and others; and some illustrating his love, worry, and care for Warnie, several ending "God save you, brother." However, Jack's letters were not just for Warnie's benefit; he genuinely feared for his brother's life, so writing to him became something of salve. His worry over Warnie is best revealed a poem he probably wrote sometime in 1939 or 1940, "How Can I Ask Thee, Father":

How can I ask thee, Father, to defend
In peril of war my dearest friend to-day,
As though I knew, better than Thou, the way,
Or with more love than thine desired the end?
When I, for the length of one poor prayer, suspend
So hardly for his sake my thoughts, that stray
And wanton, thrusting twenty times a day,
Clean out of mind the man I call my friend;
Who, if he had from thee, no better care
Than mine, were every moment dead. But prayer
Thou givest to man, not man to thee: thy laws
Suffering our mortal wish that way to share
The eternal will; at taste of whose large air
Man's word becomes, by miracle, a cause.[35]

Finally, there is an irony we should not miss. The twenty-three-year-old Warnie emerged from WWI in 1918 mentally healthy and looking forward to the future. Despite the horrific things he witnessed and experienced on the battlefield, he came out of that terrible conflict relatively unscarred and positive. Conversely, the forty-five-year-old Warnie—who almost certainly saw no direct combat—came out of WWII mentally exhausted, spiritually battered, and physically worn out. If the 1930s were the high-water mark of Warnie's life, the 1940s ushered in his slow ebb into mental, physical, and emotional crises.

When Warnie returned to life at the Kilns, Jack, of course, was elated.[36] In a letter to Greeves, Jack revealed that Warnie was living much of the time on the *Bosphorus* as a part of the Home Guard patrol of the upper Thames River: "He's painted the boat battleship-grey and bought a blue peaked cap so as to emphasise the fact that he's now part of the navy! Dear Warnie—he's one of the simplest souls I know in a way: certainly one of the best at getting simple pleasures."[37] Warnie was ecstatic to be off active duty, and his whimsical purchase of the blue peaked cap was a public way of noting he had gladly traded the life of a soldier for one of a sailor. Changes also greeted Warnie at the Kilns, chief among them was the presence of children evacuated from London. With most of these children, Warnie was shy, polite, and respectful. One of the schoolgirls, Patricia Heidelberger, later wrote that "we didn't have a great deal of rapport with him, though he was always friendly. I would describe him as 'avuncular' [like an uncle] towards us."[38] Warnie's particular favorite came to be Jill Flewett, better known within the household as June. When she left the Kilns several years later to follow her career as an actress, Warnie wrote in his diary:

Our dear, delightful June Flewett leaves us tomorrow, after nearly two years, for London and the Dramatic School where she is to be taught to be an actress. She is not yet eighteen, but I have met no one of any age further advanced in the Christian way of life. From seven in the morning till nine at night, shut off from people of her own age, almost grudged the time for her religious duties, she has slaved at The Kilns. . . . I have never seen her other than gay, eager to anticipate exigent demands, never complaining, always self-accusing in the frequent crises of that dreary house. Her reaction to the meanest ingratitude was to seek its cause in her own faults. She is one of those rare people to whom one can venture to apply the word "saintly." . . . From a personal selfish point of view I shall feel the loss of June very keenly: for in addition to her other virtues, she is a clever girl, and with her gone, it means that when J is away, there is no one to talk to in the house.[39]

June remembered Warnie with deep affection: "He was amusing and enjoyed playing the crusty old bachelor. He and Jack listened to classical music on an old gramaphone with a huge wooden horn. I was sometimes invited to join them for this in Jack's study. I do not remember ever seeing him in a bad mood. . . . In the two years that I shared his home he was consistently kind and courteous to me and I was very fond of him." It is worth noting that June never recalled seeing Warnie drunk.[40]

Jack was also pleased to have Warnie back home since he became Jack's de facto secretary. The volume of Jack's correspondence was increasing quickly because of his growing fame as a Christian apologist, particularly after the publication of *The Screwtape Letters* in 1942. Using his little Royal typewriter—the same one he used to compile the *LP*—Warnie began to answer routine letters. Although there is no way to discern precisely when this began, Walter Hooper says the first of Warnie's typed letters was to the BBC's Eric Fenn of November 30, 1942.[41] Drawing on his logistical experiences as a career RASC officer, Warnie brought his substantial organizational skills, attention to detail, and dogged persistence into service. Jack told Greeves on June 1, 1943, that his brother was helping him as a secretary, typing all his nonpersonal letters.[42] Much in the way that he tackled the enormous amount of work involved in bringing the *LP* to print, Warnie threw himself into systematically opening, arranging, and frequently answering some of the daily letters that arrived at the Kilns. In this way, Warnie relieved Jack of much literary donkeywork. However, Jack was not the only beneficiary of Warnie's assistance. Indeed, his efforts as Jack's secretary filled a large hole in Warnie's life. After his disappointing service in WWII, serving as Jack's secretary provided Warnie with meaningful work and relieved his brother of the bothersome minutiae of correspondence—acquiring stationery, envelopes, and postage, not to mention the daily grind of opening letters, deciding which were important enough to require Jack's attention and which Warnie could handle routinely. All this brought significant purpose and meaning to Warnie's life.

MRS. MOORE

In contrast to Warnie's happy return to the Kilns because of Jack, he was also entering into an almost penitentiary-like existence with Moore. By this time Warnie had a long list of grievances against her, including selfishness, egoism, inflexibility, stubbornness, know-it-all attitude, bossiness, baseless opinions, boring conversation, ignorance, overreactions to the unexpected, unreasonable worries, prejudices, dogmatic positions, condescension, bitter hatreds, petty meanness, and domineering personality.[43] His disaffection for her festered and blistered. One reason for this was that Warnie spent more time at the Kilns and with Moore than did Jack, since as an Oxford don Jack had rooms at Magdalen College to which he could retreat.[44] Warnie had no such haven, and we can only imagine how maddening it must have been for him to be in close daily proximity to someone he found so irritating.[45] Accordingly, it is not entirely surprising that as early as 1936, he began to keep a record of Moore's dogmatic, selfish, and condescending statements and dialogues. To these he added other examples of "wheezes"[46] that he overheard while living in the Kilns, eventually compiling what he called "*Mens Humana* or Kilns Table Talk."[47] Not all these wheezes involved Moore; some were spoken by others among the ill-assorted collection of people Moore gathered around herself at the Kilns. What is most revealing about these wheezes is how they illustrate something of day-to-day life in the Kilns; specifically, they show the atmosphere or tone of life as experienced by Warnie, and, taken as a whole, they reflect his sense of living among a group of people (his brother excepted) that he did not admire, value, or respect. Yet it appears he usually held his tongue, keeping instead his log of wheezes and letting them speak for themselves. In what follows I mine Warnie's "*Mens Humana*," offer explanatory comments, and focus in particular upon his comments regarding Moore, Maureen, and Vera Henry,[48] Moore's goddaughter and occasional Kilns housekeeper.

A close study of the wheezes illustrates a number of consistently appearing characteristics—sometimes singly, but more often than not, in combination.[49] First, some wheezes illustrate a failure by the person in question to understand the point being made, often times with irrelevant or tangential conclusions being reached. In one instance, Jack recounted the story of a brother in a monastery who asked the Abbot that he not be involved in making business decisions;

however, the Abbot, intending to make a point, sent the brother to buy wine for the monastery. This led Jack to surmise that whatever the Abbot's intention, the rest of the monks probably had to drink a good deal of bad wine. On hearing the anecdote, Vera made the irrelevant comment that a local priest would never let her leave his home without offering her some kind of drink.[50] In another instance, two of the Kilns housemaids, Anna and Nellie, passed two young children walking down Kilns Lane. Anna commented that the two children looked very cold. Nellie agreed, making the unwarranted point that they must have lost their father in WWII.[51] One day, Vera praised the honesty of Oxford undergraduates, and offered proof of this by stating that a local café began the term with forty ash trays on the tables and at the end of the term not one of them was missing, never considering that the owner of the café may have been regularly replacing stolen ash trays.[52] During a conversation with Moore, Warnie suggested a furniture store where she could probably find a good used wardrobe; she then asked if it was the place where Warnie bought his pork pies.[53] It is not hard to imagine Warnie scratching his head trying to figure out how such pointless or unrelated conclusions were reached.

Second, some wheezes betray an embarrassing degree of ignorance. Once after Warnie saw the film *King Kong*, the following exchange took place:

> Warren: "The fight between the prehistoric animals was amazingly well done."
> [Moore]: "Were they real prehistoric animals?"[54]

Jack, upon hearing a discussion of Mozart's clarinet quartet, asked innocently but absurdly if it was a work for five clarinets.[55] On another occasion, Warnie told Moore he had read that a man eats less in proportion to his size than other animals, excepting perhaps the elephant. Moore replied, knowingly, that such could not be the case, since an elephant eats more than a man, completely failing to see the point Warnie was making.[56] Maureen once wondered whether it would be cheaper to come back from Egypt on a boat or a vessel, as if there was some difference between the two.[57] In an exchange between Maureen and Kathleen Whitty,[58] after Maureen explained that she and her friends had travelled to the Isle of Wight by the ferry, Whitty asked if was the floating ferry.[59] Maureen once asked if the French celebrated Guy Fawkes Day, November 5, as if the French should want to celebrate this important English holiday.[60] During one Easter season, Warnie opined that one of the guests at the Kilns would want to know where the local Presbyterian Church was located. Moore strongly disagreed, arguing confidently that Presbyterians did not believe in Easter.[61] Moore, when referring to the road to Whipsnade Zoo, insisted that it was level until it began to go uphill.[62] In addition, Moore once pointed out to Maureen a group of carrion crows; in response, Maureen asked what they were carrying.[63] In her study of a map of Africa, Moore asked where Greece was.[64]

Third, some wheezes reveal a deeply held prejudice against Christianity. On one occasion Mrs. Armitage complained to Moore about the recent religious conversion of a girl from a local family. Armitage noted that only a few days before she had met one of the girls who seemed quite ordinary, but when she saw her the next day, the girl said she was about to surrender to Jesus Christ. Moore replied to the news by lamenting that it was a great pity, for the girl had in the past been such a nice person.[65] Maureen commented that she thought religion was a good thing as long as a person did not take it very seriously.[66] Moore, referring to another neighbor, said the woman was the kind of terrible person who brought her religion into her ordinary daily life.[67] In a conversation between Warnie and Moore, she remarked upon the marriage of a young girl, claiming it was a great coup for her since she was of no importance. When Warnie asked what she meant, Moore replied snobbishly that the girl was a nobody because she was the daughter of a county clergyman.[68]

Fourth, some wheezes illustrate a rigid inflexibility or unyielding dogmatism. In one case, Warnie recounted an incident when he arrived at the Kilns around 1:40 P.M. after taking lunch in town at noon. Moore and the cook were frantically working to prepare lunch. Surprised at the late hour, he asked if they had not already lunched. Moore, somewhat testily, replied that no, they had not yet had lunch. Then she complained to him, asking why he had not come to lunch at 1:00 with everyone else, concluding that he would have gotten his lunch just as soon.[69] Maureen once made the argument that when married people quarrel, there was usually fault on the part of both husband and wife. Her mother disagreed strongly, telling Maureen that she did not know what she was talking about. Actually, Moore insisted, often the entire fault was on one side, citing her own case as definitive proof.[70] Moore once complained to Warnie that seaside locations were spoiled by piers. When Warnie countered that many people found a pier to be an attraction, Moore said he was talking nonsense, since she hated piers.[71] During one cold snap, Warnie noted that Kew Observatory said that the coldest February had occurred in 1936. Moore insisted instead that the Kew Observatory was wrong, claiming authoritatively it was colder where they lived from 1922 to 1930.[72] Often a wheeze speaks for itself:

> [Moore] (shouting from hall): "Warnie!"
> Warnie (leaves study and appears): "Well?"
> [Moore]: "What's the time?"

Warnie: "6:45."

[Moore]: "Oh rubbish! It's 6:40."

Warnie (nettled): "Well why ask me?"

[Moore]: "Because I thought you'd tell me right."[73]

Moore's dogmatism was again on display when she claimed that Maureen was the most truthful person she knew, excepting, of course, herself.[74]

Fifth, some wheezes reveal an all-consuming egoism and selfishness. Once Moore was explaining a terrible night she spent recently on board a boat sitting in dock. She recounted how all the lights were turned off, and for the fifty people or so on board, there was only an old stable lantern to light the passage. She called it wicked, since people could have been sick and not been able to see where to walk. So she took the lantern and put it in her own cabin, blind to her selfishness in doing so.[75] On one occasion, an acquaintance of Moore's from Bristol came for an extended visit. Maureen bought her a ticket to a concert in Oxford and drove her into town. When they entered the hall, the woman selfishly told Maureen that if it was raining afterward, she should bring the car to the front door of the hall since she did not want to get her shoes wet.[76] On another occasion, the woman told Warnie not to hang up his coat during a concert since she wanted to wrap it around her feet as a blanket.[77] When Moore complained that the woman's baby's urinating was ruining the furniture, the woman blithely replied that she did not have any waterproof sheets to spare for that problem.[78] Once, Warnie pointed out that the sale of oranges was being limited to children under six because it would help them get the necessary vitamins they needed to grow up strong. Moore was incensed, arguing that old people needed the vitamins. What, she complained, was the point of giving children vitamins since they could not appreciate them.[79] At Moore's request that Warnie lend a guest staying at the Kilns a thimble, he wondered if Moore had a thimble. She admitted she did, but added she never lent it to anyone because thimbles were things one never got back when lent out.[80] On another occasion, Moore, who had no young children and five servants, said to Grace Havard,[81] who had no servants and five young children, that she was very sorry for Grace, feeling that she must be having nearly as bad a time as Moore.[82] When Moore learned that one of the maids was going to have a baby, she complained the maid should have known how unwell Moore was.[83]

Sixth, a great many of the wheezes are marked by irony, unintended humor, double entendres, or malaprops. In a conversation between Vera and Warnie, she noted that she often visited a friend who was married to a captain who hardly ever let a glass whisky out of his hand, going to bed drunk every night. Surprised, Warnie asked if the captain would actually get drunk in his own house before his wife and a guest. Vera replied that he would every night, unless there were other men there; then he would stay perfectly sober. Vera apparently was unable to see the irony that the husband may have gotten drunk when he had to be alone with his wife and her female guests.[84] On one occasion, Warnie asked Paxford how far it would be from the Kilns to Harwell[85] as the crow flies, expecting Paxford to say something like 10 miles; instead, Paxford's droll reply was that it would be pretty straight as the crow flies.[86] During one dinner conversation, Warnie had been grumbling about the local school mistress who had decided to resign her position in order to give birth; in summarizing Warnie's position to several latecomers to the dinner, Maureen said that Warnie did not like his mistresses to bear children.[87] In describing a balding acquaintance named Harry Legge, Maureen offered un-knowingly the *double entendre* that he no longer had any hair except around his bottom.[88] Maureen also pointed out that another of her acquaintances had been granted the power of a tourniquet regarding her father's estate[89] Regarding a mural artist, Maureen said that he covered the walls with rural paintings.[90]

Although these last entries indicate that Warnie sometimes found comedy while residing at the Kilns, more often than not "*Mens Humana*" is a montage revealing the maddening atmosphere within which he lived. With Maureen, Vera, and the others, Warnie was more annoyed or irritated than anything else. How-ever, with Moore—given her snobbery, conceit, pettiness, self-righteousness, and mean-spiritedness—he fairly boiled with anger. She was dogmatic, contentious, and irascible, so that he found her extremely hard to bear. Consider the following exchange:

> [Moore] (inspecting the interior of tea pot testily): "Lor' bless us man, put some more water in it!"
> Warnie: "You said half full; it is half full."
> [Moore] (more testily): "Well but you ought to have known when I said half, I meant three quarters."[91]

Beyond what "*Mens Humana*" tells us about Warnie's jaundiced view of Moore and the many others who passed through the Kilns, we also learn several things about him as a writer. First, he has an historian's sense of what was worth recording; we can surmise that he probably recorded dozens more of these dialogues and conversations.[92] However, instead of reproducing all of them, he is selective, sifting the wheat from the chaff and judiciously including those he thought most illustrative. Second, he has a keen ear for dialogue; in this regard, he avoids embellishment, allowing each speaker's words to reveal facets of his or her character. Third, there is an easy rhythm and measured cadence to his prose;

in the same way that he does not embellish, so he does not overwrite. There are economy and concision in his remarks, and he stays on point, allowing the words to carry the weight and significance of the moment. Finally, rather than paint in miniature his many years of frustration with Moore, he brushes on a broad canvas, noting the quirks, oddities, foibles, peculiarities, and idiosyncrasies of the Kilns menagerie he lived within for more than twenty years.

By the middle of the 1940s, Warnie's long-simmering dislike of Moore boiled over into something approaching hatred. Before exploring in more detail Warnie's reasons for his accelerating dislike of Moore, it is worth noting that Jack, at least before her death, rarely revealed anything about living with Moore. In his autobiography, *Surprised by Joy,* he only offered one veiled comment regarding their relationship. After finishing his service in WWI, he returned to Oxford in early 1919 and wrote: "But before I say anything of my life there I must warn the reader that one huge and complex episode will be omitted. I have no choice about this reticence. All I can or need say is that my earlier hostility to the emotions was very fully and variously avenged. But even were I free to tell the story, I doubt if it has much to do with the subject of this book."[93] It was only after Moore's health began to deteriorate and she was moved to a nursing home in 1950 that Lewis occasionally shared in letters what it had been like to live with her. For instance, on April 5, 1950, he wrote to Greeves that he must put off a visit to Ireland until after Moore entered the nursing home; although he dreaded the expense, "in one way it will be an enormous liberation for me. . . . I hardly know how I feel—relief, pity, hope, terror, & bewilderment have me in a whirl."[94] On June 15, 1950, he told Greeves that Moore seemed to have adjusted to the nursing home, and then added: "Remember that if you can get over to England the Kilns is *now* a house less horrible to stay in than I know it was before."[95] To another correspondent, he wrote on July 26, 1950, that Moore was more at peace now than in previous years: "She was for many years of a worrying and, to speak frankly, a jealous, exacting, and angry disposition."[96]

When Warnie wrote June on behalf of Jack, he shared their distress at Moore's deteriorating condition: "Minto continues much the same, some days recognizing us, some days not. It sounds horribly unChristian and callous, but I can't help wishing she would die. Can you imagine anything more horrible than lingering on in this state?"[97] In other letters, Jack admitted that Moore's removal to the nursing home gave him the liberty to plan his days and be free from time-consuming domestic duties for the first time in fifteen years; in one case he described his life as now being both more physically comfortable and psychologically harmonious.[98] Jack confided to Mary Van Deusen "that I have lived [most of my life] in a house wh. was hardly ever at peace for 24 hours, amidst senseless wranglings, lyings, backbitings, follies, and *scares*. I never went home without a feeling of terror as to what appalling situation might have developed in my absence."[99] And to his friend Sister Penelope (Ruth Penelope Lawson), he shared: "[Minto] died almost a year ago. . . . I beg you will often pray for her. She was an unbeliever and, in later years, very jealous, exacting, and irascible, but always tender to the poor and to animals."[100]

Jack's belated confessions about how hard it was living with Moore provide an additional context for Warnie's view of her. Not only was Warnie jealous of how Moore dominated his brother's life, but also the longer he lived with her, the more he found her personality infuriating. In many of his diary entries after WWII but before her death, he revealed how difficult it was to live with her as well as her gradual slide toward madness. On one occasion after Moore related a story in which she believed one of the servants was planning to murder her, Warnie wrote: "I am getting frightened about Minto. It is an appalling thing to say, but she seems to me to be going mad through trying to live on hate instead of love. . . . Her ideal seems to be hate. I feel that she has been dying for years, and all is white ash now except the flame of greed and hate which is burning even more brightly than it did ten or fifteen years ago."[101] In another diary entry, he related episodes of how Moore, in petty and spiteful ways, pitted servants against one another in an effort to manipulate and control them. Things were so bad that their family doctor, Havard, told him Moore might collapse at any time, begin to rave madly, and then be helpless for several weeks, after which she would die. Warnie felt guilty thinking about how relieved he would be if Moore did die.[102] In fact, Moore came near death in March 1947. Warnie wrote that while he felt some sorrow for her, her bitter, selfish dealings depressed him and made living at the Kilns a misery. "Here is a woman, who has been, if not at Death's door, at least at his front gate: and the very minute returning strength enables her to do so, she is hard at work building up again the flame of her envy, hatred and malice. When I go into her room and look at the puckered old mouth bubbling and slobbering venom, I can almost say that I feel 'literally' sick: do at least *literally* feel that she and her room stink, and that I must get out into the fresh air."[103] Six months later, he worried that Jack would never find rest from caring for Moore, and that after he died Moore would continue to haunt the Kilns. Warnie was so distraught with her that he claimed she was the human equivalent of Shelob.[104]

By the summer of 1948, Moore admitted that she was depressed and wished that she and her dog, Bruce, would die so they would no longer be burdens on the Kilns. Warnie wrote that Moore's depressing words were ones he could not bear, nor could he offer any comfort to her.[105] On January 28, 1949, Warnie related an incident in which Moore arbitrarily decided that Jack could no longer sit in his study in the afternoon because the dining room fire was to be lit instead of the study fire in order to save fuel. When Warnie asked Vera where the saving of fuel was, she replied that there was none, but Moore's nitpicking demands upon Jack were more readily made if he was in the dining room.[106] Later that summer, Warnie, dealing with his own depression, cited a line by Omar Khayyam: "Who said 'I myself am heaven and hell?' True of me, truer of Minto: but the writer forgot to note that such a hell as M[into] lives in, poisons the lives of all who come in contact with it. It is at times very, very hard to keep in mind that Christ died for her."[107] On January 17, 1950, some relief came as Bruce—an animal that Warnie had come to despise as much as Moore—died. Warnie related that in the dog's final days, as Moore's mind began to slide more quickly toward insanity, having someone walk Bruce was an obsession for her. Often Moore insisted that Jack take the dog out three times in an hour. Warnie's disgust with the entire matter culminated in his writing: "For months past [Bruce] had shit in M's tiny overheated bedroom and stunk out the house. How she stood living in what was practically an open latrine I don't know, but that was her affair. . . . I am resting now in a delicious unaccustomed peace; but I wish Paxford had been able to bury the *stench* as well as the dog!"[108]

Blessed relief came to Warnie when Moore was admitted to Restholme, a nursing home near the center of Oxford, on April 29, 1950. Warnie could hardly believe how pleasurable living at the Kilns was without Moore. Items that she had vetoed or banned, were now everywhere present, leading him to write how wonderful it was now that Moore no longer ruled the Kilns.[109] Within nine months of her being placed at Restholme, Moore died on January 12, 1951. Following her death, Warnie described with some bitterness his antipathy for her, regretting Jack's "crushing misfortune" in meeting her. Moreover, Warnie characterized Moore's domination of his brother as "the major disaster of the rape of J's life." He also emphasized Moore's selfishness, egoism, and dogmatism.[110] While Warnie's reference to Moore's years with his brother as "the rape of J's life" is hyperbolic and ungracious, there is little question that she was not an easy person to live with. However, he did express some sympathy for her: "Great though her influence on J was, it was not absolute, for she never succeeded in making him quarrel with me. And indeed, to do her justice, she put up with my debaucheries[111] in a way which many a better woman would not have done."[112]

After thinking for some time about the nature of Warnie's relationship with Moore, I offer several reflections. First, although Warnie says it was a crushing misfortune that his brother ever met Moore, I think it was also the case for Warnie since most of his life after WWI—and particularly after his retirement from the RASC—was blighted by his years of living with her at the Kilns. Within only a few years of moving to the Kilns, Warnie was profoundly unhappy there; his relationship with Moore poisoned his life, making living at the Kilns like being in an unwelcoming army billet. While it would be unfair to blame Moore for Warnie's slide into alcoholism, it has to be said that his feelings toward her certainly led him to drink excessively at times as a way of coping with being around her. Second, at the center of the conflict between Warnie and Moore was Jack. Both wanted the lion's share of his attention, and so they were jealous of each other. Moore replaced her son, Paddy, lost in WWI, with Jack; she became possessive and obsessive about him, and she fought against anything or anyone that threatened their relationship. Warnie longed to return to the idyllic days when he and Jack were in the little attic room at Leeborough; he resented Moore's hold over Jack, finding it mysterious, bizarre, and pathological. If two people ever fought each other over the soul of a third, it was Moore and Warnie. Finally, both Moore and Warnie were emotionally dependent persons. Both needed someone to serve as a beacon, to be the focus of their lives—lives that sought to find meaning and purpose in what was oftentimes an existence marked by uncertainty, confusion, and heartache. Warnie and Moore would never have known each other, much less lived together for over twenty years, had not both loved Jack so much.

There are other more kindly and generous views of Moore. For instance, George Sayer writes:

> Mrs. Moore possessed to a high degree the virtue of hospitality. Her house was always open to her daughter's friends and their friends too. Everything Jack said to me on the subject of her hospitality convinces me that he approved and learned much from it. . . . On the two occasions when I was invited to go and have tea on the lawn with Mrs. Moore, I found the atmosphere pleasant and cheerful. She was a most generous person, who gave shelter to many, usually, but not always young, men and women, who needed help and kindness. Impulsive, enthusiastic, and perhaps rather scatter-brained, she tended to be emotionally involved with all of them, which made her exaggerate their virtues when she first knew them, and then become disillusioned and even dislike them later. . . . A girlhood that had obliged her to act the role of housekeeper for her widowed father and mother for the younger children had made her bossy and self-opinionated. Age and infirmity, such as the nagging discomfort of varicose veins, unfortunately encouraged the growth of these defects.[113]

Owen Barfield claims that Warnie's portrait of Moore as "a kind of baneful stepmother and inexorable taskmistress" is inaccurate: "If she imposed some burdens on [Jack], she saved him from others by taking them on herself even against his protestations. Moreover she was deeply concerned to further his career. . . . [There were years that to all] friends and visitors, [they] looked like a normal and reasonably happy family life. I recall more than one quite jolly social evening at Hillsboro with the three of them, Lewis, Mrs. Moore and her daughter, Maureen."[114] In *C. S. Lewis Remembered,* Barfield adds:

> I know quite a lot and I have read quite a lot of what has been written about Mrs. Moore since Lewis's death, a great deal of it very unfavorable, giving a very unfavorable impression of her. Now that may be not inaccurate as to the later years of her life, and I hardly ever saw her. She may have grown into perhaps a peevish old lady. At the time when I knew him then as an undergraduate and also for quite a number of years afterward, after I was married and my wife and I both used to go and visit them in the Kilns, my wife and I both had the impression that Mrs. Moore was really extremely good to these two brothers. By that time Warnie, his brother, was also living there, and she was extremely good to them, looking after them very well. I think I remember my wife saying on one occasion, "How she spoils those two!" I mention that to add a little balance to what you may have read about Mrs. Moore. She was not by any means only an ogre. Or ogress, I suppose I should say.[115]

And Paxford remembers Moore fondly: "She was like a mother to Mr. Jack, and he always called her Mintoes. She was also very good to me. She had one funny little habit when she was bottling fruit and shaking it down in the bottles: she always had part of her tongue showing between her lips. She was also very fond of flowers, never had too many. She bottled a lot of fruit and gave a lot of it away. She gave a lot of eggs away as well. She had a kind nature. Anyone who came to the Kilns for help nearly always went away with money, and if it was a man, a handful of cigarettes."[116] Walter Hooper also suggests that "for every one who did not like Mrs. Moore, I have come across a dozen who seemed genuinely devoted to her. This includes many of her neighbours who were still living near the Kilns when I was there."[117]

These accounts of Moore are significant and worth noting. However, none of these men—Sayer, Barfield, Paxford (he lived in a separate cottage on the Kilns property) or Hooper—actually lived in the Kilns with Moore and would have had the day-to-day, private contact with her that Warnie did. While we should not discount their views, neither should we give them greater weight in comparison to Warnie's. Because he lived in close proximity to Moore, he had a more informed, intimate, and daily view of her than anyone else, excepting his brother. Moreover, Warnie's experiential reality was living with Moore, and his view of her—uncharitable as it may seem to some—nonetheless reflects his subjective, existential, and palpable everyday record of life with her.

WARNIE'S ALCOHOLISM

Contiguous with Warnie's unhappy life with Moore at the Kilns was his long-standing and increasingly uncontrollable problem with alcohol. We know from his years in the army that he had become a heavy drinker. Often his diary entries indicated that he knew he was drinking too much. During WWI, he referred to waking up with an aching head because the evening before he had one drink too many or because he had two more whiskeys than he had intended.[118] He frequented drinking parties daily or would host events that gave those attending as much alcohol as they could drink.[119] Whiskey was his preferred drink, although he expressed enjoying beer, cocktails, rum, gin, wine, port, sherry, brandy, and ale. After the war, his drinking did not slacken, and often entire days were planned around what he could find to drink or where he could go to obtain alcohol. In addition, when he went home to Belfast to be with his father, he looked for opportunities to indulge, often effectively stealing alcohol whenever his father asked him to go to the wine cellar to retrieve a bottle.[120]

His yearlong tour of duty in Sierra Leone from March 1921 to April 1922 only intensified his drinking; the weather and climate were terrible as far Warnie was concerned, and, other than his routine duties, most of his time was spent trying to find relief from the heat and boredom. Frequently the easiest way to do this was through alcohol. Late evening drinking sessions where he would get "tight" were often mentioned. Sometimes complete days were spent drinking beer and reading. Occasionally, he would rebuke himself, promising to cut down to only three drinks a day.[121] Among his New Year's resolutions for 1922 were to keep out of debt, lessen his expenses, and limit his intake of alcohol.[122] Two days later, he broke all three. After he returned to England, his cited an old drinking song in his diary:

If sadly thinking, with spirits sinking,
Could more than drinking my cares compose,
A cure for sorrow from sighs I'd borrow,
And hope tomorrow would end my woes.
But as in wailing there's nought availing,

And Death unfailing will strike the blow,
Then for that reason, and for a season,
Let us be merry before we go.[123]

Although intended as lighthearted comment on the use of alcohol, this verse also underscored Warnie's melancholic mindset. While his return to England meant less boredom and more comfortable living conditions, his drinking carried on much as it had before.

During his years in Shanghai—as in Sierra Leone—other than work, much of his time was spent filling long periods of boredom. Not surprisingly, frequently heavy drinking was the result, with many of his diary entries detailing cocktail parties, bar gatherings, communal nightcaps, sizable purchases of whiskey, and large-scale alcohol consumption at special events. In one instance, Warnie gathered with others to celebrate Russian Easter Sunday on April 15, 1928. He noted how his father would have enjoyed the event, since for the most part the participants would gulp down the alcohol, eat a little food, and then gulp down some more. The goal was to see who would be the last man standing.[124] At the time of one of the armed conflicts between the Japanese Imperial Army and China, Warnie wrote that because he and his fellow soldiers were both bored and frightened, many had become alcoholics.[125] On the morning he set sail back to England in 1930, he recorded that he felt sick and shaky; however, he attributed his feelings not to seasickness but instead to too much whiskey.[126] Many of his diary entries during the voyage home chronicled his drinking, and he was quite surprised during the stop in San Francisco when he drank and savored nonalcoholic Busch Lager.[127]

After fourteenth months serving the RASC in England, Warnie did his final fourteen-month tour of duty in Shanghai from October 9, 1931, to December 14, 1932. It appears he managed to control his abuse of alcohol to some degree, but he usually ended each day with a whiskey and soda.[128] When he retired from the RASC, Warnie wrote less in his diary about drinking and more about his walking tours with Jack, his work on the *Lewis Papers*, his travels on the *Bosphorus*, and his involvement with Inklings meetings. Although it is hard to ascertain how much he was drinking at this time, given that he was fully engaged in these other matters, throughout the 1930s Warnie was probably a moderate drinker, consuming alcohol at meals, in pubs, and other social gatherings. It is also possible that his return to Christian belief aided him in curtailing his excessive drinking. Be that as it may, I believe the turning point in Warnie's abuse of alcohol coincided with his eleven months service in WWII. I have already suggested that several of Jack's biographers believe Warnie's short time of active service strongly hints that his early dismissal was due to excessive drinking. We do not know, and we probably will never know. However, we do know that beginning in 1943, even Warnie admitted he was drinking too much. For example, in his diary entry on February 22, 1943, he admitted: "We dined and wined in [Magdalen] College, [our host] very civilly speeding the usual tempo of the circulation of the decanters, for my special benefit, as he pointed out. . . . Before going to bed I had a whiskey and soda: the first I have tasted since I was up in town in the middle of December: and I had forgotten what a delicious drink it is when one is tired, and *uses* instead of abusing it."[129]

Other matters contributed to his increasing reliance on alcohol, including his deteriorating relationship with Moore and the harsh reality of life in post–WWII England. It was not a pleasant place to live. Rationing was still in effect, so that food, clothing, medicine, and fuel were scarce. The winter of 1946 to 1947 was terrible—England's snowiest and most frigid of the twentieth century. The brutal weather added to the hardships England was experiencing as it tried to recover from the damage and deprivations the war.[130] Ruth Pitter—who Warnie came to know and admire—captured something of the dark mood of many regarding this terrible weather in her poem "The Great Winter, 1946–1947":

> The leaves die, fall and go.
> They lie all under the snow.
> In the great snow the grass dies;
> Still the deep clouds fill the skies.
> Summer wept, and now the east
> Roaring falls on man and beast.
>
> And man and beast die, fall and go;
> Under the sky's pall, rain or snow;
> Neither hut nor palace stays
> The sure ending of their days;
> Age and sickness and the wars
> Stretch them stiff beneath the stars.
>
> And the stars die, fall and go.
> Eye by eye, they cease to glow;
> Orb by orb, the storm of suns
> To its end in glory runs;
> The great wheels, the galaxies,
> Shall turn no more about the skies.

Since all must die, fall and go,
Why do we mourn that it is so?
All mourn, lament and weep
That creation falls asleep?
This was given us to make
Our spirits homeless for His sake.[131]

Warnie would have resonated with the sobering tone of this poem, and his diary reflected his slide into a weather induced depression. On February 20, 1946, he noted:

> The bitter cold continues with the same intensity, and the whole machinery of the country is slipping into chaos; we are in fact experiencing the sort of thing that one thought only happened to peoples one reads about in the papers—factories at a standstill, light and power cut off even from factories on export work, growing shortage of food etc. etc. . . . I am slowly beginning to realize that the depression which has formed the background to my mind for some weeks now must be permanent, for a very good reason; in other days I have had my bad times—very bad times—but there has hitherto always been something to look forward to. Now there is nothing, and never will be again; as the senior shop assistant said to Mr. Polly—"We're all crawling down a drain pipe: and there's no way out."[132]

Later that spring, Jack revealed for the first time in a letter to June that Warnie had been drinking heavily, writing that he had one of his alcoholic bouts but was now better.[133] Once the weather cleared a bit, Warnie went on holiday to Exmouth with Herbert Parkin for a month in May and June 1946; however, Parkin's own depression did little to help Warnie deal with his dark view of life.[134]

The atrocious weather continued into the next year. Warnie noted that there had been fifty-five straight days of terrible cold, leading him into despair. The snow was constant and the winds strong and unrelenting, causing him to fear that the chimney in his study would fall down. Trees had fallen across Magdalen College bridge, and another had crashed into a driver, injuring him badly.[135] That Jack referred to one of Warnie's drinking bouts in his letter to June suggests that his abuse of alcohol had been going on for some time, but it is not possible to discern precisely a particular date when it first started. Warnie continued his heavy drinking, but a year later he cherished a holiday with Jack in Malvern, April 4–17, 1947. However, in contemplating his return to the Kilns and Moore, he was greatly depressed since he loathed every square inch of the house.[136]

On June 11, 1946, Warnie's spirits were briefly raised when he went on holiday to Ireland. He found it incredible that he was able to get away, although he admitted guilt at leaving Jack alone with Moore.[137] Warnie had hoped that Parkin would be able to join him, but when that fell through, he was left alone to mull over his black mood.[138] The cottage he was renting in Ireland—isolated, cold, and without running water—and its melancholic atmosphere drove him into deep waves of depression, prompting him to drink heavily. Unfortunately, he unwittingly purchased a bottle of gin spiked with methanol. By June 20, Warnie knew he was experiencing alcohol poisoning, and he found a local doctor who arranged to have him admitted to the Convent Hospital of Our Lady of Lourdes in Drogheda, 30 miles north of Dublin. During his first night there, he was certain he was dying and fearful that he would never see Jack again. Despite Warnie's protests, the staff wired Jack and urged him to come see his brother. When Jack arrived on June 23, Warnie could tell he was worried and worn-out; nevertheless, his arrival did Warnie more good than any medical treatment could have because he had so feared that he might die before seeing Jack.[139]

Blind to the now obvious truth that he was an alcoholic, a few days later Warnie assumed he was "cured," giving much of the credit to the Roman Catholic Sisters of the Medical Missionaries of Mary who had nursed him along. The gentle kindness and winsome care of these women contrasted with all he had ever imagined about convents and nuns. Rather than being a place of darkness, superstition, and pinched-faced prudes, in the hospital Warnie experienced a joy and happiness he could never have imagined possible. In fact, the nuns cared for him tenderly and lovingly, and he basked in the tranquil surroundings. He said he would "not soon or easily forget this little fortress of happy, valiant Christianity."[140] Warnie's recovery at the convent was both fortuitous and a foreshadowing, since in the years to come he would return to it a number of times during repeated alcoholic binges.[141] This crucial episode in Warnie's struggle with alcoholism finished with Warnie and Jack on June 28 moving to the White Horse in Drogheda, a pub Warnie described as his sort of pub—not fancy, off the beaten track, and accommodating.[142] They spent several happy days there, taking a number of walks that reminded Warnie of their annual walking tours in the 1930s.[143] However, Jack had to return to Oxford before Warnie, leading him write on June 30: "[Today] I said goodbye to [Jack] with much depression at quarter to five; there are times when in retrospect my life seems to have consisted in saying goodbye to J. . . . I got back to my room before going to bed [and] had my solitary glass of sherry; whilst drinking it I was struck with the haunting fear that is so often with me—suppose J were to die before I did? And a sheer wave of animal panic spread over me at the prospect of the empty years; but I pulled myself together, said my prayers, and tumbled into bed."[144]

Although Warnie was particularly happy that Jack had joined him in Drogheda, he continued to avoid confronting the truth that he was an alcoholic.[145] Despite his belief that he was cured, he was not, and his excessive drinking continued for the next two years, leading to a number of crises, culminating in a series of episodes occurring in 1949.[146] In late February or early March, Warnie's drinking landed him in the Acland Nursing Home in Oxford. He was released from the Acland on March 3, 1949, and the next day he wrote in his diary: "I emerged from the Acland yesterday morning, where I had been as a finale to the wearisome cycle of insomnia—drugs—depression—*spirits*—illness. The saddest feature of the thing is that I can see that J, mine own familiar friend doesn't believe this to be the cycle, but assumes it to be *spirits*—insomnia—drugs—depression—spirits—illness. But his kindness remains unabated, and what more can I want?"[147] Importantly, this entry shows that by now it was obvious to Jack that Warnie was an alcoholic. Unhappily, Warnie's bouts with heavy drinking contributed to Jack's own emotional and physical deterioration. In fact, Jack had been admitted to the Acland in early June 1949 for exhaustion, probably related to his distress about Warnie as well as the burden of caring for the now dementia-afflicted Moore. Warnie was greatly distressed when Jack entered the Acland.[148] Furious at Moore and blaming her for Jack's illness, Warnie insisted that Jack have a break away from caring for her, in part because their doctor, Havard, recommended it. Relieved and excited, Jack planned to take a break from Moore and to recuperate in Ireland, hoping that Warnie would stay with Moore. Jack wrote Greeves on June 21: "I have been ill and am ordered a real change. I'm coming home (Belfast) for a month. . . . And of course I want to be with you as much as possible. Can you find me a nice little hotel (or decent rooms) near your cottage? If you wd. care for us to go somewhere else for part of the time together. . . . I'm your man. I shall be free for once. . . . It seems too good to be true."[149]

Indeed, it was too good to be true. Warnie continued to drink heavily, so that on July 2 Jack wrote Greeves and called off the trip, confiding that

It is much darker than I feared. W's trouble is to be called "nervous insomnia" in speaking to . . . others: but in reality (this for yr. private ear) it is Drink. This bout started about ten days ago. Last Sunday the Doctor and I begged him to go into [the Acland] Nursing Home (that has always effectively ended previous bouts) and he refused. Yesterday we succeeded in getting him in: but alas, too late. The Nursing Home has announced this morning that he is out of control and they refuse to keep him. To day a mental specialist is to see him and he will be transferred, I hope for a *short* stay, to what is called a hospital but is really an asylum.[150] Naturally there is no question of a later Irish jaunt for me this year.[151]

Three days later Jack offered even more details about Warnie's problem, telling Owen Barfield that the Acland had relented and allowed Warnie one more opportunity to stay there, as long as someone sat outside his door from 8 P.M. to 5 A.M., a task that Jack took on. Jack explained to Barfield that the idea of keeping him in the Acland was to prevent his drinking and to compel him to take bromides as prescribed. Then Jack revealed Warnie's repeated pattern of drinking:

> [Warnie's] general plan is heavy drinking for 3 days, a terrific overdose of dope[152] followed by 3 days' almost continuous sleep, and announcement that he is 'cured,' then 3 more days drink—an so on. The two things I'm chiefly afraid of are (a.) The traffic in the streets: I have found him being *led* to my rooms [at Magdalen College] by a grinning scout[153] (b.) lest he should insult someone. Drink uncovers a quite unsuspected side in him. He keeps on talking about who is or isn't a gentleman . . . and describing people as "gutter-filth."[154]

The next day, Jack declared to Greeves that Warnie was a dipsomaniac.[155] Still, Warnie was unwilling to admit the truth, naïvely believing he could control his intake of alcohol. For example, in August 1949 Warnie wrote about a trip to Euston where he tried to prove to himself that he had learned how to control his drinking. He entered a bar and purposely risked drinking a large whiskey, and then reflected that he was glad he did so. Warnie fooled himself into believing his prayers had been granted so that he could now use alcohol in moderation.[156] However, over the next three weeks his diary entries highlighted how each day revolved around ensuring that he had ready access to alcohol.

For the rest of his life, Jack would worry about Warnie's next "episode," undoubtedly undermining the quality of his own life. Despite Warnie's self-efforts, over the next two years there is no evidence he curtailed his drinking, and his diary confirms that he returned to at least the same level of drinking as he had up to the earlier crisis in June and July 1947. Certainly, Moore's downward spiral toward dementia, and Warnie's view of life at the Kilns as horrid, as well as his frequent attendance at the twice weekly meetings of the Inklings, ensured that he would not moderate his consumption of alcohol. Warnie, notwithstanding the best of intentions and numerous resolutions to manage his drinking, remained in the grip of alcohol for the rest of his life. There would be extended periods of sobriety—some lasting almost a year—but eventually something would trigger another binge. Warnie was gripped by alcohol and ineffectual in managing his addiction.

WARNIE AND THE INKLINGS: PART 2

As I suggested in the last chapter, one of Warnie's greatest pleasures after being reunited with Jack was meeting with the Inklings. Although the Inklings
formed initially in the late 1920s around Jack and Tolkien, many have noted that
once Warnie joined them as the third most frequent attendee, the group took
off. We know he was routinely attending the meetings from 1934 through late
August 1939, but when he was called to active service in WWII, he was unable
to attend their meetings until after his return to civilian life on August 16, 1940.
From that time forward, he was a fixture at the meetings, becoming the affable
de facto host of the meetings. In Warnie's "Memoir," he offered a number of
important general comments about an Inklings gathering, noting that "properly speaking [the Inklings] was neither a club nor a literary society, though it
partook of the nature of both. There were no rules, officers, agendas, or formal
elections—unless one counts it as a rule that we met in Jack's rooms at Magdalen
every Thursday evening after dinner."[157] Meetings never had an official starting
or ending time "though there was a tacit agreement that ten-thirty was as late
as one could decently arrive."[158] Occasionally, a new man would join them by
common agreement. Warnie noted that the ritual of a meeting was predictable,
marked by a gathering of six or so, the appearance of a pot of tea, the lighting
of pipes, and then Jack asking if anyone had something to read.[159] Someone
would then pull out a manuscript and begin to read. The others would listen
and "sit in judgment upon it—real unbiased judgement, too, since we were not
a mutual admiration society: praise for good work was unstinted, but censure
for bad work—or even not-so-good work—was often brutally frank. To read
to the Inklings was a formidable ordeal."[160] On the evenings when no one had
anything to read, Warnie said that the fun could be riotous, usually led by Jack's
wit and humor: "At the Inklings [Jack's] talk was an outpouring of wit, nonsense,
whimsy, dialectical swordplay, and pungent judgement such as I have rarely heard
equaled."[161] Moreover, Warnie affirmed that a second weekly gathering of the
Inklings occurred every Tuesday prior to lunch at the Eagle and Child pub. [162]

Who were the men we now think of as the Inklings? Scholar Diana Glyer
argues that nineteen men comprised the group: Owen Barfield, J. A. W. Bennett,
David Cecil, Nevill Coghill, James Dundas-Grant, H. V. D. Dyson, Adam Fox,
Colin Hardie, Robert E. Havard, C. S. Lewis, Warren Lewis, Gervase Mathew,
R. B. McCallum, C. E. Stevens, Christopher Tolkien, J. R. R. Tolkien, John Wain,
Charles Williams, and C. L. Wrenn.[163] It is almost certain that there never was
a gathering of the Inklings when all nineteen were present; indeed, most meetings had anywhere from three to eight present. Interestingly, because minutes
were never taken of Inklings' meetings, until recently we had no comprehensive

record of their meetings from 1933 to 1954, either the documented or possible gatherings.[164] However, I have cross-referenced a number of primary documents so that we now have that record, and a number of observations are worth noting.[165] First, there were 93 documented meetings and 1048 possible meetings of the Inklings from 1933 to 1954, for a total of 1141 possible gatherings. If we assume the average meeting lasted two hours, this means that the range of hours some portion of the Inklings collectively spent together falls somewhere between 186 and 2,282 (see Chart 1).[166] We can only imagine the range of serious discussions as well as the jokes, teasing, and verbal horseplay that occurred during these meetings. The most concentrated period of documented meetings occurred between May 15, 1945, and March 18, 1948, when there were 48 gatherings (or 52 percent of all documented meetings).

Chart 1: Documented and possible meetings of the Inklings

YEAR	DOCUMENTED MEETINGS	POSSIBLE MEETINGS
Fall 1933 to Fall 1937	2	Irregular, nondocumented
1938	0	Irregular, nondocumented
1939	5	27
1940	9	94
1941	1	99
1942	None	105
1943	1	103
1944	16	89
1945	6	75
1946	17	68
1947	17	61
1948	8	76
1949	3	65
1950	3	41
1951	3	37
1952	1	41
1953	0	40
1954	1	27
TOTAL	93	1048

Second, after Jack, Tolkien, and Warnie, the most frequent attendees at documented meetings were Robert Havard (32), Charles Williams (24), Colin Hardie (20), Christopher Tolkien (19), and Hugo Dyson (13). Conversely, the group most often not at documented meetings includes Owen Barfield (3), J. A. W. Bennett

(2), Adam Fox (1), and Nevill Coghill (0). Barfield's infrequent appearances are not surprising since he was a busy solicitor in London and would have had a difficult time getting back and forth to Oxford. Coghill's absence at all the documented meetings is noteworthy and challenges the argument made in *The Fellowship: The Literary Lives of the Inklings: J. R. R. Tolkien, C. S. Lewis, Owen Barfield, Charles Williams* that "Lewis, Warnie, Tolkien, Coghill, and Dyson attended most meetings, and Barfield came up from London when possible" (199). Of course, in the case of Coghill he may have been a regular attendee at the undocumented meetings of the Inklings.

Third, most of what we know about the documented Inklings' gatherings are from Jack, Warnie, and Tolkien, since of the 93 meetings, we find evidence in their letters and diaries of 84 of them. In *The Collected Letters of C. S. Lewis, Volume 2: Books, Broadcasts and the War, 1931–1949,* Jack documents 15 meetings between October 1937 and February 1943. Tolkien, in *The Letters of J. R. R. Tolkien,* writes about 18 meetings between April 1944 and February 1952. However, we owe most of what we know about the documented meetings to Warnie, since he writes in his diary of 51 (or 55 percent) of the gatherings between May 1945 and February 1951—either in *BF* (37) or in the unpublished portion of his diary (14). All three tend to give the contexts of the gatherings—what were the topics, discussions, or disputes. For instance, Jack gave a flavor of what made these gathering so special in a letter of December 21, 1941, to Dom Bede Griffiths: "[Charles] Williams, [Hugo] Dyson of Reading, & my brother (Anglicans) and [J. R. R.] Tolkien and my doctor, [Robert] Havard (your Church) are the 'Inklings' to whom my Problem of Pain was dedicated. We meet . . . in my rooms: theoretically to talk about literature, but in fact nearly always to talk about something better. What I owe to them all is incalculable. Dyson and Tolkien were the immediate human causes of my own conversion. Is any pleasure on earth as great as a circle of Christian friends by a good fire?"[167]

When Tolkien wrote about an Inklings' meeting, he tended to give a detailed account of what took place, and often mentioned Warnie. For instance, regarding the meeting on November 23, 1944, he wrote his son Christopher:

I reached the Mitre [pub] at 8 where I was joined by C[harles].W[illiams]. and the Red Admiral (Havard), resolved to take fuel on board before joining the well-oiled diners in Magdalen (C. S. L. and Owen Barfield). C. S. L. was highly flown, but we were also in good fettle; while O. B. is the only man who can tackle C. S. L. making him define everything and interrupting his most dogmatic pronouncements with subtle [distinctions]. The result was a most amusing and highly contentious evening, on which (had an outsider eavesdropped) he would have thought it a meeting of fell enemies hurling deadly insults before drawing their guns. Warnie was in excellent majoral form. On one occasion when the audience had flatly refused to hear Jack discourse on and define 'Chance', Jack said: 'Very well, some other time, but if you die tonight you'll be cut off knowing a great deal less about Chance than you might have.' Warnie: 'That only illustrates what I've always said: every cloud has a silver lining.'"[168]

Warnie's wit struck Tolkien on other occasions. When he first learned Warnie was writing a book, Tolkien said that it must be because he had been attending so many Inklings meetings and that when Warnie read a portion of it to the group, he found it witty and entertaining.[169]

Other Inklings also recalled the quality of their meetings. For instance, James Dundas-Grant offered a snapshot of their gatherings: "We met every Tuesday morning over a glass of beer. Warnie, [Jack's] brother was there; MacCallum . . . Gervase Mathew . . . Tolkien . . . and Havard. We sat in a small back room . . . back and forth the conversation would flow. Latin tags flying around. Homer quoted in the original to make a point. And Tolkien, jumping up and down, declaiming in Anglo-Saxon."[170] Havard, after Jack, Warnie, and Tolkien, the fourth most frequent Inklings attendee, shared a sense of the intoxicating flavor of a gathering: "The usual procedure [of a meeting], after drinks and gossip had been exchanged, was to settle into armchairs and then for someone to be invited to read a recent manuscript. The rest then commented, led nearly always by [Jack]. Criticism was frank but friendly. Coming from a highly literate audience, it was often profuse and detailed. . . . The talk was good, witty, learned, high hearted, and very stimulating."[171] John Wain vividly remembered the meetings in Lewis's rooms:

> I can see that room so clearly now, the electric fire pumping heat into the dank air, the faded screen that broke some of the keener draughts, the enamel beer-jug on the table, the well-worn sofa and armchairs, and the men drifting in (those from distant colleges would be later), leaving overcoats and hats in any corner and coming over to warm their hands before finding a chair. There was no fixed etiquette, but the rudimentary honours would be done partly by Lewis and partly by his brother . . . a man who stays in my memory as the most courteous I have ever met—not with mere politeness, but with genial, self-forgetful considerateness that was as instinctive to him as breathing.[172]

Owen Barfield also recalled Warnie at the meetings: "[Warnie] used to attend the meetings of the little group they called 'the Inklings.' . . . His range of interest was certainly different from his brother's in many ways, although they were so close together. Warnie Lewis hated philosophy. He couldn't stand anything to do with it, and how he managed in spite of that to enjoy attending the Inklings, I don't know, but he did. But he was, in many ways, a thoroughly well-educated man."[173] Furthermore, Diana Glyer notes that some claim "it was [Warnie's] outgoing and gracious personality that formed the social 'glue' holding" together the diverse group of personalities. She says it is easy to imagine Warnie being a genial counter to the sometimes argumentative group, "keeping the relational balance and encouraging the conversation along."[174]

Warnie certainly took pleasure in the meetings, and because of him, we know many of the topics covered at other meetings. Among the topics discussed were the following: the possibility of dogs having souls, the morality of the Nuremburg trials, the possibility of communications with the dead, the moral aspect of atomic bombing and total war, second sight or the ability to perceive future or distant events, the ethics of cannibalism, the almost impossible challenge of interesting the uneducated indifferent in religion, how far pagan mythology was a substitute for theology, the various versions of the Bible, A. E. Housman and the ferocity of his prefaces, public schools, Sherlock Holmes stories, the inexplicable problem of why some children are allowed to die in infancy, and whether poets created or reflected the mood of their time. He also remarked that Wain once won a bet by reading a chapter of *Irene Iddesleigh* without smiling.[175] Warnie noted on another occasion that after Hardie read a dense paper on an unintelligible point about Virgil, Wain remarked "To say I didn't understand it is a gross understatement."[176]

Warnie was also candid about the personalities. Although he liked Dyson, he was sometimes irritated by his loud outbursts and trenchant opinions. He had great regard for Tolkien—whom he nicknamed Tollers—and he loved both *The Hobbit* and *The Lord of the Rings*. Robert Havard and Colin Hardie were comfortable to be with, and as much as he liked Christopher Tolkien, especially his oral readings of *The Lord of the Rings*, Warnie sometimes found him odd and irritable.[177] Wain often talked a lot of nonsense, but it was the kind Warnie appreciated. About R. B. McCallum, Warnie said he improved as time went on, even if when listening to him one felt like he was sitting through a history lecture.[178] Once when Gervase Mathew made a brief stop at a meeting, Warnie said he looked like a sparrow that had accidently landed on a tree limb with a cat.[179] When the poet Roy Campbell attended one meeting, Warnie thought he was more well fed and less argumentative than he used to be.[180] One time Warnie was irritated that Tolkien brought a stranger with him, Gwynne Jones, professor of English at Aberystwyth University in Wales. However, Warnie was won over, writing that he was a fine chap and read a thrilling Welsh story.[181]

The most traumatic event in the history of the Inklings was the death of Charles Williams on May 15, 1945, especially for Jack and Warnie. Jack was devastated, since he had no idea Williams was even ill, no more expecting him to die than he expected himself to die that day. As it was a Tuesday, he walked to the Eagle and Child to share the news, and noted that "the very streets looked different. . . . The world seemed . . . at that moment primarily a *strange* one. That sense of strangeness continued with a force which sorrow itself has never quite swallowed up. This experience of loss (the greatest I have ever known) was wholly unlike what I should have expected."[182] Warnie was similarly brokenhearted, likening the effect of the news on him to having the ground cut from underneath his feet. His immediate reaction was to get a drink, but as he did so, he grieved that "there will be no more pints with Charles: no more 'Bird and Baby': the blackout has fallen, and the Inklings can never be the same again. . . . And so vanishes one of the best and nicest men it has ever been my good fortune to meet."[183] Warnie sent Williams's wife, Florence, a letter expressing profound sympathy for her loss, his own sense of privation, and apologizing "if my feelings are badly expressed, they are none the less both deep and genuine, and as time goes on, I shall I'm afraid feel it not less, but more."[184] Almost certainly, Warnie began to turn increasingly to alcohol to cope with the death of Williams.

Although Warnie believed the Inklings would never be the same after the death of Williams, his passing was not its death knell. Indeed, the evidence we have from the documented meetings of the Inklings illustrate the gatherings continued unabated, serving as a source of respite, relaxation, and renewal. For Warnie, they were the primary social events of his life, and provided him with the psychological, emotional, and intellectual energy he needed to endure living at the Kilns. However, there is one caveat important to point out. Alcohol flowed freely at Inklings meetings—as Tolkien put it above, the attendees were often "well-oiled"—and this was not a good thing for Warnie. While there is no evidence that the meetings were drunken bashes, often participants were tipsy or close to being over the limit. Given Warnie's propensity to drink too much, easily obtained alcohol was injurious to his health. In a life already racked by alcohol abuse, Warnie's downward spiral was quickened by the frequency of Inklings gatherings.

CHAPTER 6

Historian and Literary Success
(1952–1960)

The decade after the death of Moore was a momentous one for Warnie and Jack. Chief among the events was the entrance of Joy Davidman into their lives; while her eyes were for Jack only, she played no small part in Warnie's life, and he grew to care for her deeply.[1] Equally important was the seismic shift that occurred in 1955 when Jack left Magdalen College, Oxford, for Magdalene College, Cambridge. Jack's decision to leave Oxford was complicated and almost prevented by his worries that Warnie's alcoholism might intensify if he were to move to Cambridge.[2] At the same time, Warnie continued serving as Jack's secretary, thereby relieving his brother of much administrative work, and he faithfully served his parish as a churchwarden for Holy Trinity Church.[3] However, for Warnie, these years were paradoxical. On the one hand, he won critical acclaim for his books on seventeenth-century French history; in them we witness his continuing growth as a writer—the promise of which had been previewed with the *Lewis Papers* and his diary (by 1952 approaching almost 940,000 words), and first given public evidence through his eight published essays on boating with the *Bosphorus*. On the other hand, he lost close friends and acquaintances, culminating in the death of Joy. Professionally, then, he came into the light, while personally he was dogged by shadows of sorrow. Moreover, although he made faltering efforts to control his binge drinking, it was a struggle he did not win.

Much of what we know about Joy Davidman's entry into the lives of the brothers comes from her letters and Warnie's diary entries. As early as 1947, Joy had become disaffected with the Communist Party of the United States of America and started her journey to Christianity, propelled in part by reading Jack's books, especially *The Pilgrim's Regress*, *The Screwtape Letters*, *The Great Divorce*, and

That Hideous Strength. In a June 21, 1949, letter to Chad Walsh, a mutual friend of hers and Jack's, she confided:

> [Bill and I] more than share your feeling for [C. S.] Lewis; with us it was not the last step but the first that came from reading his books, for we were raised atheists and took the truth of atheism for granted, and like most Marxists were so busy acting that we never stopped to think.[4] If I hadn't picked up *The Great Divorce* one day—brr, I suppose I'd still be running madly around with leaflets, showing as much intelligent purpose as a headless chicken. . . . What I am working round to is, yes we would dearly love to talk about Lewis' work. . . . By the way, your remark that Lewis answered even asinine letters gave us courage to write to him—so we sent the unfortunate man five single-spaced pages of personal history and what not.[5]

It appears that the correspondence between Jack and Joy commenced in the latter half of 1949, for on January 27, 1950, Joy expressed delight to Walsh about a letter of response from Jack:

> Just got a letter from Lewis in the mail. I think I told you I'd raised an argument or two on some points? Lord, he knocked my props out from under me unerringly; one shot to a pigeon. I haven't a scrap of my case left. And, what's more, I've seldom enjoyed anything more. Being disposed of so neatly by a master of debate, all fair and square—it seems to be one of the great pleasures of life, though I'd never have suspected it in my arrogant youth. I suppose it's *unfair* tricks of argument that leave wounds. But after the sort of thing that Lewis does, what I feel is a craftsman's joy at the sight of a superior performance.[6]

Warnie, always somewhat circumspect in his view of women, later wrote about his first impression of Joy: "Until 10th January 1950 neither of us had ever heard of her; then she appeared in the mail as just another American fan, Mrs. W. L. Gresham from the neighborhood of New York. With however the difference that she stood out from the ruck by her amusing and well-written letters, and soon J and she had become 'pen-friends.'"[7]

After he met Joy during her first visit to England in the fall 1952, Warnie confessed: "I was some little time in making up my mind about her; she proved to be a Jewess, or rather a Christian convert of Jewish race, medium height, good figure, horn-rimmed specs., quite extraordinarily uninhibited. Our first meeting was at a lunch in Magdalen [College], where she turned to me in the presence of three or four men, and asked in the most natural tone in the world, 'Is there anywhere in this monastic establishment where a lady can relieve herself?'"[8] Joy, at Jack's invitation, spent about two weeks at the Kilns around and including Christmas 1952, and the three of them often walked the countryside together.[9] Joy later remembered a particularly memorable excursion: "One day the three of us were over Shotover to Horspath and then to Garsington, coming back by way of Wheatley . . . and getting caught in a savage rain—I blistered my feet, and Jack and Warnie practically had to pull me up Shotover on the last stretch.[10] But it was great fun."[11] She memorialized the day by giving a comic rendering of the walk in her "Ballade of Blistered Feet" and then sharing it with Jack and Warnie:

Morning a sparkle of blue
And air that one breathed with a thrill;
The world tasted fragrant and new
When we climbed over Shotover hill.
Swallows were merry and shrill;
They cavorted all over the sky,
And we had the whole day to kill,
Jack and Warnie and I.

We came to a pub that we knew,
Whose sign was a queen in a frill,
And somehow before we were through
We drank rather more than our fill;
It *was* a bit careless to spill
Half of the beer in my eye;
But we were too gay to sit still,
Jack and Warnie and I.

What started as delicate dew
Grew up into rain, dank and chill;
I got a small lake in my shoe,
And all down my spine ran a rill;
There we were, halfway to Brill,
On ground that was naked and high—
Wet enough to distill,
Jack and Warnie and I!

Envoy

Ducks, I got home slightly ill
And more than ready to die;
But we'll do it again, so we will,
Jack and Warnie and I![12]

Joy understood that in order to win Jack, she also needed to win Warnie, and it is certain that in the "Ballade of Blistered Feet," she appealed to both. Indeed, Warnie was delighted with Joy, calling her stay at the Kilns a triumph. They became friends quickly, enjoying both walks and trips to the pub. When she headed back to America early the next year, all three were disappointed but looked forward to the next time she visited.[13]

Joy, with her marriage to Bill falling apart, returned to England ten months later in November 1953, with her sons, David and Douglas, and Jack and Warnie saw more and more of her. Jack invited Joy and the boys to spend Christmas 1953 at the Kilns. Warnie was initially uncertain about entertaining the boys, writing June that he and Jack were awaiting Joy's arrival with her two sons with a certain amount of gloom. Although Joy had been there before and been entertained easily—including liking cocktails—Warnie wondered how two old bachelors would be able to keep the boys busy and not bored.[14] But the visit was a huge success, with Warnie telling June that the boys turned out to be delightful. However, they were also exhausting, since, according to Warnie, as soon as the boys reached the ground after climbing Magdalen College tower, they wanted to do it again. In addition, he found them articulate and able to converse easily.[15]

In his "Memoir," Warnie noted that by 1955 Joy and Jack were on close terms, with the initial attraction on Jack's side the result of Joy's intellect. Joy, according to Warnie, was the only woman whose brain matched Jack's "in suppleness, in width of interest, in analytical grasp, and above all in humour and sense of fun. Further, she shared his delight in argument for argument's sake, whether frivolous or serious, always good-humoured yet always meeting him trick for trick as he changed ground."[16] Warnie found her to be a person of great charity with an unbounded contempt for sentimentality. Although Joy was sometimes overly zealous because of the high standards she lived by, Warnie found her ability to laugh at herself winsome; in addition, he found her intensely feminine.[17] Not surprisingly then, Joy was a woman Warnie came to hold in genuine affection and to love deeply. Most importantly, because of her work as a poet and prose writer, and especially her knowledge of French—Joy eventually played an important part in Warnie's life as a writer. As a young woman, Joy had translated dozens of poems by French poets, including Paul Verlaine, Henri de Régnier, Charles d'Orléans, François

Villon, and Francis Jammes.[18] Accordingly, when Warnie worked on several of his books, Joy served as his editor, in the process collaborating with him.

Coincidentally, as Joy came into his life, his longtime friend at the Kilns, Vera Henry, died. Warnie first met Vera in 1934 shortly after moving into the Kilns. As had been the case with Maureen, Warnie initially disliked Vera and avoided her as much as possible; he found her voice detestable. He believed she was presumptuous and assumed privileges that were not hers, including borrowing Maureen's clothes without asking. However, she owned a small retreat, the Golden Arrow, at Annagassan near Dundalk Bay on the east coast of Ireland, 20 miles north of Drogheda, and when Warnie heard about it, he longed to go there, as it reminded him of his own desire to have such a haven. As time went by, Warnie grew to care for Vera genuinely, especially after he realized most of his ill will toward her was the result of listening to Moore's grievances and slanders; for instance, one time Moore told a number of people that Vera had attempted to murder a woman in Oxford by throwing her out of a window.[19] Warnie realized that Moore would purposely arrange things to cause Vera discomfort and inconvenience. He also came to understand that, conversely, Vera went out of her way to make things more comfortable for Jack, despite Moore's backbiting and lies about her. A key turning point in his feelings for Vera was revealed in his unpublished diary entry of July 25, 1947, written during the time of his alcoholic poisoning in Drogheda: "When I got back to the pub, having been out two hours, who should I meet at the door, but Vera: and I was very glad to see her. It's quite extraordinary how different she looks in Drogheda to what she does in Oxford: here she is a well-preserved woman, rather above the average of good looks of her sex."

On many subsequent occasions, Warnie and Vera shared a drink and commiserated about Moore. Beginning in the late 1940s, at the invitation of Vera, Warnie and Jack regularly visited Vera's retreat, the Golden Arrow.[20] For Warnie, it was a magical place, a welcomed contrast to life with Moore at the Kilns. He also enjoyed Vera's penchant for telling stories, particularly about Irish characters she knew. In his unpublished diary entry for April 28, 1951, he wrote that Vera had told a hilarious biographical anecdote the previous day about a woman named Doris who was such a good wrestler that she broke two ribs of a male opponent in less than fifteen minutes. Even though he was not sure of the veracity of the story, Warnie rejoiced that in Ireland all things were possible.[21] Subsequently, when he learned of Vera's death on April 15, 1953, he was stricken: "She was up to the limit of and perhaps beyond her means, one of the most generous people I have ever met, and no trouble was too much for her to take to make us comfortable. The holidays which she gave us . . . will be a happy memory. . . . Dear

Vera, I miss her now, and I shall miss her more as time goes on."[22] In addition, because of Vera, Warnie had struck up a friendship with her brother, Frank. The two men became good friends and enjoyed meeting each other during Warnie's annual visits to Ireland.[23]

While he keenly felt the loss of Vera, Warnie's great passion in life was not for a woman; instead, it was for seventeenth-century French history, especially the reign of Louis XIV (1638–1715), variously referred to as Louis the Great or the Sun King. As I noted earlier, Warnie's fascination with this period had its origin in March 1919 when he was browsing a bookstore in Arques, Pas-de-Calais and stumbled upon the *Memoirs* of Louis de Rouvroy, duc de Saint-Simon (1675–1755). Although he had purchased the memoirs as a diversion from French novels, the main effect was that he became addicted to seventeenth-century French history.[24] As a result, he frequently cited Saint-Simon in his books, although often disagreeing with his opinions and thoughts about Louis XIV. Furthermore, he told a friend years later that he eventually accumulated about five hundred books on the period.[25] Perhaps influenced by Saint-Simon, Warnie's primary interests in seventeenth-century France were upon the people, places, and events of the *ancien régime*—the political and social system in France before the Revolution of 1789. As a consequence, his books combine social history and biography. That is, they do not focus upon political, military, or governmental matters per se; rather, they probe how seventeenth-century French society—its codes, ethos, and manners—can be understood. In the main, he explores selected persons and events, while not neglecting the broader scope of seventeenth-century French culture. Although his books offer no new startling discoveries or investigative revelations, he sometimes engages in interpretation. However, he never purports to be original in the sense of offering an in-depth analysis of some topic never before attempted. He does not try to uncover heretofore unknown facts, documents, or archives; instead, he works with existing historical records—especially memoirs and letters—to offer his personal interpretation of the milieu. His strengths as a writer of history are collation, distillation, illustration, revisiting, sketching, summarizing, and tracing, traits similar to the ones he drew on while compiling the *Lewis Papers*. At the same time, he avoids personal biases, oddities, or quirks; instead, he writes with insight and is both entertaining and compelling. While readers might start a chapter with little understanding or appreciation for the topic at hand—maybe even thinking it a tedious subject—by the end they find themselves drawn into the often distant, unfamiliar world that Warnie skillfully sketches.

THE SPLENDID CENTURY

As early as the spring of 1934, while he was still working on the *Lewis Papers*, Warnie began writing about seventeenth-century France. For example, in April 1934 he wrote one of his very few poems, "The French Revolution," a work that gives no false impression about the romance of the French Revolution. [26] However, the poem does demonstrate Warnie's long-held fascination with French history. Five weeks after he wrote "The French Revolution," he confessed that his research was an intermittent effort to write a doggerel history of Louis XIV and his reign, mostly to amuse himself and with no illusions as to its historical value. [27] Warnie worked slowly on this project, and by 1942 he had completed a first draft of what came to be *The Splendid Century*. [28] In order to test the waters, he eventually decided to read portions of the manuscript at Inklings meetings. Cognizant of the kind of no-holds-barred criticism he would receive, he approached the first reading with some trepidation. So it eased his mind considerably when his work was received favorably; for example, after the April 13, 1944, meeting of the Inklings, Tolkien reported to his son, Christopher: "The best entertainment proved to be the chapter of Major Lewis' projected book—on a subject that does not interest me: the court of Louis XIV; but it was most wittily written (as well as learned)." [29] In addition, after the May 24, 1944, Inklings meeting Tolkien told his son that Warnie was writing a book ("it's catching") and that "the chief entertainment was provided by a chapter of Warnie Lewis's book on the times of Louis XIV (very good I thought it)." [30] Warnie offered almost no reflections in his diary about his writing process for *The Splendid Century*; in fact, from 1951 to 1963, his diary contained less than 23,000 words (by way of comparison, his diary for 1930 contained 163,000 words). This fall off indicates that the writing he did on his books largely took the place of his diary writing. [31]

When we turn to *The Splendid Century* (not surprisingly, it was dedicated to Jack), Warnie wrote in the foreword that it might have been better titled "Some Aspects of French Life in the Reign of Louis XIV." [32] In essence, this alternative title alerted readers that he was going to focus on the matters that particularly interested him—the people, practices, and protocols of seventeenth-century France. His was going to be a selective, not a comprehensive, history. This meant that he would not write about topics beyond his competence; thus, for instance, he would avoid writing about the French navy, the *Parlements* and their struggles with the Louis XIV, artists and philosophers, and the civil service. Therefore, he painted on a small canvas, not a large one. *The Splendid Century* was not macrohistory, but rather microhistory. Topics that he did write about included the king, the court, the peasants, the church, the army, rural life, the town, the medical world, the art of living, the galleys, sea travel, female education, and the world of letters. His specific concerns included: What was Louis XIV like? How did he rule? What was it like to live in his court? Who were his closest companions? What were the contrasts between living in the town vs. the country? What was the state of the French church? What were the major concerns of the army and who were its leaders? What was the nature of the medical world? What was travel like, especially on the sea? What would it have been like to be condemned to the galleys? How were women educated? Who were the important writers?

Readers of *The Splendid Century* found that Warnie, while conscious of Louis XIV's many faults, was generally sympathetic to him, especially given his less than ideal upbringing that included an impoverished court, endless wars, civil unrest, and an abysmal education. Most telling, according to Warnie, were the personal qualities of the king: charm, good nature and looks, strong sense of justice, taste for hard work, political savvy, attention to detail, common sense, decorum, memory, politeness, and approachableness. However, these qualities were offset by his iron rule, as befitted a monarch who was convinced of his divine right to reign, and this assurance bred an overweening arrogance. Warnie commented: "The most lasting and important of Louis's assets was his own deep conviction that as King of France he stood in a peculiar personal relationship with God: a conviction which was strengthened and sustained by the narrowness and rigidity of his own religious beliefs."[33] Not that the king was especially religious, since he tried to adjust religion to himself, not himself to religion. Given Louis's mind-set, it was futile and even dangerous to argue with him, as an excerpt from the king's memoir reveals: "As he (the king) is of a rank superior to all other men, he sees things more perfectly than they do, and he ought to trust rather to the inner light than to information which reaches him from the outside. . . . Occupying, so to speak, the place of God, we seem to be sharers of His knowledge as well as of His authority."[34]

Throughout *The Splendid Century*, Warnie gave readers "a day in the life of" scenarios. In an early instance, he imagined living through a day at the court in Versailles, beginning with a detailed description of the hierarchy of the court—dukes, counts, marquises, and barons—and who could sit down in the presence of whom. Social skirmishing and petty conflicts abounded. Lucky courtiers would have rooms at the Palace of Versailles, a place Warnie described as cold, drafty, smelly, and generally uncomfortable. When Warnie compared those not so lucky, he almost echoed his own experiences at Wynyard and Malvern:

> But greater than [an unlucky courtier's] material sufferings would be those of a
> kind with which most of us are familiar, the embarrassments and agonies of a

new boy at school; for there is a remarkable resemblance between the life of old Versailles and that of a public school. At Versailles was the same complex unwritten law, the same struggle for trivial distinctions, an intricate and illogical code of privilege, with public shame and biting rebuke for the man who transgressed against its provisions.[35]

One was particularly honored if given the opportunity to watch Louis dress in the morning. After chapel, Louis would attend to business, and courtiers would begin to angle for where to eat the midday meal. When the king lunched, there would be between thirty and forty dishes with little conversation because Louis preferred to do his talking between meals rather than during them. In the afternoon, if there was no business, two or three days of the week were spent hunting; afterward, he might meet with his governmental ministers.

Three nights a week were given over to entertainment, including concerts followed by billiards and cards; gambling was heavy, and small fortunes could be won or lost of an evening. Louis himself never took part. The supper hour was usually ten o'clock, and for the king this was the crowning moment of the day. When healthy, he might consume "four plates of soup, a whole pheasant, a whole partridge, two slices of ham and a salad, some mutton with garlic, followed by pastry, and finishing off with fruit and hard-boiled eggs."[36] After dinner, Louis would receive members of his family for an hour or so before feeding his dogs and going into his bedroom. He would say his prayers, and speak privately with several petitioners. His day would end with time on the commode, helped by the Gentlemen of the Bedchamber, who paid a huge amount of money for the distinction and satisfaction of aiding at this nightly endeavor.[37] These details about a day in the life at the court in Versailles, while more than some readers might desire, nonetheless indicate the extent to which Warnie went in ferreting out and sharing the history of the period.

Undoubtedly, Louis cast a large shadow over seventeenth-century France; however, Warnie wrote about other topics with genuine insight and perception, perhaps nowhere more obvious than in his chapter "The Church"—at forty-four pages by far the longest in the book.[38] His central effort was to untangle four doctrinal issues dominating the Roman Catholic Church in France: Jansensim (an effort to reconcile the theological problem of divine grace and human free will); Quietism (a Christian spiritual tradition that asserts perfection is achieved via the passivity [quiet] of the soul and the suppression of human effort in order that divine grace may be fully operational); the conflict of Gallican (those supporting the autonomy of the French church) versus Ultramontane (those supporting papal authority); and the attempt to crush Protestantism. Although not a trained theologian, Warnie discussed these four issues with a high level of perspicacity, and he offered a clear discussion of the personalities, points of crisis, and ongoing controversies. The most horrific episode was the persecution of the Huguenots—the French protestants. The Roman Catholic Church and French society in general were ruthless in their oppression of its theologically reformed subjects, intent on extirpating them. The unfortunate result was widespread Huguenot flight from the country, taking with them many able artisans, lawyers, printers, hotel keepers, shoemakers, tailors, merchants, and the like. Warnie demonstrated in this chapter that the suppression of the Huguenots was a huge black stain against the rule of Louis XIV.[39]

In his chapter, "The Medical World," Warnie pointed out that seventeenth-century French doctors often argued their disagreements via scurrilous and venomous public debates, tarnishing themselves and providing entertainment for the cynical. In addition, the medical profession, centered in Paris, was hopelessly tied to the past, thus eschewing any new treatments, medical discoveries, or scientific explorations. As Warnie put it, the medical establishment's "permanent mental attitudes may be described as a deep loathing of other physicians and a profound contempt for surgeons."[40] Moreover, bleeding reigned as the first choice of almost any ailment, although dentistry advanced to the point where false teeth were made available. Tooth extraction, however, remained unimaginably painful, and there was one nonoperational technique that Warnie drily questioned as efficacious: "First boil, then reduce to ashes, some earthworms; fill the hollow tooth with this powder, seal it with wax, and the tooth will soon fall out."[41]

Warnie's chapter "The Galleys," was first published in 1947 as "The Galleys of France," a contribution to *Essays Presented to Charles Williams*.[42] His opening sentence was striking: "Until the coming of the concentration camp, the galley held an undisputed pre-eminence as the darkest blot on Western civilization; a galley, said a poetic observer shudderingly, would cast a shadow in the blackest midnight."[43] Warships that combined sail and oars, galleys were indispensable to the Mediterranean powers. Manned almost exclusively by condemned convicts, the *galériens* were drawn from Turkish slaves, deserters, salt smugglers, violent criminals, as well as persecuted Huguenots. In his day in the life of a galley convict at sea, Warnie revealed that it was essentially a picnic in Hell.[44] There were no accommodations, no sleeping quarters, primitive cooking facilities, vermin everywhere, and the constant clashing of chains, cracks of whips on bare flesh, howls of pain, and brutish growls.[45] Rowers often were at it for twenty-four hours straight, fed on biscuits soaked with wine while they rowed, and if they died while at their posts, they were unceremoniously thrown overboard. While Warnie dwelt on the horrors of the galley, he offered an objective, almost poetic summation: "The seventeenth-century criminal is not a sympathetic subject. . . . [Ample records exist] of the horrors and atrocities which he boasted of having perpetrated. Whether the system made the criminal or the criminal made the system . . . it is all over now. The tumult and the shouting dies; the galley in all its gilded splendor and hidden misery has followed the age it symbolizes into oblivion."[46]

Throughout *The Splendid Century*, Warnie wrote perceptively and incisively. Like Jack, he did not pad or waste words. His chapter on "Female Education" was sympathetic and approving, while his "The World of Letters" briefly evaluated the important writers of the period. Readers may find this chapter akin to Jack's *English Literature in the Sixteenth Century Excluding Drama* (1954), a book he was writing at the same time; it is conceivable that the brothers consulted one another as they worked through the literature of their respective periods. Critical responses to *The Splendid Century* were overwhelmingly positive, from both popular critics and professional historians. E. T. Smith, writing in the *Library Journal*, assessed the book as "a truly distinguished work both in style and content."[47] In his review for the *Saturday Review*, Leo Gershoy noted that in the book "there is much to enjoy in the vivid picture of life in the France of Louis XIV. . . . Mr. Lewis is not only extraordinarily informative: he paints with a high color and he enlivens his graceful pages with humor and wit."[48] In a review appearing in the *Spectator*, D. W. Brogan wished for a better organized book with more critical handling of the material, "yet the book has merits. It does make plain that there was something in Louis XIV that justified [Lord] Acton's very high estimate of him."[49] Writing for the *American Historical Review*, William F. Brown pointed out that the author's "flair for the picturesque is everywhere evident" and he effectively communicated "to the reader of . . . genuine feeling for the innumerable intricacies of human experience during the reign of the sun king."[50] However, the greatest praise came from well-known scholar and novelist Albert Guerard. Writing for the *New York Times*, he referred to Warnie as a "conscientious scholar as well as delightful writer."[51] After offering a number of complimentary remarks on several of the chapters, Guerard closed his review by calling attention to the ending of "The World of Letters," calling it "a passage of unexpected and very real eloquence: 'And it is the writers, not the soldiers, grandees and politicians, who give the century its enduring place in the history of civilization; on their shoulders rest the claim of the *Grand Siècle* to the title of 'the splendid century.'"[52]

Joy raved about *The Splendid Century*, writing Bill: "Warnie's book is out; he has just sent me a copy. Lord, the way they publish here. It's a whopping big volume, beautifully printed, with fifteen black-and-white plates and handsome end papers. . . . Haven't had a chance to read it yet, but it looks good and Jack says it's getting terrific reviews."[53] Dorothy L. Sayers praised the book to Jack, and in response, he wrote: "My brother is delighted that you are enjoying the book."[54] After Arthur Greeves wrote Warnie about his enjoyment of *The Splendid Century,* Warnie responded: "I'm so glad you enjoyed the book, and it was good of you to write. . . . Whether there is to be any more book-making depends on how this book goes; the latest London report is that 'sales are steady, not sensational,' which is as good as a beginner can hope for I think. The New York edition came out on the seventeenth [of March], and of it I have as yet no news—beyond a positively rapturous review [by Albert Guerard] in the N. Y. Times, which is all to the good, as far as it goes."[55]

THE SUNSET OF THE SPLENDID CENTURY: THE LIFE AND TIMES OF LOUIS AUGUSTE DE BOURBON, DUC DE MAINE, 1670–1736

Warnie was being somewhat coy about whether or not there would be any more bookmaking since he was already working on what came to be *The Sunset of the Splendid Century: The Life and Times of Louis Auguste de Bourbon, Duc de Maine, 1670–1736.* As in the case of *The Splendid Century,* we have almost no information about Warnie's writing process for this book since his diary said nothing about his work on it; in fact, in 1952 and 1955 there are no diary entries of any kind. The few clues we have involve Joy. On July 30, 1954, she wrote Bill: "I've been reading copy on Warnie's new book for him (mostly for spelling—the Lewises have a family failing of being unable to remember when and where *i* comes before *e* or the reverse)."[56] Apparently, by October 1954, Warnie had completed the book, since the foreword cited that date, and he thanked Joy for her help in correcting the proofs.[57] The first review appeared in August 1955, so we can reasonably assume the book was published sometime after October 1954 and sometime before August 1955. The foreword also hinted that Warnie was very much at work on the book while still writing *The Splendid Century,* since he said it was essentially a follow-up to *The Splendid Century.*"[58]

Sunset continued Warnie's fascination with Louis XIV, but from a different perspective. That is, unlike *The Splendid Century,* which was a social history of seventeenth-century France, *Sunset* was a social biography focusing upon the life Louis Auguste de Bourbon, duc du Maine (1670–1736), the eldest illegitimate son of Louis. In order to throw duc du Maine's life into relief, Warnie also explored in more detail the life of Louis. In addition, he offered a number of character sketches of the key people in Maine's life, and he probed how Maine was perceived by them and by society at large. In some ways Warnie tried to correct earlier negative portraits on the duke. He was drawn to write about duc du Maine, because Warnie found him to be an everyday man in spite of his connections to Louis.[59] Accordingly, *Sunset* is a social biography tracing how Louis's favorite illegitimate son went from being a nobody, to being a somebody, to being, in the end, again a nobody; as a result, readers learn as much about seventeenth-century France as they do about Maine.

A case in point was how the death of Louis XIV on September 1, 1715, precipitated the greatest crisis in duc du Maine's life. The heir to the throne was Louis's great-grandson, Louis XV, Duke of Anjou, but he was only five years old in 1715. Until the young boy reached the age at which he could rule, France was presided over by the Regent, Philippe II, duc d'Orléans, the nephew of Louis XIV. Duc d'Orléans, who had been forced by Louis XIV to marry his bastard daughter—the now legitimized sister of duc du Maine, Françoise Marie, Mlle. de Bourbon—cared little for her or her brother, particularly after Louis in July 1714 raised duc de Maine to being in line to the throne. Warnie pointed out that duc d'Orléans had led an irreverent, licentious, dissolute life, and been implicated—although it was never proven—in the poisoning deaths of the parents and brother of Louis XV. The conflict between Maine and the Regent came to a head over provisions in the will of Louis XIV that named Maine as responsible for the education of Louis XV. On September 7, 1715, less than a week after the death of Louis XIV, the Regent assembled the French Parlement and convinced them to set aside the provisions of the king's will, stripping Maine of any power or influence over the young king.

Then, on August 25, 1718, the Regent conspired to deprive Maine of any pretensions to the throne. Several years later, Mme. du Maine—but apparently not her husband—became embroiled in an ill-advised conspiracy against the Regent. When the Regent discovered the conspiracy, he was not vindictive. Maine, however, never again lived with his wife. Warnie neatly described the downfall of Maine in two chapters entitled "Humpty Dumpty" and "Humpty Dumpty Falls Farther." After pointing out that he believed the greatest hindrance to Maine's life was his marriage, Warnie ended the book this way: "Knave, fool, nullity, or the victim of frustration? Which was he? I have produced, and endeavoured to sum up, all the available evidence. The verdict I leave to the reader."[60] The other matter worth commenting upon here is that Warnie cited frequently from the *Memoirs* of Louis de Rouvroy, duc de Saint-Simon, the very book that had first drawn his attention to seventeenth-century French history; however, Warnie often cautioned readers to take Saint-Simon's remarks about Maine with a grain of salt since Saint-Simon despised the duke.

As had been the case with *The Splendid Century*, reviews of *Sunset* were positive. The reviewer for *Kirkus* wrote that "this is the brilliant biography of

Louis XIV's bastard son, the crippled Duc de Maine. . . . One has a sense of scholarship, [and the book is] well documented without being heavy handed."[61] John Bruckman, while complimentary, also identified what many find to be the greatest weakness of the book: "The only flaw in the book is that Maine himself is too much of an abstraction, he seldom comes to life, and is almost a vacuum among the personalities that dominated his era. Scholarly, often provocative, and fascinating withal."[62] Another reviewer generously offered praise that must have pleased Warnie: "Lame, lack-lustre, and lucklessly married to a wolverine of a woman, the Duc de Maine would hardly seem an adequate eminence from which to view the decline of a glittering era, and it is a measure of Mr. Lewis's skill that this poor creature not only fulfills to perfection the function that is thrust upon him but manages to win our sympathetic understanding."[63] Albert Guerard also found much to admire, noting that "the qualities of style that made *The Splendid Century* an outstanding piece of historical writing are undimmed in this companion volume."[64] Warnie was also cheered by the news that Greeves enjoyed his book. In Jack's letter to Greeves of February 19, 1956, he wrote: "W. was pleased with yr. remarks about his book."[65]

ASSAULT ON OLYMPUS: THE RISE OF THE
HOUSE OF GRAMONT BETWEEN 1604 AND 1678

Now a critically acclaimed historian, Warnie appears to have experienced a creative phenomenon familiar to many authors—one book gave birth to another. Even before reviews of *Sunset* were published, he was engaged in research for *Assault on Olympus: The Rise of the House of Gramont between 1604 and 1678*. In his diary entry of December 10, 1954, he noted that he was researching his next book, and that it would examine the life of the Gramont family.[66] Joy added additional information about this book, writing Bill on March 23, 1955: "We're all hard at work here; the house [the Kilns] is practically a book factory. Warnie's deep in the life of Gramont (dashing seventeenth century bloke), I'm putting Mme. M. together, and Jack has started a new fantasy—for grownups."[67] Notwithstanding Joy's comments about Warnie participating in something of a writer's conclave, *Assault on Olympus* proved to be difficult. In his diary of November 5, 1956—he had not kept a diary since the December 10, 1954, date mentioned above—he wrote:

> And today, nearly two years later, this book, *Assault on Olympus* was dispatched to the agents. Nothing that I have yet written has given me so much trouble; the first version, 120,000 words, was finished in July 1955, was rejected out of hand

both by Eyre and Spottiswoode and by Sloane of New York, and then sent to J's
agent, Curtis Brown. I had long written it off as a stillborn, and in fact begun to
use it as a quarry for my new effort, Louis XIV,[68] when out of a blue sky C[urtis]
B[rown] placed it with Andre Deutsch in London and Harcourt Brace in New York:
subject to its being cut to 100,000. This I did, and retyped the whole thing. Then
. . . came an airy letter saying that both publishers were of opinion that after all
90,000 would be a better length. . . . I made the second cut and typed the damned
thing for the *third* time—doing the 90,000 in ten days, and incidentally driving
myself into Restholme thereby.[69]

Warnie never suggested that the actual writing of the book was torturous, indicat-
ing instead it was the rewriting and revising to length that were so off-putting.
Of special note is his reference to driving himself into Restholme. In fact, the
pressure of reworking *Assault on Olympus* led to another alcoholic binge, with
Jack writing Greeves on September 9, 1955: "I arrived home with a 100 horse-
power cold to find an empty house, W having been drunk for a fortnight and
now in his old nursing home."[70]

The foreword of *Assault on Olympus* is dated October 1955–1956, and since the
copyright date of the book is 1958, it was probably in various stages of production between late 1956 and 1958. A reasonable guess is that it was published in
late 1957 or early 1958. In the foreword, Warnie outlined that once again he was
writing social history—or more precisely, a social biography—this time examining how a provincial family was converted into a noble one, drawing especially
on the plethora of memoirs written by the Gramonts.[71] He also specified that he
focused upon the Gramonts because, "unlike the majority of French nobles, [the
Gramonts] were a travelled family; and consequently, instead of spending all our
time in France, we see through their eyes a good deal of their Europe—Germany,
Spain, England, Holland, and the Netherlands."[72] He concluded his foreword by
thanking Joy who again had assisted him as an editor.[73] As had been the case with
Sunset, Joy's collaboration was crucial in the writing of *Assault on Olympus.*

The particular focus of the book was Antoine III, First duc and Maréchal
de Gramont, Comte de Guiche, Comte de Gramont, Comte de Louvigny, Sou-
verain de Bidache (1604–1678). As Warnie related his story, Antoine, tiring of
his backward life in the country, made his way to Paris when he was fourteen,
intent on becoming a courtier at the court of Louis XIII (1601–1643). Adopting
the guise of a lighted-hearted, comic, rich, reckless fellow, Antoine's naturally
sharp-eyed and calculating personality looked for every chance of advancement.
Warnie then neatly traced Antoine's life from his days as a penniless, young
cadet to achieving unimagined success, eventually becoming Duke of France,

Peer of France, Marshal of France, Knight of the Saint-Esprit, Colonel of the French Guards, Sovereign of Bidache, Minister of State, Governor of Béarn and Navarre, and Governor and Mayor of Bayonne. Yet, as Warnie read Antoine's life, he wondered if Gramont ever asked "himself if it had all been worth while? His mind was ambitious, complacent, trained for acute observation in a small field, and quite lacking in power of introspection."[74] The greatest cost to Antoine had been rich and meaningful friendships, "for this is luxury with which the [social] climber dare not burden himself. . . . Like all men of his stamp, Gramont obviously failed to escape the nemesis of the unloved and friendless; and as the last darkness closed in upon him he may have seen as by a lightning flash, the emptiness of that 'magnificence' which he had always worshipped."[75]

Once again, reviewers found much to admire. From the *Manchester Guardian* came the remark that "this biography was worth writing."[76] The reviewer for the *New Yorker* wrote that Antoine had "an extraordinary, and an extraordinarily slippery, career, and Mr. Lewis leads us through it spellbound."[77] Warnie certainly must have enjoyed reading in the *San Francisco Chronicle* that "the book is full of meaty commentary."[78] The greatest praise came from the *London Times Literary Supplement:* "All this world, Mr. Lewis surveys from the point of view of an old-fashioned moralist . . . [and he] is free with judgments of great severity and rather tepid allocations of praise. . . . Few modern historians use memoirs with the same confidence or come to such positive judgments on debatable questions. . . . The common reader will enjoy himself."[79] Jack enjoyed the book and sent a copy of it to Greeves "with my compliments. It has elicited a furious letter from the present representative of the family, The Duc de Guiche: so furious I was relieved to find it did not end in a challenge!"[80]

Warnie's pleasure over the reception of *Assault on Olympus* was tempered by his second great loss of the decade; on November 9, 1958, his boon companion and fellow officer, Herbert Parkin, died—after Jack, his longest and most treasured friend. Returning from working in the Bodleian library on November 13, 1958, Warnie opened a letter from a firm of solicitors that began "Lt. Col. Herbert Denis Parkin deceased;" for a full minute or so, he was stunned and unable to read further. In his diary he wrote: "He was a friend of almost thirty years standing, and one whose place no one can fill. . . . We shared a stock of memories which were very precious to both of us, and . . . at my age I shall miss him to the end—the only real friend I ever made in the army. . . . God rest his soul."[81] Parkin's passing was not totally unexpected, since he had suffered a stroke in the spring of 1957; nevertheless, Parkin's death jolted Warnie. They had known each other for forty years, first meeting in France in 1918, and then becoming close friends in 1928 while serving in Shanghai; at one point, Parkin had even tried to convince Warnie to accompany him on what turned out to be an aborted trip to the Great Wall of China.[82] During service together, they commiserated over military life, including arcane and incomprehensible regulations, incompetent commanders, and worthless comrades; several times Parkin warned Warnie about people to avoid at various army locations. Over the years, Warnie came to know something of Parkin's extended family, including his mother and father, his brother, Alan, and a cousin, A. S. Parkin, with whom Warnie had served at various postings. After the service, the two had gone on many weekend jaunts together, met for countless drinks, lunches and dinners, attended theatrical productions, and talked on almost every subject possible. Warnie particularly enjoyed Parkin's wry sense of humor, and he had been a frequent guest on the *Bosphorus*. Parkin's death was a blow to Warnie—and had he known it—an ominous foreshadowing of more darkness and loss about to come his way.

LOUIS XIV: AN INFORMAL PORTRAIT

About the composition of Warnie's next book, *Louis XIV: An Informal Portrait*, we have a number of hints. His November 5, 1956, diary entry mentioned above, revealed that he used his preliminary work on *Assault on Olympus* as the source for his next book on Louis XIV.[83] Joy wrote friends on June 6, 1957, and said Warnie had "written his life of Louis XIV and is now cutting and rewriting."[84] A third insight came in his December 15, 1958, letter to a friend where he said he was busily trying to keep up with the cost of living by writing another book. He called it good fun, even if it would not bring him additional income.[85] Since the first review of *Louis XIV: An Informal Portrait* appeared in June 1959, the book was probably published in early 1959.[86] In the foreword, Warnie claimed twice that he was not writing a biography, although he did suggest the book might eventually provide notes for a definitive life of Louis XIV.[87] Notwithstanding his assertion, *Louis XIV: An Informal Portrait* is in fact a biography, albeit a social biography in keeping with Warnie's personal interests. In it he explored the following questions: "What, if anything, lay behind that magnificent façade [of the Grand Monarque]? What were his ambitions, hopes, and fears? How did he make love, eat, drink, and dress? What were his personal tastes and prejudices?"[88]

In some instances, Warnie covered the same ground he did in both *The Splendid Century* and *Sunset*. However, newly explored material of note was Warnie's discussion of Louis's military adventures since he did so from the perspective of one who had served in an army. Despite the fact that more than two centuries separated the campaigns of Louis in the seventeenth century and Warnie's active service in the RASC from 1914 to 1932, his intimate knowledge of the workings of armies, the attitude of the soldiers serving, and the commanders who led—particularly their blind spots—gave him penetrating insight into army life. While Warnie rarely explored the wisdom of Louis's various efforts to achieve military glory, he did neatly identify the King's regimental shortcomings. Chief among them was his tendency to micromanage, attending to matters that should have been delegated to junior staff officers. For instance, the King insisted on being roused in the middle of the night in order to answer unimportant dispatches. Warnie assessed this fault, claiming that the King bungled the distinction between strategy and tactics, thus effectively undercutting his achievements on the battle-field.[89] When battles or campaigns were successful, it was because of the expertise of the senior commanders, not Louis. Unfortunately, Louis falsely believed he was adept at both planning and conducting a war.[90] The most serious upshot of this thinking was that Louis thought he could conduct a military campaign from his desk in Versailles, thus creating a "fatal tendency to over-centralization, which robbed commanders in the field of all initiative and nearly brought the whole French military structure tottering to its fall."[91] Warnie could write with such perception about this matter because of his experiences in France during WWI and his subsequent postings in Sierra Leone, back in England, then to Shanghai, and finally his brief involvement in WWII.

Another important matter covered in *Louis XIV: An Informal Portrait* is Louis's married life. At the death of Louis's wife, Queen Marie-Thérèse in 1683, he turned to Mme. de Maintenon for both personal comfort and spiritual counsel. His days of keeping multiple mistresses were over, and at forty-four years old, he was over-weight and no longer fresh skinned nor good looking.[92] What he needed now was a mature, sensible woman he could confide in and trust implicitly. Mme. de Maintenon, who had essentially raised several of Louis's illegitimate children—including duc de Maine—now became indispensable to the king, and on June 12, 1684, the two were secretly married. One bishop wrote Louis, commending her: "You have an excellent companion, filled with God's spirit, whose tenderness for you is unequalled . . . no one loves you more tenderly or respectfully than she does. . . . It is plain that God has wished to support you . . . by giving you a woman who, like the good wife of Scripture, occupies herself with the salvation of her husband."[93] As Warnie put it, Cinderella finally married Prince Charming. Historians have debated how true this assessment may have been, but most agree this morganatic marriage was a tremendous benefit to Louis, and it was certain that he was devoted to Mme. de Maintenon for the rest of his life.[94]

In evaluating the life of Louis, Warnie affirmed that he was a controversial figure lacking a definitive appraisal, either as a man or ruler. In his view Louis, was handicapped by being seen as a demigod, leaving him proud, selfish, and arrogant. Yet in the final paragraph of his biography, Warnie ascribed three qualities to Louis that ameliorated to some degree his negative ones. First, the king "had standards and values to which he adhered unflinchingly; as *père de famille* [father of the family] to twenty million children he struggled valiantly with the impossible task of keeping them all fed with the outmoded economic machinery at his disposal." Second, he showed great kindness and generosity to his family. Third, although an absolutist, in "his innate justice, . . . his almost invariable good temper; and . . . his magnanimity to the traducers of his regime there is something of real greatness. If he aroused some hatred, he also inspired much affection." Warnie pointed out that frequently those who offered their views of Louis were jealous and ungrateful; however, he ended his study of the king with a sanguine comment: "To me it seems that few historical figures emerge better from so searching a test; and that this Louis, warped but not broken by upbringing, absolutism, and flattery, need not fear comparison with any other man whose life has been so minutely preserved for us."[95]

Overall, the reviewers were positive, although several took umbrage with one aspect of Warnie's approach: the lack of a scholarly apparatus. For instance, one reviewer argued that it "is a good and useful book, but it is a shame that it lacks a bibliography and that the author has indulged in the unfortunate habit of quoting without naming sources."[96] Another reviewer complained that "Mr. Lewis has seriously impaired the value of his contribution by omitting a bibliography and starving the reader in the matter of sources." However, the same reviewer noted that "all in all, Mr. Lewis has most successfully established the merits of his individual approach and given us a thoroughly attractive, well-balanced, and exciting book."[97] Geoffrey Bruun led a chorus of complementary voices, noting that "although the subtitle describes this biography as an informal portrait, it might be described more justly as a scrupulous and realistic effort at reinterpretation."[98] Still another reviewer said Warnie was "perhaps the most engaging contemporary authority on seventeenth-century France . . . [and] pieced together a credible likeness of a human being."[99] Richard McLaughlin best summarized Warnie's achievement: "Perhaps today's most entertaining, and certainly the most informative, guide to seventeenth century France is W. H. Lewis. . . . His books make wonderful escapist reading, yet serve every need of the scholar and urbane history lover. . . . No matter how much he may disclaim to have written a full-dressed biography. . . . Mr. Lewis comes very close to writing a definitive biography of Louis XIV."[100]

THE SCANDALOUS REGENT: A LIFE OF PHILIPPE,
DUC D'ORLEANS, 1674–1723, AND OF HIS FAMILY

Warnie probably began work on his fifth book, *The Scandalous Regent: A Life of Philippe, Duc d'Orleans, 1674–1723, and of His Family*, as early as the summer of 1958, since Joy related in a letter of July 2, 1958, that he was starting research on a new book.[101] By the late fall of 1959, he finished a draft, writing in his diary that he had just sent it to his publisher and that he thought it was good.[102] A year later on November 22, 1960, he sent the corrected proof copy of the book, including an index, to his publisher.[103] During his work on the book, Joy died on July 13, 1960.[104] Poignantly, he dedicated the book to Joy and thanked her for all the ways she had helped him.[105] So it was surely with something of a sore heart that Warnie thought back over his work on the book with Joy. Warnie went on in the foreword to say the book was a biography attempting to demonstrate how Orléans, to his credit, dealt with the aftermath of Louis XIV's extravagant spending, building, and warring that resulted in a worn-out, depleted, and bankrupt kingdom. At the same time, he admitted that Orléans was an unsavory character, since he was one of the most notorious rakes of the eighteenth century. Still, while Warnie said he would not whitewash Orléans, he intended to reveal the Regent as "the competent soldier, the hard-working statesman with ideas ahead of his time, and the man whose charm was in the eyes of his contemporaries, his most noteworthy characteristic. If his Regency is considered a failure, as I fear it must be, it was at least a gallant failure."[106]

Orléans appeared briefly in three of Warnie's previous books. However, in writing a biography of Orléans, Warnie was free to explore in much greater detail the character of the man who served as Regent—the trustee of Louis XV from 1715 until 1723. As we are introduced to Orléans and to the people around him, we soon begin to wonder if everyone within that orbit was a rascal, a sycophant, an adulterer, or a deceiver; licentiousness, venality, intemperance, immorality, and atheism mark the majority of his companions. Orléans's life was forever scarred when Louis XIV—who feared for anyone in his family to attain more glory than himself—thwarted Orléans's military career while also forcing him to marry one of Louis's illegitimate daughters, Françoise Marie, Mlle. de Bourbon. We understand the less than ideal nature of the marriage via Orléans's nickname for his wife: Mme. Lucifer. Accordingly, forced into a loveless marriage and quick to indulge his rapacious libido, Orléans maintained what was essentially a harem.[107] A predictable pattern emerged: after a day of boredom, work, or political intrigue, Orléans would retreat with his mistresses and roués, spending the hours until dawn in drunkenness, dissipation, revelry, lechery, and sensuality. Often there

would be indecent magic shows, plays enacted by naked young women, or organized orgies; the dinner service included plates portraying various obscenities.
He told companions that he did not care how morally debauched they were as
long as they did not try to reach above their given social status. He disliked those
who failed to get drunk and was especially dismissive of women who might try
to use sex with him to advance their political agendas.[108] Orléans never tried to
hide his outrageous behavior; in fact, he boasted about it publicly.

It may be that the Regent's most praiseworthy attribute was his genuine love
and care for the future Louis XV; whenever the young man took ill, the Regent
took pains to go see him, order the best treatment, and ensure his recovery. At the
Regent's death on December 2, 1723, few people other than his family mourned
his passing. In assessing the Regent's life, Warnie faulted him for setting into
motion the events that led to the French Revolution in 1789, his reckless financial decisions, and irresolute decision making. But he softened his critique a bit
when he wrote that "it was Orléans's tragedy that he attained power too late, after
years of idleness and undeserved opprobrium; and when at last the call came,
the mainspring of his character was broken, and only his likeability carried him
through his Regency. Even in rebuking him, said one who knew him well, one
could not help loving him; and by his charm he could palliate his most deplorable actions. Many a virtuous man liked him without respecting him."[109]

Warnie was not the only one who liked *Regent*. David Finch in the *Library
Journal* writes that "Mr. W. H. Lewis . . . has composed an extremely spirited and
witty narrative."[110] Another reviewer noted that the book, along with Warnie's
The Splendid Century and *Sunset*, "constitute a fascinating trilogy on the reign
of Louis XIV and its aftermath. Few historians have mastered the details of an
age more completely than Mr. Lewis or described them with greater charm and
intimacy."[111] Leo Gershoy said, "Orléans has waited long for an understanding
biographer. In this moving work, where the chronicle of his scandals is joined
to a probing and sympathetic assessment of his virtues, the calumniated Regent
has found him."[112] However, some reviewers were critical of Warnie's focus on
Orléans. For instance, L. C. Breunig, writing in the *New York Times Book Review*,
argued that "Mr. Lewis has made the famous rake . . . a very likeable character.
The reader's sympathy, however, is all but swallowed up in a more violent sentiment of disgust for the whole period—and one wonders whether the author's
fascination with the more unsavory aspects of . . . [Orléans's life] has not dis-
torted the picture."[113] Ved Mehta also took issue with Warnie's biography, while
at the same time tipping his hat toward Jack: "Mr. Lewis (a shade too worldly
the brother of C. S. Lewis) has a wry and trenchant style . . . [and] he has written a painstaking, thorough, and sometimes brilliant biography. . . . [But] his

few attempts to rescue the drowning Duke from the sea of history simply sealed his fate as a roué: hardly a justification for another book on the Regent. . . . The tragedy remains buried under the weight of Mr. Lewis's passion for scandals."[114]

Before considering Warnie's sixth book, *Levantine Adventurer: The Travels and Missions of the Chevalier d'Arvieux, 1653–1697,* it is necessary to turn to the matter of Joy's death—after the losses of Vera Henry and Herbert Parkin—the third great personal blow to Warnie during these years. After Joy's return with her boys to England in 1953 and the renewal of her relationship with Jack, Warnie saw what was coming, so it was no real surprise to him that Jack married Joy in a civil ceremony on April 23, 1956.[115] To Warnie, Joy was the antithesis of Moore, and he delighted that after many years of being chained to Moore, Jack was blessed to find happiness with Joy. Warnie volunteered to move out of the Kilns so that Jack and Joy would have privacy, but they insisted that he stay. Joy, unlike Moore, was "a witty, broad-minded, well-read and tolerant Christian, whom I had rarely heard equalled as a conversationalist and whose company was a never-ending source of enjoyment."[116] Jack was elated with Joy, she was thrilled with him, and Warnie was delighted for them. But their shared jubilance was rocked by Joy's tragic turn in October of 1956. On December 30, 1956, Warnie wrote June that Jack had gone off quietly one morning in April and married Joy—who he described as a fascinating woman, an American, and just the perfect age for Jack. But then, only a few weeks later, she had to go into the Winfield hospital where she was diagnosed with cancer. Warnie went on to tell June that Joy had been recently suffering from fibrositis, but now only had a 40 percent chance of life. He confessed that he was bitter about the misdiagnoses, but found Joy's attitude heroic, writing about her marvelous courage, and how she talked about her condition as if she was speaking of a woman she only slightly knew and did not care for. Her attitude, Warnie said, made it harder for them, since a courageous woman moved men in a way tears never did. He ended by asking June to pray for Joy.[117]

Warnie loved Joy so much, in part, because she was everything Moore was not: intelligent, witty, funny, flexible, physically attractive, literate, religiously informed, and devoted, in the best possible sense, to Jack. He also admired how Joy bore the pain and suffering of her cancer and inevitably contrasted her upbeat attitude with the many years he lived with Moore who indulged in self-pity, bathos, and selfish melodrama. But he also loved her because of her genuine interest in him; he was not simply someone to be won over as a means to winning Jack. For the first time since the death of his mother, Warnie realized in Joy how a woman could enrich, enhance, and even nurture his life. During the early days of her battle with cancer, Warnie's affection for her was keen; he admired her bravery and good mood in the face of such terrible odds. In particular, he marveled at the way she treated her illness as if it was someone else's.[118]

Joy's love for Warnie went well beyond her assistance and collaboration with the writing of his books. Given that her divorced husband, Bill, was an alcoholic, she knew all the signs.[119] On several occasions, she tried to help Warnie, at first with some success. After Warnie's two weeks at Restholme in August and September 1955 drying out from a binge, he resolved to stop drinking.[120] Joy wrote Bill on November 28, 1955, and told him that Warnie "is now T[ee] T[otalling]."[121] Three months later, she shared that "Warnie didn't need the A[lcoholics] A[nonoymous] programme—though I bombarded him with AA propaganda and literature, and it may have helped to convince him that he couldn't be a normal drinker. At any rate, he finally admitted this and just stopped! He's been on the beam for about four months now."[122] Unfortunately, Joy's efforts to help Warnie were only temporarily helpful, with Jack writing Greeves on May 13, 1955: "After 9 months of perfect tee-totalism (we flattered ourselves it was a real cure) W. has started drinking again."[123] In Joy's letter to Bill on December 7, 1956, she gives the most comprehensive picture we have of Warnie's struggle with alcohol:

> W.'s off again. He *still* won't hear of AA and tries will power. It worked for about nine months, then he started a series of slips and now he's nearly as bad as ever. His pattern is a bit unusual; he drinks by himself about two quarts of gin, sitting up night and day; then feels terribly ill; then, gentle as a lamb, submits to a nursing home—or even goes there himself, though he may try to smuggle a bottle in. His conversation remains lucid, even scholarly, and perfectly polite, but he can't walk. I wish he'd listen to AA talk! After a bout he is usually all right for a week or more. He stayed heroically sober for about a month to look after me (run errands, etc.) while Jack was in Cambridge, but the prospect of a visit to some friends finally set him off. Jack is far more patient with him than any wife could be and I suppose he'll never really *need* to stop except for physical reasons—that hasn't happened yet; his health is good, and it doesn't take much alcohol to satisfy him.[124]

Despite his battle with alcohol, once Joy's cancer was discovered, Warnie often watched over her, particularly during term when Jack was away in Cambridge.[125]

Warnie was also present at Jack and Joy's "second" marriage performed by Peter Bide on March 21, 1957, and he was deeply moved by it: "I found it heart-rending, and especially Joy's eagerness for the pitiable consolation of dying under the same roof as J; though to feel pity for anyone so magnificently brave as Joy is almost an insult."[126] Once she moved into the Kilns, Jack noticed how Warnie's concern for Joy had the unanticipated benefit of tempering the frequency of his brother's alcoholic binges, confiding to Dorothy L. Sayers on July 1, 1957: "Between you and me, [Warnie] had been for years a periodical dipsomaniac. The blessed & unexpected result of my marriage and the consequent disorganisation of his life . . . and the responsibilities wh. inevitably rest on him when I'm at Cambridge, has been to keep him absolutely sober and angelically helpful for months. It is wonderful. He was almost as much a friend of Joy's as I when I was only a friend and they have French history in common."[127] Joy appreciated Warnie's support, writing Chad Walsh "Warnie is well too; having the responsibility of looking after me and assisting the nurse now and then seems to be doing him good."[128]

Although Joy's initial diagnoses had been grim, her cancer went into remission, and for three years she and Jack enjoyed a love neither could have imagined. Warnie watched Joy and Jack with great happiness, both amazed at the remission and hopeful for the future. As early as July 27, 1957, Warnie joked to June that he had become the equivalent of an unpaid hospital orderly since he was the primary caregiver for Joy when Jack was at Cambridge. Yet he said it had been so rewarding because Joy's condition had improved marvelously, even though they could not be certain of a permanent cure. But what Warnie delighted in most was that her cancer had for several months gone into remission. As a result, Joy was getting stronger, eating and sleeping well, and as happy as anyone could be under such circumstances.[129] He wrote another friend on March 1, 1958, that everyone at the Kilns was filled with happiness at Joy's good health, confessing that two years earlier none of them imagined she would ever see another spring. He added that Joy was spending her time having the house refurnished and painted.[130] Nine months later, he wrote the same friend that Joy kept surprising them by her wonderful recovery and now even walked twice a day up to the top of the wood at the back of their garden. Moreover, Joy gave parties, went shopping, and did whatever else she wanted.[131] Warnie gave June a very optimistic report on December 6, 1958, sharing that Joy had been particularly active laying a barbed wire fence and using a rook rifle to drive away trespassers on the grounds of the Kilns.[132]

However, the remission did not last, and in the spring of 1960 the cancer returned with a vengeance. In May, Joy had her right breast removed, and in June she went into the Acland hospital. For a time, she rallied, with Warnie noting that she had made fools of the doctors again; she was even able to go out with Jack to a luncheon at one of their favorite pubs and take a day trip to the Cotswolds with another friend. Moreover, Warnie was touched that Joy, despite her own intense suffering, acted graciously toward him, giving him a dozen handkerchiefs on June 16, 1960, his sixty-fifth birthday.[133] But Joy's rally was only a rearguard action since a complete recovery was impossible. Warnie noted that her fighting spirit and grim humor served her well, as during her final afternoon she forbade Jack to get her an expensive coffin, insisting that "posh coffins are all rot."[134] The end came on the evening of July 13, 1960.[135] Warnie was brokenhearted, surprised at how much he had come to love Joy. He wrote: "God rest her soul, I miss her to a degree which I would not have imagined possible."[136] On the day of her funeral, Warnie was upset that only a few of Jack's friends bothered to come, and he reflected with sadness on Joy's having left his life: "There is no doubt that cremation is the most dignified ending; Joy really has become dust, returned to dust in clean sunlight, and one does not have the customary nightmare thoughts of a mass of worm-eaten putrescence in a graveyard. At times during the morning I felt Joy very close to me."[137] As much as Warnie had despised Moore, it is important to note how much he loved Joy—as a confidante, counselor, collaborator, sister, and beloved friend. After his mother, Joy was the woman he most loved in his life. In subsequent letters to friends, he commented on his loss. To one he confessed that Joy's death had left a hole in him that no one else could fill. Although he knew his loss was nothing compared to Jack's, he affirmed that he missed her dreadfully; he especially admired her fun-filled life despite her pain and suffering.[138]

The five books Warnie published from 1952 to 1962 are noteworthy for a number of reasons. First, Warnie's alcoholism was often disruptive and problematic. About yet another binge—this time in August 1957 during a trip to Ireland—Jack wrote Greeves: "Telephone call from Eire to say that W was dead drunk and they were trying to get him into the Lourdes Hospital. Then, a day or two later, letter from W, not in Lourdes Hospital, to say he has been diagnosed as having a heart complaint wh. will kill him in a year. It may be true—he says anything in his alcoholic spasms—and I've written to the Rev. Mother asking for the facts. It's weary waiting for an answer. It always might be true this time."[139] Fourteen months later in October 1958, Warnie returned from vacation in Ireland where a binge led to a case of jaundice and another stay in Our Lady of Lourdes Hospital. He wrote June about this and seemed at least partially aware that it was his drinking that caused the illness. Ironically, however, he said he tried to cure himself with an old remedy from his days in China by drinking brandy and ginger ale.[140] The remedy did not work. Warnie also wrote a friend several times about his jaundice, sharing that it had contributed to his depression; yet he would be glad to trade the physical pain of jaundice rather suffer with depression.[141] Despite repeated binges like this and the obvious effects on his physical and mental health, Warnie's literary output reveals that he was a highly functioning alcoholic. Drawing on his finely honed skills as a researcher, Warnie explored energetically the historical period that had captured his imagination since 1919.

Second, as a social historian and biographer, he exercised a piercing, informed perspective on seventeenth-century French history, one that was lauded by popular and scholarly reviewers. Although he had to sift through mountains of already published information, he did so resourcefully, making thoughtful assessments and judgments. For instance, he was careful to comment on the questionable assertions made in some of the memoirs he used, especially those of Saint-Simon. Third, Warnie displayed an intimate understanding of the sources he drew from, demonstrating that he was a careful, judicious researcher; in particular, his use of memoirs, biographies, and letters illustrates how well-read he was and how able he was at marshalling historical artifacts. Fourth, Warnie's understanding of the human condition gave him the grace to write sympathetically about those characters he admired; yet he was not a hagiographer, and he never shied away from penetrating the veneer of human pride and vanity he found among those many persons who populated seventeenth-century France. Perhaps the most serious charge that can be leveled regarding Warnie's books is their lack of psychological insight. Of all the persons that he wrote about—Louis XIV, Mme. de Maintenon, duc de Maine, duc de Gramont, and duc d'Orleans—readers come to the end of their stories without having really learned much about their interior lives. Warnie gives his audience the external view of these historical personages, so that in many ways they remain in the shadows. Why did they do what they did? What internal struggles did they experience? What was the nature of their spiritual lives? What did they most love? What were their greatest disappointments and heartfelt joys? These are not questions Warnie chose to investigate. However, to criticize Warnie for not exploring the psychology of his characters is to complain about something he never intended. He approached their lives from the outer perspective that he best understood. To critique the results as psychologically limited, is as much as to say that Warnie wrote the wrong kinds of books.

Despite the literary success of these years, Warnie was often unhappy, especially with life at the Kilns. Although he no longer had to endure Moore, Joy's death meant that he and Jack had to concern themselves with the care of her sons, David and Douglas Gresham. This responsibility was not one that Warnie was well equipped—either by temperament or inclination—to handle. Warnie sensed a growing darkness, particularly regarding Jack's now obviously failing health. Frequently, Warnie wrote in his diary about his fears of losing Jack, praying that he would die before his brother. Subsequent events would not follow that narrative, ushering him into the final years of his life—ones marked by profound grief, psychological suffering, physical pain, and alcoholic abuse.

CHAPTER 7

Men Must Endure
(1960–1973)

A number of issues dogged Warnie beginning in 1960, the first being his grief over the loss of Joy; related to this was Jack's gradually weakening health. Since WWI, Warnie worried almost constantly about his brother's health, fearing especially that Jack would die before him. Second, matters related to his finances and living arrangements were uppermost in Warnie's mind. Although Warnie was actually financially stable, he nonetheless lived in a state of constant misgivings—convinced he was on the verge of bankruptcy. Third, Warnie had uneasy relationships with a number of people. However, his final years also had some bright spots. He wrote four more books, and while only three were subsequently published, his work on them was an important day-to-day anodyne. In addition, several new friendships tempered his apprehensions, bringing him some degree of happiness.

Jack and Warnie responded to Joy's death as might have been expected: they wrote. Jack composed *A Grief Observed* within six months of her death. A prose poem lament of searing anguish, *A Grief Observed* is Jack's most emotionally powerful book, and passages of raw agony are everywhere.[1] In some ways, Jack worked at and worked out his grief through his pen. Warnie, too, used words to move on from the great loss of Joy. However, unlike Jack, whose intense suffering was that of a lover undone, Warnie's pain was a dull ache, a sense of something forever lost, a melancholy soreness for that which could never be.[2] While Jack went to work on *A Grief Observed* almost immediately, Warnie floundered during the six months after Joy's death, and went on several binges. For instance, Jack wrote to Arthur Greeves on August 30, 1960: "W is away on his Irish holiday and has, as usual, drunk himself into hospital."[3] To another correspondent, Jack later

made a veiled but wry joke about Warnie's alcoholism, writing about "a dipsomaniac retired major I once knew who refused the suggestion that he shd. try
A. A. on the ground that 'it would be full of retired majors!'"[4] However, Warnie
eventually found a project wherein to submerge himself and to alleviate some
of his sorrow. He recalled having read in 1930 the memoir of Laurent d'Arvieux
(1635–1702), a French traveler and diplomat. In January 1961, as he reread the
memoir, he started taking notes with an eye toward writing his sixth book. He
began outlining the book on May 22, finished a draft by August 9, and sent the
completed manuscript to his publisher during the first week of September 1961.
Although uncertain with the result, he was pleased to have it done, particularly
since throughout the writing he was worried about Jack's health.[5] Working on
the book also helped curtail his drinking. In his diary for October 20, 1961, he
wrote: "During the year which ended today I have been a teetotaler for 355 days."[6]

LEVANTINE ADVENTURER: THE TRAVELS AND MISSIONS
OF THE CHEVALIER D'ARVIEUX, 1653–1697

The text Warnie produced after reading the memoirs of d'Arvieux is his most
self-indulgent work; that is, because he so enjoyed reading the memoirs, he decided to highlight those aspects of them that he found most interesting and to
supplement them by translating key portions of the memoirs from the originals.
In addition, Warnie thought *Levantine Adventurer* might appeal to several different audiences at the same time since it was part travelogue—at the time of its
appearance travel books were all the craze—part seventeenth-century history
and part exotic adventure story. He hoped enthusiasts, devotees, and aficionados
of these tastes would find the book appealing. It was published in November
1962. In the foreword, Warnie briefly sketched the early life of d'Arvieux and
offered his impression of him: "[He was] a man who enjoyed every minute of
the business of living, whether he was eating, drinking, money-making, sight-
seeing, or engaged in . . . diplomacy. . . . With all his gusto d'Arvieux was neither
ingenuous nor an enthusiast, but a good-humoured cynic who observed the follies of mankind with an indulgent eye, qualities which stood him in good stead
as a memoir writer, where he is crisp, vivid, and generous."[7] He concluded the
foreword by citing d'Arvieux's first editor, Jean-Baptiste Labat: "One never tires
of reading these memoirs because they are a continuous blend of the useful, the
instructive, and the pleasing."[8]

As a travelogue, *Levantine Adventurer* more than satisfies, since d'Arevieux
had an unquenchable interest in all the places he visited.[9] D'Arvieux sailed from

Marseilles in October 1653 and arrived in the Turkish port of Smyrna in early 1654, but only after a dangerous sea battle with a Dutch warship. After four years in Smyrna, d'Arvieux traveled to Egypt and the Levant—Lebanon, Syria, and Palestine. Additional trips took him to Alexandria, Rosetta, Tyre, Acre, Seide, Samaria, Jaffa, Rama, Jerusalem, Jordan, Jericho, the Dead Sea, Bethlehem, Hebron, Emmaus, Mt. Carmel, Beirut, Tripoli, Cedars of Lebanon, Nazareth, Cannobin, and Damascus. D'Arvieux eventually settled in Seide, where he lived until 1664. Because of his journeys, he became fluent in Arabic, extremely knowledgeable about Turkish culture, customs, and politics, and familiar with the beliefs and practices of Islam. Warnie, himself an experienced world traveler, surely enjoyed vicariously the treks of d'Arvieux, and they must have recalled his own knockings about in France, West Africa, China, and the United States.

The story of d'Arvieux also satisfies readers curious about French interests in the Ottoman Empire in the seventeenth century. A case in point concerns Louis XIV's response to the very real problem of piracy in the eastern Mediterranean. Worn out by the constant attacks on French shipping, in 1664 the king established a French base in North Africa at Algiers. Warnie noted that this action incensed the Turks, so much so that they conspired to get revenge by wiping out all remaining Frenchmen under Ottoman rule.[10] In total, d'Arvieux spent twenty-five years interacting with the Arabs, leading him to appreciate them very much. In addition, because he was fluent in the Arabic, Turkish, Persian, Hebrew, and Syriac languages, he was able to provide Louis XIV essential inside information about how to negotiate and manage diplomacy in the Levant.[11] The last striking quality of *Levantine Adventurer* is Warnie's account of exotic traditions, adventures, and incidents. For instance, Warnie highlighted that d'Arvieux found the Arab reverence for beards fascinating, including the claim that a Muslim would sooner lose his head than his beard. Moreover, horses were widely honored and treated as one of the family—caressed, fondled, and allowed to sleep in tents where children were sprawled all over. An Arab never struck a horse, but instead kissed and talked to it as if were human. A horse that tossed its head when tethered was esteemed because it was believed the animal was reciting verses of the Koran.[12]

Throughout *Levantine Adventurer* Warnie found much to extol about d'Arvieux and his Middle East travels. Although Warnie did not visit all the places d'Arvieux did, both sailed along the French and North African coasts, and Warnie saw Algiers, Tunisia, Malta, the northern coast of Egypt—places well known to d'Arvieux. Accordingly, Warnie felt a kinship with d'Arvieux. As he read about d'Arvieux's involvement in financial and governmental affairs, political appointments, commercial dealings, and bureaucratic in-fighting, he recalled his own military experiences. Of particular pleasure for Warnie was reading through d'Arvieux's memoirs and letters, and it was from those sources that he drew much of what he wrote about in *Levantine Adventurer*. In telling d'Arvieux's story, Warnie identified much that was most captivating, enthralling, gratifying, and reminiscent of his own travels. The reviewer for *Kirkus* praised *Levantine Adventurer*, calling it a "fascinating book" about a man who had "gone Turk." The review ended with high praise: "Mr. Lewis has brought d'Arvieux's story into clearer focus for us with pertinent references to other early travellers in the area, and, unobtrusively, with his own impressively detailed knowledge of the 17th Century European scene. It is an out of the way book, yes, but one well worth going out of one's way to enjoy."[13]

MEMOIRS OF THE DUC DE SAINT-SIMON

The critical praise for *Levantine Adventurer* was surely the catalyst for Warnie's next book. Indeed, it was almost inevitable that his seventh book dealing with seventeenth-century France would be the *Memoirs of the Duc de Saint-Simon,* his edition of Bayle St. John's translation of the volume Warnie first read while stationed in France in 1919. Saint-Simon's memoirs had long been the impetus for Warnie's fascination with Louis XIV and all things related to him.[14] In his first six books, Warnie had drawn extensively from Saint-Simon's memoirs, so in his edition he selected passages that he found most informative—ones that drove his perceptions about the people, places, and events of the reign of the Sun King. In the introduction, Warnie asserted that Saint-Simon was something of an anachronism, since he yearned for the return to power of the old French aristocracy: "In [Saint-Simon's] reading he was as divorced from his century as in his political theories; he devoured old memoirs, genealogies, and the like, and from them he acquired a style which derives nothing from the great writers of his own day. And apparently in his favourite books he found nothing to disturb his belief that rule by the Peers [the French nobility] was the ideal government for France."[15] Given Saint-Simon's views, Warnie argued that it was easy to understand the duc's hatred of Louis XIV, whose theory of government was the exact opposite. With such a bias, Saint-Simon was incapable of seeing the King's good sense in disestablishing the nobility in favor of a new bourgeois civil service. Warnie argued that while Saint-Simon believed that Louis was a fool, the king actually knew Saint-Simon to a much greater degree than Saint-Simon knew himself, a truth which embittered the duc even more toward the king.[16] In reading Warnie's edition of the *Memoirs*, readers come away cognizant of how Warnie was able both to use and to critique Saint-Simon's character sketches; for instance, although Saint-Simon was invariably critical of Louis XIV, Mme. de Maintenon, and M. du Maine—it is not going too far to claim he hated them— Warnie saw through the enmity. Accordingly, his portraits of these characters offered more enlightened and generous insights.[17]

Contiguous with his work on the *Memoirs*, on October 1, 1962, Warnie, apparently in response to an invitation by the New York magazine, *Horizon*, began work on another book, what he called a 28,000-word teenage Louis XIV.[18] In less than a fortnight, he wrote a synopsis of the entire book as well as the first chapter, mailing both to America on October 12.[19] Two weeks later, he was miffed by the less than complimentary editorial response from *Horizon*. He wished he had never started the job and sensed it would be an endless project.[20] Nevertheless, by November 1, he sent his revisions back, and on November 12 he started working on the full-length manuscript.[21] Writing quickly—probably because he was drawing extensively upon his earlier biographies of Louis XIV—he mailed the finished draft of the book to *Horizon* on December 4, although he had little hope it would be acceptable.[22] Over the next two months, he sent several other revisions to New York, noting on February 15, 1963, that he had just sent the umpteenth version to *Horizon*'s editor.[23] By this time, he was thoroughly frustrated with how *Horizon* was handling his work: "The fact and fancy and frustration of this last revise has upset me quite a lot in fits of blasphemy at trivial annoyances, rage at the tedium of life and so on. I probably should have chucked up the contract after his first, & at any rate his second demand for revision."[24] As this book was never published and no copies of the manuscript survive, what Warnie meant by calling it a "teenage Louis XIV" is unclear. Was it a biography of the teenage years of the king or was it a full biography of Louis XIV intended to be pitched to American teenage readers? Although we have no way of answering these questions, Warnie's frustrations with the whole *Horizon* Louis XIV biography come through clearly.

Warnie's *Levantine Adventurer, Memoirs of the Duc de Saint-Simon*, and the *Horizon* biography were important not only because they illustrated his continuing interest in writing, but also because they helped take his mind off Jack's failing health. Since the death of Joy, Jack's physical ailments had gradually increased. Especially worrisome were his heart, kidneys, and prostate, resulting in a medical "horns of a dilemma"; that is, while he needed an operation on his prostate, the doctors did not want to perform one until his heart and kidneys were stronger, but his heart and kidneys could not get stronger until his prostate was operated on. Throughout the summer and fall of 1961, Jack was in medical limbo, writing one correspondent: "The state of my kidneys and heart which the prostatic trouble had set up has to be put right before they can operate and it is not right yet. It looks as if they can't cure it except by doing what can't be done till it is cured! So I'm in a vicious circle—or, as a Cambridge undergraduate said in his Tripos paper, by a happy slip of the pen, 'a viscous circle.' But I've no pain and am seldom either bored or depressed."[25]

Warnie worried constantly about his brother, dreading that Jack's health would turn for the worst. Still, at times he was optimistic, writing a friend on January 4, 1962, that Jack was very much better, with a vastly improved blood count. Warnie admitted to being more happy and hopeful than he had been for some time.[26] For almost a year Jack's condition stabilized, so Warnie could tell another friend that his brother was keeping wonderfully well; and despite Warnie's anxiety about Jack, his better health had been a great weight lifted. In fact, Jack was so much better that he was able to return to Cambridge during the autumn term 1962 and had no problems. Warnie also shared that he thought Jack's return to the intellectual comradery of Cambridge was of especially great benefit to his brother.[27] Indeed, Jack was well enough that he taught at Cambridge from the spring of 1962 through the spring of 1963.[28] Throughout this period, Warnie took a great deal of stress off Jack by continuing to handle his routine correspondence. George Sayer says Warnie was able to do this because "he was having a sober year."[29]

Since Jack's condition seemed stable, Warnie decided to take his annual vacation to Ireland, leaving Oxford in late May 1963; once there, he began drinking heavily. Jack was cognizant of Warnie's binge, writing Mary Van Deusen on June 20, 1963: "Warren is on a holiday in Ireland and at the moment ill in hospital there."[30] At the same time, Jack, who himself had planned to visit Ireland that summer, became very ill, was admitted to the Acland Hospital on July 16, had a heart attack, fell into a coma, and was given the sacrament of extreme unction. Everyone believed he would not survive the night. However, the next afternoon he awoke from the coma and asked for a cup of tea. Jack, now extremely weak, was fearful about not being able to handle his correspondence without Warnie's help. Fortuitously, Walter Hooper, an American devotee of Jack, was available.[31] Jack told Sayer he had engaged Hooper as his secretary: "I want you to like him. I want all my friends to like him. He is a young American. Very devoted and charming. He is almost too anxious to please, but no fool. Certainly not a fool. I must have someone in the house when I go home. Warnie has deserted me. . . . There will be hundreds of letters. I must have a secretary."[32] Jack, who rarely complained about Warnie, confessed to Sayer: "I have not had a word from [Warnie] since he went to Ireland, except a note from the hospital at Drogheda to say that they had taken him in, as usual, drunk. I don't suppose he reads any letters. How am I to let him know what has happened to me?"[33]

In fact, Warnie knew nothing about his brother's setback and was on another binge. Sayer went to Drogheda to break the news to Warnie, but the sisters there told him Warnie was in Dublin. When Sayer explained why he needed to see Warnie, the sisters shared that "he was not fit to travel, and he would certainly drink himself insensible if he were told that his brother was dangerously ill."[34] Since Warnie had not opened any mail from Oxford, the sisters told Sayer they were sure Warnie had no idea of what had happened to Jack. They offered to inform Warnie at the right time about what had happened to Jack. When Sayer returned to Oxford without Warnie, he said Jack was disappointed and felt Warnie had forsaken him. One difficulty in understanding Warnie's thoughts and actions of this period is that he was writing very little in his diary; in fact, from March 7 to October 31, 1963, there are no diary entries and only a few letters survive.[35] In addition, although we cannot know with certainty when the sisters told Warnie about Jack's condition, he must have known by the end of July. But August passed and September came, and Warnie remained in Ireland.[36] Jack was bereft by his brother's failure to come to him, writing Greeves on September 11: "W., meanwhile, has completely deserted me. He has been in Ireland since June and doesn't even write, and is, I suppose, drinking himself to death. He has of course been fully informed of my condition and more than one friend . . . has written him strong appeals but without the slightest result."[37] Nine days later, on September 20, Jack confessed to Hooper that his brother was still in Ireland, and he feared that Warnie would kill himself with drink if he continued his binge.[38] However, sometime in late September or early October, Warnie finally made a belated return to the Kilns.[39]

There is no way to excuse Warnie's unforgiveable desertion of his brother. Although we have no diary entries to prove it, it seems obvious that he avoided returning because he would have to face Jack's deteriorating condition and its implications. He did not want to confront the possibility of Jack's impending death, for he had long feared that Jack would die before him. Warnie was no coward, but the tremendous void he faced were Jack to die before him, led him to act ignobly. Under the power of alcohol, Warnie shrank from facing a life without Jack. Moreover, he could not bear to witness Jack's diminished quality of life. If only the two of them could go back to their early, idyllic days at Leeborough, living vicariously in Animal Land and Boxen, perhaps all could be well. But Warnie knew that was a dream, and that dream could not avert the nightmare that awaited him when he returned to Oxford. Throughout his life, Warnie had leaned on Jack, emotionally and psychologically; to brave life without him was unthinkable. This dread, in combination with the alcohol that now ruled his judgment, led Warnie to act badly. Rather than steel himself for Jack's benefit and face the future with grim resolve, Warnie gave in to his fears and escaped into an extended binge when Jack needed him most. Despite Warnie's deeply held affection for Jack—after all, he was not only his beloved brother, but he was also his best friend—Warnie forsook Jack at his most critical time. Moreover, it is worth emphasizing that this was one of the few instances in his adult life when Jack needed Warnie psychologically and emotionally; regrettably Warnie failed Jack miserably on this occasion.

Nonetheless, once back at the Kilns, Warnie proved a genuine help to Jack, handling routine correspondence and helping to care for his brother. During their final six weeks together, they almost recaptured the spirit of their early days at Leeborough. Warnie recalled their conversations were long on happy memoires and that when Jack remembered them, his spirits would brighten and his smile would return; together they experienced laughter and merriment. Many of the days were filled with cheer, and they drew as much delight from them as they could, squeezing out every last drop of fun.[40] Warnie was comforted to some degree since he knew Jack was ready to die. On the day Jack died, they had spent the morning handling routine correspondence and after lunch Jack took a nap. In his "Memoir," Warnie wrote: "Our few words then were the last: at five-thirty I heard a crash and ran in, to find him lying unconscious at the foot of the bed. He ceased to breathe some three or four minutes later. The following Friday would have been his sixty-fourth birthday. Even in that terrible moment, the thought flashed across my mind that whatever fate had in store for me, nothing worse than this could ever happen to me in the future. 'Men must endure their going hence.'"[41] The elegance of this description of their final moments together illustrates that regardless of his own misery, Warnie found solace in putting on paper his thoughts—a lifetime practice the two brothers shared. However, the pain of losing Jack was such that Warnie did not attend his brother's funeral on November 26 at Holy Trinity Church, almost certainly having drunk himself into unconsciousness.[42] The stone he later had placed on Jack's grave reads:

In Loving Memory of My Brother
CLIVE STAPLES LEWIS
Born Belfast 29th November 1898
Died in this Parish 22nd November 1963
Men Must Endure Their Going Hence[43]

Warnie's grief over Jack was initially put on hold as he had to attend to hundreds of letters of sympathy—for example, one day he responded to seventy-seven such letters. He complained that while he had to deal with huge snow drifts a year earlier, this year he had to deal with overwhelming letter drifts.[44] However, in the midst of such drudgery, Warnie was able to share his personal pain with Greeves, writing: "Of all the letters I have dealt with . . . yours is outstanding. For the simple reason that you and I knew Jack as no other people did. No doubt we both saw a different Jack, but still we share memories of him which go back further than those of anyone. . . . Of all the people I know, we two are the only ones who can really sympathize with each other."[45] Oddly enough, Warnie did not keep a record of his grief in the one place we might have expected: his diary. As had been his recent practice, he wrote very little in his diary during this time. For example, there are no entries between October 31, 1963, and May 19, 1964—the very period he might have reflected on his loss of Jack. Of course, the most reasonable explanation for his silence is that it was simply too painful for him to write about.[46] By early December, he decided he could no longer live in the Kilns. He wrote one friend on December 7 that the lonely evenings in the Kilns, a house he felt filled with ghosts, was a bad time for him. In fact, Warnie really could not stand it, so he purchased a smaller house in the neighborhood of the Kilns. There he believed he would not have to recall so many things that would torment him about having lost Jack.[47] The house Warnie secured was at 51 Ringwood Road, only a few streets over from the Kilns; however, he did not move into the new house until several months later.[48]

THE LETTERS OF C. S. LEWIS

Even as he handled the avalanche of correspondence, by early January 1964 Warnie also began planning to write a biography of Jack. His first step was to advertise for the loan of Jack's letters, and happily he received many letters. Hooper offered to help with copying the letters, but after only three weeks of work, Warnie went on a binge, left for Ireland, and ended up in Our Lady of Lourdes Hospital. Hooper wrote and offered to come to Ireland to help Warnie return to Oxford. In his letter of February 8, 1964, Warnie shared with Hooper the kind of biography he wanted to write: "I am my old self again [and] hope to get home under my own steam about the 18th. When I get back I intend to see what sort of hand I make at a 'Life and Letters' of dear Jack. Not exactly an L & L in the usual sense. . . . It will be more what the French 17th Cent. writers used to call '*Memories pour Servir* etc. . . . ' That is, Memories in order to help the understanding of a man, or a period."[49] On February 28, 1964, after his return to Oxford, Warnie offered Jock Gibb at Geoffrey Bles Ltd. more on his idea of a biography for Jack. He wrote that he wanted to write a personal biography of his brother and best friend. As such, he did not plan to offer critical discussions of Jack's books. Instead, he wanted to gather and publish as many of Jack's letters as possible, especially those in which Jack had offered spiritual and personal comfort.[50] In effect, Warnie wanted to produce a social biography of his brother, something he was used to doing . With the letter, Warnie included a draft of the first chapter so that Gibb could get a sense of what the book would look like.

Warnie and Hooper worked on copying and arranging the letters, and at first all went well. However, Warnie was grieving not only for Jack, but also for his old life with Jack. On May 19, 1964, he moved into 51 Ringwood Road, feeling the loss of Jack even more than if he had stayed at the Kilns.[51] Although he thought moving out of the Kilns would cause him less sorrow, he had a difficult time getting used to the new house, and so would spend most of his days back at the Kilns, returning to 51 Ringwood Road only to sleep. He and Hooper continued working on the letters, but Warnie started drinking heavily again and retreated to Drogheda on June 11; on June 16 he celebrated his sixty-ninth birthday while on another binge. Hooper went to Ireland and managed to persuade Warnie to return to Oxford on July 27 in order to finish the biography. Warnie so disliked his new home that he asked Hooper to spend the nights there with him. At one point, Hooper confided to Warnie that Jack had spoken about him very lovingly: "During the course of a chat with Walter this evening he told me that while I was in Ireland last summer J said, 'Warnie is my dearest and closest friend, and I can never be sufficiently thankful for the way in which he accepted my marriage.' I had always hoped it was like this, but did not *know*; for this is the sort of thing neither of us could have said to the other. It made me very happy—happier I suppose than I shall ever be again."[52] However, Warnie was usually despondent. He appreciated Hooper's help and enthusiasm, but they did little to solace Warnie since he missed Jack more, not less, with each passing day. He also worried constantly about his financial situation.[53] Soldiering grimly on, Warnie completed his manuscript—C. S. *Lewis: A Biography*—in the second week of October 1964, and returned to Ireland for the last two weeks of that month.[54]

Jock Gibb was not satisfied with the manuscript, which essentially imitated what Warnie had done with the *Lewis Papers*. Rather than deal with Gibb's concerns, Warnie, taking Hooper with him, left for Drogheda on November 14, and authorized his literary agents to give his publisher complete control of his manuscript.[55] Gibb faced a difficult dilemma since Warnie's manuscript was mostly excerpts from Jack's letters with Warnie's comments interspersed here and there.[56] Because he was uncertain as to how to proceed with the manuscript, he asked Christopher Derrick to evaluate it and offer a way forward.[57] Derrick offered a lengthy, blistering critique of the manuscript, calling its effect "broken-backed, as if W. H. L. had started to write a full detailed life, but lost heart half-way through." Other objections included no explanations for the omission of some passages in selected letters; the questionable verbal integrity of some letters; the biases of both Warnie and Hooper; and the lack of letters to important people in Jack's life such as Tolkien, Barfield, Charles Williams, and others. The chief suggestion Derrick made had to do with how the book should be targeted: "The book should be aimed specifically at a particular public, a large and growing one here and in America and elsewhere—the audience of those interested in Lewis's mind and thought."[58] Gibb agreed and set Derrick to work on a thorough revision.

Warnie's difficulties with his alcoholism were magnified when Our Lady of the Lourdes Hospital decided that intoxicated patients would no longer be permitted to use it as a place to sober up. Accordingly, with Hooper's assistance, Warnie left the hospital on December 3, 1964. He returned to life at 51 Ringwood Road, and although now more used to living there, he still was not happy; in fact, he was profoundly depressed. In his diary for February 22, 1965, he reflected on how bored he was as well as his fears that his mental state was slipping. Nothing really satisfied him—not reading, not walks in the neighborhood, not even trips to pubs—nor did anything lessen the anguish of life without Jack. He also mused that it was not the recent Jack he often thought about, but the young Jack: "It is the J of the attic and the little end room, the J of Daudelspiels and walks and jaunts, the J of the early and middle years whom I miss so cruelly."[59] He continued to drink heavily. The only place he could go in Oxford to sober up and receive treatment was the Warneford Hospital—a place Warnie called a hellhole and that he was regularly in and out of. He confided to one friend that life in the Warneford was like a prison, noting that he spent the days in his hospital "cell" but was allowed to go home to Ringwood for overnight. Warnie did not like his fellow "convicts" and despised the atmosphere of intrigue, backbiting, and conspiracy.[60] In his diary, he wrote that he thought the hospital atmosphere was killing him. Warnie worried he was losing his mental capacity, and he even wished that he would have a stroke that would kill him.[61] Hooper points out that "one advantage of the Warneford was that [Warnie] hated it so much that it made him want to get better. . . . After being in and out of the Warneford more times than I care to remember, I threatened on one of his visits home to nail a giant-sized photograph of the Warneford over his mantelpiece to remind him of [how much he hated it]—and he immediately began to improve."[62]

The abuse to his body from years of alcohol abuse did cause him to suffer a mild stroke toward the end of 1965 affecting his speech and right hand. Although he recovered, for much of the rest of his life his right hand felt as if being pricked with pins and needles. During this period, Warnie had nothing to do with how his biography of Jack was being radically changed. When Warnie received in early 1966 an advance copy of what was now called the *Letters of C. S. Lewis* edited by W. H. Lewis and including a memoir, he was piqued. Hooper wrote Warnie about the "new" book, and he replied that he was dispirited with the revision, threatened to withdraw it, and burn his original manuscript. He claimed that he never wanted anything to with it, since it really was no longer his book.[63] To other friends regarding the book he expressed frustration, exasperation, and irritation; he feared it would be seen as his "bastard child." He resented Derrick's arbitrary omissions, the removal of details about Jack's early life, and how most readers would find the book unreadable.[64] To one friend, he said he was only partially satisfied with the book, complaining that the publisher turned to a literary editor to revise the book, resulting in a book he did not recognize. Most of all, Warnie was angry that Gibb had not let him preview the proof pages of the book. As a result, material appeared in the book that Warnie knew nothing about, and good content he had supplied in his draft had been omitted.[65]

Despite Warnie's misgivings about the *Letters of C. S. Lewis,* reviewers were very positive. Roger Hazelton of the *New Republic* wrote: "This collection of letters made by his devoted brother strengthens and confirms the impression of the man which comes through his previously published work. The letters sparkle with insight and a low-keyed natural eloquence but never dazzle or bemuse."[66] After giving a thorough survey of the topics covered by the letters, Hazelton offered an observation that must have pleased Warnie: "The dominant impression of these letters is that C. S. Lewis lived as he taught. His Christian humanism was no unstable compound of churchly beliefs and worldly habits, but the healthy avowal and exercise of both."[67] James W. Sire of the *Prairie Schooner* was also enthusiastic: "A heavy responsibility rests on those who forage through a dead man's correspondence and publish it indiscriminately. In those books of Raleigh's we find as you say, letters "like a glass of good champagne" side by side with mere squibs thrown off in high spirits, or mere grumbles written when he was liverish.' So writes the young C. S. Lewis. To what extent C. S. Lewis's brother has been selective in his choice of letters to publish can only be judged by one familiar with the total corpus of letters at his disposal. But surely W. H. Lewis need not fear that his brother's reputation will be weakened by this collection; there are surely no squibs here, no mere grumbles, and nothing liverish."[68] In addition, Warnie would have delighted to read: "W. H. Lewis's 26-page Memoir is alone worth for its handling of his brother's personal life."[69] The most complimentary review was by John Ryan in the *Cambridge Review* who observed: "Whether the [*Letters of C. S. Lewis*], edited by his elder brother, soldier and historian of

France, W. H. Lewis, will be the last or the most penetrating commentary on him remains to be seen. Yet it is certainly true that in his introductory 'Memoir' and his actual editing of the letters selected, Warren Lewis has done signal service, both for what he reveals, and for the taste and manliness with which he carries out his role as editor, brother (and thus fellow childhood sufferer), and friend."[70] In addition, *Letters of C. S. Lewis* brought Warnie praise from his friends and a welcomed addition to his income. For instance, during a gathering with friends, Warnie noted that "all who spoke to me appeared to have read the *Letters* and seem to have really enjoyed the Memoir."[71] And to a friend, he wrote that he was happy to hear how pleasing his memoir was since many others had been writing him with similar praise.[72]

The last seven years of Warnie's life were marked by something of a gentle retreat from involvement in the outer world; while he maintained a distant interest in what was going on politically, culturally, religiously, and philosophically, he spent most of his time in a predictable, regular fashion. In letters to friends written during this time, Warnie discussed his spiritual life, his church attendance, his Bible reading, the Vietnam War, American politics and race problems, student riots, governmental intrusions, excessive taxes, his deep love for Ireland, the Irish "troubles," his great distress at IRA bombings, labor strikes, the moon landing, UFOs, his pleasure at being a published author, and a number of other topical matters. Hooper says Warnie loved the "cosy," so most days he would take a short walk and then return to his study where he would read and reread books on seventeenth-century France, as well as familiar novels by Kipling, Trollope, and others.[73] Another favorite pastime was to reread portions of his diary. At one point, he edited a selection of more than sixty of his diary excerpts that gave him great pleasure to revisit. He titled the excerpts "Happy Times" covering the years between 1918 and 1954.[74] It is worth noting that the majority of Warnie's happy times occurred between 1930 and 1939—a total of forty (66 percent) of all his favorite memories. Almost all of these involved Jack and their eight walking tours. Warnie included no happy times from early 1939 to early 1943, the period before and throughout his service in WWII. In the period from 1944 to 1954, his happy times included various outings with Jack and numerous meetings with the Inklings. Tellingly, he lists no happy times from 1955 to 1966.

Another great pleasure was tobacco. Because Warnie constantly smoked, either pipes or cigarettes, his study retained a bluish haze, and Warnie himself gave off an aroma of old books and tobacco. Moreover, Hooper affirms that Warnie "drank vast quantities of tea and even carried a flask up to bed with him every night so that he could enjoy an 'early-early-morning cup' without having to get up.... Warnie was [relaxed] and, despite all the ups and downs caused by his drinking, he was at all times the most courteous man I have ever known."[75] Warnie also maintained a regular daily schedule of devotional reading. Among his favorite works were the Bible (he read a Psalm every day), the poetry of George MacDonald, William Law's *Holy Life*, Henry Latham's *Pastor Pastorum*, G. K. Chesterton's *The Everlasting Man*, William Neill's one volume *Commentary* on the Bible, and two of Jack's books, *Letters to Malcolm* and *Reflections on the Psalms*. In his diary, Warnie mused on a number of theological matters, including the problem of pain, the death of the young, God's will, heaven and hell, the authority of Scripture, life after death, reincarnation, and the like. Also noteworthy and related were his devoted attendance at and steadfast support of his local parish church, Holy Trinity.[76] He took Communion regularly and observed all aspects of the ecclesiastical calendar; moreover, despite his anguish over the loss of Jack, he retained a resolute commitment to his Christian faith and a steady belief in God. For instance, to one friend he agreed that Christ was alive and vigilant, and caring for his followers. In addition, he recommended to his friend G. K. Chesterton's *The Everlasting Man*, which he said was the best piece of apologetic literature ever published.[77]

At one point, also he reread the diaries of his maternal grandfather, Thomas Hamilton, who for a time was vicar of St. Mark's, the local parish church in Belfast attended by the Lewis family. The experience was sobering, and Warnie wrote one friend, referring to Hamilton as his savagely evangelical grandfather; he said that his grandfather introduced him to a kind of Christianity that burned with vivid, everlasting fire pits where Warnie would go if he did not lead the straight and narrow path. When Warnie's mother, Flora, discovered that her young son was having nightmares because of her father's sermons, Warnie was never again allowed to visit his grandfather unless his mother was with him. He went on to tell his correspondent that it now horrified him to realize that his grandfather was so self-righteous that he believed he was on a first-class train ticket to heaven while he was living on the earth.[78]

Almost certainly the greatest irritation to Warnie during this time was his relationship with David and Douglas Gresham. When he first met them in the fall of 1953, he was staggered by their energy and curiosity. As Warnie got to know the boys better, he thought David was a "detestable spoilt brat," and Douglas "a decent little kid."[79] As long as Joy was alive, Warnie bore no responsibility for the two boys; however, after her death in 1960, it fell to Jack and Warnie to, in effect, parent the brothers.[80] It was not a post Warnie welcomed, especially, since with Jack away at Cambridge for much of the year, Warnie was left to cope with two teenagers. On December 13, 1960, he wrote June that meals with the boys were a trial since they spent the whole time asking him questions he could not answer—from the existence of God to the relative merit of rugby versus soccer. He sighed that this kind of thing was not for an old, morose bachelor.[81] By the middle of 1961, Warnie had a distinctly negative view of David, complaining that he sickened him; however, he found Douglas to be a high-spirited lad.[82] A year later, Warnie's growing displeasure with both boys was coming to a head. He thought Douglas terribly messy, but he saved his most bitter evaluation for David, railing that the less he saw of him the better. Warnie accused him of being spiteful, insolent, and untruthful. Worst of all, since David had become a strict Orthodox Jew, Warnie claimed he was intolerably self-righteous. As an example, Warnie noted that while David had always seemed to hate Douglas, both he and Jack were profoundly shocked one day when David explained it was his religious duty to hate his brother. Moreover, David refused to eat with the rest of them because to do would defile him; he insisted on having his own separate cooking utensils, plates, and cutlery.[83]

As far as Warnie was concerned, Douglas was an irresponsible profligate and David was an insufferable zealot. Yet Warnie's opinion of the brothers eventually switched. Most disconcerting for Warnie was what he saw as Douglas's disregard for schoolwork. To one friend, he confided that although Douglas was pleasant company, nothing would make him work. Warnie worried that Douglas's disinterest in academic success would doom him to a life of earning a living with his hands.[84] Over the next few years, Warnie grew more and more troubled by what he saw as Douglas's feckless waste of money and lack of purpose. Eventually Douglas married, immigrated to Tasmania, and became a successful farmer. In his diary entry of December 27, 1967, Warnie wrote that Douglas had surprised him, since now he was working hard and facing all his responsibilities.[85] Thus, despite Warnie's worries about Douglas having to earn a living with his hands, he not only did so, but did so very successfully.[86] By contrast, the David that Warnie had once found detestable was now a pleasure to be around. On March 8, 1967, Warnie invited David to lunch at the Kilns and was amazed at what he called David's remarkably radical change; the teenager he had once called detestable, self-righteous, and insensitive was now well-mannered and interesting. Warnie found him an intelligent young man who he enjoyed entertaining, even to the point of hoping he came visit again.[87] Several months later, David visited the Kilns again, and Warnie found him polite, undemanding, and given to reading in his own room; when with Warnie, David was articulate and approachable.[88] Warnie's difficulties with David and Douglas were most certainly the result of Warnie having been a bachelor all his life. Having never been a parent, he could hardly have known how to deal with two teenagers growing into adulthood. Although in many ways a gracious person, Warnie was also insular and self-interested when it came to dealing with David and Douglas.[89]

Warnie's relationship with Walter Hooper was also problematic. On the one hand, Hooper had become Warnie's "minder," effectively taking the place of Jack when it came time to pick up the pieces after an alcoholic binge. The role was not one Hooper was eager to assume, writing: "The fact was that while I was forced to be a 'goaler' of sorts I hadn't the authority to do it well and Warnie often reminded me, when I tried to curb his drinking, 'Walter, remember that you are not Jack, and therefore you can't *force* me to anything!'"[90] In addition, Warnie found that Hooper could not assuage the ache of life without Jack. What Warnie longed for was intimate conversation with Jack, but that being impossible, he desired to talk about the man and the brother he knew. It was unfair of him to blame Hooper for being unable to meet this need, as Hooper never had an intimate relationship with Jack. He knew Jack primarily through his books, so it is no surprise that his was a bookish approach to discussing Jack. Moreover, Warnie resented the way Hooper would often invite guests to the Kilns as well as Hooper's efforts to get him to attend events celebrating Jack, especially the annual gatherings Hooper put together. For instance, about the first of these gatherings on July 22, 1966, Hooper wrote that "Warnie was delighted to be with his old friends again."[91] However, Warnie was less sanguine about the gathering and found having to talk with people he did not know irritating and tedious.[92]

On the other hand, Warnie did not fully appreciate Hooper's honest concern for him. While the object of Hooper's admiration and affection may have been Jack, he nevertheless cared deeply for Warnie. In many letters, Hooper worried over Warnie. In a letter to Owen Barfield, Hooper reported dolefully that Warnie had started heavy drinking again. Hooper said that Warnie would barely finish supper before he would take off for the pub. When Hooper queried Warnie throughout the day about whether he had been drinking spirits, Warnie replied that no, he had not. This caused Hooper to wonder if Warnie was deliberately lying or if he simply imagined he had not been drinking. With some resignation, Hooper told Barfield that they should expect a repeat performance of Warnie's last binge.[93] On other occasions, Hooper tried to assure Warnie that he need not worry about money, a subject Warnie called a nightmare. In fact, Jack had arranged for Warnie to receive all the royalties from his books, so Hooper frequently went out his way to persuade Warnie that his income was more than adequate.[94] Hooper always acted in good faith toward Warnie, although sometimes his enthusiasm for Jack led him to do things that irritated Warnie. Although Hooper is most often remembered as Jack's devoted literary executor—and a wonderful one he was—Hooper was also a friend and loyal supporter of Warnie. Hooper once wrote to me about Warnie: "He's a man the more I think about the more I love."[95]

Although on the whole Warnie had gotten used to and was content at 51 Ring-wood Road—calling it a comfortable house in which he had been as happy as he supposed he could ever hope to be—he moved back to the Kilns on April 17, 1967, citing in part his fears of being alone at night. Mollie Miller, the longtime Kilns housekeeper, and her husband, Len, became increasingly important in Warnie's life from this time forward.[96] Not only did they provide his meals, run errands for him, and offer companionship, but also they drove Warnie on many trips around the Oxford countryside; to Malvern on visits to George Sayer and his wife, Moira, as well as Leonard and Maureen (née Moore) Blake; to June's cottage in Walberswick on the Suffolk coast of England; and, most importantly, around Ireland on his annual return trips to Eire.[97] In addition to returning to the comfort and familiarity of the Kilns, Warnie embarked on a plan to read or reread some of the towering works of Western literature—books he believed he needed to value. He found the *Iliad,* tedious, perplexing, and the most dull long poem he ever read,[98] while he enjoyed the *Aeneid* for its "stateliness," likening it to a great literary work carved out of marble.[99] Best of all, however, was the *Odyssey:* "Far the best of the three great poems, and indeed as excellent, fast moving romance as anything else I can think of."[100] His only regret was that Jack was not around for him to have a good talk with about the poems.

His more ambitious reading scheme was to revisit the plays of William Shake-speare, confiding in his diary that he wanted to make one more attempt to come to grips with what made Shakespeare so well-regarded; he was also humiliated by his past failure to appreciate what the rest of world acclaimed.[101] He began with the tragedies, calling *Macbeth* a fair melodrama, shot through with gleams of magnificent rhetoric.[102] Warnie found *King Lear* filled with some of the sor-riest stuff he had ever come across, adding:

The real trouble of this play is that there are no *characters* in it, just a set of ranting dummies; the villains are so villainous that they become ridiculous, whilst the good people are just plain bores, and one doesn't care what happens to either class. Shakespeare might have borrowed from a later playwright and called this work "The Three Loonies." Lear to be sure had some reason for being mad. I certainly would have been had I been compelled to listen to the conversation of A Fool *plus* Edgar disguised as A Fool. I lost count of the number of deaths and could not be bothered at the end to count them up, but retain an impression that by the end of the last scene the stage is pretty well littered with corpses. I wonder how they man-age this when the play is acted? But the Fates preserve me from ever *seeing* Lear![103]

When he turned to *Othello,* he found it a relief after *King Lear,* calling it a really good melodrama worth seeing because it portrays characters whose existence he can believe in.[104] He was disappointed with *Romeo and Juliet* and decided to move on from the tragedies.[105]

Predictably, Warnie found most of Shakespeare's histories delightful. After reading *Henry IV, Parts 1 and 2,* and *Henry V,* Warnie praised the speeches, the prologues, and the epilogues, and declared that his favorite character was Hotspur; moreover, he asserted that Henry's wooing of Katherine bettered all of *Romeo and Juliet.* He was so moved that he determined "to sample the other historical plays, none of which are known to me. From them I shall at last get, if not a quantity of English history quite unknown to me, at least a mass of English legend circle about our history between 1499 and 1547."[106] After reading *Richard II,* he judged it clumsily put together although containing superb poetry,[107] and he referred to *Henry VIII* as Shakespeare's best play.[108] When he turned to the comedies, Warnie was pleased with the *Comedy of Errors, The Taming of the Shrew, All's Well that Ends Well,* and *Much Ado About Nothing. A Midsummer Night's Dream* came in for particular high praise, while he called *The Merchant of Venice* the best comedy of all.[109] He enjoyed *As You Like It*—it had "a fresh, clean, countrified air about it which is most refreshing, and the two girls are about the nicest of S[hakespeare]'s women I've met so far"[110]—and *Twelfth Night*—"the girls are as good as they can be in such an absurd plot."[111] Other plays coming in for high compliments were *Measure for Measure, A Winter's Tale,* and *The Tempest.* After completing his reading of Shakespeare's plays, he noted he hoped at some point to reread *Othello, Macbeth,* and *Romeo and Juliet;* but someone would have to pay him to revisit *Hamlet* and *King Lear.* He might also reread a half dozen or so of the comedies, but surprisingly only *Henry IV, Part 1* might lure him back for another read. In the end, Warnie "regretfully confirmed [his] old opinion that Shakespeare is not for me."[112]

Two late friendships brought Warnie a great deal of pleasure. The first was with Clyde Kilby, Professor of English at Wheaton College in Wheaton, Illinois. One day, Kilby surprised Warnie by knocking on the door, but instead of reacting negatively to him as he often did when someone showed up unexpectedly, Warnie remembered him as an old pen friend of Jack's and so warmed to him almost immediately, writing: "I took to him tho' he is a teetotaler and a non-smoker, being a Baptist to whom both these things are forbidden. . . . I think I'm going to like Kilby, and am looking forward to seeing more of him during his stay in Oxford."[113] Over the next several years, whenever Kilby visited Oxford he and Warnie would meet and travel to spots nearby that Kilby was keen to see. The more they were together, the more Warnie admired Kilby because he was charm-

ingly modesty and innocently good.[114] Warnie found Kilby a comfortable person
to be with, and he appreciated Kilby's interest in him as a person—and not just
as the brother of C. S. Lewis. Warnie's admiration for and trust in Kilby led him
to ensure that after his death, Wheaton College would receive a number of Jack's
manuscripts as well as the *Lewis Papers*, Warnie's diaries, and related materials.

The second friendship was with Dr. Blanche Biggs, an Anglican medical missionary in Papua, New Guinea. Biggs, who had long admired Jack's work, found
Warnie's *Letters of C. S. Lewis* delightful, so she wrote him a letter noting that
his book helped her complete a mental picture of Jack.[115] A lengthy correspondence followed, with each sharing details of their personal lives. In addition, they
discussed a number of topics of mutual interest, including current events, their
spiritual lives, ecclesiastical issues, and the challenges of working with colleagues.
Warnie found Biggs to be a fine writer, and encouraged her to write a book based
on her experiences as a missionary: "As regards your own material I would
strongly urge you neither to burn it or hand it over to anyone else, but retain it
and when you retire, have a go at making a book out of it yourself.... You are the
kind of person who would have no difficulty in writing and I regard 'nearing 60'
as middle age—being myself 73. I had no experience in writing—except official
minutes—when I got my first book published at 58; and my seventh and last was
written when I was 69."[116] Between October 1968 and February 1973, Biggs wrote
Warnie a total of thirty-eight letters and Warnie wrote her thirty-seven letters. It
was a pen friendship that Warnie very much enjoyed.[117]

Although there was genuine affection between Warnie and Biggs, theirs was
not a romantic relationship. The matter of why Warnie never married led several
of his female pen friends to ask him about it. On March 13, 1969, he wrote to one
explaining that he had never married or even been engaged. Warnie shared that
he was not sure why he had never married since he was attracted to women.
One possible deterrent may have been that since he had no sisters, and since his
father had been a widower, female visitors to Leeborough were infrequent so he
had never learned how to interact engagingly with women. He wondered if he
may have simply gotten off on the wrong foot as a boy.[118] On January 4, 1971,
he explained to another friend that during his career the only women he might
have married were the daughters of his senior officers or the sisters of his fellow
officers. Because he did not like the idea of marrying a woman who would be
forced to be as deferential to the wife of his commander as he had to be to his
commander, and because he did not relish the idea of returning to his married
quarters—identical with every other officer's married quarters—to an evening of
discussion with his wife on regimental sport and scandal, he avoided marriage in
the army. Moreover, because he was not handsome, rich, or popular, he claimed

that he had no chance to captivate a rich civilian's daughter.[119] Having grown into adulthood living primarily in male-dominated societies—initially at Wynyard, Malvern, and Sandhurst and then later throughout his army career—Warnie was essentially segregated from female companionship until he was thirty-seven years old, when he retired from the army. Unfortunately, the women he then came into regular contact with at the Kilns—especially Mrs. Moore—were persons with whom he had little in common. Moreover, by this time Warnie was used to living as a bachelor with the inevitable result that he was in some ways selfish and self-contained. He neither knew how to nor desired to have an intimate, long-term, romantic relationship with a woman. On March 22, 1969, he wrote in his diary: "In bed I reflected on my extraordinary good fortune in never having married."[120]

Warnie never recovered from losing Jack. While with time the pain was less sharp, becoming instead a dull throb, still the sense of his loss was ever-present. At times, his sorrow caused him to dream about Jack. In one dream, Warnie thought Jack was among the dead, although he himself was alive. He described the place as a flat, red-colored plain, covered with flints, under a leaden sky, with a great many listless, bored people mulling about. Suddenly, he saw Jack coming toward him, but when Warnie tried to hug him, there was nothing but empty air.[121] On another occasion, Jack appeared in a dream and asked for the return of his prayer book. But when Warnie went to fetch it, Jack vanished and Warnie woke up.[122] Five years to the day after Jack's death, Warnie wrote gravely: "It is five years ago today that I lost my dear SPB and it still hurts; not of course any longer a constant ache, but only rarely does a day pass in which I do not miss him acutely and momentarily."[123] He also reflected on how different he and Jack were. For instance, after giving up trying to read Jack's *Studies in Words*, Warnie wondered: "He and I, born of the same parents, he so brilliant, I so much the reverse. How and why?"[124]

The three great joys of Warnie's life were being with Jack, reading books , and enjoying landscape scenery; about the latter, whenever he recalled the walking tours he did with Jack, the pleasure was so intense it was almost palpable. Unfortunately, because of low blood pressure and poor circulation, in the summer of 1970 his doctors advised him against taking any more long walks, a limitation he sorely regretted . Eventually, Warnie was fitted with a pacemaker; while the device helped his circulation and heart rate, he often felt dizzy, a state of affairs that he found most unpleasant. He sensed that the end was near, so in August 1972 he arranged for a return to Our Lady of Lourdes Hospital in Drogheda, Ireland, where he hoped he might regain some measure of health; instead, once there he got worse, developing gangrene in both feet. Due to his poor health, he remained at the hospital in Drogheda until the following April when he was well enough to return to Oxford. On April 9, 1973, Warnie died a peaceful death at the Kilns, and was buried in the same grave as Jack in his parish church graveyard. Ironically, given Warnie's dislike of *King Lear*, carved onto the gravestone he shares with Jack is the quote from that play that followed him throughout his life: "Men must endure their going hence."

Epilogue

Up until this point, I have, with few exceptions, avoided comparing and contrasting Jack and Warnie. In this epilogue, I briefly turn to that effort. I begin with some of the things they had in common:

1. Both born into a loving, secure, family.
2. Both loved their mother deeply; both struggled with their relationship with their father.
3. Both deeply loved the Irish landscape in and around Belfast; both loved returning annually to the Irish countryside.
4. Both cared nothing for Irish politics.
5. Both loved the ships and the sea.
6. Both hated Wynyard School and were traumatized by the headmaster.
7. Both went to Malvern College. Warren loved it, while Jack hated it.
8. Both had W. T. Kirkpatrick as a tutor.
9. Both fought in WWI.
10. Both purchased, along with Mrs. Janie Moore, the Kilns.
11. Both came back to Christian faith at about the same time and remained committed Christians the rest of their lives.
12. Both faithfully attended Holy Trinity Church, Headington Quarry, a ten-minute walk from the Kilns.
13. Both loved Oxford and spent most of their adult lives there.
14. Both were voracious readers.
15. Both were gifted writers, writing between them almost fifty books, as well as thousands of letters.

16. Both spent the majority of their lives as bachelors until Jack's late marriage to Joy Davidman. Warren loved Joy as the sister he never had.

17. Both loved tobacco and alcohol; Jack was temperate in his use of the latter, while Warren eventually became an alcoholic.

18. Both did a poor job taking care of their health.

19. Both, along with J. R. R. Tolkien, were original members of the Inklings.

20. Both struggled with besetting sins; for Jack it was pride, and for Warren it was indolence.

21. Both loved going on walking tours; indeed, throughout the 1930s a much anticipated and enjoyed holiday was their annual trek. Related to this was their love of the landscape in and around Oxford.

22. Both had a good sense of humor and could laugh at themselves and each other.

23. Both loved a good joke, or "wheeze" as they called them.[1]

Despite these commonalities, the brothers were very different in their personalities, temperaments, and life experiences. A trivial example is that as a young man, Warnie liked driving an automobile or motorcycle; however, Jack had absolutely no interest in motoring. A more serious—and never resolved—difference was their sharply differing attitudes toward Mrs. Moore. Jack loved and cared for her for over thirty years. However, Warnie, who lived at the Kilns with Jack and Moore, despised Moore. In the following chart, I capture some of their other notable differences:

WARNIE	JACK
Melancholic/phlegmatic	Melancholic/sanguine
Practical, pragmatic	Imaginative, sensory
What there is	What could be
Realist	Romantic
More active than reflective	More reflective than active
Prosaic/prose	Poetic/poetry
Of the world	In the world
Tactile; the workings of every day	Intuitive; aesthetics
Hands on	Hands off
Mechanical	Abstract
How things work	Why things work
Things, machines	People, ideas
Facts	Notions
Read newspapers	Almost never read newspapers
Adapting to current society/culture	Reserved approach to current society/culture
Doer	Thinker
Observer	Scholar

WARNIE	JACK
Average mind	Brilliant mind
Down to earth	Intellectual
Continuous flow of life	Narrative flow of life
Historian	Cultural critic
Focus on the day to day	Focus on the eternal
Interest in daily affairs	Interest in the long view
Chronicles life minute to minute	Tells "timeless" stories
Present/current	Past/eternal
Read memoirs	Read epic poetry
Outer life; the exterior world	Inner life; the interior world
Hated cold weather	Loved cold weather
Moderately developed spiritual life	Highly developed spiritual life
Self-focus; peevish	Others focus; even-tempered
Dependent	Independent
"Younger"	"Elder"
Clubbable early on; nonclubbable later	Nonclubbable early on; clubbable later
Many acquaintances early on; fewer later on	Few acquaintances early on; many later on
Approachable	Reserved
Taker	Giver
Impatient with people	Patient with people
Linear	Broad
Interested in the visible church	Interested in the invisible church
Abused alcohol	Tempered use of alcohol
Comfortable with the collective; soldier's life	Hated the collective; scholar's life
Army career	Civilian career
Average memory	Profoundly retentive memory
Verbally noncombative	Verbally combative
Nonpolarizing	Polarizing
Well-traveled	Not well-traveled
Left brain	Right brain

This chart is not exhaustive; instead, it is offered as a snapshot emphasizing some of the key differences between Jack and Warnie. Although some may disagree with my contrasts, I use them to paint in broad brush strokes some of the distinctions between them.

Perhaps the most significant contrast between them is the one I noted in chapter 4 where I suggested that Jack was a sanguine melancholic, but Warnie was a phlegmatic melancholic. Moreover, I argued that while Jack found in Christianity an answer to his melancholy, Warnie found only a partial answer. Here I push this contrast even further. At the risk of hyperbole, my sense is that Jack knew God while Warnie knew *about* God. That is, Jack opened himself up to a full gaze of God; Warnie was only able to glimpse a partial view of God. Jack dove in and risked all; Warnie waded in, hedging his bets. In the fullness of God's gaze, Jack found freedom; Warnie, instead, found discomfort. Although it sounds as if I am finding fault with Warnie's faith, it is probably the case that most Christian believers are more like Warnie than like Jack—and I include myself in the group with Warnie. The following analogies also illustrate the spiritual contrast between Jack and Warnie:

Jack is George Herbert to Warnie's Dr. Samuel Johnson.
Jack is William Wordsworth to Warnie's Samuel Taylor Coleridge.
Jack is George MacDonald to Warnie's William Thackeray.
Jack is Lucy Pevensie to Warnie's Trumpkin the Dwarf.
Jack is Jewel the unicorn to Warnie's Bree the warhorse.
Jack is Reepicheep to Warnie's Trufflehunter the Badger.
Jack is Psyche to Warnie's Orual.

One final comparison. John Wain, himself an Inkling, had great affection for Warnie, noting among many other qualities, his penchant for excellent writing. In discussing the published portions of Warnie's diary, he linked the two brothers: "I think C. S. Lewis is the best writer of expository prose that modern England has to show. . . . He sets out his subject matter absolutely correctly, and his style is perfect from one sentence to the next. It's always rhythmical, cogent, economical, memorable. The words are right, the rhythms are right. The words are in the right order, the images are right, there is no clumsy sentence anywhere. It's absolutely superb prose." The he adds: "W. H. Lewis is exactly the same. In his less ambitious way, there is no clumsily written sentence anywhere in his work. He had the same gift."[2]

If there were ever two brothers devoted to one another, it was Jack and Warnie. That they share a grave on the grounds of Holy Trinity Church is a fitting demonstration of this devotion; they are linked even in death. Perhaps it is best to conclude with the quote from *King Lear* that followed Warnie though life. However, unlike earlier references that only cite part of the quote, I end with the full quotation:

Men must endure
Their going hence, even as their coming hither.
Ripeness is all.[3]

Appendix

A Summary of Warren Lewis's Military Service

- Appointed to a Commission as a second lieutenant from the Royal Military Academy at Sandhurst on September 30, 1914, serving in the Army Service Corps. His initial training occurred at Aldershot and then in France at the Le Havre base depot.
- Served with the Fourth Company, Seventh Divisional Train of the British Expeditionary Force (BEF) in France from November 4, 1914, to September 1915.
- Served with the Third Company, Seventh Divisional Train of the BEF September 1915 to November 1916; promoted to lieutenant on September 24, 1916.
- Served as the officer commanding the Fourth Company, Seventh Divisional Train November 13, 1916, to November 21, 1916.
- Promoted to the rank of temporary captain on October 1, 1916.
- Served with the Thirty-Second Divisional Train November 1916 to December 1917.
- Promoted to captain on November 29, 1917.
- Attended the Mechanical Transport School of Instruction, St. Omer, France, December 23, 1917, to March 4, 1918.
- Served with the Royal Garrison Artillery in an ammunition column, the Twenty-Fifth Brigade, Fourth or D Corps Siege Park, from March 4, 1918, to late May 1918.
- Served with the Thirty-First Divisional Mechanical Transport Company late May 1918 to April 1918.
- After the war ended, he returned to England on November 18, 1918.
- Served with the Sixth Pontoon Park, Namur, Belgium, April 1919 to November 1919.

- Attended training course at Aldershot Military Garrison, UK, March to June 1920.
- Served with the 487th Company (Fifteenth Company), June 1920 to January 1921.
- Served in Sierra Leone, March 1921 to April 1922.
- Served as officer in charge of supplies, Colchester, UK, October 1922 to December 1925.
- Served as officer commanding No. 17 Mechanical Transport Company, Woolwich, UK, December 1925 to March 1927.
- Served as second in command, Fifteenth Infantry Brigade, Kowloon, China, June to November 1927.
- Served as an officer at supply depot, Shanghai, April 1927 to April 1930.
- Served as officer commanding supply company, Bulford, UK. June 1930 to October 1931.
- Served as officer commanding, Shanghai, November 1931 to March 1932.
- Served as officer commanding supply depot, Shanghai, April 1932 to October 1932.
- Retired on retired pay from the Royal Army Service Corp, December 21, 1932.
- Returned to active service with the Royal Army Service Corp, Catterick, Yorkshire, September 4, 1939.
- Served with No. 3 Base Supply Depot, Le Havre, France, October 1939 to June 1940.
- Promoted to the rank of temporary major, January 27, 1940.
- Transferred to reserve of officers, August 16, 1940.
- Ceased to belong to reserve of officers, March 29, 1947.

The primary source of Warren's military service during WWI is a twenty-six-page document from the Army Personnel Centre in Glasgow, UK. This source is supplemented by a one-page summary, "The Military Record of Warren Lewis." Reference 79/P21857/OS9a/EO. Middlesex, UK: Ministry of Defence. Letter from Joe Treble to Ruth Parker, November 16, 1979. See also Joel Heck, "Chronologically Lewis," http://www.joelheck.com/chronologically-lewis.php.

Notes

1. See *BF,* 291.

1. EARLY LIFE (1895–1914)

1. *SJ,* 7.

2. In fact, at various times he did let his diary-keeping lapse.

3. *BF,* 2 (June 8, 1919).

4. *SJ,* 233.

5. J. L. McCracken in his "Early Victorian Belfast" writes: "The early Victorian age was a formative period [for Belfast] in many spheres: it saw the emergence of major industries, the development of its communications, the modernization of its institutions, and it saw also the growth and hardening of the political and moral attitudes which were to characterize the outlook of the majority of its citizens." In Beckett, *Belfast,* 97.

6. Lynch, *An Unlikely Success Story,* 1–2.

7. Edward Harland of Harland & Wolff was the person most responsible for the flourishing of shipbuilding in Belfast. While Harland handled the details of building the ships, his partner Gustav Wilhelm Wolff ran the finances and secured the contracts. Known for the high quality of their work, by 1900 Harland & Wolff employed nine thousand workers. At the conclusion of WWI, the company had launched or had in production more than five hundred ships. For more on Harland & Wolff, see Moss and Hume, *Shipbuilders to the World.* The company is still in operation; see http://www.harland-wolff.com/.

8. Among the ships they manufactured was the first *Titanic;* for more on this, see McCreary, *The Titanic Port,* 115.

9. In 1885, the firm changed its name to MacIlwaine and MacColl. George Sayer, in his biography of C. S. Lewis, *Jack: C. S. Lewis and His Times,* suggests the breakup in the partnership may have been the result of a dispute over a defective boiler. He also argues

that Richard Lewis's character suffered from the early success of the firm: "He soon came to love wealth and became arrogant and snobbish. . . . During the last years of his life . . . he was helped with money by his sons, especially by Albert. He was a difficult man to live with, his moods alternating violently between the heights of optimism and the extremes of depression, a characteristic inherited by . . . Albert. Although a snob, Richard's table manners were appalling. He insisted on being served first at meals, even if there were visitors, and ate rapidly and greedily" (23).

10. For a recent incisive and sanguine appraisal of Albert Lewis, see Hurd, "An Imaginative Tale," 81–90.

11. For examples of Warnie's early drawings of ships, see the Warnie H. Lewis Papers (1850–1972) at the Marion E. Wade Center, Boxen—Leeborough Studies (1905–1916).

12. Jack writes: "From our front door we looked down over wide fields to Belfast Lough and across it to the long mountain line of the Antrim shore. . . . This was in the far-off days when Britain was the world's carrier and the Lough was full of shipping; a delight to both us boys, but most to my brother" (SJ, 11).

13. McCracken, "Early Victorian Belfast," 96–97.

14. Flora's letter appears in LP, 2:299 (May 8, 1900). See chapter 4 for Warnie's work on compiling LP. Badgie or Badge was a family nickname for Warnie; indeed, many of Albert's later letters to Warnie begin with the salutation "My dear old Badge."

15. This in contrast to Jack who was only out of England three times—during a family vacation to France in August and September 1907, later in France from 1917 through 1918 (when he fought in the trenches of WWI), and lastly when he flew to Greece in 1960 with his wife, Joy Davidman.

16. LP, 2:306–7 (Aug. 6, 1900).

17. LP, 2:321–22.

18. "Memoir," 1.

19. Regarding the unhealthy living conditions of Belfast at this time, Brenda Collins writes in "The Edwardian City": "The persistence of typhoid, which accounted for 219 deaths in 1896, was evidence of an inadequate water supply, and it was said in 1906 that the extent of endemic typhoid was such that no other city or town of the United Kingdom equals or even approaches [Belfast] in this respect. . . . Consumption [tuberculosis] continued to be the major killer of adults, accounting for nearly one in every six notified deaths in the city." In Beckett, Belfast, 181.

20. SJ, 13.

21. SJ, 14.

22. For more on the brothers' earliest imaginary worlds, see Hooper, Boxen.

23. Warnie's work on LP began in the early 1930s. For more on LP, see chapter 4.

24. Portions of Warnie's 1967 unpublished diary include comments he made after reading several dozen Shakespeare plays. I discuss these matters in chapter 7.

25. Biographia Literaria, chap. 13; emphasis in original.

26. "Memoir," 1–2.

27. Initially, Flora and Albert had sought the advice of William Thompson Kirkpatrick, Albert's former teacher and future tutor to Warnie and Jack, regarding the choice of an English preparatory school. He expressed a good deal of skepticism about the value of such schools, citing the example of his own son who, after seven years at two different schools, left knowing nothing; Kirkpatrick recommended the firm of Rhyl (LP, 3:25, 28).

28. Lewis, *Jack*, 58.

29. *LP*, 3:33.

30. *LP*, 35.

31. For more, see "Concentration Camp" in *SJ*, 22–41; this is the longest chapter in *SJ*, an unconscious construction by Jack underscoring his terrible experience while at Wynyard.

32. *LP*, 3:35.

33. These excerpts come from Warnie's unpublished manuscript housed at the Marion E. Wade Center, *C. S. Lewis: A Biography*, 21.

34. Rounders is similar to baseball. A batter scores a point or *rounder* by running through four bases after hitting a pitched ball with a one-handed swing of the bat. There is no foul territory in *rounders*, so a ball must simply be hit, regardless of whether it is in front of or behind the plate. Conkers is a game played using the seeds of a horse chestnut tree; the game is played by two players, each with a conker threaded onto a piece of string: they take turns striking each other's conker until one breaks.

35. *LP*, 3:35.

36. *LP*, 3:40.

37. Jack echoes Warnie's assessment of this in *SJ*: "My brother . . . announced every morning with perfect truth that he had done five sums; he did not add that they were the same five every day. It would be interesting to know how many thousand times he did them" (28–29).

38. *LP*, 3:97. The *Lusitania* was the ill-fated British passenger ship sunk by the Germans on May 7, 1915; almost 1,200 lives were lost, including 128 Americans. This incident caused American sentiment about the war to shift in favor of the Allies although it was two more years before America officially entered the war.

39. *LP*, 3:148 (Oct. 3, 1908).

40. *LP*, 3:34.

41. Lunn, *The Harrovians*, 75.

42. *LP*, 3:97.

43. *LP*, 3:150 (Oct. 22, 1908).

44. For more on Flora's death and Jack's and Warnie's reactions to losing her. I offer further discusion of this later in the chapter.

45. *LP*, 3:151.

46. *LP*, 3:147 (Sept. 29, 1908).

47. *LP*, 3:151 (Oct. 25, 1908), 3:153 (Nov. 22, 1908).

48. In a lengthy letter of October 27, 1908, Albert responded to Capron's allegation that Warnie was a liar; see *LP*, 3:152 (Oct. 27, 1908).

49. See "Memoir," 3–4. Years later, Warnie reflected additionally on his experience at Wynyard after a visit he and Jack made on August 9, 1944: "Wynyard itself we found in decay and desolation, being apparently a stores depot of some kind. The unkempt garden showed that it had been long untenanted, so we walked in; it is the same size, as ugly as ever, and filled me with the old half pleasant, half painful disgust and fear. How much of the evil of my life is directly due to Wynyard, and how much to innate badness, who can now say?" He then adds that they had visited Wynyard on a number of earlier occasions:

J looks at the accursed place not only with the obvious thoughts which arose at the sight of it, but also with a sort of bewilderment at the huge cantle [portion] of our lives covered by successive visits to it. On getting home I saw that only thirteen years separated my sufferings from my first visit, and that the old Wynyard days then seemed incredibly remote; that was twenty-two years ago almost to the very day. On Tuesday, 8th August 1922—and it seems as yesterday when compared with the vast space dividing 1922 from 1909. I shall always be glad we made the 1922 visit; for then we saw Watford just as it was in our childhood. I don't think a single thing was altered. ("Diaries")

50. Male head of the family.

51. Benson's memoires of Wynyard and Capron appear in Warnie's unpublished diary entry of July 23, 1960.

52. *LP*, 3:41. Warnie also commented extensively upon Capron's tyranny over his family and employees, as did Jack in *SJ* (see 22–37). The degree to which the latter resented Capron is reflected in his poem, "Heart-breaking School"; see King, *The Collected Poems of C. S. Lewis*, 127.

53. Guthrie, *Vice Versa*, 147. Published under the pseudonym F. Anstey in 1882. In *SJ*, Jack compared Capron to Grimstone: "The reader will notice that [Wynyard] was thus coming to reflect a pattern I had already encountered in my home life. At home, the bad times had drawn my brother and me closer together; here, where the times were always bad, the fear and hatred of Oldie had something [of] the same effect upon us all. His school was in some ways very like Dr. Grimstone's school in *Vice Versa;* but unlike Dr. Grimstone's it contained no informer. We stood foursquare against the common enemy" (32). In Warnie's unpublished diary ("Diaries") for September 28, 1933, he commented on his rereading of *Vice Versa:* "It really is a most admirable book: it reminds me of Wynyard just as much as I had expected it to do—not that Crighton House is very like Wynyard in detail, but there is a common resemblance in that C. H. is a bad prep. school of the eighties, and that is what Wynyard was in the nineteen hundreds. J points out to me that its attraction for us as boys was that it 'was then the only true to life story of school:' and this is so."

54. Warnie also included the grim memories of two other former students at Wynyard in *LP*, 3:33. One said, "I shall never forget that ghastly place," while the other spoke of it with "sad contempt."

55. "Memoir," 3–4.

56. In a letter written just four months before his death, Jack wrote Mary Willis Shelburne on July 6, 1963: "Do you know, only a few weeks ago I realised suddenly that I at last *had* forgiven the cruel schoolmaster who so darkened my childhood. I'd been trying to do it for years.... Each time I thought I'd done it, I found, after a week or so it all had to be attempted over again. But this time I feel sure it is the real thing." From *CL3*, 1438; emphasis Lewis.

57. *SJ*, 21.

58. See *SJ*, 18–21.

59. Albert's father, Richard, died April 2, 1908, and his brother died September 3, 1908.

60. Shakespeare, *King Lear*, act 5, sc. 2. This line is spoken by Edgar.

61. "Memoir," 3.

62. At the same time, I would not be the first to note that the storyline in *The Magician's Nephew* concerning Digory's seriously ill and apparently dying mother may owe something

to Flora's lingering illness and subsequent death. In addition, in Jack's December 31, 1953, letter to Phyllis Sandeman, he did briefly reference his mother's death: "I first met this 'cold blast on the naked heath' at about 9, when my Mother died, and there has never really been any sense of security and snugness since. That is, I've not quite succeeded in growing up on that point: there is still too much of 'Mammy's little lost boy' about me'" (CL3, 398).

63. *LP*, 3:180.

64. *LP*, 3:181.

65. *LP*, 3:182.

66. Warnie cited an example of James's ability to laugh at himself: "On one occasion [James] was voted to the chair at a meeting of the school debating society, and in that capacity saw fit to call to order a speaker whose language he thought to have exceeded the bounds of permissible abuse. . . . [The speaker] accepted the ruling of the chair, but added 'I am surprised that the rebuke should have been thought needful by a gentleman who on the last occasion he addressed me, apostrophized me as 'You measley squirm.' James joined with genuine amusement in the subsequent roar of laughter'" (*LP*, 3:238–39). For more on James, see Blumenau, *A History of Malvern College*, 48–85.

67. Lewis, "Malvern in My Time," 14.

68. Lewis, "Malvern in My Time," 14.

69. Lewis, "Malvern in My Time," 15. Warnie's later alcoholism, perhaps principally caused by grief over his mother's death, may have been abetted by such easy and frequent access to drink.

70. Lewis, "Malvern in My Time," 16. To some degree, Warnie was like Peter in *The Harrovians*: "He found in books the companionship that he needed. . . . He made a few boy friends among the neighbours, but his real life was lived in books" (4). For Jack's panegyric on the Grundy Library, see *SJ*, 113–14.

71. Lewis, "Malvern in My Time," 16. Chief among the Malvern College lovers of golf was the Headmaster, Mr. James. In his memoir, *Seventy Years*, James writes, "What made my own life specially healthy and pleasant at Malvern was the game of golf . . . [so] I always kept two hours open in the afternoon, and I should think I must have had a round of golf on an average of four times a week, sometimes oftener. The nearest point of the course . . . was not two minutes' walk from my house" (184). Moreover, according to "Interesting Golfers":

Malvern has taken so prominent a position of recent years among our great public schools that golfers will be glad to know that its present Headmaster, Mr. S. R. James, . . . is not only a keen lover but also a most capable exponent of Golf. . . . Though it is only since his appointment to the Head-mastership of Malvern that he has had the opportunity of playing regularly, he has been a golfer for many years, and has played on many links, notably Westward Ho!, North Berwick, Bembridge, Felixstowe, and Aldenburgh. He now, of course, plays principally at Malvern, on the well-known green of the Worcestershire Golf Club. Mr. James' handicap at Malvern is seven. He plays better in a match than in Medal competition, as, although he is a good driver and approacher, he finds it difficult to acquire sufficient steadiness in putting to return a good card.

Golf Illustrated, (Apr. 1900): 47.

72. Lewis, "Malvern in My Time," 16–17.

73. For Jack's counter view about life at Malvern, see *SJ*, 83–126.

74. Lewis, "Malvern in My Time," 15.

75. Lewis, "Malvern in My Time," 16. When Albert discovered that Warnie wrote essays for others, he penned a stern letter insisting that Warnie stop the practice. He likened what Warnie was doing "to obtaining by false pretenses," something he said he prosecuted daily. He appealed not only to Warnie's sense of honesty but also to his sense of fair play, a proper respect for playing the game, and the necessity of walking uprightly in the sight of God (*LP*, 3:314–15 [Dec. 7, 1912]). Warnie's response was disingenuous, arguing that it was for his own benefit that he wrote essays for others since it kept him in practice and gave him opportunities to explore new subjects (*LP*, 3:316–17 [Dec. 12, 1912]). However, he did promise to stop writing for others; this was a promise Warnie did not keep. See also Albert's letter to Warnie of December 14, 1912 (*LP*, 3:317–18).

76. Lunn, *The Harrovians*, 37.

77. Lunn, *The Harrovians*, 121.

78. Lewis, "Malvern in My Time," 16.

79. *LP*, 3:202. Without Flora, Albert's grief and loneliness festered, as he admitted in a January 29, 1910, letter to Warnie; see *LP*, 3:199.

80. *LP*, 3:208.

81. *LP*, 3:209.

82. Later letters and diary entries make it clear that Warnie was often attracted to pretty women and had no penchant for romantic attachments to men.

83. See *SJ*, 86–99.

84. "Memoir," 5.

85. "Memoir," 5. Warnie added: "When I first read *Surprised by Joy* I pointed this out to him, and drew his attention to his absurd statement that 'there was only one topic of conversation' in the house. I could well remember many others—theatrical, sartorial, sporting, and so forth. I record the incident with pride, because on that occasion, and then only, I persuaded Jack to admit that he had been wrong" ("Memoir," 5).

86. After Malvern, Hilton spent a brief period at London University. Upon the outbreak of WWI, he joined the Royal Air Force and achieve acclaim as a test pilot. Olphert was commissioned from Sandhurst and joined the Oxford and Buckinghamshire Light Infantry in 1914; he was killed in action at La Bassée in May 1915.

87. Something of the nature of the relationship between Warnie and Jack with their father is captured in *The Harrovians*. Peter's uncle, Hampden, who had adopted him, "was fond of explaining that Peter was to look upon him as a friend, and Peter smiled and said nothing. Wiser men than Hampden know that not even a father can bridge the generation and penetrate the reserve of a boy.... Peter, like most boys, detected affectation and resented it" (3).

88. This incident is more fully described in Warnie's unpublished work, *C. S. Lewis: A Biography*, 24–25.

89. *LP*, 3:246.

90. He only keeps this diary from January 1 through February 10, 1912; the diary does not pick up again until January 1, 1918.

91. *LP*, 3:261–62. Regarding Smith, Warnie wrote about him with great affection. See *LP*, 3:262–63. I offer further discussion of Smith in chapter 4. In addition, Headmaster James lavished praise on Smith in his *Seventy Years:*

Henry Wakelyn Smith was perhaps the most remarkable character on the staff. An excellent scholar and a particularly competent teacher, he had charge of the Upper Fifth Form, in which the newly elected scholars were almost all of them placed on their arrival. Smith combined rigourous drill in points of scholarship with the power of arousing real keenness about the subject matter of the author studied. His "cycle" was not very extensive, but his methods were so thorough that no boy could pass through his hands without having mastered a great deal of very important groundwork, and very few failed to acquire some real interest in the Classics. He was very highly strung and never enjoyed robust health, but he was devoted to his boys and to the school, and when he died (as he would have wished to do) in harness, some years after I left, a very large number of those who had passed through his hands expressed their loving appreciation of what he had done for them. The form-room which he had occupied was decorated with paneling . . . in his memory. (165–66)

Years later upon visiting Malvern, Warnie was delighted to find an inscription honoring Smith. See "Diaries," Sept. 9, 1933. For more on Smith, see Blumenau, *A History of Malvern College,* 58–60.

92. *LP,* 3, 272; Feb. 18, 1912.

93. Warnie wrote Jack about his move to the science curriculum. See *LP,* 3:285 (May 10, 1912).

94. *LP,* 3:274.

95. *LP,* 3:317 (Dec. 12, 1912).

96. *LP,* 3:318.

97. See *LP,* 3:320.

98. See Warnie's letter of March 23, 1913, *LP,* 4:14–15.

99. *LP,* 4:18 (May 12, 1913).

100. *LP,* 4:18.

101. *LP,* 4:18. The Army Service Corps was a noncombatant, though essential, element of the British Army. During WWI, its role was crucially important. According to "The Army Service Corps in the First World War":

The officers and men of the ASC . . . were the unsung heroes of the British Army in the Great War. Soldiers cannot fight without food, equipment and ammunition. They cannot move without horses or vehicles. It was the ASC's job to provide them. In the Great War, the vast majority of the supply, maintaining a vast army on many fronts, was supplied from Britain. Using horsed and motor vehicles, railways and waterways, the ASC performed prodigious feats of logistics and were one of the great strengths of organisation by which the war was won. At peak, the ASC numbered an incredible 10,547 officers and 315,334 men.

102. *LP,* 4:19 (May 15, 1913).

103. *LP,* 4:21.

104. "Diaries," Aug. 30, 1968. In *SJ,* Jack noted that Albert was unhappy with Warnie's public school education: "My brother's reports had grown worse and worse. . . . A certain glazed insolence, an elaborate, heartless flippancy . . . [was] how my father envisaged my brother at this period: flippant, languid, emptied of the intellectual interests which had appeared in his earlier boyhood, immovable, indifferent to all real values, and urgent in

his demand for a motor bicycle. It was, of course, to turn us into public-school boys that my father had originally sent us to [Malvern]; the finished product appalled him" (127).

105. *BF*, 252–53 (Dec. 19, 1962). Warnie went on to fault his father: "For the average boy it is as bad if not worse for him to be condemned to live with those three to five times as rich as himself as it is for an adult. At least the adult can try to increase his income. But [my father] always had a relish for vicarious poverty. He positively *enjoyed* the thought of curates and bank clerks 'keeping a stiff upper lip on £90 a year,' though during the years I knew him he never denied himself anything" (253; emphasis in original). In a later reflection in his unpublished diary, Warnie is chagrinned by his memories of his poor performance at Malvern:

> I've been amusing myself for the last couple of days with putting my little Malvern pocketbook and the log together to form Volume One of my diaries—a saddening task, tho' shot with very happy memories here and there. But the record makes me on the whole ashamed of myself and only now, nearly forty years too late, do I appreciate how much unhappiness my Malvern "career" must have given poor P. Though to be sure the blame was not entirely mine for some of it must attach to his choice of Malvern for me—a choice which only he could have made. With all but four of the Public Schools within his means he must select the one which (as any ex-Public School boy could have told him) hardly troubled to conceal the fact that its raison d'etre was to collect good Prep. School cricketers and send them on to the Universities as expertly trained as possible to compete there for their Blues? What hope was there at Malvern for a mentally neglected boy like me with the crowning handicap of not being brought up to play any game. What could I do but stagnate in an atmosphere in which even scholarship boys of my time more often than not withered. Nevertheless while this explains it cannot excuse my instant surrender to the spirit of the place. Another thing that struck me [was] . . . the fact that I've long viewed my Coll. days through rose-tinted spectacles. The dominant impression left on reading the fragment is one of *boredom*. Now, when I look back on these early years, I realize that I was happier at Bookham than I ever was at the Coll. little though I thought it at the time. ("Diaries," May 24, 1967; emphasis in original)

106. Warnie may have had little choice if he wanted to be successful at Malvern. As Peter found out in *The Harrovians*, "'conform or be kicked' is the command written over the portals of every [public] school" (43).

107. Headmaster James once wrote Albert, "[Warnie] is rather inclined to be what I shd. call 'happy go lucky'" (*LP*, 4:274 [Mar. 6, 1912]).

108. Lunn, *The Harrovians*, 46.

109. Jack writes appreciatively about Smith in *SJ*, 110–13; in addition, he composed a poem honoring Smith, "And After This They Sent Me to Another Place," in King, *The Collected Poems of C. S. Lewis*, 128–29.

110. *SJ*, 126–27.

111. See, for instance, *LP*, 4:71 (Sept. 21, 1913); *LP*, 4:89 (Oct. 18, 1913); *LP*, 4:136 (Feb. 15, 1914). Calling Jack "It" turns into a private joke between Warnie and Albert.

112. "Memoir," 4–5. Warnie's comments on the public schools are similar to those articulated in *The Harrovians*: "Of the public schools especially it was only too true that

they had been, and in some degree still were, the homes of the average and the common-place. They had applauded mediocrity if it conformed to the rules made by the masters for the boys and the yet stricter rules made by the boys for one another" (43–44). Later we read: "'The Public Schools aim at something higher than mere culture. They build up character and turn out the manly, clean-living men that are the rock of empire.' . . . 'They teach boys something which is more important than the classics. They teach them to play the game'" (67). Moreover, "'when we find a boy cultivating his mind at the expense of his body, what do we say? We dub that boy a prig. . . . For it is precisely the discipline of the Playing Fields, the suppression of individual display in the interest of the side, it is precisely this spirit of disinterested loyalty that wins not only the mimic warfare of the playing field . . . but the more real battles on which England's glory depends'" (67–68).

113. His maternal grandfather, the Rev. Thomas Robert Hamilton (1826–1905), was a clergyman in the Church of Ireland and beginning in 1876 he was the Rector of the family's church, St. Mark's Church. Both Lewis brothers spent many hours in church and would have had more than a passing knowledge of the central tenants of the Protestant faith. See Warnie's thoughts—largely negative—about his grandfather in chapter 7.

114. *LP,* 4:15.

115. Lunn, *The Harrovians,* 97–98, 101.

116. For more on Kirkpatrick's influence on C. S. Lewis, see "The Great Knock" in *SJ,* 132–48; Jack's poem, "Old Kirk, Like Father Time Himself," in King, *The Collected Poems of C. S. Lewis,* 129–30.

117. Cited in Fisher and Robb, *Royal Belfast Academical Institution,* 122–23.

118. This difficultly was solved by having Warnie tutored by a local science teacher.

119. *LP,* 4:60.

120. The remarkable parallels between Warnie's and Jack's accounts of their experi-ences with Kirkpatrick suggest at the least that they had long conversations about those encounters; it could also be the case that Jack read Warnie's account in *LP* and freely drew upon them when he came to write *SJ.* Jack's own memories of Kirkpatrick—ones that influenced his portrait of the old man in *SJ*—are found in *LP,* 4:64–67.

121. *LP,* 4:61–62.

122. *LP,* 4:62.

123. *LP,* 4:62.

124. *LP,* 4:62–63.

125. *LP,* 4:63. Warnie wrote that "Kirk undid the bungling of the succession of incom-petents which had begun with [Capron] in 1905" (*LP,* 4:63).

126. Kirkpatrick's letters to Albert covering the months leading up the Sandhurst exams were frank, candid, and straightforward regarding Warnie's capabilities, strengths, weak-nesses, and possible future in the ASC. The one consistent item he reported on was how much affection he had for Warnie, praising him for his congenial spirit, his affability, and his eagerness to succeed. For more, see *LP,* 4:74–126.

127. Kirkpatrick congratulated Warnie on his success in a letter of January 15, 1914: "After the systematic depreciation you suffered for years . . . [at Malvern], this ought to be an encouragement to you, because it shows you in a very convincing way what you can do when you try. I am sure you will work in the same methodical and determined way in Sandhurst" (*LP,* 4:124).

128. Thomas, *The Story of Sandhurst,* 162.

129. Thomas, *The Story of Sandhurst,* 178.

130. Thomas, *The Story of Sandhurst,* 133.

131. "Sandhurst and the First World War: The Royal Military College, 1902–1918." For more on Sandhurst and WWI, see "History of the Royal Military Academy, Sandhurst"; "Royal Military College Sandhurst, Camberley: Changes in Military."

132. *LP,* 4:195 (Apr. 7, 1914).

2. THE GREAT WAR (1914–1918)

1. Mosse, *Fallen Soldiers,* 3. Mosse adds: "Some thirteen million men died in the First World War, while Napoleon in the war against Russia [1812], the bloodiest campaign before that time, lost 400,000 men—some 600,000 fewer than fell on all sides in the inconclusive battle of the Somme in 1916" (3–4).

2. Tuchman, *The Guns of August,* 439.

3. Fussell, *The Great War and Modern Memory,* 7.

4. The primary source of Warnie's military service during WWI is a twenty-six-page document from the Army Personnel Centre, Glasgow, UK. This source is supplemented by a one-page summary, "The Military Record of Warnie Lewis." See also Heck, "Chronologically Lewis."

5. For more on C. S. Lewis and the Great War, see Bremer, *C. S. Lewis, Poetry, and the Great War;* Gilchrist, *A Morning after War;* Green and Hooper, *C. S. Lewis: A Biography;* King, *C. S. Lewis, Poet;* McGrath, *C. S. Lewis: A Life;* Sayer, *Jack.* For more on Warnie and the Great War, see Heck, *Warnie Hamilton Lewis,* 3–22; Mead, "Profiles in Faith," 1–6.

6. *LP,* 4:224. In this letter, Warnie also shared that he had recently been with his Malvern chum, Blodo (Edward Goodwyn Hilton), who was serving as a private in another regiment. He confided to his father that were Blodo to be killed during the war, it would leave a huge hole in his life.

7. Latin for "they pass on the torch of life."

8. *LP,* 4:227.

9. *LP,* 4:227–28.

10. *LP,* 4:243 (Nov. 13, 1914).

11. Michael Young outlines the importance of the ASC in his *Army Service Corps:*

What can one say in general terms about the ASC? Much of what they did was pioneer work. After all, the 1914–18 war was the first war in which mechanical transport played an important, even decisive, part, and it would not be too much of an exaggeration to say, when comparing the situations in 1902 [during the Boer War] and 1918, that a quiet revolution had taken place. Behind the army of men in the trenches on the Western Front was another army which was no less important. Theirs was not the task of person-to-person combat with the enemy, but it was theirs to support, largely unseen and unsung, the men who had that task. . . . The ASC may not have been seen as front-line troops, but in practice they were always up behind the front trenches, either with essential supplies, ammunition, water or the ubiquitous ambulance; and any Gunner will tell you that a good proportion

of their targets are formation administrative areas or key crossroads where moving traffic
on replenishment duties is bound to concentrate (i.e. the enemy's transport and supply
organization. . . . [Above all else, an ASC officer needed] to be efficient at [his] job. . . .
On balance, most ASC officers had a particular skill when they joined, perhaps the sort
of background or ability in practical matters of life which was easy to sneer at but which,
nevertheless, was essential to the efficiency of the army. . . . [The ASC soldier] did not
attract media attention as a hero, but he knew his work was part of a team effort which
contributed just as much to the success of British arms as the efforts of any infantryman.
Together they made it work. The position of the ASC in supporting the army during the
First World War was second to none and the result of their work was that the British
soldier was not only better looked after than he had been at home but also had the best
administrative support of all the armies in the western alliance. (3–4)

12. Rawson, *British Army Handbook*, 125.

13. Young, *Army Service Corps*, 40.

14. According to Rawson, "the ASC was responsible for transporting thousands of tons
of supplies from the ports on the coast to divisional refilling points a few miles behind
the front, sorting them along the way. Some goods were bought locally but the bulk of
the supplies were brought to the base depots on the French coast by transport ships. . . .
Local labour and convicts helped the ASC men unload the ships at the Army Ordnance
Corps' base depots and pack the waiting supply trains" (130). The chart below suggests
the enormous increases over time in the kind of supplies the ASC had to distribute:

MONTHLY TONNAGES	AUGUST 1914	NOVEMBER 1918
Meat	1,600 tons	30,100 tons
Bread	2,600 tons	40,200 tons
Forage	2,600 tons	14,400 tons
Petrol	842,000 gallons	13 million gallons

Rawson, *British Army Handbook*, 133. Young also notes, "Initially the feeding strength
of the army in France was 12,000 men and 40,000 animals; by the end of the war the
figures were 3,000,000 and 500,000 respectively" (73–74).

15. *Regimental Standing Orders*, 36.

16. The largest section of the ASC was the Horse Transport section. Most Horse Transport Companies were under orders of Divisions, with four normally being grouped into
a Divisional Train. Others were part of the Lines of Communication where they were
variously known by subtitles as Auxiliary Supply Companies or Reserve Parks. For more
on this, see "Horse Transport." For a history of the Seventh Division in WWI, see http://
www.longlongtrail.co.uk/army/order-of-battle-of-divisions/7th-division/. While with the
Seventh Division, Warnie was a part of some of the bloodiest battles in WWI, including
the Battle of Loos (September 25–October 8, 1915) and the Battles of the Somme 1916 in
the following phases: the Battle of Albert (July 1–13), the Battle of Bazentin (July 14–17),
the attacks on High Wood (July 20–25), the Battle of Delville Wood (July 15–September
3), and the Battle of Guillemont (September 3–6).

17. Rawson, *British Army Handbook*, 127. Rawson notes that by 1916 the number of
horses had risen to more than four hundred thousand.

18. Warnie offers a full description of Prendergast in *LP,* 5:6–8.

19. *LP,* 4:260–61.

20. Although this is not the place for an exhaustive discussion of the notorious conditions of the trenches during WWI, Paul Fussell notes in *The Great War and Modern Memory* that "the British trenches were wet, cold, smelly, and thoroughly squalid. Compared with the precise and thorough German works, they were decidedly amateur, reflecting a complacency about the British genius for improvisation" (43).

21. Wohl, *The Generation of 1914,* 93.

22. *Regimental Standing Orders,* 7.

23. For information about WWI military structure and ranks, including the size of a company, see "Military Structure and Rank."

24. *Regimental Standing Orders,* 44.

25. For more on this, see *Regimental Standing Orders,* 36–37.

26. *LP,* 4:287–89 (Jan. 30, 1915).

27. *LP,* 4:295 (Feb. 6, 1915).

28. For more on this, see "The Enemy Within."

29. *LP,* 4:312.

30. *LP,* 5:6 (July 26, 1915).

31. *LP,* 5:26–27.

32. For the remainder of the war, the two men met regularly, and their friendship deepened. For example, Warnie's diary for 1918 mentions Collins more than forty times. In addition, after the war Warnie traveled frequently to visit Collins.

33. *LP,* 5:20.

34. *LP,* 5:32 (Nov. 17, 1915).

35. It is worth noting that Warnie's musings on the fate of Germany were almost prophetic, although the partition occurred after WWII not WWI. Moreover, the Allies did in fact punish Germany severely after WWI, inadvertently creating the conditions for the rise of Nazism and WWII.

36. In fact, the Military Service Act introducing conscription went into effect on February 10, 1916. For more on this, see "The 1916 Military Service Act."

37. *LP,* 5:57–58. Jack remained with Kirkpatrick in Great Bookham until March 20, 1917.

38. *LP,* 5:58.

39. *LP,* 5:62.

40. *LP,* 5:69 (Mar. 27, 1916).

41. This is a reference to the Battle of the Somme that had begun on July 1, 1916. By the end of the first day of action, sixty thousand British troops had been either killed or wounded.

42. An allusion to Daniel 9:27: "And he shall confirm the covenant with many for one week: and in the midst of the week he shall cause the sacrifice and the oblation to cease, and for the overspreading of abominations he shall make it desolate, even until the consummation, and that determined shall be poured upon the desolate." The phrase also appears in Mark 13:14: "So when you see the abomination of desolation standing where it should not be (let the reader understand), then let those who are in Judea flee to the mountains."

43. *LP,* 5:109–10 (July 16, 1916).

44. Cited in Wohl, *Generation of 1914,* 97.

45. *LP,* 5:126. See Army Service Records for Warren Hamilton Lewis. For more on this, see Warnie's letter to his father of December 13, 1916 (*LP,* 5:161–62).

46. For a history of the Thirty-Second Division in WWI, see http://www.longlongtrail.co.uk/army/order-of-battle-of-divisions/32nd-division/. While with the Thirty-Second Division from November 1916 to December 1917, Warnie was a part of the operations on the Ancre and the pursuit of the German retreat to the Hindenburg Line.

47. *LP,* 5:148 (Nov. 29, 1916).

48. *LP,* 5:149–51.

49. *LP,* 5:149.

50. *LP,* 5:161 (Dec. 13, 1916).

51. Graves, *Goodbye to All That,* 196.

52. The Hindenburg Line—named by the British for the German commander in chief, Paul von Hindenburg—was a heavily fortified zone running several miles behind the active front between the north coast of France and Verdun, near the border of France and Belgium.

53. *LP,* 5:200.

54. Jünger, *Storm of Steel,* 127–28.

55. *LP,* 5:219.

56. *LP,* 5:225 (June 20, 1917).

57. *LP,* 5:238 (Oct. 16, 1917).

58. "Memoir," 9.

59. *LP,* 5:245–46 (Dec. 2, 1917).

60. *LP,* 5:250.

61. *Regimental Standing Orders,* 6–7. For a more detailed listing of the kinds of training Warnie underwent during this period, see also 37–41.

62. "Diaries," Jan. 1, 1918.

63. "Diaries," Jan. 2, 1918.

64. "Diaries," Jan. 7, 1918.

65. "Diaries," Jan. 23, 1918.

66. "Diaries," Jan. 23, 1918.

67. "Diaries," Jan. 31, 1918.

68. *LP,* 5:277–78.

69. Our emperor.

70. Although America had declared war on Germany on April 6, 1917, its first full division did not enter the front lines until January 1918.

71. *LP,* 5:282 (Feb. 9, 1918).

72. "Diaries," Feb. 9, 1918.

73. For a history of ammunition columns in the Royal Garrison Artillery, see https://www.longlongtrail.co.uk/army/definitions-of-units/the-divisional-ammunitioncolumn/. Warnie was one of four officers in a unit of just over 250 men that oversaw 21 riding horses and 310 draught horses.

74. "Diaries," Mar. 8, 1918.

75. "Diaries," Mar. 18, 1918.

76. Cited in Young, *Army Service Corps,* 81.

77. Hemingway, "A Way You'll Never Be," in *The Nick Adams Stories,* 135–36.

78. From March 21 to April 5, 1918, the German offensive—the Second Battle of the Somme—had limited success, but it was a hollow victory since the German losses in manpower and equipment were greater than the Allies.

79. Diaries summary for March 1918.

80. Cited in Young, *Army Service Corps,* 73.

81. *LP,* 5:305.

82. From April 7 to April 29, 1918, the second phase of the German spring offensive, the Battle of the Lys, occurred. The final results were a great disappointment for the Germans.

83. *LP,* 5:306.

84. Albert had received the following telegram from the War Office: "2nd Lt. C. S. Lewis Somerset Light Infantry wounded April fifteenth" (*LP,* 5:308).

85. "Diaries," Apr. 24, 1918.

86. *LP,* 5:309 (Apr. 24, 1918). Almost certainly, Albert had been the one to exaggerate the wounds to "severely."

87. *LP,* 5:309 (Apr. 24, 1918). For more exact information on Jack's wounds and the death of Sergeant Ayers, see C. S. Lewis's letters to his father, *CL1,* 367 (May 4, 1918); *CL1,* 368–39 (May 14, 1918); *SJ,* 194–95.

88. Diaries summary for April 1918.

89. For a history of the Thirty-First Division in WWI, see http://www.longlongtrail. co.uk/army/order-of-battle-of-divisions/31st-division/. While with the Thirty-First Division, Warnie was involved in the following actions: the Battle of St, Quentin, the Battle of Bapaume, the First Battle of Arras, the Battle of Estaires, the Battle of Hazebrouck, the Defence of Nieppe Forest, the Battles of the Lys, and the Battle of Ypres.

90. The Victoria Cross is the highest award for gallantry that a British serviceman or woman can achieve. The VC is linked with acts of extreme bravery and is only merited for those who have demonstrated "gallantry of the highest order." The award is presented to those who, in the presence of the enemy, displayed conspicuous gallantry, a daring or preeminent act of valor or self-sacrifice, or extreme devotion to duty.

91. According to Young: "There were two reasons why the ASC soldier did well: firstly he wanted to help the fighting units as best he could. He saw enough dead and wounded to know that those units needed his personal support, and he was not going to let them down; and, secondly, he had great pride in his work, often as a skilled tradesman, doing a job he knew no one in an infantry battalion could do" (*Army Service Corps,* 4).

92. *LP,* 5:316. The best-known and longest-lasting nickname of the ASC was "Jam Stealers" (Young, *Army Service Corps,* 74). Warnie added in the letter that this was actually the second VC awarded to a member of the ASC.

93. "Diaries," June 6, 1918.

94. *LP,* 5:324 (June 7, 1918).

95. "Diaries," May 20, 1918.

96. "Diaries," Oct. 22, 1918; *LP,* 6:41 (Sept. 24, 1918).

97. *LP,* 6:14–15. French general, Ferdinand Foch (1851–1929), led the Allied forces during the Second Battle of Marne.

98. *LP,* 6:29 (Sept. 8, 1918).

99. Diaries summary for September 1918.

100. Flares shot by a gun.

101. *BF,* 3–4 (Nov. 10, 1918).

102. One motto about the armistice marking the end of the war put it this way: "On the eleventh month, on the eleventh day, on the eleventh hour."

103. *BF,* 4 (Nov. 11, 1918).

104. *LP,* 6:73 (Nov. 29, 1918).

105. *LP,* 6:79.

106. Fussell, *The Great War,* 8.

107. Johnston, *English Poetry of the First World War,* 13.

108. *LP,* 4:308 (Apr. 9, 1915). Warnie's tender yet ironic musing on the beauty of the sunset is reflected in many WWI writings. According to Paul Fussell: "When a participant in the war wants an ironic effect, a conventional way to achieve one is simply to juxtapose a sunrise or sunset with the unlovely physical details of the war" (*The Great War,* 55).

109. *LP,* 5:192–93 (Mar. 9, 1917).

110. *LP,* 6:30 (Sept. 8, 1918).

111. *LP,* 4:143.

112. *LP,* 5:7.

113. *LP,* 6:35–36 (Sept. 18, 1918). Warnie's favorable account of Grant stands in stark contrast with the previously described "rotter," Ronald Maclear.

3. ARMY CAREER (1919–1932)

1. Poet Ruth Pitter (1897–1992) recalled that because so many young English men had been killed in WWI, it seemed inevitable that she and thousands of other women would never be able to marry. She said she belonged to a generation of "surplus women" (cited in King, *Hunting the Unicorn,* 26).

2. Montague, *Disenchantment,* 77.

3. Sassoon, *War Poems,* 57.

4. For more on this, see Graubard, "Military Demobilization in Great Britain Following the Great War," 297–311; "Demobilisation after the First World War"; "Demobilisation and Discharge"; "Demobilisation in Britain, 1918–20."

5. For more on this, see Seipp, *The Ordeal of Peace,* 1–24; "Military Structures and Rank." As noted in the previous chapter, of the 6.2 million mobilized British soldiers, 750,000 were killed during the war.

6. Graubard, "Military Demobilization in Great Britain Following the Great War," 304.

7. Churchill, *The World Crisis,* 46.

8. The Army Service Corps was renamed the Royal Army Service Corps (RASC) in 1918 in recognition of its role in WWI.

9. Jack had been demobilized on December 24, 1918. After a brief time in Belfast, he returned to his studies in Oxford on January 13, 1919.

10. The precise way in which Jack and Moore came to set up house together was something Warnie never learned, but Jack made clear the subject was off-limits. For more on this, see Lewis, *C. S. Lewis: A Biography,* 66.

11. For more on this, see Green and Hooper, *C. S. Lewis: A Biography*; McGrath, *C. S. Lewis, A Life*; Sayer, *Jack*; Wilson, *C. S. Lewis: A Biography*. In a 2009 interview that Chris Mitchell, late director of the Marion E. Wade Center, had with Walter Hooper but only made public in December 2021, Hooper revealed for the first time what Owen Barfield said about the nature of the relationship between Jack and Mrs. Moore:

> Owen Barfield told me that yes, Lewis told him there had been a sexual relationship and it began really at the time, right after he came out of the army. And [Lewis], as he himself has said about himself he was not a moral man at that time. He believed in morality, he believed in goodness, but anyway, he—they did have an affair. And it lasted until Lewis was converted to Christianity. And Lewis told Owen Barfield that part of his reparation for all of that took the form of, first of all he stopped having the sexual relationship with Mrs. Moore as soon as he was converted to Christianity, and he thought that his penance should be and was looking after that lady for the rest of his life.

Oral history interview excerpt with Walter Hooper, December 21, 2009, used with permission.

12. Fortescue adds: "So much damage was thereby done to the [Royal Army Service] Corps that in 1925 the authorities agreed to restore two-thirds of the former allowance. But this is not the fashion in which a highly skilled body of men, of proved worth and of vital importance to the Army, should be treated" ("Introduction," *The Royal Army Service Corps*, lii–liii).

13. *LP*, 6:84.

14. Smith had been the victim of a severe influenza outbreak. In a letter to Warnie of February 11, 1919, Albert recalls how many of Smith's remarks are embedded in their everyday home conversations, so much so that he thinks of Smith as a second Kirkpatrick; he believes that Smith must have known how much affection the boys had for him and that must have provided some consolation for having never married nor had children of his own (*LP*, 6:88). Years later upon visiting Malvern, Warnie was delighted to find an inscription on a panel honoring Smith (to which both he and Jack had contributed): "This memorial is erected to a man who, having dwelt here a long time, during his mastership charmed the minds of boys with his kindly teaching, so that, nothing loath, they tended the flowery precinct of the muses. Death stayed him from his loved task, and he lives, having an imperishable name, an honoured friend." For more see "Diaries," Sept. 9, 18, 1933.

15. This conflict began on January 21, 1919, and lasted until July 11, 1921. One curious fact about Albert Lewis and his two sons was their lack of interest in these Irish conflicts, at least as reflected in their letters. Although they did on occasion mention events related to these troubles, for the most part they appeared to be outsiders watching the events from a distance.

16. For instance, see Sassoon, *Memoirs of a Fox-Hunting Man*.

17. *LP*, 6:93 (Feb. 23, 1919).

18. Later, he published his own translation of these memoirs, *Memoirs of the Duc de Saint-Simon*; for more on his translation, see chapter 7. For an excellent recent translation, see Norton, *Saint-Simon at Versailles*.

19. From the publisher's biographical note on the dust jacket of Warnie's *Levantine Adventurer*.

20. *LP,* 6:95.

21. Neither Albert nor Jack thought much of Warnie's request to see service in Russia. Albert said it made him depressed and miserable (*LP,* 6:103 [Apr. 2, 1919]). Jack, employing some hyperbole, was incredulous, wondering why in the name of all that was holy would his brother want to join the Russian Expeditionary force. He predicted Warnie would be bereft of drink, books, and tobacco and eventually be captured by the Bolshevists, who would nail him on a stake or cross (*CL1,* 445 [Apr. 2?, 1919]). For more, see "Britain and the Russian Civil War."

22. "Death in Battle" was first published in *Reveille* 3 (Feb. 1919): 508; it later appeared as the final poem in *Spirits in Bondage.* See King, *The Collected Poems of C. S. Lewis,* 116.

23. *LP,* 6:101–2.

24. The Battle of Waterloo occurred on June 15, 1815, and resulted in the final defeat of Napoleon Bonaparte (1769–1821) and the French army.

25. The biography Warnie read was probably R. Bosworth Smith's *Life of Lord Lawrence.*

26. *LP,* 6:108–10.

27. *LP,* 6:114.

28. For more on Warnie's suspicions and dislike of Moore, see Green and Hooper, *C. S. Lewis: A Biography,* 66; Sayer, *Jack,* 89, 94–96, 103–4, 203; Wilson, *C. S. Lewis: A Biography,* 139–41, 153, 224–25; McGrath, *C. S. Lewis: A Life,* 124–27, 245–47; King, "Warnie Lewis, Mrs Janie King Moore, and the Kilns," 103–18. In addition, see chapter 5.

29. When he learned of Paddy's death, Albert wrote Moore a letter of condolence. On October 1, 1918, Moore replied, telling Albert that she had lived her life for Paddy, and that she was struggling to go on living. All her hopes had been focused on her son, and they were now buried along with many others at the Somme battlefield. She noted that of the five boys who used to visit her regularly in prewar Oxford, only Jack survived. She gave way to her pain and bitterness, claiming that the war was terribly wicked and cruel. Yet she was thankful that Jack had helped her immensely, staying true to his word to Paddy that he would look after her if he did not survive (*LP,* 6:44–45).

30. In his "Memoir," Warnie offered an explanation for why Albert did not respond to Jack's pleas. He admitted it seems unlikely that a father would refuse such a request from a wounded son. However, Warnie noted that his father was idiosyncratic, especially when faced with altering his daily, if dull, routine. Albert had an almost pathological hatred of varying his day-to-day activities, so Jack remained unvisited. In Warnie's opinion, Jack was profoundly hurt by Albert's callous and unforgiveable indifference. Since his father abandoned him and rejected his requests for a visit, Jack turned to Moore instead, realizing the parental affection that Albert would not or could not provide (9–10).

31. *LP,* 6:118.

32. *LP,* 6:123.

33. *LP,* 6:129.

34. The treaty was signed on June 28, 1919.

35. Letters from Jack during this period noted that Albert was becoming more and more difficult to be around. On June 9, 1919, he told his brother that life with their father was becoming unbearable. Although he knew that Warnie understood how hard it was to live with their father, during his last visit home Jack found it insufferable. Albert was intrusive, fussy, and sulking. This letter also suggests Albert was prone to fits of solitary

drinking; if this was true, there may be a strong genetic case to be made for Warnie's own growing reliance on alcohol (*CL1*, 455).

36. He had applied for a tour of overseas service; I offer further discussion of this later in the chapter.

37. *BF,* 2 (June 8, 1918).

38. It was popular to keep a diary in England when Warnie decided to start his. For more on this, see Rodriguez, "Writing for the Record."

39. His assigned military servant.

40. "Diaries," June 24, 25, 1919.

41. "Diaries," summer 1920 (?).

42. For more, see "The Sex Life of Samuel Pepys" and "Samuel Pepys Diary: Coded Passages."

43. Pepys used a mixture of Spanish, French, and Italian. Moreover, the entirety of Pepys's diary was written in kind of shorthand, probably as way of thwarting any of his family or friends from understanding his text were they to come upon it.

44. "Diaries," July 2, 1919.

45. "Diaries," Aug. 22, 1919. In a letter to Arthur Greeves on August 24, 1919, Jack said that he and Warnie had a nice day in Dublin and that he very much enjoyed meeting Collins (*CL1*, 463).

46. For more on this, see *CL1*, 462–63.

47. "Diaries," Aug. 9, 1919. Albert wrote in his diary of September 5, 1919, about how devastating this incident was. He said that he had just passed through one of the most miserable periods of his life, claiming that Jack had insulted him by saying terrible and despicable things to him. Albert believed Jack had rejected his love, devotion, and sacrifice, and no longer respected him. He also admitted to one of Jack's most serious complaints against him—that he did not visit his son while he was recovering from his war wounds in London. Even so, Albert was defensive: "I should have sacrificed everything [to visit him in hospital] . . . had he not been comfortable and making good progress. . . . The loss of Jack's affection, if it be permanent, is irreparable and leaves me very miserable and heart sore" (*LP,* 6:167).

48. "Diaries." Summary for 1920.

49. According to Joel Heck in "C. S. Lewis Serendipities: Things You Never Knew about Jack and Warren," there is no motorcycle brand named Daudel, so the term was probably Warnie's slang for a Triumph motorcycle. Daudel "is perhaps related to the Swiss word Badautle, which means 'simple person.'" Heck points out that Warnie often referred to taking Jack for a ride on his Daudelspiel. "The word spiel is German for 'play,' 'game,' or 'sport.'" Heck believes "if the word spiel is a foreign word, then the word Daudel likely is also" (5). The motorcycles of this time were not particularly fast, so Daudel also may be a pun on dawdle.

50. *BF,* 5.

51. "Diaries," Feb. 24, 1921.

52. "Diaries," Feb. 15, 1921. For more on Warnie's antipathy for his grandfather, see chapter 7.

53. For more on the history of Sierra Leone, see Fyfe, *A History of Sierra Leone;* Alie, *A New History of Sierra Leone;* "History of Sierra Leone."

54. Indeed, his control of the ice factory made him a force to be reckoned with; he writes amusingly about this in his June 13, 1921, letter to his father. See *LP,* 7:9.

55. Conrad, *Heart of Darkness and the Secret Sharer,* 88. Conrad's double meaning is clear—Europeans working the tropics need to have strong digestive systems to survive (straight pipes), while at the same time they need to have no moral consciences.

56. In a letter of March 26, 1921, he offers his father a full account of his typical day. See *LP,* 6:267.

57. "Diaries," Apr. 8, 1921.

58. "Diaries," Apr. 24, 1921.

59. "Diaries," Jan. 1, 1922.

60. "Diaries," Aug. 11, 1921.

61. "Diaries," Aug. 16, 1921.

62. In an ironic coincidence, Warnie's suffering with anal boils is something that also afflicted the French king he would later write about so extensively, Louis XIV.

63. "Diaries," Apr. 19, 1921. Also, see in his April 20, 1921, letter to his father (*LP,* 6:283).

64. *LP,* 6:276–77 (Apr. 8, 1921).

65. "Diaries," Mar. 19, 1921.

66. "Diaries," Jan. 14, 1922.

67. "Diaries," Apr. 7, 1921. When Jack learns of Warnie's penchant for Milton, he says he is glad to hear Warnie is a convert to his work (*CL1,* 538 [Apr. 20, 1921]).

68. "Diaries," Apr. 15, 1921.

69. *LP,* 7:8 (June 13, 1921).

70. *LP,* 6:275–76.

71. "Diaries," June 2, 1921.

72. *AMR,* 82. Warnie disliked Maureen in the early days of their relationship. However, he quickly grew to appreciate and care greatly for her. For more on Warnie and Maureen, see chapter 4 and *BF,* 129, 198–99, 217, 232.

73. *AMR,* 81 (Aug. 3, 1922).

74. *AMR,* 81 (Aug. 4, 1922).

75. *ARM,* 84 (Aug. 11–14, 1922).

76. *ARM,* 84. After the death of Moore on January 12, 1951, Warnie reflected with some bitterness about his initial encounters with her. See *BF,* 236–39 (Jan. 17, 1951). I offer further discussion of Warnie's disaffection with Moore in chapters 4 and 5.

77. *AMR,* 82–83.

78. *BF,* 10. Apparently, Maureen was given to pestering Warnie. On August 14, 1922, Jack writes that a day of punting had been good, "tho' Maureen was rather a nuisance. No doubt it is good for W. to be teased by her, but it is very bad for her to learn this sort of licensed buffoonery" (*AMR,* 85).

79. *BF,* 12–13 (Sept. 29, 1922).

80. D. was one nickname Jack had for Moore.

81. *AMR,* 90.

82. *AMR,* 93 (Aug. 25, 1922).

83. *SJ,* 6.

84. *BF,* 13 (Sept. 29, 1922).

85. "Diaries," Oct. 1, 1922. He also remarked that the sermon was pathetic.

86. *AMR,* 88 (Aug. 19, 1922).

87. *AMR,* 158 (Dec. 25, 1922).

88. *AMR,* 164 (Dec. 30, 1922). Moreover, Albert was giving Warnie a regular financial supplement and covering some of his debts as well. See "Diaries," Jan. 1, 1923; his letters to Albert, *LP,* 8:237–38 (June 8, 1924); *LP,* 8:248–50 (June 24, 1924).

89. Pudaita was the nickname Jack and Warnie gave their father. The nickname is explained in *BF:* "Products of the English public school system, both boys soon learned to despise dialects that differed from the King's English; this of course particularly applied to the strong Northern Irish accent of their youth. One day, when Albert accidentally slipped from his normally dignified manner of speech into a working class pronunciation of potatoes ('pudaitas'), his delighted sons discovered a new name: 'Pudaita' or alternately, 'Pudaitabird'" (6). Warnie commented on the origins of "Pudaita Pie" on September 29, 1922: "A feature of this holiday which I have not touched upon I find, is 'Pudaita Pie': I had suggested to J that it would be a good thing to keep a written record of the most amusing remarks of the OAB and he took up the idea very keenly: between us we harvested more than forty of his historic utterances, which J has written up with a very excellent little preface" (*BF,* 13).

90. Lewis and Lewis, "*The Pudaita Pie,*" 59–68. For more on this, see Hurd, "*The Pudaita Pie,*" 47–58.

91. "Memoir," 21.

92. *BF,* 278 (Aug. 20, 1967); emphasis in original.

93. Moore, *The Ulsterman,* 172.

94. Moore, *The Ulsterman,* 252.

95. *BF,* 279.

96. See his letter to Albert, *LP,* 8:220 (May 4, 1924).

97. From January 1924 and through January 1925 Warnie read more than 100 books; the list of the books he read serves as his complete diary for this time period.

98. "Diaries," Sept. 25, 1925.

99. "Diaries," Sept. 30, 1925.

100. "Diaries," Oct. 1, 1925.

101. "Diaries," Oct. 3, 1925.

102. For examples of the many trips they took together, see *AMR,* 315–17 (Apr. 18, 1924); *AMR,* 341–44 (July 3–7, 1924).

103. *AMR,* 226 (Mar. 30, 1923).

104. *AMR,* 234 (May 22, 1923).

105. "Diaries," Oct. 5, 1933.

106. About this time, Warnie wrote that his only happy memories of Woolwich were the summer weekends spent at Sandgate just outside Folkestone. He also had one good leave when he spent ten days alone at Leeborough with the Daudel, and then a few days in Oxfordshire village of Appleton with Jack and the Moores ("Diaries," Apr. 3, 1927).

107. For more, see Nish, "An Overview of Relations between China and Japan, 1918–1945," 601–23.

108. *LP,* 9:184.

109. *BF,* 15.

110. *BF,* 15.

111. *LP,* 9:239 (June 7, 1927).

112. *LP,* 9:243 (June 14, 1927).

113. *LP,* 9:279 (Sept. 12, 1927).

114. "Diaries," Apr. 7, 1928.

115. "Diaries," Jan. 25, 1929.

116. On Albert's religious musings, see *LP,* 9:138–39.

117. Jack began as a lecturer at Magdalen College in June 1925.

118. *LP,* 9:139.

119. See *CL1,* 799 (July 7, 1929).

120. *BF,* 16.

121. *CL1,* 827; emphasis in original.

122. *LP,* 10:208.

123. *BF,* 66 (Oct. 1, 1930).

124. *BF,* 31 (Apr. 6, 1930). For more on this trip, see *BF,* 17–35.

125. *CL1,* 888 (Apr. 3, 1930).

126. I can only guess that Jack's reference to Moore's "burnetto-desmondism" refers to her tendency to be angry and demanding.

127. This is Jack's shorthand description of the idealized life he and Warnie had enjoyed in their early days at Leeborough.

128. This is Jack's shorthand description of his less than rosy current life living with Mrs. Moore, Maureen, and the odd assortment of characters that often gathered around them.

129. *CL1,* 869–71 (Jan. 12, 1930).

130. For Warnie's fullest musings on the pros and cons of moving into Hillsboro, see *BF,* 51–52 (May 25, 1930).

131. The Kilns, located in Headington Quarry, was built in 1922, most probably for those making bricks in the kilns located next to the house. The agreement between the three was that Moore was the nominal owner but after her death the Lewis brothers would live there until their death; after that the house and property would pass to Maureen. For more on the Kilns and related matters, see *BF,* 86 (Sept. 5, 1931).

132. See *BF,* 72 (Nov. 2, 1930). In the unpublished diary portion of this date, Warnie wrote that he considered the pros and cons of living at the Kilns; on balance, he decided that he preferred the Kilns at its worst to army life at its best. However, he did wonder if he had seen the Kilns at its worst. It would not be long before he would be able to answer this question. See also "Diaries," May 21, 1931.

133. For more on this see, "Diaries," Mar. 1, 1931.

134. *CL1,* 959–60 (Mar. 29, 1931); emphasis in original.

135. For more on this, see *SJ,* 229. Recently, Lewis's biographers have argued Jack's movement from atheism to theism must have occurred in 1930, not 1929. For more on this, see McGrath, *C. S. Lewis: A Life,* 141–56; and Lazo, "Correcting the Chronology," 51–62.

136. For more on this, see *SJ,* 237. Warnie later wrote in his "Memoir":

> I well remember that day in 1931 when we made a visit to Whipsnade Zoo, Jack riding in my sidecar: as recorded in *Surprised by Joy,* it was during that outing that he made his decision to rejoin the Church. This seemed to me no sudden plunge into a new life, but rather a slow steady convalescence from a deep-seated spiritual illness of long standing—an illness that

had its origins in our childhood, in the dry husks of religion offered by the semi-political church-going of Ulster, in the similar dull emptiness of compulsory church during our schooldays. With this background, we both found the difficulty of the Christian life to lie in public worship, rather than in one's private devotions. (19)

137. For more on this, see *BF*, 18; "Diaries," Feb. 28, 1930.

138. For more on this, see *BF*, 19–20; "Diaries," Mar. 4, 1930.

139. *CL1*, 948; emphasis in original.

140. *BF*, 80 (May 13, 1931).

141. For another example of their attending church together at this time, see "Diaries," Aug. 16, 1931.

142. Warnie's diary for 1930 refers to Parkin almost forty times.

143. "Diaries," Mar. 25, 1931.

144. Years later, Warnie regretted that he had thrown away the written logs he had made of his trips on his Daudels. See "Diaries," May 27, 1966.

145. *CL1*, 968–69 (Sept. 5, 1931); emphasis in original.

146. For more on this, see chapter 4.

147. For more on this, see chapter 4.

148. See *BF*, 79 (Mar. 31, 1931).

149. See *BF*, 73 (Nov. 14, 1930).

150. For more on this, see *BF*, 92 (Dec. 25, 1931).

151. For more on this, see *CL2*, 30 (Dec. 25, 1931).

152. For more on this, see *BF*, 93 (Jan. 19, 1932).

153. For more on this, see *BF*, 94 (Feb. 13, 1932).

154. Warnie's application to retire is dated August 8, 1932. For more on this, see Army Form B, 174 (Dec. 15, 1932).

155. For more on this, see "Diaries," Dec. 21, 1932.

156. These are lines 22–23 from Book I of William Wordsworth's *The Prelude or Growth of a Poet's Mind*.

157. *BF*, 95–96 (Dec. 21, 1932). For a summary of Warnie's military service, see the Appendix.

158. Wilson connects Warnie's growing dependence upon alcohol to Albert: "How far Warnie emulated at this stage of his life his father's fondness for a little drop of whiskey, and at what point he began his calamitous descent into alcoholism is not easy to determine. He was not actually dismissed from the service, though it was because of alcohol that he was asked to volunteer his own early resignation" (*C. S. Lewis: A Biography*, 114–15). While I agree that Warnie may have been genetically predisposed to alcoholism, Wilson provides no evidence that Warnie was asked to retire early. There is no hint of this in his army records. Instead, Warnie's diaries provide ample evidence that he had long been planning to retire when he did.

4. BEGINNING THE BUSINESS OF LIVING (1933–1939)

1. Warnie's diaries are filled with accounts of adventures with Parkin; for instance, between 1933 and 1935 more than 150 references are made to Parkin. A representative outing occurred on January 18, 1934, when they went to a circus. Warnie was entranced

by the sea lions, the boxing kangaroo, the lions (but which he thought too tame), and the tigers (which he thought ugly and sinister). For more, see "Diaries," Jan. 18, 1934.

2. See Green and Hooper, *C. S. Lewis: A Biography*, 66; Sayer, *Jack*, 151–67, 335–36; Wilson, *C. S. Lewis: A Biography*, 139–41, 153, 224–25; McGrath, *C. S. Lewis: A Life*, 124–27, 245–47.

3. "Diaries," Feb. 8, 1933.

4. For example, see *BF*, 104 (June 17, 1933).

5. A laced underbodice, stiffened by the insertion of strips of whalebone, metal, or wood worn to give shape and support to the figure.

6. "Diaries," Mar. 10, 1933. For another example, see "Diaries," Apr. 15, 1933.

7. *BF*, 115 (Aug. 23, 1933).

8. *BF*, 122 (Oct. 20, 1933).

9. *BF*, 120 (Sept. 14, 1933). See also *BF*, 117 (Sept. 10, 1933).

10. For more instances of Warnie's growing dissatisfaction with Moore, see also "Diaries," Nov. 6, 24, 1933, Dec. 21, 1933; *BF*, 126 (Nov. 24, 1933), 128–30 (Dec. 21, 1933).

11. *BF*, 128.

12. "Diaries," Dec. 21, 1933.

13. *BF*, 129.

14. For more, see chapter 5; *BF*, 9, 13, 35, 55, 101, 104, 117, 119–20, 126, 128–29, 148, 152, 164, 170–71, 174, 196, 198, 224–26, 232–33, 236–39, 265, 269–70.

15. For more, see *BF*, 129. On December 21, 1933, in his diary Warnie was very thankful to Maureen (1906–1977) for helping him to learn to play the piano and especially enjoyed trying to compose music. Not that he thought he would ever be any good, but still he was happy with his efforts (130). Warnie's relationship with Maureen eventually grew into a genuine friendship. On August 27, 1940, she married Leonard Blake, who eventually became the Director of Music at Malvern College. Later, on several occasions, Maureen came to the Kilns to care for her mother, while Jack and Warnie went to Malvern and stayed in Maureen's home. These breaks away from Moore and the Kilns were welcomed by both brothers. Maureen eventually became Dame Maureen Daisy Helen, Baronetess, or Lady Dunbar of Hempriggs.

16. For more, see *BF*, 129.

17. *CL2*, 128 (Nov. 5, 1933).

18. For more, see *BF*, 129. He ended his December 21, 1933, diary entry in a most positive fashion declaring that moving into the Kilns had been a triumphant success (130). As late as November 24, 1934, Warnie was still happy living at the Kilns, writing that a great wave of happiness had swept over him leading him to recognized with thankfulness how wonderful his life is (163).

19. See also examples in *BF*, 144, 148, 152–53, 160, 164–65, 170–71.

20. "Memoir," 21–22.

21. *BF*, 153.

22. *BF*, 148 (July 2, 1934).

23. See "Diaries," Aug. 1, 5, 1934. See also *BF*, 152 (Aug. 7, 1934).

24. See "Diaries," Aug. 9, 1934.

25. For more, see "Diaries," Aug. 16, 1934.

26. More than twenty years before this, Warnie had dreamed of creating a small retreat in Kilkeel where he could go any time he wanted. See "Diaries," Nov. 14, 1934.

27. "Diaries," Jan. 21, 1950; emphasis in original. See also *BF*, 238 (Jan. 17, 1951).

28. For Warnie's additional opinions about Moore throughout the 1930s, see "Diaries," Jan. 6, 17, 1934; Feb. 1, 7, 1934; Mar. 1, 4, 10, 23, 1934; Apr. 17, 1934; June 24, 1934; Aug. 1, 5, 7, 9, 11, 15, 16, 25, 27, 30, 1934; Oct. 6, 1934; Nov. 14, 30, 1934; Dec. 1, 8, 1934; Feb. 7, 16, 1935; Mar. 18, 1935; Jan. 25, 1936; Feb. 12, 1936. See also *BF*, 142 (Feb. 16, 1934); 143–44 (Mar. 1, 1934); 144–45 (Mar. 24, 1934); 148 (July 2, 1934); 151–52 (Aug. 7, 1934); 153 (Aug. 16, 1934); 157 (Sept. 26, 1934); 163 (Nov. 30, 1934); 163 (Dec. 1, 1934); 164–65 (Dec. 4, 1934); 170–71 (Mar. 18, 1935).

29. *BF*, 45–46.

30. *BF*, 62.

31. Jack also asked Greeves to send him all the letters he had written to Greeves so they could be considered for inclusion in the *LP*. See *CL1*, 971 (Sept. 22, 1931).

32. *CL2*, 46.

33. For more on Albert and Edie, see "Diaries," Jan. 9, 1931.

34. For more on Warnie's approach to editing the *LP*, see his "Foreword" in *LP*, 1:iii–iv (May 19, 1933).

35. *LP*, 1:iii.

36. *CL2*, 95; emphasis in original.

37. For more on this, see "Diaries," Jan. 9, 1931.

38. *CL2*, 101. Jack goes on in this letter to comment upon his and Warnie's return to Christian faith now that they are living together at the Kilns: "What a mercy that the change in his [Warnie's] views (I mean as regards religion) should have happened in time to meet mine—it would be awkward if one of us were still in the old state of mind" (101).

39. *BF*, 103.

40. Bound and printed version received by Warnie on June 2, 1933. See "Diaries" on this date.

41. Bound and printed version received by Warnie on September 17, 1933. See "Diaries" on this date.

42. Bound and printed version received by Warnie on November 8, 1933. See "Diaries" on this date.

43. Bound and printed version received by Warnie on August 31, 1934. See "Diaries" on this date.

44. Of the final volume, on December 19, 1934, Warnie writes that he just finished Volume XI of the *LP*, having finished the entire project three months and twelve days ahead of the schedule he had set ("Diaries").

45. Green and Hooper, *C. S. Lewis: A Biography*; McGrath, *C. S. Lewis: A Life*; Sayer, *Jack*; Poe, *Becoming C. S. Lewis* and *The Making of C. S. Lewis*.

46. See, for instance, King, *The Collected Poems of C. S. Lewis*.

47. And, of course, this present biography draws extensively from *LP*.

48. Readers will recall that in the portions of chapter 1 that deal with Wynyard and Capron, I cited from *LP*. Here I also draw from *LP* but cite details not covered earlier.

49. For more, see *LP*, 3:36.

50. Readers will recall that in the portions of chapter 1 that deal with Kirkpatrick, I cited from *LP*. Here I also draw from *LP* but cite details not covered earlier. See also Jack's memories of Kirkpatrick that immediately follow Warnie's in *LP*, 4:65–67; many of these memories are revised and included later in *SJ*, 132–48.

51. *LP*, 4:61.

52. For more, see *LP*, 4:63.

53. *LP*, 3:261–62.

54. For more on the idea of Jack and Warnie as collaborators, see Glyer, *The Company They Keep*.

55. As agreed upon by Jack, after *LP* were completed and bound, all the original family papers were destroyed.

56. Now named Salter's Steamers, the company continues operations to this day; see http://www.salterssteamers.co.uk/.

57. See Hooper, *Boxen*. References to the *Bosphorus* appear on pages 60–61, 63, 133, and 138. Other named vessels in Boxen include the *Thrush* (78, 120, 122–30, 132, 134–38, 152, 155, 159, 166), the *Indian Star* (120, 122–25), the *Cygnet* (120, 123–24, 127, 129), the *Player* (127), the *Puffin* (138, 142), the *Penguin* (142), the *Albatross* (145–48), the *Greyhound* (154–58, 165–79, 182), and the *Ariadne* (182). Hand drawings of the *Bosphorus* appear on page 60, the *Indian Star* on page 125, the *Puffin* on page 143, the *Albatross* on pages 145–46, the *Thrush* on pages 128 and 152, and the *Greyhound* on pages 156–57. A hand drawing of an unnamed vessel appears on page 57.

58. According to Simon Wenham in *Pleasure Boating on the Thames:* "Salters was able to specialize in boats with a small draft, which were suitable for shallower waters. One of these was *Bosphorus* (1936), a cabin cruiser built for Warren Lewis (and often used by his brother, C. S. Lewis). . . . Yet such craft were not widely marketable, because the small draft not only rendered them less suitable for deeper waters, but also restricted the internal space" (59).

59. The specifications describing *Bosphorus* appear in Warnie's essay, "'But What's It Going to Cost?' Three Seasons' Detailed Figures for a 20-ft. Inland Waterways Cruiser" (482–83). For all eight of the essays Warnie writes about inland cruising, he includes photographs; he was a keen amateur photographer dating back to his early post-war years.

60. According to Daniel Zawada of Salter's Steamers, the same boat today would cost £40,000. Email to the author, Feb. 13, 2019. According to https://www.measuringworth.com/index.php, that £40,000 would be about $54,000 in 2019.

61. Lewis, "'But What's It Going to Cost?,'" 482–83.

62. Lewis, "'But What's It Going to Cost?,'" 482.

63. This comes to about £2,350 in 2019, according to the inflation calculator of the Bank of England (www.bankofengland.co.uk/monetary-policy/inflation/inflation-calculator), used for all calculations hereafter.

64. His 1937 expenses would be about £5,216 in 2019, and those for 1938 about £5,425 in 2019.

65. Lewis, "'But What's It Going to Cost?,'" 483.

66. Lewis, "'But What's It Going to Cost?,'" 483.

67. This comes to about £339 and £2,713, respectively, in 2019.

68. Lewis, "'But What's It Going to Cost?,'" 483.

69. See Lewis, "Through the Oxford Canal: Part 1," 5–7; "Through the Oxford Canal: Part 2," 54–55.

70. Lewis, "Through the Oxford Canal: Part 1," 7.

71. See Lewis, "Exploring the Wey," 198–99.

72. Lewis, "Exploring the Wey," 199.

73. This comes to about £543 in 2019.

74. See Lewis, "The Great Ouse," 180–83.

75. Lewis, "The Great Ouse," 181.

76. Lewis, "The Great Ouse," 182.

77. See Lewis, "The Winter of Our Discontent," 158–59.

78. Lewis, "The Winter of Our Discontent," 158.

79. Lewis, "The Winter of Our Discontent," 158.

80. Lewis, "The Winter of Our Discontent," 159.

81. See Lewis, "A Ditchcrawling Discourse," 485–86.

82. Lewis, "A Ditchcrawling Discourse," 485.

83. Lewis, "A Ditchcrawling Discourse," 485. Rising political tensions in Europe precipitated the beginning of WWII on September 1, 1939, when Germany invaded Poland, less than five months after this essay was published.

84. See Lewis, "'Sailing P. M. 13th,'" 635.

85. Lewis, "'Sailing P. M. 13th,'" 635.

86. Lewis, "'Sailing P. M. 13th,'" 635.

87. In Warnie's unpublished diary entry of May 27, 1966, he refers to life aboard the *Bosphorus* as Arcadia-like.

88. From Jack's letters we know that he spent time on the *Bosphorus*, but it is doubtful that he took any long voyages since he was busy with college business and taking care of matters at the Kilns. On one occasion, he retrieved the portable toilet from the boat, and other occasions he brought back bottles of red wine that Warnie kept there. See *CL2*, 270–71 (Sept. 2, 1939); *CL2*, 312 (Dec. 31, 1939); *CL2*, 312 (Mar. 29, 1940).

89. WHL letter to Mrs. Frank Jones, cited in *BF*, 174 (Apr. 4, 1966).

90. "Diaries," Sept. 17, 1945. In addition, Kilby and Mead offer this assessment: "The vast majority of Warren's time on the *Bosphorus* was spent alone, though not infrequently a friend from the Army would join him for a brief holiday cruise. There were happy times for Warren, for the *Bosphorus* afforded him both a freedom and a privacy which he found increasingly lacking in his home situation at the Kilns. Though still genuinely fond of Mrs. Moore, Warren began to resist her interest in his daily activities—much as he had resisted the overtures of his father, Albert, in earlier days. Thus the *Bosphorus* provided Warren with an escape from household tensions he was incapable of resolving" (*BF*, 174).

91. "Diaries," Mar. 26, 1946.

92. "Diaries," June 21, 1950. See also *BF*, 265 (Aug. 15, 1966).

93. *BF*, 174. In addition, Warnie's unpublished diary confirms that he had kept a log. See May 12, 1969.

94. *AMR*, 317.

95. Jack had long been taking walking tours with Tolkien and others.

96. "Memoir," 16.

97. "Memoir," 16. On another occasion, Jack's requirement that they stop for tea led to a comical encounter. On July 5, 1924, the brothers biked to Wantage Rd. so that Warnie could take a picture of "the fastest train" in England. Afterward, they looked for a place to have tea. A countryman directed them to a place they thought he called the Dog House. Jack wrote:

> Here we had strange adventures. I rang at the closed door—it is a little red house under
> a woodside—and waited for ten minutes: then rang again. At last a very ancient beldame

appeared. I asked if we could have some tea. She looked hard at me and asked "Are you golfers?" [On] my answering "no" she shut the door softly and I could hear her hobbling away into the bowels of the house. I felt like Arthur at Orgolio's Castle. Anon the ancient dame appeared again and, looking even harder at me, asked me a second time what I wanted. I repeated that we wanted some tea. She brought her face closer to mine and then with the air of one who comes at last to the real point asked "How long do you want it for?" I was quite unable to answer this question but by God's grace the witch left me . . . and hobbled away once more. This time she left the door open and we walked in and found our way to a comfortable dining room where a plentiful and quite unmagical tea was presently brought us. We sat here for a very long time. A storm of wind got up (raised, I make no doubt, by our hostess, who, by the by, may have been the matriarchal dreadfulness) and the ivy lashed the windows. (*AMR*, 343–44)

98. For all of the walking tours taken by Warnie and Jack, I cite the mileage that Warnie wrote down in his diary. However, as Warnie admitted, the pedometer he was using was not entirely reliable. Accordingly, the walking distances he cited may be slightly higher than the actual distances they covered. It is important to note here that there are three rivers named Wye in England. At 185 miles long, the River Wye that Warnie and Jack followed in their first three walking tours is the fifth largest river in England. Its source is in the Welsh Mountains at Plynlimon near Aberwrystwith; the river flows southeasterly through Wales into England at Chepstow, where it meets the River Severn and eventually empties into the Bristol Channel. Wye means either wanderer or crooked. I offer additional information about the other two Wye rivers in England later in the chapter.

99. The villages they passed through between Chepstow and Hereford were St. Arvans, Tintern Abbey, Tintern Parva, Brockweir, St. Briavels, Rebrook, Monmouth, Symonds Yat, Goodrich, Weston, Ross-on-Wye, Wilton, Hoarwithy, and Little Dewchurch,

100. See "Diaries," from Jan. 9, but citing Jan. 1, 1931.

101. See "Diaries," from Jan. 9, but citing Jan. 2, 1931.

102. "Diaries," from Jan. 9, but citing Jan. 3, 1931.

103. "Diaries," from Jan. 9, but citing Jan. 4, 1931; emphasis in original.

104. *BF*, 76 (from Jan. 9, but citing Jan. 4, 1931).

105. "Diaries," from Jan. 9, but citing Jan. 4, 1931.

106. *CL1*, 948 (Jan. 10, 1931); emphasis in original.

107. "Diaries," Jan. 3, 1933. As they remembered their earlier days in Malvern, they began to plan a return.

108. Other villages they passed through included passing through the villages of Boughrood, Erwood, Aberedw, and Llanelwedd.

109. "Diaries," Jan. 6, 1933.

110. Towns they visited along the way included Newbridge-on-Wye, Rhayader, Llangurig, Pant Mawr, and Ponterwyd.

111. See *BF*, 124 (Nov. 17, 1933).

112. See *BF*, 132 (Jan. 2, 1934).

113. *BF*, 135 (Jan. 4, 1934).

114. See *BF*, 137–38 (Jan. 5, 1934).

115. *BF*, 138 (Jan. 5, 1934).

116. *BF,* 140 (Jan. 6, 1934). In total, they had walked approximately 124 miles in their effort to trace the source of the Wye River.

117. The Chiltern Hills, northwest of London, are a popular tourist destination. The hills form a chalk escarpment across Oxfordshire, Buckinghamshire, Hertfordshire, and Bedfordshire. Interestingly, during this walking tour the brothers probably passed near the second of three Rivers Wye in England. This River Wye is in Buckinghamshire and has its source in the village of Bradenham near High Wickham; it flows 11 miles southward, emptying into the River Thames at Bourne End. The villages they passed through included Northend, Turville, and High Wycombe, and then northward through Little Kingshill, Great Missenden, and Tring, and finally southwest to Wendover, Great Kimble.

118. "Diaries," Jan. 3, 1935.

119. See Dairies, Jan. 4, 1935.

120. Dairies, Jan. 5, 1935.

121. This is the third River Wye, a 15-mile-long stream that flows southeasterly through the county of Derbyshire. The river's source is near the town of Buxton, and it empties into the 66-mile-long River Derwent at the village of Rowsley.

122. "Diaries," Jan. 14, 1936.

123. "Diaries," Jan. 15, 1936.

124. "Diaries," Jan. 16, 1936.

125. Jack had visited portions of this area in when he was on a rare holiday with his father and his uncle, Augustus (Gussie), and his aunt, Anne Hamilton, Flora's brother-in-law and sister. See *CL1,* 570–84 (Aug. 7, 1921).

126. "Diaries," Jan. 5, 1937.

127. "Diaries," Jan. 6, 1937.

128. "Diaries," Jan. 9, 1937.

129. Eighteen months later, Jack befriended one of the nuns of this order, Sister Penelope (Ruth Penelope Lawson) after she had written him about how much she enjoyed his *Out of the Silent Planet.* For more on Sister Penelope, see *CL2,* 1055–59.

130. *BF,* 175.

131. See "Diaries," Jan. 12, 1938. Littlecote House is a large Elizabethan country house now serving as a hotel. For more, see https://historicengland.org.uk/listing/the-list/list -entry/1000479.

132. See "Diaries," Jan. 13, 1938.

133. "Diaries," Jan. 13, 1938.

134. "Diaries," Jan. 14, 1938.

135. "Diaries," Jan. 2, 1939.

136. "Diaries," Jan. 3, 1939; emphasis in original.

137. "Diaries," Jan. 4, 1939.

138. Jack also wrote about this walking tour in a letter of January 11, 1939, to A. K. Hamilton Jenkin. See *CL2,* 239–43.

139. George Sayer says Jack "liked country walking and thought a good walk almost every afternoon important for his health. But he did not like walking alone. Warnie was for him the perfect walking companion. They enjoyed the same scenery, though they often had different impressions of it, and both relished the halts for bread and cheese and beer in old-fashioned pubs. It is a mistake to think that in their conversation Warnie was

always the junior partner. He often took the lead, for he had a far greater experience of ordinary life than his brother and was probably shrewder in his assessments of character" (Sayer, *Jack*, 420).

140. In 1929, an undergraduate at Oxford, Edward Tangye Lean, had called his essay club "The Inklings." He invited Lewis and Tolkien to join the group, in hopes that it would carry on after Lean graduated. It did not. Lewis eventually took the name for the group that he and Tolkien formed. The two most notable books on the Inklings are Diana Glyer's *The Company They Keep: C. S. Lewis and J. R. R. Tolkien as Writers in Community* and Philip and Carol Zaleski's *The Fellowship, the Literary Lives of the Inklings: J. R. R. Tolkien, C. S. Lewis, Owen Barfield, Charles Williams.* In both, readers will find a wealth of information on the history, meetings, influences, and personalities of this remarkable group of writers. Humphrey Carpenter's earlier study, *The Inklings: C. S. Lewis, J. R. R. Tolkien, Charles Williams and Their Friends* is also a valuable resource for further reading; at one point he offers the scenario of an imagined meeting of the Inklings. See also Walter Hooper's summary about the beginnings of the Inklings in *CL2*, 181–83; Hooper, *C. S. Lewis: Companion and Guide*, 731; and Hooper, "Introduction," *They Stand Together*, 27. In addition, Clyde Kilby and Marjorie Mead write: "Though it is not possible exactly to determine the beginnings of the Inklings, the possible date is 1933. It also appears likely the regular (i.e., weekly) Thursday meetings of the Inklings did not begin until April 1940" (*BF*, 182–83). Humphrey Carpenter seems to agree with this dating (see *The Inklings*, 73). Colin Duriez does as well (see his *Tolkien and C. S. Lewis*, 81). Joel Heck agrees and states that in the fall of 1933 "The Inklings meet for the first time." See his "Chronologically Lewis."

141. John Ronald Reuel Tolkien (1892–1973) was one of Jack's closest friends. He was professor of Anglo-Saxon at Oxford, and in 1943 he became Professor of English at Merton College, Oxford. He is best celebrated as the author of *The Hobbit* (1937) and *The Lord of the Rings* (1954–55). He became good friends with Warnie who nicknamed him Tollers. In a letter Jack wrote to Warnie on November 22, 1931, we find a prototype for later gatherings of the Inklings: "It has also become a regular custom that Tolkien should drop in on me of a Monday morning and drink a glass. This is one of the pleasantest spots in the week. Sometimes we talk English school politics: sometimes we criticise one another's poems: other days we drift into theology or 'the state of the nation': rarely we fly no higher than bawdy and 'puns'" (*CL2*, 16).

142. In chapter 5, I offer additional details about the Inklings, including a list of those usually known as members of the group, when and where the meet, and matters discussed at many of their gatherings.

143. *BF*, 97 (Feb. 18, 1933). Henry Victor Dyson (1896–1975), generally known as Hugo Dyson, was a Shakespeare expert, Lecturer in English at Reading University, and later Fellow and Tutor at Merton College, Oxford. His books include *Pope* (1933) and *The Emergence of Shakespeare's Tragedy* (1950). He was one of Lewis's oldest friends and, along with Tolkien, was instrumental in Jack's movement toward Christianity.

144. *BF*, 106 (July 26, 1933). Nevill Henry Kendal Aylmer Coghill (1899–1980) was a Fellow of Exeter College, Oxford, and in 1957 he was elected Professor of English Literature. He produced major translations of Chaucer's poetry and produced and directed a number of theatrical performances in Oxford. Like Tolkien and Dyson, Coghill was a close friend of Jack's. About this evening, Warnie added: "We adjourned [to the common room] for drinks:

there was a spirit case and siphons on a side table, all the decanters in the case being low, with the result that we had a most mischievous selection of drinks—some got whiskey, some brandy, and I myself gin. While we were drinking Dyson kept us in fits of laughter with an account of a visit he had recently paid—or states he has paid—to a bone setter. We broke up reluctantly at about twenty past ten after a thoroughly enjoyable evening" (107).

145. *BF*, 145–46.

146. *CL2*, 183 (Mar. 11, 1936).

147. *CL2*, 219 (Sept. 23, 1937).

148. For more on Havard, see the next chapter. For more on this trip, see Havard, "Philia," *C. S. Lewis at the Breakfast Table*, 218–20, and Griffin, *Clive Staples Lewis*, 162–63.

149. For more on Warnie's return to active duty, see *CL2*, 270; Charlton. "On W. H. Lewis's Military Rank," 36.

150. It is notable that Jack's first two books—*Spirits in Bondage* (1919) and *Dymer* (1926)—are largely inwardly focused. See, for instance, in *Spirits in Bondage*, "To Sleep," "Dungeon Grates," "Alexandrines," "Death in Battle"; in *Dymer*, cantos 1–4.

151. Walter Hooper largely agrees with my assessment of this reversal. Writing about Warnie's alcoholism, Hooper says: "Although the reasons for Warnie's alcoholism were numerous and complex, one of them was his shyness. In their youth, Warnie was gregarious, and Jack was to some extent a recluse. As time went on, they exchanged positions. Jack's fame as a Christian apologist drove him to mingle with all sorts of people, most of whom he came to like. Warnie withdrew more and more into the company of French history and very few friends" ("'Warnie's Problem,'" 13). See also Hooper, "Introduction," 31–32.

152. The very shy character in Kenneth Graham's *The Wind in the Willows*.

153. *CL3*, 589–90 (Apr. 2, 1955).

5. TURNING AND DRIFTING (1939–1951)

1. For more on Warnie's probable feelings at this time, see *BF*, 177–78; Sayer, *Jack*, 161–62; and McGrath, *C. S. Lewis: A Life*, 192–96.

2. *BF*, 178. Darlington is 15 miles north of Catterick. Jack's lectures were later published as *The Abolition of Man*.

3. *CL2*, 274 (Sept. 15, 1939).

4. *CL2*, 275, 277 (Sept. 18, 1939).

5. Earlier in his career from June 1930 to October 1931, Warnie served as assistant to the commanding officer of the supply company at Bulford. See Chapter 3.

6. Warnie's first overseas posting in WWI was to Le Havre in November 1914. See Chapter 2.

7. *CL2*, 280–81 (Nov. 5, 1939). Regarding the evidence of censorship, Jack wrote: "The newspaper cutting did not arrive, not, I think, for the usual reason that you never enclosed it, but because the censor removed it; at any rate the letter had been opened and re-addressed. This, in all the circumstances is as good as any of the anecdotes about the censorship at present in circulation" (280).

8. See *CL2*, 286 (Nov. 11, 1939).

9. See *CL2*, 294 (Nov. 19, 1939).

10. *CL2*, 294–95 (Nov. 24, 1939).

11. *CL2*, 285–86.

12. *CL2*, 301.

13. Johnson was a particular favorite of the brothers, and a writer Warnie had mentioned in a December 8, 1939, letter to Jack. Cited in *CL2*, 303–7.

14. *CL2*, 304–5 (Dec. 18, 1939).

15. *CL2*, 305.

16. *CL2*, 308, 309, 310.

17. *CL2*, 311–12.

18. *CL2*, 312.

19. *CL2*, 313.

20. See *CL2*, 316–22 (Jan. 9, 1940); *CL2*, 322–25 (Jan. 14, 1940).

21. See *CL2*, 328–32 (Jan. 21, 1940).

22. For the rest of his life, Warnie was referred to as Major Lewis. His promotion to the rank of temporary major was later changed to that of honorary major when he ceased to belong to the Reserve of Officers on March 29, 1947. He was entitled to be called major, but his retirement pay was that of a captain. For a longer explanation of this, see his letter to Jane Douglas (Lewis, "Letters to Jane Douglas" [Nov. 4, 1969]).

23. See *CL2*, 337–43 (Feb. 3, 1940).

24. See *CL2*, 343–44 (Feb. 11, 1940).

25. See *CL2*, 347–53 (Feb. 18, 1940); *CL2*, 358–62 (Mar. 3, 1940).

26. See *CL2*, 358–59 (Mar. 3, 1940).

27. In *CL2*, see Jack's letters to Warnie of March 17 (Palm Sunday), 1940 (363–67); March 21 (Maundy Thursday), 1940 (367–71); and March 29, 1940 (376–80). In these letters, Jack noted that he was cheered to hear of Warnie's gradual recovery, was hopeful for Warnie's leave, how he was constantly on his mind, happy Easter wishes, and his enjoying another bottle of wine that had been stored on the *Bosphorus*. We also learn that Warnie shared snippets of encounters and conversation with French soldiers and officers.

28. See Jack's letters to Warnie, *CL2*, 381–90 (Apr. 11, 1940); 397–401 (Apr. 21, 1940); 401–6 (Apr. 28, 1940); 406–12 (May 4, 1940). The latter letter is especially interesting as in it Jack explored ideas about the four love that eventually lead twenty years later to his *The Four Loves*.

29. See *CL2*, 413 (May 9, 1940).

30. See *CL2*, 431–34 (Aug. 11, 1940).

31. Letter by Sergeant H. L. Wilson, Aug. 16, 1940 (Army Service Records for Warnie Hamilton Lewis). For a summary of Warnie's military service, see the Appendix.

32. In May 1940, Anthony Eden, Secretary of State for War in England, asked men between 17 and 65 to sign up for a home defense force, the Local Defense Volunteers (LDV). Thousands of men registered—many were veterans of WWI—and in July 1940, Prime Minister Winston Churchill changed the name LDV to the Home Guard. Jack also served in the Oxfordshire Home Guard. For more on the role of private soldiers in home guards, see http://www.oxfordshirehomeguard.uk/ldv-to-hg.html.

33. McGrath, *C. S. Lewis: A Life*, 196.

34. Sayer, *Jack*, 161–62.

35. "How Can I Ask Thee, Father?," 325.

36. See *CL2*, 450–52 (Oct. 24, 1940).

37. See *CL2*, 486 (May 25, 1941). See also *CL2*, 504 (Dec. 23, 1941). "Warnie is still at home. As I think I told you he spent the summer as part of the floating H.G.127 in his motor boat, but is now in winter quarters at the Kilns"; *CL2*, 549 (Jan. ? 1943): "Warnie has grown thin. It's quite interesting seeing the shape of the face coming out: like unpacking a parcel"; *CL2*, 596 (Dec. 20, 1943): "I've had a lot of examining work and been pretty busy. I have a cold of course but none of us has flu' so far, thank God. Warnie is flourishing."

38. Schofield, *In Search of C. S. Lewis*, 54.

39. *BF*, 180–81 (Jan. 2, 1945). For more of Warnie's thoughts about her departure from the Kilns, see "Diaries," Jan. 2, 1945. June later wrote to Walter Hooper about her departure from the Kilns:

> It was very difficult to leave the Kilns—I had been some sort of "mother's help"—looking after the hens and feeding them was one of my duties—for two years. Paxford was working at Cowley and could only keep a few things going in his spare time. There was no other help apart from Vera Henry who came up and cooked a couple of times a week. Minto had open and painful varicose ulcers and was supposed to lie on a sofa with her leg up as much as possible. I suppose I felt they couldn't manage without me. Also I knew that the burden would fall on Jack as he was already under strain with the demands of his work at Magdalen, the broadcasts and his own writing, while looking after Minto as much as he could. (Cited in *CL2*, 622 [Jan. 27, 2003])

40. Email to the author, Aug. 26, 2016. See also her remarks in Schofield, *In Search of C. S. Lewis*, 55–59. Jack was equally stricken with June's departure, writing on January 4, 1945, to her mother, Winifred Flewett:

> Oh what a sad waking up this morning when we realised that June was gone!—but I try to comfort myself by realising that there was a correspondingly happy waking in your house and thinking how long you and she had waited for it and how you deserve it. This is really just a covering letter (as one might say, "Daughter enclosed") and to try, once again, to express some part of our great gratitude. I have never really met anything like her unselfishness and patience and kindness and shall feel deeply in her debt as long as I live. . . . Tell June that the Hens were asking for her first thing this morning: that Warnie is even more depressed than usual: and that the cats, under this shared calamity, sank their common differences and slept, mutually embracing, in the same box. . . . Mrs. Moore sends her love to June and you with best wishes for the year. . . . We are the ghost and ruin of a house. . . . Ichabod, Ichabod! God bless her (indeed that is just what I keep on telling Him). (*CL2*, 636)

41. For more on Warnie's work as Jack's secretary, see, see *CL2*, xiii–xiv.

42. *CL2*, 579 (June 1, 1943).

43. This list is drawn from Warnie's diary entries during this time period.

44. Moreover, Jack's job as a don at Magdalen College kept him very busy and frequently away from the Kilns. Conversely, Warnie's retirement ensured he would spend a great deal of time in daily contact with Moore.

45. For a while he did have the *Bosphorus* as a retreat, but several physical ailments led his doctor to recommend that he give up sailing. He sold the boat in 1945.

46. Bits of "wisdom" or amusing anecdotes.

47. *Mens Humana* is Latin for "the human mind." Quotations from *"Mens Humana* or Kilns Table Talk" by Warnie H. Lewis are published by permission of the Marion E. Wade Center, Wheaton College, Illinois. The provenance of *"Mens Humana"* is uncertain. Although the document came to the Wade Center in 1973 as directed by Warnie's will, there is no date noting when it was compiled. However, we know from an unpublished diary entry of January 25, 1936, that he was already assembling entries. On that date, he wrote about the unwelcomed and extended visit to the Kilns of Molly Askins, the widowed daughter-in-law of Moore's brother, Dr. Robert Askins. After chronicling Molly's various impositions, Warnie noted that he had never met a woman more in need of male attention. In addition, she forced Maureen to act as her chauffer and to pay for any expenses when the two went out for coffee or tea. At the same time, if they attended a concert together, Molly would isolate Maureen from any men present and expect the men to fawn over her. Based on my reading, and taking into account some internal clues, I suggest the final version of *"Mens Humana"* containing 72 wheezes was probably composed between 1940 and 1951.

48. Irishwoman Vera Henry (?–1953) ran a holiday resort where the two Lewis bothers sometimes stayed. When Henry served as the housekeeper of the Kilns, she and Moore often quarreled, and it was left to Jack to act as peacemaker. In the unpublished portions of Warnie's diary, he wrote that he initially disliked Vera, but as happened with his feelings toward Maureen, over time he came to admire and value her deeply. For more on Vera, see chapter 6.

49. In what follows, I refer to each wheeze by the Roman numeral assigned it by Warnie.

50. II.

51. X.

52. XXXVIII.

53. LXV.

54. IX. In *BF,* Warnie wrote about having seen *King Kong* on September 1, 1933, noting that it was one of the best films he had ever seen. He was especially intrigued by the representations of the prehistoric monsters (116).

55. XII.

56. XX.

57. XXIII.

58. Whitty, formerly Maureen Moore's music teacher when she and her mother resided in Bristol, was a frequent visitor at the Kilns.

59. XXV.

60. XXXIII. Guy Fawkes, a Catholic, and his coconspirators spent months planning to blow up King James I of England during the opening of Parliament on November 5, 1605. Their plan was thwarted the night before when Fawkes was discovered in the cellar below the House of Lords next to thirty-six barrels of gunpowder. Immediately, bonfires were set celebrating the failed plot, and Parliament later declared November 5 a public day of thanksgiving. Guy Fawkes Day, also known as Bonfire Night, has been celebrated in Great Britain ever since. Maureen's ignorance of the history behind this national holiday must have caused Warnie to throw up his hands in exasperation.

61. XL.

62. XLII.

63. XLIII.

64. L.

65. VI.

66. XIX.

67. XXVII.

68. XXXVII.

69. XXXVII.

70. XXXV.

71. XXXVI.

72. XLI.

73. LIX.

74. LXIII.

75. VII.

76. XXX.

77. XXX.

78. XXX.

79. LII.

80. LVI.

81. Grace Havard was the wife of C. S. Lewis's physician, friend, and fellow Inkling, Robert "Humphrey" Havard.

82. LVII.

83. LXXII.

84. V.

85. A village 13 miles south of Oxford.

86. XLV.

87. LVIII.

88. LX.

89. LXVIII.

90. LXIX.

91. LIV.

92. See *BF* for more examples. In addition, the unpublished portion of his diary contains scores of additional examples.

93. *SJ*, 198.

94. *CL3*, 28–29.

95. *CL3*, 37–38; emphasis in original.

96. *CL3*, 45.

97. *CL3*, 56 (Sept. 29, 1950).

98. *CL3*, 79 (Dec. 30, 1950).

99. *CL3*, 108 (Apr. 18, 1951); emphasis in original.

100. *CL3*, 158 (Jan. 10, 1952).

101. "Diaries," Oct. 14, 1946.

102. See "Diaries," Feb. 20, 1947. See also *BF*, 224 (Nov. 23, 1948).

103. The first sentence in this quote comes from *BF*, 198 (Mar. 17, 1947). The second sentence beginning "When I go . . ." immediately follows the first sentence and has never been published before. See "Diaries," Mar. 17, 1947; emphasis in original.

104. "Diaries," Nov. 18, 1947. Shelob is the name of the monstrous, bloated spider in Tolkien's *Lord of the Rings.*

105. "Diaries," July 26, 1948; emphasis in original.

106. *BF,* 225 (Jan. 28, 1949).

107. "Diaries," June 15, 1949. In context the quote from *The Rubáiyát of Omar Khayyám* is: "I sent my Soul through the Invisible, / Some letter of that After-life to spell; / And by and by my Soul returned to me, / And answered, 'I Myself am Heav'n and Hell.'"

108. "Diaries," Jan. 17, 1950; emphasis in original.

109. "Diaries," Oct. 5, 1950.

110. *BF,* 236–37 (Jan. 17, 1951). See also in his "Diaries" additional comments on this date about Moore.

111. His alcoholic binges.

112. *BF,* 238. See also his comments about Moore sixteen years later. *BF,* 270 (Feb. 6, 1967).

113. Sayer, *Jack,* 166–67.

114. From the "Foreword" to *AMR,* ix–x.

115. Poe and Poe, *C. S. Lewis Remembered,* 28.

116. Graham, *We Remember C. S. Lewis: Essays and Memoirs,* 123.

117. *TST,* 23.

118. See "Diaries," Jan. 2, Feb. 28, 1918.

119. "Diaries," June 25, 1918.

120. For instance, see *BF,* 6–7 (Jan. 15, 1922).

121. "Diaries," Apr. 24, 1921.

122. "Diaries," Jan. 1, 1922.

123. "Diaries," Aug. 14, 1922.

124. "Diaries," Apr. 15, 1928.

125. "Diaries," May 29, 1928.

126. *BF,* 17 (Feb. 25, 1930).

127. *BF,* 24 (Mar. 17, 1930).

128. "Diaries," Jan. 21, 1932.

129. "Diaries," Feb. 22, 1943; emphasis in original.

130. See https://forum.netweather.tv/topic/33821-the-winter-of-1946–47/.

131. Pitter, "The Great Winter 1946–47," in *Sudden Heaven,* 244–45.

132. "Diaries," Feb. 20, 1946.

133. Letter to June Flewett, *CL2,* 706 (Apr. 17, 1946).

134. "Diaries," June 20, 1946.

135. "Diaries," Mar. 17, 1947.

136. *BF,* 200 (Apr. 17, 1947).

137. *BF,* 201 (June 11, 1947).

138. As already noted, Parkin's own depression during 1947 was acute. See "Diaries," Oct. 29, 1947.

139. *BF,* 201 (June 30, 1947).

140. *BF,* 201–2.

141. According to Walter Hooper, from Warnie's "initial stay in 1947, he retreated to Drogheda and Our Lady of Lourdes Hospital at least once a year." See Hooper, "Warnie's Problem," 6.

142. *BF*, 202. For more on this, see Warnie's diary entry of June 30, 1947, in his "Diaries."

143. In a July 6, 1947, letter to Ruth Pitter, Jack mentioned this incident: "My Brother, thank God, was out of danger when I reached him on Monday morning last but was at the unearthly city of Drogheda where almost every building is a church or a tavern and what men do but pray and drink or how life is supported in their bodies I can't conceive. . . . My Brother was in the care of the most charming nuns" (*CL2*, 789–90).

144. *BF*, 203. Warnie's holiday in Ireland continued until July 26, 1947. For more on this holiday, see *BF*, 203–7; "Diaries," esp. July 2, 13–15, 17–19, 22–23, 25–26, 1947.

145. Hooper, "Warnie's Problem," 3–21.

146. Another contributing factor to Warnie's abuse of alcohol was news that Parkin was contemplating moving to Mauritius. See "Diaries," Jan. 21, 1948. In the end, Parkin did not move to Mauritius, so meetings between the two friends continued sporadically. See "Diaries," Oct. 14, 1949; *BF*, 133–34 (June 21, 1950); and "Diaries," Feb. 4, 1951.

147. *BF*, 225; emphasis added.

148. See *CL2*, 944–45 (June 18, 1949).

149. *CL2*, 945.

150. The Warneford Hospital on Warneford Road, Oxford.

151. *CL2*, 952–53; emphasis in original. Founded in 1882, the Acland Nursing Home was renamed the Acland Hospital in 1964. In 2004, it was again renamed, this time as the Manor Hospital, when it moved to Headington.

152. A sleeping sedative.

153. A college servant.

154. CSL to Owen Barfield, July 5, 1949, in "'Warnie's Problem': An Introduction to a Letter from C. S. Lewis to Owen Barfield," *Journal of Inklings Studies* 5, no. 1 (Apr. 2015): 20–21; emphasis in original.

155. *CL2*, 957 (July 6, 1949). See also *CL2*, 959 (July 27, 1949).

156. *BF*, 228 (Aug. 14, 1949.

157. "Memoir," 13.

158. "Memoir," 13.

159. "Memoir," 13.

160. "Memoir," 13–14.

161. "Memoir," 14.

162. "Memoir," 14.

163. Glyer also argues that the four who attended meetings most frequently were the Lewis brothers, Havard, and J. R. R. Tolkien. See Glyer, *The Company They Keep*, 11.

164. Documented meetings refer to ones where a written summary of the meeting was recorded—either in letters or diaries.

165. For more on this, including a complete listing of the Inklings meetings, see my essay, King, "When Did the Inklings Meet?," 184–204.

166. Assuming two hours for the length of an average meeting is probably conservative.

167. *CL3*, 501.

168. Tolkien, *The Letters of J. R. R. Tolkien*, 103.

169. Tolkien, *The Letters of J. R. R. Tolkien*, 71 (Apr. 13, 1944). He is referring to what becomes Warnie's first published book on seventeenth-century France, *The Splendid Century: Some Aspects of French Life in the Reign of Louis XIV*. See also Tolkien's comments

on Warnie's writings in Tolkien, *The Letters of J. R. R. Tolkien,* 83 (May 31, 1944); 84 (June 10, 1944); 92 (Sept. 23–25, 1944).

170. Dundas-Grant, "From an 'Outsider,'" 231.

171. Havard, "Philia," 217. See also Green, "In the Evening," 212.

172. Wain, *Sprightly Running,* 184.

173. Barfield, "C. S. Lewis as Christian and Scholar," 29.

174. Glyer, "The Centre of the Inklings," 32. See also Glyer, *The Company They Keep.*

175. *BF,* 197 (Nov. 28, 1946). *Irene Iddesleigh* (1897) is a novel by Anna Margaret Ross, also known by her pen name, Amanda McKettrick Ros.

176. *BF,* 198 (Feb. 6, 1947).

177. *BF,* 218 (Mar. 4, 1948).

178. *BF,* 225 (Feb. 4, 1949).

179. *BF,* 196 (Oct. 24, 1946).

180. *BF,* 197 (Nov. 28, 1946).

181. *BF,* 200 (Apr. 24, 1947).

182. See *Essays Presented to Charles Williams,* xiv; emphasis in original. See also his poem "On the Death of Charles Williams," in *The Collected Poems of C. S. Lewis,* 334.

183. *BF,* 182–83 (May 15, 1945).

184. Lewis, Letters to Florence (Michal) Williams, May 16, 1945.

6. HISTORIAN AND LITERARY SUCCESS (1952–1960)

1. The story of Joy and Jack is so well known, it need not be recounted here. For example, see *Bone;* Dorsett, *And God Came In;* Lewis, *A Grief Observed;* Kilby and Mead, *Brothers and Friends;* Santamaria, *Joy.*

2. For more on this, see *CL3,* 469–85; Sayer, *Jack,* 217–20; Hooper, *C. S. Lewis: Companion* and Guide, 65–77; McGrath, *C. S. Lewis: A Life,* 309–21; Zaleski and Zaleski, *The Fellowship,* 430–32.

3. Minutes of vestry meetings at Holy Trinity throughout the 1950s confirm Warnie's contributions as a church warden. For instance, see the minutes of May 1952, May 1955, May 1956, and May 1957. The minutes of the latter meeting read in part: "At the Vestry Meeting the Vicar thanked the Churchwardens for their work over the past year, and paid tribute to Major W. H. Lewis for his many years' service on his retirement as Vicar's Warden." Although Warnie served faithfully, he sometimes tired of the work, especially because of the petty personal disagreements that would sometimes occur between church members.

4. Joy is referring to herself and to her husband at the time, Bill Gresham.

5. *Bone,* 104–6. The five single-spaced page letter Joy refers to here has not survived.

6. *Bone,* 116; emphasis in original. For other letters where she referred to Lewis's influence, see *Bone,* 109 (Aug. 19, 1949); *Bone,* 118 (May 29, 1951).

7. *BF,* 244 (Nov. 5, 1956). There is some confusion about when Joy first wrote Jack since her letter cited previously to Walsh of June 21, 1949, suggests she first wrote him in the latter half of 1949.

8. *BF,* 244 (Nov. 5, 1956).

9. Joy had made the trip to England alone, leaving her sons, David and Douglas, in the care of her husband, Bill, and her cousin, Renee Pierce (née Rodriguez).

10. Shotover Hill is behind the Kilns.

11. See *Bone*, 138–39 (Jan. 25, 1953).

12. This poem appears in King, *A Naked Tree*, 267–68; emphasis in original.

13. *BF*, 244–45. In addition, Warnie told George Sayer: "We treated her just as if she were a man. She loved the pubs, walked fairly well considering that she was not used to it, drank her pints of beer and often made us laugh" (Sayer, *Jack*, 353).

14. Lewis, Letters to June Flewett, Dec. 14, 1952.

15. Lewis, Letters to June Flewett, Dec. 31, 1952.

16. "Memoir," 23.

17. "Memoir," 23.

18. King, *A Naked Tree*, 5–7.

19. *BF*, 196 (Oct. 14, 1946). His unpublished diary entry of April 17, 1953, provided additional information about his relationship with Vera, noting that what came to be a close friendship resulted from him becoming less unchristian and Vera becoming less aggressive and more comfortable about her role at the Kilns. However, most of all, Warnie said that he grew to care for Vera because Moore hated her and treated her abusively. Moore's petty, mean-spirited rants about Vera had actually caused Warnie to want to know Vera better.

20. Warnie described her retreat in his unpublished diary entry of September 3, 1949, noting that it was larger and more sophisticated than he had thought it would be. It included two railway cars, linked by a porch that faced the sea. A third railway car joined the porch at right angles to the other two, resulting in a T-shaped building. Two other huts and a caravan provided beds for sixteen people as well as two comfortable sitting rooms.

21. "Diaries," Apr. 28, 1951; emphasis in original.

22. *BF*, 241–42 (Apr. 17, 1953).

23. According to Walter Hooper, Major Frank Henry (1901–2004) would drive Warnie around Ireland during his visits: "I knew Warnie well during the last ten years of his life, and on a number of occasions I was asked to go to Drogheda and escort Warnie back to Oxford. The 'deal' he always struck was that if I stopped in Drogheda for a week and accompanied Major Henry and him on his little motor tours around Drogheda he would return to Oxford with me" (Hooper, "Warnie's Problem," 6).

24. See the publisher's biographical note on the dust jacket of Warnie's *Levantine Adventurer*. Later he published his own translation of these memoirs, *Memoirs of the Duc de Saint-Simon*; for more on his translation, see chapter 7. For an excellent recent translation, see *Saint-Simon at Versailles*.

25. Lewis, Letters to Blanche Biggs, Nov. 11, 1969.

26. For the poem, see "Diaries," Apr. 29, 1934.

27. *BF*, 147 (June 3, 1934). See also *BF*, 182 (May 15, 1945); *BF*, 195 (Sept. 5, 1946). See also "Diaries," Jan. 24, 1934; Oct. 4, 1946; Jan. 9, 1947; Aug. 19, 1948.

28. See footnote 199 in *BF*, 182.

29. Tolkien, *The Letters of J. R. R. Tolkien*, 71.

30. Tolkien, *The Letters of J. R. R. Tolkien*, 83 (May 31, 1944. Tolkien also mentioned Warnie reading other portions of the manuscript in Tolkien, *The Letters of J. R. R. Tolkien*, 92–93 (Sept. 23–25, 1944).

31. His unpublished diary entry of June 13, 1951, does offer one insight into his work on *The Splendid Century*. He reported having just finished reading a biography of Orsini Delesse de Montmenny that gave him a new idea regarding seventeenth-century cleanliness; after her husband's death, she became a boarder in a convent, and while not in training for a religious life, she observed faithfully the rules of the order. This included having clean linen once a week in imitation of the nuns. Warnie drew the conclusion that those living in the seventeenth century must have been a much less smelly group of people than he had imagined.

32. Some editions of the book include this phrase as the subtitle.

33. Lewis, *The Splendid Century*, 28. The exact publication date of *The Splendid Century* is not certain. Warnie dated his completion of the book's foreword as May 2, 1953 (xiv). On June 27, 1953, Jack wrote a friend that Warnie was reading the proofs (see *CL3*, 342), and Jack promised to send Arthur Greeves a copy as soon as it was published in a letter of October 17, 1953 (*CL3*, 372). Therefore, *The Splendid Century* must have appeared sometime between October 17 and November 18, 1953 (for additional information on this, see Joy Davidman's letter later in this chapter). In addition, on December 16, 1953, Jack wrote Dorothy L. Sayers: "I hope you are reading my brother's Splendid Century. It is his first book, tho' he is three years my senior, but he has been at the court of Louis XIV pretty well all his life. It seems to be going down well" (*CL3*, 387).

34. Lewis, *The Splendid Century*, 30. Another early weakness was the King's inability to pass up a woman, made particularly easy since women eagerly threw themselves at him. Warnie explored Louis's sexual life in some detail in his fourth book, *Louis XIV: An Informal Portrait* discussed later in this chapter.

35. Lewis, *The Splendid Century*, 41.

36. Lewis, *The Splendid Century*, 58.

37. Lewis, *The Splendid Century*, 59.

38. The average chapter length is about twenty-five pages.

39. For more on Louis's persecution of the Huguenots, see Lewis, *Louis XIV: An Informal Portrait*.

40. Lewis, *The Splendid Century*, 178.

41. Lewis, *The Splendid Century*, 194.

42. Lewis, *Essays Presented to Charles Williams*.

43. Lewis, *The Splendid Century*, 214.

44. Lewis, *The Splendid Century*, 220.

45. Lewis, *The Splendid Century*, 220.

46. Lewis, *The Splendid Century*, 220.

47. *Library Journal* 79 (Mar. 15, 1954): 546.

48. *Saturday Review* 37 (Mar. 27, 1954): 10.

49. *Spectator*, Dec. 11, 1953, 704.

50. *American Historical Review* 60 (Oct. 1954): 83–84.

51. "At the Top Was the King," *New York Times*, Aug. 15, 1954, 10.

52. Lewis, *The Splendid Century*, 286.

53. *Bone*, 160–61 (Nov. 19, 1953). In spite of their marital estrangement, Joy and Bill continue to write one another frequently. The subject of their letters usually concerned their sons, David and Douglas. However, since both were writers, they also often breezily discussed their works in progress and related matters.

54. *CL3*, 438 (Mar. 9, 1954).

55. *CL3*, 450–51 (Apr. 2, 1954).

56. *Bone*, 210–11.

57. Lewis, *The Sunset of the Splendid Century*, 10. Joy also compiled the very detailed index for the book. On March 16, 1955, she told Bill: "I finished the index of Warnie's new book for him—he's in a nursing home with fibrositis and flu—and his publisher was so pleased with the job I did on it that she asked if I would do indexes professionally and said she'd send me some now and then (*Bone*, 241). Many will read her comment about Warnie's "fibrositis and flu" as a likely veiled reference to an alcoholic binge. In addition, in his letters Jack often veiled Warnie's alcoholic binges as times of "illness."

58. Lewis, *The Sunset of the Splendid Century*, 9.

59. Lewis, *The Sunset of the Splendid Century*, 9.

60. Lewis, *The Sunset of the Splendid Century*, 299.

61. *Kirkus* 23 (Aug. 15, 1955): 162.

62. *Library Journal* 80 (Oct. 1, 1955): 2156.

63. *New Yorker*, Nov. 12, 1955, 231. Much later, John B. Wolf wrote that Warnie's study of duc de Maine "well exemplifies the writer's ability to bring out the color and flair of his subject even though he does not always probe very deeply." See Wolf, "The Reign of Louis XIV," 132.

64. "The Underworld of a Classical Age," *New York Times*, Dec. 18, 1955, 6.

65. *CL3*, 710.

66. *BF*, 243.

67. *Bone*, 242. At Warnie's suggestion, Joy was researching a book on Mme. de Maintenon, the second wife of Louis XIV. The reference to Jack's book is *Till We Have Faces*.

68. This refers to what became Warnie's fourth book, *Louis XIV: An Informal Portrait*.

69. *BF*, 243–44; emphasis in original.

70. *CL3*, 648.

71. Lewis, *Assault on Olympus*, 8.

72. Lewis, *Assault on Olympus*, 8.

73. Lewis, *Assault on Olympus*, 9.

74. Lewis, *Assault on Olympus*, 228–29.

75. Lewis, *Assault on Olympus*, 229.

76. *Manchester Guardian*, Mar. 28, 1958, 7.

77. *New Yorker*, June 28, 1958, 94.

78. *San Francisco Chronicle*, June 22, 1958, 29.

79. *Times Literary Supplement*, Mar. 7, 1958, 124.

80. *CL3*, 948–49. Walter Hooper said in his footnote to this letter that "the member of the family who wrote Warnie was Antoine (XII) Agénor Armand de Gramont (1879–1962), Duc de Guiche and Duc de Gramont 1925–62. Warnie had probably infuriated the Duc de Guiche by some error of fact in his book" (949).

81. *BF*, 246–47.

82. About this adventure, Warnie wrote that Parkin never got to the Great Wall because he had gotten caught up in a four-hour ride on a cattle truck that carried Chinese soldiers, seventeen black pigs, a madman, a blind man, and their guide who kept falling down whenever the train started or stopped. As Parkin was telling this story, Warnie and the others fell on the ground laughing (Aug. 1, 1929).

83. *BF,* 244.

84. *Bone,* 327.

85. Lewis, Letters to Edward Allen; *CL3,* 998–99.

86. See the review in the *Times Literary Supplement,* June 5, 1959, 334.

87. Lewis, *Louis XIV,* 9.

88. Lewis, *Louis XIV,* 9. The foreword also included something of an apology as War-nie explained that he omitted a bibliography, for reasons of space, and also because he did not want to appear to promise more than he actually provided (9). Several reviews criticized this omission (see the reviews later in this chapter).

89. Lewis, *Louis XIV,* 95.

90. Lewis, *Louis XIV,* 96.

91. Lewis, *Louis XIV,* 96.

92. Lewis, *Louis XIV,* 126.

93. Lewis, *Louis XIV,* 130–31.

94. Although Warnie never wrote a book on Mme. de Maintenon, he collected a good deal of information about her, and eventually he suggested that Joy write a book about her. On February 19, 1954, she wrote Bill: "Warnie keeps suggesting that I collaborate with him on a life of Mm. de Maintenon, Louis XIV's morganatic wife" (*Bone,* 179). In her May 17, 1954, letter to Bill, she said: "Warnie's sent me a full outline of the lady's life complete with book and page references all the way, and *what* a life; born in the workhouse, mysterious childhood visit to America, married as a girl to brilliant paralyzed poet, widowed, gets to be governess to the king's bastards and next thing you know she's reformed the king and married him! Her hobby was a girls' school she founded and she used to pop out of the royal bed at dawn, tear off to the school, help get the children up and teach a few classes herself" (*Bone,* 197). Joy took to the idea with enthusiasm, telling Bill six months later she was still doing research for the book, but apparently had not begun writing the manuscript: "I'm getting my teeth into *Queen Cinderella*—provisional title for my biography of Mme. de Maintenon; what do you think of it? Warnie's lent me some of his treasured books. There's miles of reading to do, but I think I ought to be able to sell it on an outline and a few speci-men chapters; the story's sure-fire . . . [and] smells to me like a money-maker if I can get it done" (*Bone,* 224–25 [Nov. 4, 1954]). A month later, she wrote Chad Walsh that she had "plunged into research for the life of Mme. de Maintenon which Warnie suggested to me and provided me with an outline for. So I'm living a very quiet life, deep in the seventeenth century. (*Bone,* 228 [Dec. 13, 1954]). On January 19, 1955, she wrote other friends about her work: "I've been doing research for the life of Mme. de Maintenon that Major Lewis started me on—I've got a pile of his most cherished books here to work my way through, and it's going very well . . ." (*Bone,* 234–35). However, eventually she was thwarted by the research the book required, complaining about it in many of her letters. Throughout the spring of 1955, she worked steadily on *Queen Cinderella,* sending out a 5,000-word outline to several publishers. On July 11, 1955, she wrote Bill with the bad news: "Macmillan, drat them, has turned down the synopsis of my *Queen Cinderella,* and so has H[odder] and S[toughton]. Looks as if I'll have to write it first" (*Bone,* 253). Her last reference to the book is August 26, 1955 (*Bone,* 258), after which she effectively abandoned it.

95. Lewis, *Louis XIV,* 217.

96. B. R. Redman, *Saturday Review* 42 (Oct. 17, 1959): 24.

97. *Times Literary Supplement,* June 5, 1959, 334.

98. *New York Herald Tribune*, Oct. 25, 1959, 4.

99. *New Yorker*, Oct. 10, 1959, 206.

100. *Springfield Republican*, Dec. 6, 1959, 3.

101. *Bone*, 338.

102. *BF*, 247 (Dec. 1, 1959).

103. *BF*, 251.

104. I discuss the impact of Joy's death on Warnie later in this chapter.

105. Lewis, *The Scandalous Regent*, 7.

106. Lewis, *The Scandalous Regent*, 7.

107. Lewis, *The Scandalous Regent*, 33.

108. Lewis, *The Scandalous Regent*, 93.

109. Lewis, *The Scandalous Regent*, 77.

110. *Library Journal* 86 (May 1, 1961): 1768.

111. Geoffrey Bruun, *New York Herald Tribune Lively Arts*, June 4, 1961, 26.

112. *Saturday Review* 44 (Apr. 29, 1961): 19.

113. *New York Times Book Review*, May 28, 1961, 7.

114. *New Yorker*, Apr. 22, 1961, 175.

115. For more, see Warnie's January 2, 1957, letter to Moira and Sayer, in *Jack*, 223–24. See also *BF*, 244–51.

116. "Memoir," 24.

117. Lewis, Letters to June Flewett.

118. *BF*, 245 (Mar. 21, 1957).

119. Bill and Joy had divorced on August 5, 1954.

120. Jack confirms this, writing Greeves on October 30, 1955, that Warnie had determined to stop drinking and was even doing very well at that time (*CL3*, 669).

121. *Bone*, 267.

122. *Bone*, 274 (Jan. 8, 1956).

123. *CL3*, 749.

124. *Bone*, 302; emphases in original.

125. Jack was thankful for Warnie's help with Joy, writing Greeves on November 25, 1956: "I know you will pray for her and for me: and for W., to whom also, the loss if we lose her, will be great" (*CL3*, 812).

126. *BF*, 245–46; emphasis in original.

127. *CL3*, 862 (July 1, 1957). In another letter, this time to Greeves, Jack reports the good news that Warnie is "as sober as a judge" (*CL3*, 986 [Nov. 3, 1958]). And Jack writes Tolkien on November 10, 1958: "Warnie, for the first time this many years, came back from his Irish holiday sober" (*CL3*, 988).

128. *Bone*, 327 (June 6, 1957). Certainly, Joy's encouragement helped Warnie to control his drinking. For instance, in his diary entry of March 30, 1960, Warnie writes about his efforts: "Another Lent over, and I make a note of my doings; not as a Pharisee, but that if I am spared until Lent 1960, I may do better. . . . I was a teetotaler, drank tea for breakfast, and had only bread and butter on Friday mornings" (*BF*, 247). Also, on October 1, 1960, he wrote in his unpublished diary: "In the year which ended yesterday I drank alcohol on 83 days and was a teetotaler for 282."

129. Lewis, Letters to June Flewett, July 27, 1957. In another positive report, Warnie wrote that Joy's recovery was miraculous. See Lewis, Letters to Mary Van Deusen, Oct. 1, 1957.

130. Lewis, Letters to Mary Van Deusen, Mar. 1, 1958.

131. Lewis, Letters to Mary Van Deusen, Nov. 8, 1958.

132. Lewis, Letters to June Flewett, Dec. 6, 1958.

133. *BF*, 249 (June 21, 1960).

134. *BF*, 250.

135. For Warnie's detailed comments on the main events leading up to Joy's death, see *BF*, 244–51.

136. *BF*, 250 (July 13, 1960).

137. *BF*, 251 (July 18, 1960).

138. Lewis, Letters to Mary Van Deusen, Dec. 12, 1960; Lewis, Letters to Belle Allen, Oct. 7, 1961.

139. *CL3*, 878.

140. Lewis, Letters to June Flewett, Oct. 23, 1958.

141. Lewis, Letters to Mary Van Deusen, Feb. 26, 1959. See also his letter to her of Nov. 8, 1958.

7. MEN MUST ENDURE (1960–1973)

1. For more on this, see my "Poetic Prose: Lewis's Poetic Legacy," in *C. S. Lewis, Poet*, 237–44.

2. See "Memoir," 24.

3. *CL3*, 1181–82.

4. *CL3*, 1312 (Jan. 17, 1962).

5. *BF*, 251 (Sept. 5, 1961).

6. *BF*, 252. See also "Diaries," Oct. 20, 1961.

7. Lewis, *Levantine Adventurer*, 8.

8. Lewis, *Levantine Adventurer*, 9.

9. Cited on the inside front of dust jacket of *Levantine Adventurer*.

10. Lewis, *Levantine Adventurer*, 95.

11. At one point, d'Arvieux assisted in a translation of *Abub Feda* or Arab Geography and he later wrote a Latin-Turkish dictionary. It may be that d'Arvieux was the first Lawrence of Arabia.

12. Lewis, *Levantine Adventurer*, 109.

13. *Kirkus* 56 (Jan. 1, 1962).

14. Lewis, *Memoirs of the Duc de Saint-Simon*. Warnie made no mention of this book in his diaries. I surmise he began work on the book almost immediately after the publication of *Levantine Adventurer* in 1962. Bayle St. John (1822–1859) published his four-volume edition of *Memoirs of the Duke of Saint-Simon in the Reign of Louis XIV* in 1857.

15. Lewis, *Memoirs of the Duc de Saint-Simon*, xi.

16. Lewis, *Memoirs of the Duc de Saint-Simon*, xi.

17. No reviews of the *Memoirs* appeared. The original dust jacket of the book offers the following favorable appraisal:

The Memoirs of Louis, Duc de Saint-Simon (1675–1755), became celebrated long before it was thought fit, in 1829, to publish the first edition. Whatever violence they may have done to the previously impressive image of the *Roi Soleil* (and, occasionally, to the truth), their effect was to bring the reader closer to the court of Versailles than to almost any other group of individuals in history. Every subsequent historian has of necessity seen Louis XIV and his court largely through the eyes of this supremely gifted if idiosyncratic observer. For Saint-Simon, for all his prejudices, was too inquisitive, and much too concerned to obtain the greatest effect (which for the memoir-writer means telling all), to be of value only to those who shared his political views. The nature of the original text suggests that Saint-Simon's honesty of purpose was constitutional. Passages of great descriptive power and examples of psychological portraiture by comparison with which his near-contemporary John Aubrey appears, charmingly, provincial and ingenuous, intersperse far larger tracts of matter than was never remarkable. In making this selection from the still vast mass of admirable material, W. H. Lewis has concentrated on showing the range of the Memoirs as a source for the history of France between 1691 and 1723, and, in more detail, Saint-Simon's achievement as a narrator of events [as] the portraitist of the King, his family, ministers and friends, and as historian of the manners and customs of the most splendid of European courts. There are eight pages of illustrations from contemporary sources.

18. *BF*, 252 (Oct. 1, 1961). *Horizon,* subtitled *A Magazine of the Arts,* was published from 1958 to 1989 as a hardback by *American Heritage.* The table of contents for the years 1959 to 1977 reveal no contribution by Warren Lewis. See http://notearama.blogspot.com/2013/09/horizon-magazine-hardcover-issues-1959.html.

19. "Diaries," Oct. 11, 1962.

20. *BF,* 252 (Oct. 24, 1961).

21. "Diaries," Nov. 1, 12, 1962.

22. *BF,* 252 (Dec. 4, 1961).

23. *BF,* 253 (Feb. 15, 1963).

24. "Diaries," Feb. 15, 1963.

25. *CL3,* 1298 (Nov. 30, 1961).

26. *CL3,* 1309. Because of his poor health, Jack was not in Cambridge for the Hilary term in 1962.

27. *CL3,* 1392 (Dec. 14, 1962).

28. Jack was in Cambridge in April 1962 for the Trinity term, the Michaelmas term in October 1962, the Hilary term in January 1963, and the Trinity term in April 1963.

29. Sayer, *Jack,* 401. Warnie gave himself mixed marks regarding his consumption of alcohol, writing that out of the preceding 365 days, he avoided alcohol for 298 of them. Compared to the previous year, he said it was poor record (*BF,* 253).

30. *CL3,* 1431.

31. In *They Stand Together,* Hooper writes: "I met C. S. Lewis early in 1963 and Warren had already gone off on what was to me (then) one of his inexplicable binges. Meanwhile, Lewis and I became more intimate, and finally he asked me to become his companion-secretary and I moved into his house. It was then that the facts about Warren came to light. They did indeed explain why Jack was in such open need of help. No one knew any more than that Warren was somewhere in Ireland on one of his more or less regular sprees" (30).

32. Sayer, *Jack,* 405. For Hooper's account of this period, see *CL3,* 1442–46.

33. Sayer, *Jack,* 405.

34. Sayer, *Jack,* 406. Sayer also noted:

The nuns were plainly very fond of him. The Warren they knew seemed rather different from the Warren we knew in Oxford. "Very devout in a simple way," one sister said. "Certainly a Catholic in the heart," said another. "If it had not been for his brother, he would be a full practicing member of the church," said still another, who thought that at one time or another he had made a confession to the convent chaplain. I was surprised to hear that he had gone as far as this. The hospital was a curiously happy place. Warren had often said to me, "If you know you are going to have an operation or a serious illness, go there at once, and you'll enjoy it." Certainly it was his spiritual and happiest physical home. (406)

35. Warnie's diary keeping had fallen off noticeably since 1949 when his diary ran to 37,000 words. Throughout the 1950s, his dairy keeping steadily became more sporadic, although, as I have suggested, this was probably because of the books he was writing. By the early 1960s, Warnie is writing little in his diary. For instance, his diary for 1960 contains 4,700 words; in 1961, 920 words; in 1962, 1725 words; in 1963, 1,856 words; and in 1964 1,110 words.

36. On August 1, 1963, Hooper wrote Roger Green and told him Warnie was expected back at the Kilns in a fortnight (*CL3*, 1444). On August 5, Hooper wrote Green again and affirmed that Warnie was expected back on August 14, 1963 (*CL3*, 1446).

37. *CL3*, 1455. Hooper notes about this time:

[Jack] was anxious as to what would happen to [Warnie] after his own death. In an effort to be as generous and, yet, as practical as possible he made Warnie the sole beneficiary of his literary Estate, having also appointed two of his friends as Executors and Trustees [Owen Barfield and Cecil Harwood] to prevent his brother converting that Estate, for as long as he should live, into ready cash. Even then the thought of Warnie's future so troubled him that he told me he wished, for Warnie's sake, that his brother might die first to prevent him ending up in a ditch uncared for and unloved. He always lamented, "'*Who* is there to look after him when I'm gone?' The thought that I might be the one to do that never entered my head" (Hooper, *They Stand Together*, 31; emphasis in original).

38. *CL3*, 1458.

39. In Jack's October 11, 1963, letter to Hooper he noted that Warnie had finally come home (1461). Jack added a caution to Hooper about returning to the Kilns too soon: "There's always the chance W. might resent your presence (if he did, you wd. never know. He is the politest of men). Also, that he might welcome it as finally excusing him from all responsibilities to me, and so go more often on the binge" (1462). It is obvious that Jack was growing tired of dealing with Warnie's alcoholism.

40. Lewis, *A Biography of C. S. Lewis*, 468.

41. "Memoir," 24–25.

42. The Kilns housekeeper, Mollie Miller, wrote Hooper the day after Jack's death, giving him an account of what had happened, and confided that Warnie was unable to handle Jack's passing. Southern Historical Collection, Wilson Library, UNC; Nov. 23, 1963.

43. Shakespeare, *King Lear*, act 5, sc. 2. This quote from Edgar was printed on the family calendar on August 23, 1908, the day Flora Lewis died. Albert preserved that calendar page for the rest of his life. For more on this, see chapter 1.

44. Lewis, Letters to Jock Gibb, Jan. 19, 1964.

45. Hooper, *They Stand Together,* 37.

46. For more on this, Walter Hooper's "Introduction" to *They Stand Together* provides excellent background and commentary on Warnie's life after Jack's death, especially 29–36.

47. Lewis, Letters to Mrs. Frank Jones. Hooper suggested that Warnie panicked and made the move because he feared he would not be able to maintain the Kilns (Hooper, "Warnie's Problem," 10).

48. Warnie spent his first night at 51 Ringwood Road on May 19, 1964.

49. Hooper, "Warnie's Problem," 10.

50. Lewis, Letters to Jock Gibb, Feb. 28, 1964.

51. *BF,* 254.

52. *BF,* 254 (Aug. 23, 1964); emphasis in original.

53. *BF,* 254 (Sept. 1, 1964); emphasis in original.

54. This unpublished manuscript is available at the Wade Center.

55. Hooper, "Warnie's Problem," 12.

56. Hooper points out that "of the approximately 230,000 words which made up the original 'biography' (as [Warnie] insisted on calling it), only about 23,300 were narration, and most of those were in the early chapters" (Hooper, "Warnie's Problem," 12).

57. Christopher Hugh Derrick (1921–2007) had been a former pupil of Jack's. He was a writer, reviewer, publisher's reader, and lecturer.

58. Christopher Derrick to Jock Gibb, Dec. 7, 1964.

59. *BF,* 255.

60. Lewis, Letters to Edward Allen, Dec. 26, 1965.

61. *BF,* 256 (Jan. 1, 1966).

62. Hooper, *They Stand Together,* 34–35.

63. Lewis, Letters to Walter Hooper, Jan. 12, 1966; emphasis in original.

64. *BF,* 256–57 (Apr. 16, 1966).

65. Lewis, Letters to Edward Allen, Apr. 19, 1966. In the preface to Walter Hooper's revised and enlarged edition of Warnie's *Letters of C. S. Lewis* (1988), he includes a November 16, 1987, statement by Christopher Derrick regarding his revision of Warnie's original manuscript:

> Here's how I see the question. Over the years, I have done a good many jobs of editorial carpentry for various publishers, ranging from petty correcting to full ghosting. This was one such job among many. Jock Gibb asked me to do it, on lines specified by himself: I did it to the best of my ability and to his satisfaction: I feel neither pride nor shame at the outcome, apart from the general satisfaction of pleasing a friend and ad hoc employer. . . . Do tell this aspect of the story exactly as you see fit, with or without any mention of my name. I don't suppose you'll want to cast me for the villain of the piece! In so far as there is any villain, it is doubtlessly the drink, as then making it impossible for Warnie to do a proper job or even supervise it. . . . If Warnie were still alive I believe he would consider all my corrections as pedantic, not really necessary but not wrong either. I think he would be more cheerful about my attempts at restoration, a job he incidentally helped with by giving me the original typescript of his book. (12)

66. Hazelton, "C. S. Lewis: No Further Than Gethsemane," 25.

67. Hazelton, "C. S. Lewis: No Further Than Gethsemane," 27.

68. Sire, "The Many Faces of C. S. Lewis," 364.

69. Sire, "The Many Faces of C. S. Lewis," 366.

70. Ryan, "The Man behind the Mask," 421.

71. "Diaries," July 22, 1966.

72. Lewis, Letters to Belle Edwards, Dec. 9, 1966.

73. Hooper, *They Stand Together*, 32.

74. For more on this, see *BF,* 256 (Apr. 8, 1966).

75. Hooper, *They Stand Together*, 32.

76. On occasion, Warnie did express frustration with what he viewed as poor services and the local vicar.

77. Lewis, Letters to Vera Gebbert, May 27, 1966.

78. Lewis, Letters to Jane Douglas, Oct. 16, 1970.

79. Lewis, Letters to June Flewett, Dec. 12, 1957.

80. After Joy's death, Jack provided financial support for David and Douglas until they turned twenty-one.

81. Lewis, Letters to June Flewett, Dec. 13, 1960.

82. Lewis, Letters to Mary Van Deusen, July 19, 1961.

83. Lewis, Letters to Belle Allen, June 8, 1962; emphasis in original.

84. Lewis, Letters to Mary Van Deusen, Dec. 15, 1962.

85. *BF,* 283.

86. For Douglas Gresham's view of Warnie, see Gresham, *Lenten Lands,* 40–46, 189–92. In emails to the author of July 17 and 18, 2021, Gresham praised Warnie for his bravery in WWI and WWII and affirmed that he was a "gentle, gracious man and one who was a good friend until the Gin got to him." On one occasion when he came to the Kilns and found Warnie passed out from excessive drinking, Gresham started to cry. "He and I had been good friends for years and here he was deliberately fading into destruction." Gresham also noted that Warnie's final years were very sad because he had lost Joy and Jack, "the only people whom he really and deeply loved." The Kilns became "a doleful home and . . . Warnie was alone deep in himself. The three people in all the world whom I [Gresham] loved, were gone, Warnie was gone too but still living and hurting and there was nothing I could do to help him. I do still feel a bit sad for him and angry with myself for not spending more time with him, but it would have done no good to him nor for me had I done so. . . . A few years later, I went back to England to be at Warnie's Funeral, and again I wept but kept that hidden." See in addition Lyle Dorsett's oral interview with Gresham of June 4, 1982.

87. "Diaries," Mar. 8, 1967.

88. *BF,* 277 (Aug. 10, 1967).

89. It is ironic that Warnie was unable to sympathize with David and Douglas as they grew up since when he was their age, he had found fault with his father for similar reasons.

90. Hooper, *They Stand Together,* 34; emphasis in original.

91. Lewis, "Warnie's Problem," 16.

92. For more, see "Diaries," July 22, 1966.

93. Walter Hooper to Owen Barfield, Feb. 27, 1965.

94. In addition, George Sayer reported that after probate Jack's estate was valued at £37,772, so Warnie really need not have worried about his finances. Nevertheless, Warnie feared that sales of Jack's books would eventually slacken, and he would face financial ruin. Owen Barfield confirmed Warnie's anxiety about money; see his oral interview with Lyle Dorsett; July 19–20, 1984.

95. Email to the author, July 25, 2016.

96. Hooper believed the Millers had a genuine concern for Warnie's well-being. Douglas Gresham, however, had a more jaundiced view of the Millers, believing that they encouraged and enabled Warnie's drinking, hoping in the end to benefit financially after Warnie's death. For more on Gresham's view, see Gresham, *Lenten Lands*, 189–92. Frank Henry also had a negative view of the Millers; see his oral interview with Lyle Dorsett, Dec. 12, 1984.

97. June had married Clement Freud (1924–2009) in 1950. Together they owned Westons, a beach cottage in Walberswick on the west coast of Suffolk, and she often invited Warnie to use it for holidays.

98. "Diaries," May 7, 1966.

99. *BF,* 260 (June 15, 1966).

100. *BF,* 262 (July 13, 1966).

101. "Diaries," Mar. 11, 1967.

102. "Diaries," Mar. 11, 1967.

103. *BF,* 272–73 (Mar. 24, 1967); emphasis in original.

104. "Diaries," Mar. 27, 1967.

105. "Diaries," Apr. 3, 1967.

106. "Diaries," Apr. 9, 1967. Other history plays he read were *King John* and *Henry VI,* parts 1, 2, and 3.

107. *BF,* 280 (Sept. 26, 1967).

108. *BF,* 284 (Jan. 15, 1968).

109. "Diaries," June 26, 1967.

110. "Diaries," July 8, 1967.

111. "Diaries," July 22, 1967.

112. *BF,* 284–85 (Jan. 15, 1968).

113. *BF,* 261 (June 26, 1966).

114. *BF,* 266 (Aug. 19, 1966).

115. Lewis, Blanche Biggs to WHL; Oct. 5, 1968.

116. Lewis, Letters to Blanche Biggs, Oct. 22, 1968.

117. For more on the relationship between Warnie and Blanche—including the letters—see Glyer, *The Major and the Missionary.*

118. Lewis, Letters to Sister Joseph Damien, Mar. 13, 1969.

119. Lewis, Letters to Dorothy Thibaut, Jan. 4, 1971.

120. *BF,* 290 (Mar. 22, 1969). In a July 20, 2021, email to the author, Douglas Gresham reported that Warnie told his mother that he had been jilted early on by a woman he had proposed to. Warnie never wrote about or referred to this event.

121. *BF,* 260 (June 23, 1966). For a similar dream, see *BF,* 269 (Jan. 19, 1967).

122. *BF,* 276 (July 12, 1967).

123. *BF,* 288 (Nov. 22, 1968).

124. *BF,* 275 (July 4, 1967). Warnie is referring to Jack's *Studies in Words.*

EPILOGUE

1. An example of a joke/wheeze occurred while the brothers were enjoying a lunch once with Ruth Pitter, the well-known poet and friend. Pitter engaged Jack in a comic argument. She recalls:

I asked C. S. if I might catechize him a bit about the delectable "Lion, Witch, and Wardrobe," in which I thought I had detected a weakness. Permission courteously given:

R. P.: The Witch makes it always winter and never summer?
C. S.: (In his fine reverberating voice) She does.
R. P.: Does she allow any foreign trade?
C. S.: She does not.
R. P.: Am I allowed to postulate a *deus ex machina,* perhaps on the lines of Santa Claus with the tea-tray? (This is where C. S. lost the contest. If he had allowed the deus-ex-m., for which Santa gives good precedent, he would have saved himself).
C. S.: You are not.
R. P.: Then how could the Beavers have put on that splendid lunch?
C. S.: They caught the fish through holes in the ice.
R. P.: Quite so, but the drippings to fry them? The potatoes—a plant that perishes at a touch of frost—the oranges and sugar and suet and flour for the lovely surprise Marmalade Roll—the malt and hops for Mr. Beaver's beer—the milk for the children?
C. S.: (With great presence of mind) I must refer you to a further study of the text.
Warnie: Nonsense, Jack; you're stumped and you know it. Cited in King, *Hunting the Unicorn,* 209–10.

2. Wain, "Brother and Friends," 228.
3. Shakespeare, *King Lear,* act 5, sc. 2, ll. 9–11. Alexandra Como so loved Warnie's seven books on seventeenth-century French history that in August 1971 she wrote him a highly complimentary letter, sharing that she thought he was a better writer than Jack. When the letter arrived at the Kilns, Warnie asked Walter Hooper to open the letter and read it to him. After Hooper read the letter and her comment that she thought he was a better writer than Jack, Warnie exclaimed forcefully, "That makes two of us!"

Bibliography

Alie, Joe A. D. *A New History of Sierra Leone*. New York: St. Martin's Press, 1990.

"A Novice's Guide to Yacht Insurance: The Cost of Covering a 30-ft. Cruiser in Various Circumstances." *Motor Boat and Yachting* 65 (Dec. 11, 1936): 632–33.

Archives, Royal Military College, Sandhurst.

The Army Service Corp. http://www.1914-1918.net/asc.htm.

Army Service Records for Warren Hamilton Lewis. http://www.joelheck.com/resources /Warren%20Hamilton%20Lewis%20Military%20Record.pdf.

"Army Service Corps in the First World War." http://www.longlongtrail.co.uk/army /regiments-and-corps/the-army-service-corps-in-the-first-world-war/.

"Army Service Corps Mechanical Transport Companies." http://www.longlongtrail. co.uk/army/regiments-and-corps/the-army-service-corps-in-the-first-world-war /army-service-corps-mechanical-transport-companies/.

Audion-Rouzeau, Stéphane, and Annette Becker. *14–18: Understanding the Great War*. Translated by Catherine Temerson. New York: Hill and Wang, 2002.

Bardon, Jonathan. *A History of Ulster*. Belfast: Blackstaff Press, 1992.

Beadon, R. H. *The Royal Army Service Corps: A History of Transport and Supply in the British Army. Vol II*. Oxford: Oxford Univ. Press, 1931.

Beckett, J. C., ed. *Belfast: The Making of the City, 1800–1914*. Belfast: Appletree Press, 1983.

Beckett, J. C., and Robin E. Glasscock, eds. *Belfast: The Origin and Growth of an Industrial City*. Chatham, Kent, UK: W & J Mackay & Company, 1967.

Blumenau, Ralph. *A History of Malvern College: 1865 to 1965*. London: St. Martin's Press, 1965.

Bond, Brian. "The Army between the Two World Wars 1918–1939. In *The Oxford Illustrated History of the British Army*, edited by David Chandler. Oxford: Oxford Univ. Press, 1994.

Bremer, John. *C. S. Lewis, Poetry, and the Great War, 1914–1918*. Plymouth, UK: Lexington Books, 2012.

Breunig, L. C. "Review of *The Scandalous Regent: A Life of Philippe, Duc d'Orleans*,

1674–1723, and of His Family." *New York Times Book Review.* May 28, 1961, 7.

"Britain and the Russian Civil War." https://warwick.ac.uk/services/library/mrc/explore further/digital/russia/civil_war/.

Brogan, D. W. "Review of *The Splendid Century.*" *Spectator.* Dec. 11, 1953, 704.

Brown, William F. "Review of *The Splendid Century.*" *American Historical Review* 60 (Oct. 1954): 83–84.

Bruckman, John. "Review of *The Sunset of the Splendid Century.*" *Library Journal* 80 (Oct. 1, 1955): 2156.

Bruun, Geoffrey. "Review of *The Scandalous Regent: A Life of Philippe, Duc d'Orleans, 1674–1723, and of His Family.*" *New York Herald Tribune Lively Arts.* June 4, 1961, 26.

"Canal and River Trust." https://canalrivertrust.org.uk/.

Carpenter, Humphrey. *The Inklings: C. S. Lewis, J. R. R. Tolkien, Charles Williams and Their Friends.* Boston: Houghton Mifflin, 1979.

Cecil, David. "Oxford's Magic Circle." *Books and Bookmen* 24, no. 4 (Jan. 1979): 10–12.

Center for First World War Studies. http://www.birmingham.ac.uk/research/activity /warstudies/index.aspx.

Chandler, David, and Ian F. W. Beckett, eds. *The Oxford Illustrated History of the British Army.* Oxford: Oxford Univ. Press, 1994.

Charlton, B. G. "On W. H. Lewis's Military Rank." *The Chronicle of the Oxford University C. S. Lewis Society* 4 (2007): 36–37.

Churchill, Winston S. *The World Crisis, 1918–1928: The Aftermath.* New York: Charles Scribner & Sons, 1929.

Collins, Brenda. "The Edwardian City." In *Belfast: The Making of the City, 1800–1914,* edited by J. C. Beckett. Belfast: Appletree Press, 1983.

Como, James T. *C. S. Lewis at the Breakfast Table and Other Reminiscences.* New York: Macmillan, 1979.

———. "Routes of Regression: Brothers and Friends, Then and Always." *CSL: The Bulletin of the New York C. S. Lewis Society* 14, no. 2 (Dec. 1982): 1–6.

"Cruisers for Inland Waterways: Advice to Those Who Are Thinking of Acquiring Their First Boat." *Motor Boat and Yachting* 65 (Sept. 18, 1936): 288–90.

Daniell, David Scott. "The Men at the Wheel: Motor Yachtmen Classified." *Motor Boat and Yachting* 69 (Dec. 9, 1938): 626–27.

Davidman, Joy. *A Naked Tree: Joy Davidman's Love Sonnets to C. S. Lewis and Other Poems.* Edited by Don W. King. Grand Rapids, MI: William B. Eerdmans, 2015.

———. *Out of My Bone: The Letters of Joy Davidman.* Edited by Don W. King. Grand Rapids, MI: William B. Eerdmans, 2009.

Davies, Mark J., and Catherine Robinson. *A Towpath Walk in Oxford: The Canal and River Thames between Wolvercote and the City.* Oxford: Oxford Towpath Press, 2012.

"Demobilisation after the First World War." http://www.mylearning.org/demobilisation -after-the-first-world-war/p-4744/.

"Demobilisation and Discharge." http://www.longlongtrail.co.uk/soldiers/a-soldiers -life-1914–1918/demobilisation-and-discharge/.

"Demobilisation in Britain, 1918–20." http://www.nationalarchives.gov.uk/pathways/first worldwar/spotlights/demobilisation.htm.

Edwards, Bruce, ed. *C. S. Lewis—Life, Works, and Legacy.* 4 vols. Westport, CN: Praeger, 2007.

"The Enemy Within: The Battle over Alcohol in World War I." http://theconversation
   .com/the-enemy-within-the-battle-over-alcohol-in-world-war-i-30441.

Examination for Admission to the Royal Military Academy, or the Royal Military College. Army Personnel Centre. http://www.army.mod.uk/home.aspx.

Finch, David. "Review of *The Scandalous Regent: A Life of Philippe, Duc d'Orleans,
   1674–1723, and of His Family.*" *Library Journal* 86 (May 1, 1961): 1768.

First World War.Com: A Multimedia History of World War I. http://firstworldwar.com
   /index.htm.

Fisher, John H., and Joseph R. Robb, eds. *Royal Belfast Academical Institution: Centenary
   Volume, 1810–1910.* Belfast: M'Caw, Stevenson & Orr, 1913.

Fortescue, John. *The Royal Army Service Corps: A History of Transport and Supply in the
   British Army.* Vol 1. Cambridge: Cambridge Univ. Press, 1930.

———. *A History of the British Army.* London: Macmillan, 1930.

Foster, Mike. "'That Most Unselfish Man': George Sayer, 1914–2005: Pupil, Biographer, and
   Friend of Inklings." *Mythlore* 26, no. 3/4 (2008): 5–26.

French, David. "Doctrine and Organization in the British Army, 1919–1932." *The Historical
   Journal* 44, no. 2 (2001): 497–515.

———. *Military Identities: The Regimental System, the British Army, and the British
   People, c. 1870–2000.* Oxford: Oxford Univ. Press, 2005.

Freud (née Flewett), Jill. Email to author. Aug. 27, 2016.

Fussell, Paul. *The Great War and Modern Memory.* Oxford: Oxford Univ. Press, 1975.

Fyfe, Christopher. *A History of Sierra Leone.* London: Oxford Univ. Press, 1962.

Gershoy. Leo. "Review of *The Scandalous Regent: A Life of Philippe, Duc d'Orleans,
   1674–1723, and of His Family.*" *Saturday Review* 44 (Apr. 29, 1961): 19.

———."Review of *The Splendid Century.*" *Saturday Review* 37 (Mar. 27, 1954): 10.

Gilchrist, K. J. *A Morning after War: C. S. Lewis & WWI.* New York: Peter Lang, 2005.

Glyer, Diana. "Warren Hamilton 'Warnie' Lewis (1895–1973)." *The C. S. Lewis Readers'
   Encyclopedia.* Grand Rapids, MI: Zondervan, 1998.

———. "The Centre of the Inklings: Lewis? Williams? Barfield? Tolkien?" *Mythlore* 26,
   no. 1/2 (2007): 29–39.

———. *The Company They Keep: C. S. Lewis and J. R. R. Tolkien as Writers in Community.*
   Kent, OH: Kent State Univ. Press, 2006.

Graham, David, ed. *We Remember C. S. Lewis: Essays and Memoirs.* Nashville, TN:
   Broadman & Holman, 2001.

Graubard, Stephen Ruchards. "Military Demobilization in Great Britain Following the
   Great War." *Journal of Modern History* 19 (Dec. 1947): 297–311.

Graves, Robert. *Goodbye to All That.* London: Jonathan Cape, 1929.

The Great War Society. http://www.iwm.org.uk/.

The Great War Timeline. http://www.pbs.org/greatwar/timeline/.

Green, Roger Lancelyn, and Walter Hooper. *C. S. Lewis: A Biography.* London: Collins, 1974.

Gresham, Douglas. Emails to the author. July 17, 18, and 20, 2021.

———. *Jack's Life: A Memoir of C. S. Lewis.* New York: Broadman Holman: 2005.

———. *Lenten Lands.* San Francisco: HarperSanFran, 1988.

Griffin, William. *Clive Staples Lewis: A Dramatic Life.* New York: Harper & Row, 1986.

Guerard, Albert. "At the Top Was the King," *New York Times.* Aug. 15, 1954, 10.

———. "The Underworld of a Classical Age," *New York Times*. Dec. 18, 1955, 6.

Guthrie, Thomas Anstey [F. Anstey, pseud.]. *Vice Versa: A Lesson to Fathers*. London: Smith, Elder & Co., 1911.

Hammond, Gerald Bruce. "Memories of Dunkirk: In the RASC." *WW2 Peoples War: An Archive of World War Two Memories*. https://www.bbc.co.uk/history/ww2peopleswar /stories/19/a2313019.shtml.

Haswell, Jock, and John Lewis-Stempel. *A Brief History of the British Army*. UK: Thames and Hudson, 1975.

Haythornthwaite, Philip. *The World War One Source Book*. London: Arms and Armour Press, 1993.

Hazelton, Roger. "C. S. Lewis: No Further than Gethsemane." *New Republic* 156 (Feb. 18, 1967): 25–27.

Heck, Joel D. "C. S. Lewis Serendipities: Things You Never Knew about Jack and Warren." *CSL: The Bulletin of the New York C. S. Lewis Society* 47, no. 4 (July/Aug. 2016): 1–14.

———. "Chronologically Lewis." http://www.joelheck.com/chronologically-lewis.php.

———. *No Ordinary People: Twenty-One Friendships of C. S. Lewis*. Hamden, CT: Winged Lion Press, 2021.

———. "Warren Hamilton Lewis: His Brother's Brother." *The Chronicle of the Oxford University C. S. Lewis Society* 6, no. 3 (2009): 3–22.

Hemingway, Ernest. *The Nick Adams Stories*. New York: Bantam, 1973.

The History of the RMA Sandhurst. http://www.army.mod.uk/documents/general/history _of_rmas.pdf.

"History of the Royal Military Academy, Sandhurst." http://www.army.mod.uk/training _education/24487.aspx.

"History of Sierra Leone." http://www.historyworld.net/wrldhis/PlainTextHistories.asp ?historyid=ad45.

Hooper, Walter. *C. S. Lewis: Companion and Guide*. New York: HarperCollins, 1996.

———. Email to the author. July 25, 2016.

———. "'Warnie's Problem': An Introduction to a Letter from C. S. Lewis to Owen Barfield." *Journal of Inklings Studies* 5, no. 1 (Apr. 2015): 3–21.

———. "Warren Hamilton Lewis: An Appreciation." *CSL: The Bulletin of the New York C. S. Lewis Society* 5, no. 6 (Apr. 1974): 5–8.

"Horse Transport." http://www.longlongtrail.co.uk/army/regiments-and-corps/the-army -service-corps-in-the-first-world-war/.

Hurd, Crystal. "An Imaginative Tale from the Father of C. S. Lewis." *Sehnsucht: The C. S. Lewis Journal* 14 (2020): 81–90.

———. "*The Pudaita Pie*: Reflections on Albert Lewis." *VII: Journal of the Marion E. Wade Center* 32 (2015): 47–58.

Imperial War Museum. http://www.iwm.org.uk/.

"Interesting Golfers." *Golf Illustrated*. Apr. 20, 1900, 47.

James, Sydney Rhodes. *Seventy Years: Random Reminiscences and Reflections*. London: Williams & Norgate Ltd., 1925.

Jenkins, Philip. *The Great and Holy War: How World War I Became a Religious Crusade*. New York: HarperCollins, 2014.

Johnston. John. *English Poetry of the First World War: A Study in the Evolution of Lyric and Narrative Form.* Princeton, NJ: Princeton Univ. Press, 1964.

Jones, David. *In Parenthesis.* London: Faber and Faber, 1937.

Jünger, Ernest. *Storm of Steel.* Trans. Michael Hoffman. Stuttgart: J. G. Cotta'sche Buch-handlung NachfolderGamH, 1920; London: Penguin, 2003.

Keegan, John. *The Face of Battle: A Study of Agincourt, Waterloo, and the Somme.* New York: Viking, 1976.

———. *The First World War.* New York: Vintage, 2000.

King. Don W. *C. S. Lewis, Poet: The Legacy of His Poetic Impulse.* Kent, OH: Kent State Univ. Press, 2001.

———. "The Early Life of Warren Hamilton Lewis (1895–1913)," *Journal of Inklings Studies* 8, no. 1 (Apr. 2018): 1–30.

———. "Warnie at War (1914–1918)." *VII: Journal of the Marion E. Wade Center* 35 (2018): 87–110.

———. "Warren Lewis and the Lewis Papers." *VII: Journal of the Marion E. Wade Center* 37 (2020): 111–22.

———. "Warren Lewis, Mrs Janie King Moore, and The Kilns." *Journal of Inklings Studies* 7, no. 1 (Apr. 2017): 103–18.

———. "Warren Lewis: The Soldier Sailor." *Journal of Inklings Studies* 11, no. 1 (Apr. 2021): 58–69.

———. "When Did the Inklings Meet? A Chronological Survey of Their Gatherings: 1933–1953." *Journal of Inklings Studies* 10, no. 2 (Oct. 2020): 184–204.

———. *Yet One More Spring: A Critical Study of Joy Davidman.* Grand Rapids, MI: William B. Eerdmans, 2015.

Lazo, Andrew. "Correcting the Chronology: Some Implications of 'Early Prose Joy,'" *SEVEN: An Anglo-American Literary Review* 29 (2012): 51–62.

Lewis, C. S. *All My Road Before Me: The Diary of C. S. Lewis, 1922–1927.* New York: Harcourt Brace, 1991.

———. *Boxen: The Imaginary World of the Young C. S. Lewis.* Edited by Walter Hooper. London: Collins, 1985.

———. *The Collected Letters of C. S. Lewis.* Vol. 1, *Family Letters 1905–1931,* edited by Walter Hooper. London: Harper Collins, 2000.

———. *The Collected Letters of C. S. Lewis.* Vol. 2, *Books, Broadcasts and the War, 1931–1949,* edited by Walter Hooper. London: Harper Collins, 2004.

———. *The Collected Letters of C. S. Lewis.* Vol. 3, *Narnia, Cambridge, and Joy, 1950–1963,* edited by Walter Hooper. London: Harper Collins, 2006.

———. *The Collected Poems of C. S. Lewis: A Critical Edition.* Edited by Don W. King. Kent, OH: Kent State Univ. Press, 2015.

———, ed. *Essays Presented to Charles Williams.* Oxford: Oxford Univ. Press, 1947.

———. "How Can I Ask Thee, Father?" In *The Collected Poems of C. S. Lewis: A Critical Edition,* edited by Don W. King. Kent, OH: Kent State Univ. Press, 2015.

———. *Surprised by Joy: The Shape of My Early Life.* London: Geoffrey Bles, 1955.

———. *They Stand Together: The Letters of C. S. Lewis to Arthur Greeves (1914–1963).* Edited by Walter Hooper. London: Collins, 1979.

———. "Wain's Oxford." *Encounter* 20, no. 1 (Jan. 1963): 81.

Lewis, C. S., and Warren Lewis. "*The Pudaita Pie:* An Anthology." *VII: Journal of the*

Marion E. Wade Center 32 (2015): 59–68.

Lewis, Warren H. *A Biography of C. S. Lewis.* Unpublished typescript. Marion E. Wade Center.

———. "A Ditchcrawling Discourse: Some Thoughts on Inland Waterways Cruising." *Motor Boat and Yachting* 70 (May 12, 1939): 485–86.

———. *Assault on Olympus: The Rise of the House of Gramont between 1604 and 1678.* London: Andre Deutsch, 1958.

———. *Brothers and Friends: The Diaries of Major Warren Hamilton Lewis.* Edited by Clyde S. Kilby and Marjorie Lamp Mead. San Francisco: Harper & Row, 1982.

———. "'But What's It Going to Cost?' Three Seasons' Detailed Figures for a 20-ft. Inland Waterways Cruiser." *Motor Boat and Yachting* 69 (Nov. 4, 1938): 482–83.

———. *C. S. Lewis: A Biography.* Unpublished typescript. Marion E. Wade Center.

———. "The Diaries, Correspondence, Papers, and Walking Tours of W. H. Lewis." Warren H. Lewis Collection. Marion E. Wade Center.

———. "Exploring the Wey: A Three Days Cruise on a Tributary of the Thames." *Motor Boat and Yachting* 68 (Feb. 25, 1938): 198–99.

———. *Letters of C. S. Lewis.* New York. Harcourt Brace Jovanovich, 1966.

———. Letters to Belle Allen. Marion E. Wade Center.

———. Letters to Blanche Biggs. Marion E. Wade Center.

———. Letters to Dorothy Thibaut. Marion E. Wade Center.

———. Letters to Edward Allen. Marion E. Wade Center.

———. Letters to Florence (Michal) Williams. Marion E. Wade Center.

———. Letters to Mrs. Frank Jones. Marion E. Wade Center.

———. Letters to Jane Douglas. Marion E. Wade Center.

———. Letters to Jock Gibb. Bodleian Library.

———. Letters to June Flewett. Taylor University Center for the Study of C. S. Lewis & Friends.

———. Letters to Mary Van Deusen. Marion E. Wade Center.

———. Letters to Sister Joseph Damien. Marion E. Wade Center.

———. Letters to Vera Gebbert. Marion E. Wade Center.

———. Letters to Walter Hooper. Southern Historical Collection, Wilson Library, UNC.

———. *Levantine Adventurer: The Travels and Missions of the Chevalier d'Arvieux, 1653–1697.* London: Andre Deutsch, 1962.

———. *Lewis Papers: Memoirs of the Lewis Family: 1850–1930.* 11 volumes. Unpublished typescript. Marion E. Wade Center.

———. *Louis XIV: An Informal Portrait.* London: Andre Deutsch, 1959.

———. "Malvern in My Time." *The Beacon* (Malvern College) 1954: 14–17. Reprinted in *CSL: The Bulletin of the New York C. S. Lewis Society* 12, no. 8 (June 1981): 1–3.

———. "Memoir of C. S. Lewis." In *Letters of C. S. Lewis,* edited by Warren H. Lewis. London: Geoffrey Bles, 1966.

———. *Memoirs of the Duc de Saint-Simon.* London: B. T. Batsford, 1964.

———. "'Sailing P. M. 13th.'" *Motor Boat and Yachting* 70 (June 23, 1939): 635.

———. "The Galleys of France." In *Essays Presented to Charles Williams,* edited by C. S. Lewis. Oxford Univ. Press. Oxford, 1947.

————. "The Great Ouse: A Week with "Bosphorus on Fenland Waterways." *Motor Boat and Yachting* 69 (Aug. 12, 1938): 180–83.

————. *The Scandalous Regent: A Life of Philippe, Duc d'Orleans, 1674–1723, and of His Family.* London: Andre Deutsch, 1961.

————. *The Splendid Century.* London: Eyre & Spottiswoode, 1954.

————. *The Sunset of the Splendid Century: The Life and Times of Louis Auguste de Bourbon, Duc de Maine, 1670–1736.* London: Eyre & Spottiswoode, 1955.

————. "The Winter of Our Discontent: It Is Not So Bad, After All, Thinks This Ditch-crawler." *Motor Boat and Yachting* 70 (Feb. 17, 1939): 158–59.

————. "Through the Oxford Canal: A Whitsun Cruise on a Secluded and Attractive Waterway, Part 1." *Motor Boat and Yachting* 67 (July 2, 1937): 5–7.

————. "Through the Oxford Canal: A Whitsun Cruise on a Secluded and Attractive Waterway, Part 2." *Motor Boat and Yachting* 67 (July 9, 1937): 54–55.

————. Warren Hamilton Lewis Letters Collection. Marion E. Wade Center.

The Long, Long Trail: The British Army in the Great War, 1914–1918. http://www.1914–1918.net/index.html.

Lunn, Arnold. *The Harrovians: A Tale of Public School Life.* London: Methuen 7 Co., 1913.

Lynch, J. P. *An Unlikely Success Story: The Belfast Shipbuilding Industry, 1880–1935.* Belfast: Belfast Society, 2001.

"Major W. H. Lewis: Soldier and Writer, Obituary" *The (London) Times.* Apr. 16, 1973.

"Major Warren H. Lewis." *CSL: The Bulletin of the New York C. S. Lewis Society* 3, no. 10 (Aug. 1972): 1–4.

McCaughan, Michael. *The Birth of the Titanic.* Montreal: McGill-Queen's Univ. Press, 1998.

McCreary, Alf. *The Titanic Port: An Illustrated History of Belfast Harbour.* Belfast: Booklink, 2010.

McGrath, Alister. *C. S. Lewis: A Life.* Carol Stream, IL: Tyndale House, 2012.

Mead, Marjorie Lamp. "Profiles in Faith: Major Warren Hamilton Lewis (1895–1973)." *Knowing and Doing* (Spring 2006): 1–6.

Messenger, Charles. *Call to Arms: The British Army 1914–18.* London: Weidenfeld & Nicolson, 2005.

Michelson, Paul E. "W. H. Lewis: Writer and Historian, A Prolegomena." *CSL: The Bulletin of the New York C. S. Lewis Society* 50, no. 5 (Sept./Oct., 2019): 1–9.

"Military Structures and Rank." http://www.bl.uk/world-war-one/articles/military-structures-and-ranks.

Montague, Charles Edward. *Disenchantment.* London: Chatto and Windus, 1922. Reprinted by MacGibbon and Kee, 1968.

Morton, Anthony. "Sandhurst and the First World War: The Royal Military College, 1902–1918." http://www.army.mod.uk/documents/general/rmas_occ_paper_17.pdf.

Moss, Michael, and John R. Hume. *Shipbuilders to the World: 125 Years of Harland and Wolff, Belfast 1861–1986.* Belfast: Blackstaff Press, 1986.

Mosse, George L. *Fallen Soldiers: Reshaping the Memory of the World Wars.* New York: Oxford Univ. Press, 1990.

"Motor Boats and Defence: An Unsatisfactory Position." *Motor Boat and Yachting* 71 (July 21, 1939): 51.

Murphy, Joan. "The Lewis Family." In *C. S. Lewis & His Circle: Essays and Memoirs from the Oxford C. S. Lewis Society*, edited by Roger White, Judith Wolfe, and Brendan N. Wolfe, 169–74. Oxford: Oxford Univ. Press, 2015.

National Army Museum. https://www.nam.ac.uk/collections.

"The 1916 Military Service Act." http://www.longlongtrail.co.uk/soldiers/a-soldiers -life-1914-1918/enlisting-into-the-army/the-1916-military-service-act/.

Nish, Ian. "An Overview of Relations between China and Japan, 1918–1945," *The China Quarterly* 124 (Dec. 1990): 601–23.

Noetzel, J. T., and M. R. Bardowell. "The Inklings Remembered: A Conversation with Colin Havard." *Mythlore* 31, no. 1/2 (2012): 29–46.

Norton, Lucy, ed. and trans. *Saint-Simon at Versailles*. London: Hamish Hamilton, 1980.

"Oxford Canal and Stretton History." https://rose-narrowboats.co.uk/oxford-canal-and -stretton-history.htm.

Parker, Peter. *The Old Lie: The Great War and the Public-School Ethos*. London: Constable, 1987.

Patterson, Nancy-Lou. "Warnie and Jack." *Mythlore* 9, no. 3 (1982): 33–34.

Pitter, Ruth. *Sudden Heaven: The Collected Poems of Ruth Pitter: A Critical Edition*. Edited by Don W. King. Kent, OH: Kent State Univ. Press, 2018.

Poe, Harry Lee. *Becoming C. S. Lewis: A Biography of Young Jack Lewis*. Wheaton, IL: Crossway Books, 2019.

Poe, Harry Lee. *The Making of C. S. Lewis: From Atheist to Apologist*. Wheaton, IL: Crossway Books, 2021.

Poe, Harry Lee, and Rebecca Poe. *C. S. Lewis Remembered: Collected Reflections of Students, Friends & Colleagues*. Grand Rapids, MI: Zondervan, 2006.

Pollard, Sidney, and Paul Robertson. *The British Shipbuilding Industry: 1870–1914*. Cambridge, MA: Harvard Univ. Press, 1979.

Rawson, Andrew. *British Army Handbook 1914–1918*. Phoenix Mill, UK: Sutton, 2006.

Redman, B. R. "Review of *Louis XIV: An Informal Portrait*. *Saturday Review* 42 (Oct. 17, 1959): 24.

The Regimental Standing Orders of the Army Service Corps of 1911. London: Harrison & Sons, 1911.

Remarque, Erich Maria. *All Quiet on the Western Front*. Translated by A. W. Wheen. Berlin: Ullstein A. G., 1928. Reprint, New York: Ballantine, 1982.

Report of Medical Board, Register No. 100/L/4050 (Jan. 17, 1914). Army Personnel Centre. Glasgow, UK. http://www.army.mod.uk/home.aspx.

"Review of *Assault on Olympus: The Rise of the House of Gramont*." *Manchester Guardian*. Mar. 28, 1958, 7.

"Review of *Assault on Olympus: The Rise of the House of Gramont*." *New Yorker* 34 (June 28, 1958): 94.

"Review of *Assault on Olympus: The Rise of the House of Gramont*." *San Francisco Chronicle*. June 22, 1958, 29.

"Review of *Assault on Olympus: The Rise of the House of Gramont*." *Times Literary Supplement*. Mar. 7, 1958. 124.

"Review of *Levantine Adventurer: The Travels and Missions of the Chevalier d'Arvieux, 1653–1697*." *Kirkus* 56 (Jan. 1, 1962).

"Review of *Louis XIV: An Informal Portrait. New York Herald Tribune.* Oct. 25, 1959), 4.

"Review of *Louis XIV: An Informal Portrait. New Yorker* 34 (Oct. 10, 1959): 206.

"Review of *Louis XIV: An Informal Portrait. Springfield Republican.* Dec. 6, 1959, 3.

"Review of *Louis XIV: An Informal Portrait. Times Literary Supplement.* June 5, 1959, 334.

"Review of *The Sunset of the Splendid Century.*" *Kirkus* 23 (Aug. 15, 1955): 162.

"Review of *The Sunset of the Splendid Century.*" *New Yorker.* Nov. 12, 1955, 231.

Rodriguez, Mariel. "Writing for the Record: Nineteenth Century Diarists." June 20, 2017. http://historytothepublic.org/nineteenth-century-diarists/.

Royal Army Service Corps. http://www.nam.ac.uk/research/famous-units/royal-army -service-corps.

Royal Army Service Corps: British Military History. https://www.britishmilitaryhistory .co.uk/docs-services-royal-army-service-corps/.

Royal Logistics Corps. http://www.royallogisticcorps.co.uk/heritage/museum/.

"Royal Military College Sandhurst, Camberley: Changes in Military." http://www.bbc.co .uk/programmes/po2b36vc.

Ryan, John S. "The Man behind the Mask." *Cambridge Review* 88 (1966): 421–23.

"The Salonika Front, 1915–1918." http://www.nzhistory.net.nz/media/photo/salonika -front-19151918.

Salters Steamers, Limited. http://www.salterssteamers.co.uk/.

"Samuel Pepys Diary: Coded Passages," http://www.pepys.info/bits.html.

Sassoon, Siegfried. *Memoirs of a Fox-Hunting Man.* London: Faber and Gwyer, 1928.

———. *Memoirs of an Infantry Officer.* London: Faber and Faber, 1930.

———. *Sherston's Progress.* London: Faber and Faber, 1936.

———. *The War Poems.* Edited by Rupert Hart-Davis. London: Faber and Faber, 1983.

Sayer, George. *Jack: A Life of C. S. Lewis.* Rev. ed. Wheaton, IL: Crossway Books, 1994.

Schofield, Stephen, ed. *In Search of C. S. Lewis.* South Plainfield, NJ: Bridge Publishing, 1983.

Seipp, Adam R. *The Ordeal of Peace: Demobilization and the Urban Experience in Britain and Germany, 1917–1921.* Burlington, VT: Ashgate, 2009.

"The Sex Life of Samuel Pepys." https://www.rmg.co.uk/discover/behind-the-scenes/blog /sex-life-samuel-pepys.

Sheffield, Gary. *Forgotten Victory: The First World War: Myths and Realities.* London: Headline, 2001.

Simkins, Peter. *Kitchener's Army: The Raising of the New Armies 1914–16.* Manchester, UK: Manchester Univ. Press, 1988.

Sire, James W. "The Many Faces of C. S. Lewis." *Prairie Schooner* 40, no. 4 (Winter 1966/1967): 364–66.

Smith, E. T. "Review of *The Splendid Century.*" *Library Journal* 79 (Mar. 15, 1954): 546.

Smyth, John. *Sandhurst: The History of the Royal Military Academy, Woolwich, the Royal Military College, Sandhurst, and the Royal Military Academy, Sandhurst 1741–1961.* London: Weidenfield and Nicolson, 1961.

Taylor, A. J. P. *The First World War: An Illustrated History.* London: Hamish Hamilton, 1963.

Thomas, Hugh. *The Story of Sandhurst.* London: Hutchinson & Co., 1961.

Tolkien, J. R. R. *The Letters of J. R. R. Tolkien.* Rev. ed. Edited by Humphrey Carpenter, with Christopher Tolkien. Boston: Houghton Mifflin, 2000.

———. "Letter to W. L. White, Sept. 11, 1967." In *The Image of Man in C. S. Lewis,* edited by William Luther White. Nashville, TN: Abingdon Press, 1969.

Todd, John. *Cruising the Oxford Canal (with One Eye on Its History).* Self-published, 2011.

Treble, Joe. "The Military Record of Warren Lewis." Letter to Ruth Parker, Nov. 16, 1979. Reference 79/P21857/OS9a/EO. Middlesex, UK: Ministry of Defence.

Tuchman, Barbara. *The Guns of August.* New York: Macmillan, 1962.

Unit History. Royal Army Service Corps. https://www.forces-war-records.co.uk/units /4495/royal-army-service-corps.

Ved, Mehta. "Review of *The Scandalous Regent: A Life of Philippe, Duc d'Orleans, 1674–1723, and of His Family.*" *New Yorker* 37 (Apr. 22, 1961): 175.

Wain, John. "Brothers and Friends: The Diaries of W. H. Lewis." In *C. S. Lewis & His Circle: Essays and Memoirs from the Oxford C. S. Lewis Society,* edited by Roger White, Judith Wolfe, and Brendan N. Wolfe, 223–38. Oxford: Oxford Univ. Press, 2015.

———. *Sprightly Running.* London: Macmillan & Co. Ltd., 1962.

The Wartime Memories Project: The Great War. http://www.wartimememoriesproject .com/greatwar/allied/armyservicecorps.php.

Wenham, Simon. *Pleasure Boating on the Thames: A History of Salter Bros., 1858–Present Day.* Stroud, Gloucestershire, UK: History Press, 2014.

West, Richard C. "W. H. Lewis: Historian of the Inklings and of Seventeenth-Century France." *SEVEN: An Anglo-American Literary Review* 14 (1997): 75–86.

Williams, Charles. *To Michal from Serge: Letters from Charles Williams to His Wife, Florence, 1939–1945.* Edited by Roma A King Jr. Kent, OH: Kent State Univ. Press, 2002.

Wilson, A. N. *C. S. Lewis: A Biography.* New York: Norton, 1990.

Winter, Jay. *Sites of Memory, Sites of Mourning: The Great War in European Cultural History.* Cambridge: Cambridge Univ. Press, 1995.

Wohl, Robert. *The Generation of 1914.* Cambridge, MA: Harvard Univ. Press, 1979.

Wolf, John B. "The Reign of Louis XIV: A Selected Bibliography of Writings since the War of 1914–1918." *The Journal of Modern History* 36, no. 2 (June 1964): 127–44.

Wood, William, and A. J. Mann. *The Salonika Front.* London: A. C. Black, 1920.

"Yachting—A Disease: A Sufferer Describes Its Symptoms and Progress." *Motor Boat and Yachting* 67 (Aug. 13, 1937): 184–85.

Young, Michael. *Army Service Corps 1902—1918.* South Yorkshire, UK: Leo Cooper, 2000.

Zaleski, Philip, and Carol Zaleski. *The Fellowship: The Literary Lives of the Inklings: J. R. Tolkien, C. S. Lewis, Owen Barfield, Charles Williams.* New York: Farrar, Straus and Giroux, 2015.

Index